Transnational Competence

Transnational Competence
Empowering Professional Curricula
for Horizon-Rising Challenges

Peter H. Koehn and
James N. Rosenau

Paradigm Publishers
Boulder • London

Copyright © 2010 Paradigm Publishers

Published in the United States by Paradigm Publishers, 2845 Wilderness Place, Suite 200, Boulder, CO 80301 USA.

Paradigm Publishers is the trade name of Birkenkamp & Company, LLC, Dean Birkenkamp, President and Publisher.

Library of Congress Cataloging-in-Publication Data

Koehn, Peter H.
  Transnational competence : empowering professional curricula for horizon-rising challenges / Peter H. Koehn and James N. Rosenau.
    p. cm.
  Includes bibliographical references and index.
  ISBN 978-1-59451-678-8 (hardcover : alk. paper)
  ISBN 978-1-59451-679-5 (paperback : alk. paper)
  1. Professional education—Curricula. 2. Professional employees—Training of.
3. Globalization—Economic aspects. I. Rosenau, James N. II. Title.
  LC1059.K64 2009
  378'.013—dc22

                                                                                    009014134

Printed and bound in the United States of America on acid-free paper that meets the standards of the American National Standard for Permanence of Paper for Printed Library Materials.

Designed and Typeset by Straight Creek Bookmakers.

14 13 12 11 10   2 3 4 5

To Justin, Jason, Sophia, Fan, Patrick, Nicole, and Alexandria.
And a future graced with transnational competence.

Contents

Foreword

SUSTAINABLE DEVELOPMENT, infectious disease, climate change, converging applications of nanotechnology, partnered education, transcontinentally connected financial and economic futures—tomorrow's challenges require transnational competence. Higher-education leaders, starting with presidents, chancellors, vice-chancellors, and provosts, increasingly are expected to shoulder responsibility for articulating an institutional vision of pathways to creating transnationally competent faculty, students, and staff. While more remains to be done, our colleges and universities are making remarkable progress in educating internationally focused undergraduates through additional-language training, academically informed experiences and service-learning opportunities in less-visited countries, and expanded and enriched major and minor degree opportunities. I am particularly heartened by prospects that Congress will enact legislation authorizing and funding the Paul Simon Study Abroad Foundation and help send one million U.S. students abroad each year within the next decade.

Tertiary-level institutions around the world now are challenged to take a bold next step in campus internationalization. Higher education's next challenge is two-fold. First, we must push beyond student awareness of and appreciation for diversity into the realm of ingrained and animated transnational competence. To realize this objective, societies must direct attention and resources to preparing transnationally empowered professionals. Our practicing professionals already are called upon to address both the rapidly unfolding crises and the complex long-term challenges of interdependence through participation in multinational and far-flung teams. Looking ahead, university leaders of the new century can foresee in emerging economic, communications, mobility, and security developments the stimulus for dramatic escalation in the number and urgency of cross-border, transdisciplinary, and multisited expectations that will confront future generations of professionals. Without question, specialized and post-graduate education merits the level of concern, energy, transformative thinking, and resource investment that we have devoted to undergraduate internationalization initiatives over recent decades.

Fortunately, we have experience to guide us in this venture. U.S. public and land-grant universities, for instance, have been in the forefront of innovative science-based efforts to prepare specialists of many nationalities for international assignments in a number of critical fields, including agriculture, health, climate stabilization, governance and project management, engineering, ecotourism, water development, and natural-resource management. Historically, they also have initiated and collaborated in transnational research and development partnerships of mutual benefit to participating faculty members, post-graduate students, campuses, local communities, and the broader interests of nations. It is encouraging in this regard that, at the April 2009 G20 meeting, President Barack Obama called for a doubling of U.S. financial support for agricultural development in developing countries to more than $1 billion in 2010 and outlined a major role in this renewed effort for land-grant universities. In the health sector, the Tom Lantos and Henry J. Hyde United States Global Leadership Against HIV/AIDS, Tuberculosis, and Malaria Reauthorization Act of 2008 calls for the training of 140,000 new health-care workers in the developing world, especially in sub-Saharan Africa, and includes a connective strategy to encourage postsecondary educational institutions in partner countries, in collaboration with U.S. colleges and research universities, to develop human and institutional capacity that will sustain the fight against these diseases.

In *Transnational Competence: Empowering Professional Curricula for Horizon-Rising Challenges*, Peter H. Koehn and James N. Rosenau draw upon the exemplary features of U.S. and overseas higher-education approaches in constructing an integrated framework for transnational-competence education. Public and state university initiatives have contributed prominently to their composite framework and to the linked pedagogical suggestions they provide. From Purdue University's Global Engineering Program to the University of Massachusetts Medical School's Global Multiculturalism Track, these experiences are appropriately captured, effectively applied, and creatively adapted in this book.

At the same time that it incorporates institutional experience, *Transnational Competence* challenges educational leaders to move their vision of 21st-century professional-career preparation a giant step forward. Instead of fragmented and eclectic approaches, Koehn and Rosenau demonstrate that the time has arrived for a common and comprehensive vision of transnational-competence education that transcends disciplinary boundaries. Their interdisciplinary vision is reflected in the foundation curriculum they elaborate and then tailor to preparation in teacher education, business management, engineering, social-justice work, agricultural sciences, development administration, environmental studies, and health and medicine. Their insights merit serious consideration separately and across advanced fields of study. Institutional leaders, chief academic officers, and deans and faculty with responsibility for delivering state-of-the-art professional programs nationally and transnationally will be well-served to consider embedding the skills and learning approaches detailed in *Transnational Competence* in their professional-education programs and using the book in advanced classes and training programs.

The visionary educational themes developed in *Transnational Competence* will have appeal between and beyond U.S. shores. Transnational partnerships and joint-degree programs that aim to prepare technically qualified professionals who are globally competent will be enhanced by the analytic, emotional, creative, communicative, and functional insights contributed here.

The Association of Public and Land-Grant Universities (A·P·L·U) is committed to promoting stronger relationships and collaborative development projects among educational institutions throughout the world. In this connection, it is especially rewarding that the A·P·L·U-led Africa-U.S. Higher Education Initiative has been successfully launched. With startup funding from the U.S. Agency for International Development and the Bill & Melinda Gates Foundation, twenty new transcontinental partnerships will strengthen higher-education programs, promote human-resource development, transfer scientific knowledge and valuable insights, and develop high-quality, future-centered curricula in the United States and across sub-Saharan Africa. Since these capacity-generating partnerships concentrate precisely on the professional fields addressed in *Transnational Competence,* the book offers a profoundly valuable resource for the leaders of such educational initiatives and for graduates of their professional programs.

While Koehn and Rosenau illuminate the pathway, additional resources are needed to ensure that transnational preparation becomes a national priority and a sustainable reality for future generations of practicing professionals. A·P·L·U experience has shown that the way forward on major international-education initiatives calls for an integrated approach involving government in partnership with the university community and its associations, concerned nongovernmental organizations (NGOs), foundations, and the private sector. We *can* graduate professionals who possess the transnational competence needed to address the coming challenges of an interconnected world. With *Transnational Competence* as a guide, the government of the United States is in a position to take the lead in supporting the authors' promising vision for advancing professional education.

M. Peter McPherson, President
Association of Public and Land-Grant Universities (A·P·L·U)

Introduction

The greatest public service higher education can perform is to develop people prepared to help solve society's emerging problems....

—Philip Werdell[1]

BOTH SINGULARLY AND COLLECTIVELY, individuals are central to the course of events. This book is about preparing individual specialists for the rising challenges that they will face in a world that is pervasively interconnected yet richly and perpetually filled with contextual diversity. It is directed principally to higher-education leaders and faculty throughout the world who shoulder responsibility for educating the new generation of professionals and are open to reinvigorating and enriching international education by focusing on transnational competence.

Managing the emerging problems of the 21st century requires all kinds of boundary-busting and boundary-spanning initiatives. We were inspired to collaborate on this work because our unique scholarly trajectories invoked a common direction for educating tomorrow's professionals. That shared educational path, which Rosenau reached by focusing on the dynamics of international affairs and Koehn discovered through local and micro-level research and experience, centers on interpersonal skills along a frontier-traversing web of transnational interactions.[2] For reasons that will become clear, we refer to this galvanizing pathway, which expands upon and applies the global skill revolution and builds on the notion that "people count,"[3] as *transnational competence* (TC).

Transnational Skills and Campus Internationalization

Today's universities are bee hives of global problem-solving and innovation. University-based professional programs are educating the men and women who will lead their fields in the 2030s, 2040s, 2050s, and into the 2060s. "If you think our world is interconnected now," notes Earl Kellogg, Emeritus Professor of Agricultural Economics at the University of Illinois, "wait until 2030!"[4]

xiv

Whether the issue is climatic change, applications of nanoscale technologies,[5] or pro-poor health care, renewed urgency and intensity energizes the transboundary learning objectives of today's hope-filled youth across the globe.[6] Among our multiple objectives, we aim for *Transnational Competence* to inspire, reinforce, and extend the graduating professional's thirst to engage the complex interdependent challenges of today and tomorrow. At the same time, we recognize that "people are more productive when they are having fun."[7] At its core, TC professional education is about linking passion with skills.

Active Skill Expectations

The rising challenges of our time and the professional-education needs of the people who will confront them are complex, interwoven, and transnational. In its May 2000 "strategic vision statement for learning, scholarship and engagement in the new century," the U.S.-focused National Association of State Universities and Land Grant Colleges (NASULGC) foresaw that cross-border influences on all fields of human endeavor necessitate "infusing the curriculum and all related co-curricular activities with an international perspective" and "ancillary skills."[8] In a later "call to presidential leadership," the NASULGC Task Force on International Education emphasized that educational "expectations for students prepared to live, work and contribute to an interconnected world" are "high."[9] Community colleges that prepare workers for a vast array of technical positions in the new global economy also are responding to changed employment calculations. At the 32nd Annual Meeting of Community Colleges for International Development, attending educators stressed the importance of incorporating transboundary skill training in the curriculums provided to the widest possible range of workers.[10]

The challenges facing first-degree and professional programs are not restricted to North American institutions of higher education. Because "*globalization is de-territorializing the skills and competencies it rewards,*"[11] the leaders of tertiary-education institutions throughout the world confront converging transnational skill-development and curricular-building expectations. In some cases (e.g., Mexico and Australia), faculty members are more likely to introduce global perspectives in their courses than are their counterparts in the United States.[12]

Higher-education visionaries have vigorously promoted competency-centered campus internationalization since 1980.[13] What does this long-sought international competency involve? After nearly three decades of concern, there remains little clarity or certainty regarding the skills required for professional transboundary interactions.[14] In addition, as the president of one of our universities, whose career has been distinguished by commitment to international education, recently lamented, "while globalization indicates many graduates will spend at least part of their careers in other countries, no one knows quite how to prepare them for it."[15]

Current Curricular Limitations

Among those responsible for educating tomorrow's professionals, awareness of the limitations associated with narrowly focused international-educational endeavors is growing. Based on results from a turn-of-the-century survey of high-level officials in business, government, and not-for-profit nongovernmental organizations, a study supported by the Starr Foundation, the Rockefeller Brothers Fund, the United Nations Foundation, and RAND concluded that "the traditional ways that universities conceived of 'internationalizing' their curriculums—by developing academic area studies and language training—may no longer be the best ways of producing broad-gauged professionals. Instead, universities need to devise ways to give students a grounding in thinking and acting across cultures."[16] Among other limitations, from the perspective of professional schools, joint programs with area studies fail to equip graduates with the core skills required for effective transnational collaborations.[17] Without jettisoning area and foreign-language studies, the future-centered TC approach to professional education elaborated in this volume moves beyond traditional geographic place- and linguistic group–constrained and skill-neglecting endeavors.

Portable TC Expectations

For students who graduate from professional-education programs, demonstrated technical expertise offers one key to a successful career. The discussion developed in this book rests on the premise that portable transnational competence constitutes an equally indispensable dimension of cooperation, competition, conflict resolution, and governance in boundary-spanning 21st-century working environments. The TC framework we elaborate here is intended to offer the basis for breakthroughs in the way universities prepare graduating professionals from varied country, ethnic, social-class, and academic backgrounds to navigate a deeply interconnected and increasingly interdependent world. Over time, transnational competence is likely to assume even greater value as a lifelong learning asset, as specialized knowledge rapidly becomes obsolete[18] and people increasingly change occupations and encounter new professional mobility challenges.

While we recognize that human-resource demands are immense and growing everywhere[19] and anticipate that the opportunity to develop transnational competence will be valuable, even expected, in all professional-degree programs, its transformative potential is likely to be greatest at educational institutions in the developing world that urgently seek to graduate professionals who are connected to workforce needs[20] and qualified to shrink South-North divides. In the words of Mamphela Ramphele of the World Bank, there is "a cruel irony in the inverse relationship between the size of the development challenges that nations face and the capacity of their university systems to rise to meet them."[21] We are encouraged, in this connection, that "after being shunted to the side by national governments and international agencies alike for almost two decades, higher education is again recognized as a key sector in African development."[22]

Multiple Boundary Interfaces

As we move toward identifying useful transnational skills, it is helpful to think in terms of boundaries. The concept of boundaries and the challenge of working across multiple spatial and cognitive boundaries are critical for professional development in a world replete with interconnectivity, transdisciplinarity, and network and alliance building. In Joel Migdal's enlightening conceptualization, "boundaries signify the point at which something becomes something else, at which the way things are done changes, at which 'we' end and 'they' begin, at which certain rules for behavior no longer obtain and others take hold."[23] Permeable boundaries surround the political jurisdictions delineated on maps as well as professions, languages, ethnic groups, cultures, literary and musical genres, organizations, ideological and political party affiliations, social classes, generational groupings, and a host of other identifications. As widening and overlapping action sites where "different ways of doing things meet,"[24] boundary interfaces often involve uncertainty, tension, and creative opportunity.

There is general agreement in scholarly and professional circles that competence across boundaries—variously termed[25] transnational, international, global,[26] transdisciplinary, or (inter)cultural competence—is necessary if one is to succeed in an expanding list of social and technical initiatives,[27] and that it can be created and developed through the educational process.[28] One encounters less consensus regarding precisely what such competence entails and how this desired goal is attained.[29]

The Need for Comprehensive Frameworks

In the words of William B. DeLauder, President Emeritus of Delaware State University and Executive Director of the Abraham Lincoln Study Abroad Fellowship Program that developed the recommendation that the U.S. Congress support a national program with resources that would enable one million students to complete part of their education abroad each year,[30] the paramount educational challenge of our time is "how do we better prepare future leaders, managers, and other professionals to be effective in the global environment in which we live?"[31] In *Transnational Competence*, we develop and defend a comprehensive framework for transnational competence and, then, center on the crucial *how* questions—how are people empowered for transnational interactions in variable contexts through professional learning and how should transnational skill preparation be provided in the specialized preparation offered by higher-education institutions?

Professionals, Professional Education, and Laypersons

Professionals are persons skilled in a specialized field who make a livelihood applying "somewhat abstract knowledge"[32] in their chosen occupation. They generally occupy positions of considerable privilege.[33] Globalization's powerful boundary-spanning processes are sustained and reshaped, in part, by identifiable professionals who frequently engage in intense and temporary interactions with other professionals.[34] In this study, we are concerned with new and returning professionals who receive training at institutions of higher education and with professional roles, relationships, networks, and partnerships that cross borders and boundaries.[35]

Focal Professions

One is struck by the vast number and "breathtaking diversity" of existing professions,[36] many of which evoke intense attachment. We could not consider more than a hand- ful in a book project. In selecting professions for attention in this discussion of the competence with which people manage their work and lives, we were primarily guided by two considerations. First, we were interested in professions that aim to graduate men and women who are prepared to engage a range of complex interdependence issues—from policies and governance structures that are sensitive to greenhouse- gas emissions to measures that mitigate threats to global public health. Our second consideration was academic ferment—that is, we gravitated toward professions that have evidenced initiative with respect to enhanced preparation for intense transna- tional interaction challenges. Based on these considerations, readers of *Transnational Competence* will find chapters devoted to teacher education, business management, engineering, social-justice work, sustainable development, and health.

Established professions are represented by members holding recognized creden- tials who interact in various fora, including conferences, and are recruited for their disciplinary expertise. Some formally recognized professions (medicine comes to mind) have endured and evolved for centuries, while others (nuclear physics, for instance) are of recent derivation. Many more loosely bounded professions remain open to participants from multiple and diverse educational backgrounds (e.g., en- vironmental sciences and conflict management). All professionals develop official and private networks through which individuals cope with complexity, seize trans- boundary opportunities, and address evolving and emerging local, transnational, and glocal challenges.

Professional Schools and Associations

Throughout the world, professional schools exert enormous influence within academe and the broader society. Many U.S. professional schools not only graduate experts; they also "set a global normative standard of what professional excellence is ... "[37] Formally defined professions rest on knowledge and learning criteria created, debated, revised, and transmitted by intellectual gatekeepers who typically are connected to universities.[38] Although one encounters different orientations and varied academic positions, rather than a single orthodoxy, within and/or across professional schools,[39] gatekeepers establish and apply rules and procedures for regulating membership— typically by screening (inflexible entry standards),[40] performance assessments, and certification. Formalized bodies, including accrediting agencies, set educational standards, monitor practice, and assess outcomes.

When professional organizations "do not transcend national boundaries in their deliberations with regard to practice implications," they impede progress.[41] Increasingly, therefore, the learning objectives and assessment criteria established by professional schools and associations and the standards insisted on by accrediting bodies encompass internation and intercultural competency considerations.[42] The U.S. National Council for Accreditation of Teacher Education (NCATE) has insisted since 1995 that future teachers receive education in global perspectives.[43] Since 2002, the Council on Social Work Education's accreditation standards have included development of the skills needed to "analyze organizational, local, state, national, and *international* issues in social welfare policy and social service delivery [emphasis ours]."[44] In 2004, moreover, the International Association of Schools of Social Work (IASSW) and the International Federation of Social Workers adopted voluntary global standards for social-work education.[45] The "common professional component" accreditation standards of the U.S. Association of Collegiate Business Schools and Programs (ACBSP) mandate a minimum of thirty hours of curriculum coverage devoted to "global dimensions of business."[46] ABET, which accredits U.S. engineering programs, includes understanding "the impact of engineering solutions" in a global economic, environmental, and societal context among its criteria.[47] The Liaison Committee for Medical Education (LCME), the accrediting authority for U.S. and Canadian medical schools, specifically calls upon schools to "document objectives relating to the development of skills in cultural competence, indicate where in the curriculum students are exposed to such material, and demonstrate the extent to which the objectives are being achieved."[48] The criteria for accrediting schools and programs of public health set in 2005 by the Council on Education for Public Health (CEPH) require the preparation of practitioners "who are competent to carry out broad public health functions in local, state, national, and *international* settings [emphasis ours]." While they are expected to graduate students who are competent to address global issues and to practice in transnational and transcultural settings, professional programs that embrace internationalization receive little specific guidance from external sources when it comes to determining exactly what skills their students require and how to provide the requisite preparation.[49]

One goal of education is to enhance the micro-level role-performance skills of individual graduates who will later participate in meso and macro structures and processes. We submit that a TC approach will enable professional programs to keep up with the need to provide graduates with the new and evolving skills demanded by increasingly connected local and global labor markets and expected by accrediting bodies and service-seeking publics. However, there are additional reasons for professional programs at institutions throughout the world to demonstrate commitment to building sustainable transnational skills. The occupational successes of TC-prepared professional graduates promise to redound to the benefit of programs, universities, communities, nations,[50] and humanity as a whole.

Professionals and Laypersons

Although we have elected to focus on professionals and professional education in this book, it is important from the outset to recognize that others, including persons who lack professional training and those with nefarious objectives,[51] are advantaged by transnational-competence preparation. By cultivating links "to the resources, experiences, and opportunities that place [of origin] provides,"[52] more persons in more places around the world are opting to pursue transnational lives than ever before. Moreover, as people are thrust into relationships with those they have never previously been in contact with,[53] growing numbers of individuals function (often unselfconsciously[54]) as glocal contacts and resource people, role models, imagination cultivators, and intercultural mediators. As Arjun Appadurai has observed, "few persons in the world today do have not a friend, relative, or coworker who is not on the road to somewhere else or already coming back home, bearing stories and possibilities."[55]

Transmigration and "global neighborhoods" that are sustained by residents' frequent border-crossing relations[56] promote transnational competence in subtle as well as apparent ways. The movement of exiles, refugees, displaced persons, documented and undocumented workers, and legal immigrants, along with family members, across porous state borders enables people who are proficient in a culture of origin to develop competency in new receiving-society cultures.[57] With proven skill portability, bicultural and multicultural individuals have a head start on transnational competence that endows them with valuable personal assets for prospering in today's socially, politically, economically, culturally, technologically, and environmentally interconnected world.[58]

The TC of nonprofessionals is crucial for another, more practical, reason. The outcome of prevailing responses to highly interdependent challenges is determined largely by the nature of collaboration/conflict that professionals experience with activists and lay publics. Complex interdependence challenges typically are accompanied by profound uncertainties, power differentials, and high risks. Information is at a premium. For effective policy making/implementation and improvements in conditions and outlooks, professionals are dependent upon the knowledge, influence, and behavioral decisions of laypersons.[59] Indeed, in making boundary-spanning judgments, the street smarts of informally educated people can be more useful than the prescriptions of highly educated "experts."[60] As boundaries interpenetrate, professional-nonprofessional interactions have assumed increasing relevance because "global communications are not only dense but also very cheap. This factor gives any two people who have some minimum resources, wherever they may be on the globe, the ability to speak to each other, to exchange documents and funds rapidly, to travel to meet face to face and, hence, to work together in transnational structures."[61]

In short, the transnational competence/incompetence of *all* engaged parties affects the outcome of professional-lay transactions.[62] When a professional interacts with a layperson, both individuals simultaneously are transmitters and receptors, teachers and learners.[63] In the case of professionals, however, educational preparation offers a unique opportunity to advance TC learning in reasoned and systematic, rather than in ad hoc and fortuitous, fashion. Education uniquely provides skill learners with ethical context (e.g., a sense of social justice) and direction regarding the humanist promise of TC applications.

Opportunities for TC Professionals

We also are aware that workforce demographics in the United States and elsewhere forecast an "unprecedented opportunity" for transnationally competent men and women to fill leadership positions in organizations with global reach.[64] Employers of all kinds—business, government, not-for-profit—are on the lookout for technically trained personnel who have honed their transnational interpersonal-interaction skills.[65] Their principal interest, and the focus of this book, is on graduates with technical skills who can *perform* locally and across physical and intangible boundaries.

Although the central narrative of *Transnational Competence* covers similar ground for each professional field of study, our primary sources for the six focused TC learning discussions are educators with combined and diverse expertise in international education and the specific field of study. The rich source notes and parenthetical insights we provide throughout the book are designed to encourage adventurous readers to initiate their own voyage of discovery while navigating the narrative directed by the authors.

Chapter 1

Transnational Competence and the Skill Revolution

Given the growing interdependence among nations as a result of trade, increased communications, and migratory flows, it will be crucial for people to develop the skills to understand and help resolve ... urgent [shared planetary] challenges.
—Fernando Reimers[1]

THE SKILL REVOLUTION offers a launching pad for further exploration of the more encompassing concept of transnational competence. Skill involves the mental and physical "capacity to use knowledge in accomplishing a task."[2] Spurred by advances in information technology and means of human mobility, people everywhere at all levels of society—from rich to poor, from elites to ordinary persons—are enhancing their skills and capabilities.[3] As time and distance continue to contract, individuals around the world, by necessity, are developing new and extended skills.

The "empowerment of individuals to act globally is the most important feature" of the flattened and shrinking world popularized by Thomas Friedman.[4] People have gained an increased ability to grasp the underlying dynamics of situations they encounter and an expanded working knowledge of how their world operates. One impressive aspect of the global skill revolution involves enhanced information processing and interpretation. While this dimension of the skill revolution is assisted by technological advances, the overall competency progression is derived from a multiplicity of sources.[5] Our focus in *Transnational Competence* is on how specialists can increase portable transnational skills through one of these sources: advanced education.

1

The Interpersonal Nexus

The diverse and multidimensional talents that comprise competence are individually based. They encompass street smarts and advanced learning, experiential wisdom and intellectual curiosity, judgmental and reflective capacities, native intelligence, and technical mastery. It is safe to assume, therefore, that each individual possesses a unique, imperfect, and constantly changing competence profile. One's competence profile is pivotal when professionals are called upon to engage in boundary-spanning roles.[6]

If it is to make a difference, professional competence must, in most cases, be expressed interpersonally. While it often is valuable in knowledge-building exercises to master virtual links, face-to-face interactions remain the nexus of empowerment in our interconnected age.[7] While cyberspace is useful for engaging disparate professionals in shallow encounters, it also offers "an escape from many of the difficulties of deeper more involved human relations."[8] Person-to-person relationships even turn out to be "paramount when building an electronic network for information exchange."[9] In the application of technical knowledge to challenging problem situations, specialists primarily depend on human connections and relational attributes that build social capital.[10] As individuals increasingly are called upon to translate pressing proximate concerns into transnational deliberations and to transform intruding distant complexities into locally contextualized actions and products,[11] the most relevant interactions and experiences are simultaneously face-to-face and deterritorialized.

In short, individuals manifest or fail to demonstrate transnational competence in their boundary-spanning interactions with other individuals. In managing complex interdependent issues, people and human transactions remain decisive. Working with diverse individuals is difficult and cooperating as a network member adds a demanding measure of challenge to the task. It is crucial, therefore, that all professional training incorporates interpersonal skills that facilitate interactions with persons who are different from oneself.[12]

Governance and Transnational Epistemic Communities

The skill revolution is developing alongside more widespread and deeper borderless involvement by individuals and nongovernmental collectivities in steering rule systems, framing goals, and shaping policy and resource-allocation outcomes.[13] A variety of mechanisms and institutions have come into being as influential webs of governance that transcend national borders. Today, a vast and shifting network of informal and decentralized forms (spheres) of authority supplement long-established formal and institutionalized structures, such as national governments and international organizations, that have diminished capacity to steer socio-technical systems.[14] The goals and interests of the individuals, groups, and organizations crowding the global governance stage are so numerous, diverse, and disaggregated that a hierarchical global structure with a single mechanism for governance is not likely to arise in the foreseeable future. Some steering mechanisms (e.g., markets) possess wider scope for influencing the course of events than do others, but none is capable alone of dominating the processes of governing.[15]

With the wide dispersion of centers of authority at every level of community, people around the world have witnessed a vast extension of rule systems and steering mechanisms.[16] The result is an ever-widening realm in which governance is undertaken as new role challenges arise that offer opportunities for rapid-network-mobilizing nonstate actors to seize the advantage.[17] Epistemic communities,[18] including horizontally as well as vertically organized groups of professionals, are deeply involved in this multilevel and multicentric world of global governance. Compliance is the key to ascertaining the presence of formally and informally constituted spheres of authority. Professional associations offer excellent examples of how civil-society collectivities in our multicentric world use expertise to create rules and to evoke compliance with their issue-specific recommendations among members, policy makers, other nongovernmental actors, and lay publics.[19]

Increased participation by highly educated professionals will not resolve the democratic deficit that vexes global governance.[20] Input legitimacy will remain a challenge in the absence of a transnational public sphere. By effectively addressing serious global problems, however, collaborating professionals can enhance output legitimacy. The influential, if often low-profile, output roles that individual experts and epistemic communities have assumed in global governance underscores the importance of preparing transnationally competent professional scientists, engineers, architects, physicians, economists, and other specialists who are committed to ensuring that global steering mechanisms are inclusive, responsive, flexible, accountable, and promote social justice.

Building Transboundary Social Capital

Effective global governance is contingent upon the construction and activation of transboundary social capital. Our conceptualization of social capital emphasizes human-resource enhancements. Social capital encompasses the building of influential nonhierarchical "networks of civic engagement" among actors who "are bound together by trust and reciprocity"[21] and the development of multilevel/multiple-context interaction skills. When professional stakeholders are challenged by complex interdependencies, transboundary social capital expands the scope for cooperative action and enriches both the individual professional and transnational teams. In a linked but fragmented world, characterized by the proliferation of authority networks and the relative absence of cross-cutting cleavages among them, human-relations skills in conflict-management and in transboundary bridging will be at a premium.

As one available means of building social capital, governments, foundations, and other nongovernmental organizations can encourage and facilitate the development of transnational competency through education and training. At the end of the 20th century, for instance, the U.S. Social Science Research Council launched a *human research capital initiative* aimed at addressing the worldwide need for research professionals capable of "understanding local situations in relationship to global, transnational and international trends and impacts."[22] Developing transnational skills helps to enhance the performance of the organizations and networks within which professionals operate and increases people's capacity to participate effectively in global governance.

Transnationally Empowering Professional Connections and Projects

For today's universities, external networks, alliances, and partnerships are a central mechanism for campus internationalization.[23] Kent Buse and Gill Walt suggest that "partnership can be placed at one end of a continuum, with networks at the other end, and alliances somewhere in between. The partnership end involves more formalized agreements and consequently fewer parties, while the network involves a looser grouping of a greater number of parties who share common interests."[24] While some networks are purposive, the occupants of others "may be entirely unaware of one another—for example, people who ... visit the same website."[25] All networks are useful, however, in identifying the potential for alliance or coalition formation.[26] In an information-driven age, it is not surprising that universities have positioned themselves at the hub of globally interconnected networks.[27]

By necessity in an interdependent world, professionals cooperate on projects through alliances and partnerships that cross disciplinary, institutional, and nation-state boundaries. The potential benefits of transnational and transprofessional linkages include positioning at the cutting edge of information flows, emerging ideas, resource opportunities, impending policy changes, and technical and social breakthroughs.[28]

The potential of transnational professional connections that arise around shared concerns and purposes is fully realized when they result in concrete projects. The U.S. National Science Foundation (NSF), for instance, encourages transnational research by providing the opportunity for all principal investigators (PIs) awarded an NSF grant to add an international dimension to their projects via supplemental funding that would support overseas partners in any country.[29] For large-scale projects, PIs increasingly seek out consortia of domestic-based institutions and foreign partners. When informed that one of us was constructing a database of international research and development projects covering the 218 Association of Public and Land-Grant Universities (APLU) members, a number of forward-looking PIs indicated that they would explore the posted profiles as part of their technology-prospecting and consortia-building processes.[30] The likelihood of success in transboundary partnership-building and in constructing complex consortia is enhanced when transnationally competent professionals in both the South and North take the lead in designing projects and arranging the details of collaboration.

Transnational alliances are difficult to sustain.[31] From project design to implementation, skills in interacting with professional counterparts of diverse nationalities and across specialization boundaries are pivotal. Although professional networks and partnerships vary in size, purpose, scope, coherence, intensity, location, and duration, those that experience the most extensive and reciprocally fruitful interpersonal interactions are likely to be the most effective when addressing arising interdependence challenges. Our challenge in the chapters that follow is to demonstrate how TC can enable diverse, horizon-preparing professionals to make the most of their specialized training as they serve distant and proximate individuals, collectivities, and societies.

Chapter 2

The Case for Transnational Competence

How do we better prepare future leaders, managers, and other professionals to be effective in the global environment in which we live?
—William B. DeLauder[1]

THOSE CONCERNED with advancing higher-education study and practice stand to gain from clarity and closure on terms and their relationships.[2] Why should we privilege "transnational" over its closest conceptual competitors—"global" and "cultural" or "intercultural" competence? First, we need a term that captures the porous nature of nation-state borders in a time of unparalleled human mobility and interconnectedness. Once fixed borders became fluid and permeable frontiers, domestic-foreign exchanges proliferated in *intra*nation as well as *inter*nation human endeavors and professional networks.

Transnational phenomena and dynamics "cross, alter, transcend, and even transform borders and boundaries."[3] "Transnational" directs attention to activities that traverse and interlink levels (urban, rural, national, regional) at the same time that it recognizes the permeable status of physical borders and intangible boundaries that have not disappeared. "Transnational" also galvanizes change and transforms curricular visions by explicitly integrating and building on the efforts and advances contributed by advocates of internationalizing higher education and of multicultural education.[4]

When attached to competence in human interactions, transnational is less universalistic than "global"; yet, it encompasses more than culture. Since few, if any, individuals interact on a worldwide scale,[5] global competence is neither practicable nor necessary. Increasingly, however, human interactions occur across interconnected boundaries, many of which are not primarily culturally defined. We need a construct that does not sacrifice attention to the capacity to cross multiple and fluid frontiers in the process of addressing complex interdependence challenges. "Transnational" captures the diversity and multiplicity of contemporary domestic-foreign boundary exchanges without requiring global reach.

Limitations of Cultural and Intercultural Competence

The versatility and power of TC in comparison with cultural competence (CC) is revealed when considered in the context of the medical consultation.[6] In an era of migration, transmigration, and global-local connectivity, many health outcomes are shaped by transnational interactions among care providers and recipients who meet in settings where nationality/ethnic match is a diminishing option. In many parts of the United States as well as in other industrialized nations, physicians encounter patients who are in transition from an unprecedented multitude of dissimilar, often low-income, nation states. In addition to multiple nationalities, physicians are challenged by bicultural (even multicultural) patients, and diasporic and third-culture (different from both origin and host) interactions. Culture-competence medical education, initially intended for mastery of specific domestic two-culture interactions,[7] is of limited utility in today's diverse, hybrid, shifting, and transnationally demanding patient-care environment.

Income, education, occupation, and wealth differences, along with the multidimensional nature of human experience, generate considerable intragroup variation.[8] In individual medical encounters, therefore, physicians are confronted by the dynamic interplay with culture of gender, socio-economic status, place of residence, power position, discrimination/persecution, and transborder connections. Patient variability means that the single-dimension and standardized-list approach to diagnosis and treatment associated with some CC approaches is problematic. By focusing on a lengthy and elaborate list of presumably internally homogenous, static, and timeless culture-specific characteristics,[9] "groups of people are often essentialized, lumped together, all of their members possessing traits unilaterally."[10] Among other gaps, recipes of cultural characteristics miss the complexity and diversity of perspectives and behaviors that exist *within* ethnic groups due to mixed origins, class differences, unique historical experiences, multiple national identities, and sustained transnational participation.[11] The learning outcome is likely to be a "facile interpretation" of incomplete and inapplicable content; competence *in* a culture is rarely approximated.[12] In today's interconnected and interactive world, cultural diversity only can be fully appreciated in the context of transnational conditions that shape, sustain, elaborate, modify, and transform identities. Rather than referencing cultural lists and centering on static descriptions of ethnic identity, the most promising health-care approaches focus on ethnographic inquiry regarding dynamic transnational as well as domestic influences, on socio-economic and political status along with individual cultural/ subcultural/blended-culture orientations,[13] on unrecognized commonalities as well as subtle differences, and on building interpersonal therapeutic alliances that are sufficiently powerful to transform the conditions that underlie poor health and suffering.[14] These demands for versatile skills require an approach that moves beyond cultural, or intercultural, training.[15]

Prevailing disparities in health status largely reflect lifestyle practices that are mediated by socio-economic position and (in)ability to access/use health-care opportunities.[16] Individuals and families in transnational spatial transition frequently confront inequities in health-care access and medical treatment alongside new health risks associated with "health-compromising" living and working conditions.[17] Responding to the voice of the least advantaged through social and political action that would mitigate contextual sources of distress has not been integral to the cultural-competence medical curriculum.[18] Unsurprisingly, many medical students emerge from CC education believing that it is unnecessary, optional, or impossible for physicians to mitigate social, economic, and political barriers to equity in health care and health status.[19] Moreover, the CC curriculum typically fails to prepare medical students for alliance building across professions and with patients, for networking across national borders (especially in the global South, where one finds the gravest health disparities), and for effective participation in the policy process.[20]

According to Kenneth Cushner, *inter*cultural education utilizes "comparisons, exchanges, cooperation, and confrontation between groups."[21] While multicultural education, in Cushner's view, is limited to "unrelated juxtapositions of knowledge about particular groups without any apparent interconnection between them," intercultural education addresses problems and situations "through the convergence and combination of different view points."[22] Given the dynamic and interactive emphasis of this perspective, the intercultural-education approach found in some schools of education is in a stronger position to prepare graduates for diverse, complex, and shifting identities and behaviors relative to the CC approach or to multicultural education. However, cultural backgrounds (regardless of location) continue to constitute the preoccupation of intercultural education[23] at a time when, in Derek Bok's provocative assessment, students cannot foresee "just which cultures and languages will prove important to them after they graduate."[24] Consequently, the intercultural-education approach (along with multicultural education) remains limited in its capacity to prepare for multidimensional transboundary challenges that encompass social, economic, and political influences. A more holistic framework of skill development is needed so that graduates will be able to "adapt and respond effectively to *whatever* international problems and opportunities may confront them in their later lives."[25]

The TC Framework

The earliest published resource highlighting the term transnational competence appears in a 1997 volume issued as an Institute of International Education (IIE) Research Report. The report, *Towards Transnational Competence: Rethinking International Education (A U.S.-Japan Case Study)*, was prepared by the Task Force for Transnational

Competence with support from the U.S.-Japan Foundation. The narrow focus of the IIE report, and the edited book published three years later,[26] is on ways to improve "international education" in the United States and Japan.[27] Task force members recognized that "education in the future will need to place greater emphasis" on TC.[28] In addition, the task force's capsule description of TC's "core elements" touched on analytic, creative, and communicative abilities as well as on technical skills.[29]

In 2002, we published our independently constructed comprehensive TC framework based on cross-disciplinary meta analysis.[30] Our vision of transnational competence is fundamentally a transactional one. Transnational capacity is expressed (or not expressed) in human encounters and in role performance. We approach transnational encounters as micro-level *interpersonal interactions* that occur in a *social/power context* and are shaped by *macro-level forces* (global, regional, cross-border, national, and local).

In our conceptualization, transnational competence involves applications of five sets of clearly differentiated capacities: analytic, emotional, creative/imaginative, communicative, and functional. These skill sets are presented in outline form in List 2.1. The sections that follow elaborate on the explicitly transboundary dimensions of each skill domain.

List 2.1: Dimensions of Transnational Competence

Analytic competence

- Ability to achieve a reasonably complete understanding of the central beliefs, values, practices, and paradoxes of counterpart culture(s) and society(ies)— including political and ethnic awareness
- Ability to link conditions in new settings to one's own circumstances and vice versa
- Ability to discern risks and benefits and to assess complex alternative socio-technical paths
- Ability to discern effective transboundary interaction strategies and to learn from past successes and failures

Emotional competence

- Motivation and ability to open oneself up continuously to divergent cultural influences and experiences
- Ability to assume genuine interest in, and to maintain respect for, different values, traditions, experiences, feelings, and challenges
- Ability to read emotional messages conveyed by people with vastly different backgrounds
- Ability to manage multiple identities
- Sense of transboundary efficacy

Creative/imaginative competence

- Ability to foresee and exploit the synergistic potential of diverse group perspectives in collective problem solving
- Collaborative ability to articulate novel and shared transboundary syntheses
- Ability to envision viable mutually acceptable alternatives
- Ability to tap into diverse cultural, societal, and technical sources for inspiration

Communicative competence

- Proficiency in and use of counterparts' spoken/written language
- Skill in interpretation and in using an interpreter
- Proficiency in and relaxed use of interculturally appropriate nonverbal cues and codes
- Ability to listen to and discern different messages
- Ability to engage in meaningful transboundary dialogues and to facilitate mutual self-disclosure
- Ability to avoid and resolve communication misunderstandings across diverse communication styles

Functional (project/task) competence

- Ability to relate to counterpart(s) and to develop and maintain positive interpersonal relationships
- Ability to apply/adapt procedural insights, empathy, and imagination in transboundary interactions
- Flexible ability to employ an extensive and complex range of accommodative organizational strategies and interaction paths
- Ability to overcome problems/conflicts and accomplish goals when dealing with transnational and transboundary challenges and globalization/localization pressures
- Ability to build and activate professional and societal resources that mitigate socio-economic inequities, power differentials, exclusionary policies, and other institutionalized constraints

Analytic Competence

Transnational competence places priority on skill acquisition and application. Central to TC are probing, reflecting, and converting information into usable understanding, reasoning, and action. The skills-first nature of TC is particularly important in understanding the facilitative promise of analytic competence. Among professionals, analytic competence primarily involves developing the ability to search for, locate, select, assemble, organize, interpret, critically assess, and apply relevant generic and context-specific knowledge, data, and rules.[31] The paramount objective of transnational analytic preparation is mastering the processes and tools that provide access to a reliable repository of concepts and useful procedural insights that illuminate previously unfamiliar circumstances.

Transnational analytic competence includes the process of acquiring a reasonably complete understanding of the complex beliefs, values, practices, and paradoxes of interface individuals, groups, networks, and societies along with the ability to render culturally accurate attributions of interpersonal behavior. However, the TC framework moves beyond exclusive reliance on cultural analysis.[32] Awareness of political and ethnic interests in one's own and counterpart societies—what Kimberly Maynard refers to as "the fault lines of tension" and "areas for potential cross-identity cooperation"[33]—is a particularly important analytic ability among trained practitioners. Professional skills are further enhanced by systematic capacity to comprehend the interacting economic, political, technical, historical, and cultural forces behind globalization and localization[34] and the complex and changing relationships involving integration and fragmentation,[35] unity and diversity,[36] and benefits and costs at subnational, national, supranational, and transnational levels. The transnationally competent professional possesses the ability to analyze how the intersection of local, national, and international opportunities and constraints influences his/her role in contributing to and shaping the interdependent challenge at hand.[37] As Merry Merryfield has shown, developing the habit of identifying, discriminating among, consulting, comparing, and evaluating diverse perspectives and indigenous sources of information is crucial in these analytic processes.[38]

In transnational interactions, the ability to grasp unfamiliar settings, operations, and underlying dynamics is essential. In such situations, "successful players benefit from knowing who the key people are … , knowing the local rules that apply to their activities, and having an understanding of local negotiating practices."[39] Valuable analytic abilities include "alertness to the political consequences of behavior in everyday work and social settings" and skill in analyzing the institutional structure that frames decision-making processes in specific transboundary contexts.[40] Analytic skill in developing accurate and reasonably comprehensive understandings of power relationships and other key contextual determinants of behavior facilitates professional transnational competence by reducing prospects for costly and dangerous mistakes due to false assumptions and/or insufficient information, by revealing ignored needs and uncovering opportunities, and by minimizing unrealistic expectations.[41]

The ability to link unfolding economic, social, technical, environmental, and political conditions in the counterpart's context to one's own circumstances and outcomes (and vice versa) constitutes another analytic skill promoting transnational competence. Interdependence challenges inherently involve an extraordinary interconnectivity of settings, issues,[42] events,[43] processes, and variables. Skillful transnational actors are able to define, trace, and anticipate the complex, circuitous, and rapidly evolving connections and reactions among distant developments and proximate conditions and to connect their own actions to transboundary objectives and consequences.

Transnational analytic competence also involves assessments of alternative technical and cultural paths. The transnational path-assessment process begins with the selection and sequential arrangement of relevant features from the transboundary context "for elaborating a course of action."[44] Skillful professionals are able to identify numerous, detailed, and complex strategic action paths and assess their appropriateness for particular problem-addressing situations.[45] This skill requires simultaneity of consciousness (that is, being able to sustain and mine multiple complex world views without collapsing them into simple dichotomies) and simultaneity of place (that is, being simultaneously engaged in knowledge building and comprehension at virtual sites alongside one's physical location).

Finally, transnational analytic competence involves discerning where, when, and how transboundary collective action can be effective and selecting viable interaction and transaction strategies. In this connection, the skillful professional seeks to identify and understand the underlying rules, processes, and ethical standards at work in specific collaborative situations and to determine how diverse individuals and organizations are likely to confront new situations and manage long-standing ones.[46]

Emotional Competence

Emotional competence is a valuable professional resource that draws upon five principal skills. The first is centered on motivation. Nation-state "transcenders" are distinguished by "their curiosity and willingness to explore the complexities of diversity."[47] Specifically, the emotionally skillful person possesses the motivation (even eagerness) continuously to open up and adapt to unfamiliar and ambiguous cultural influences and transboundary experiences and the "resolve not to run away" that stems from persistence in managing anxiety and frustration.[48] Furthermore, the committed and passionately motivated professional often is found inspirational by colleagues and laypersons. The capacity to address challenges with passion can contribute "the spice that enhances all other ingredients with greatness."[49]

The ability to assume a genuine interest in new patterns of language, family life, cuisine, customs, and so on, and to maintain respect for a multiplicity of different (including nonmainstream) values, beliefs, traditions, experiences, challenges, and preferred communication styles comprises a second TC-enhancing emotional skill. The complexity and richness of diversity and hybridity are explored in depth and celebrated.[50] This skill requires recognition that there are many values worth living by[51] and withholding judgmental attributions based on perceived socio-economic, ethnic, religious, and/or political differences.

A third dimension of transnational emotional competence involves the ability to discern unspoken emotional messages conveyed by people with vastly different backgrounds and to judge them as welcoming or threatening.[52] For professionals, this skill centers on empathizing and emotionally connecting with the unique feelings, needs, experiences, motivations, and/or work styles of a diverse set of associates and laypersons.[53] Transnational empathy includes learning to understand how others with different backgrounds view one's own decision-making process.[54] Forging empathic bridges and connectedness with other people, Kenneth Cushner adds, involves recognition that one's "individual as well as collective fate is inextricably linked to that of others."[55] Furthermore, persons "who can 'reason from the point of view of others' are better equipped to resolve, and resolve fairly, the challenging transboundary issues that create overlapping communities of fate."[56]

Transnational emotional competence also requires the ability to manage multiple identities—one's own and others'. When confronted by interdependence challenges, people can employ a multiplicity of identifications (e.g., nation-state, world citizen, ethnicity or nationality, religious affiliation, gender, professional, organizational, relational) in particular situations.[57] It is rare for people to present themselves in constant, fixed ways in transboundary relationships, and increasingly easy to move from one identification to another without fear of losing any. Indeed, the salience and intensity of enacted identities vary across situations, collaborators, and/or time. Boundary-transcending professionals must be skilled at identifying, activating, enriching, and guiding multiple identities in transnational problem-solving situations.

Self-confidence, or a sense of personal transnational efficacy tempered with compassion,[58] constitutes the culminating emotional skill. Transnational self-confidence, which often is developed through perseverance, "involves learning that one can do things with a certain likelihood of success and, moreover, with a fair likelihood of being able to run the course again should one fail."[59] Transnational self-efficacy strengthens the professional's willingness to "take risks and seek out more demanding challenges."[60] To be effective in addressing complex interdependence challenges, technically prepared participants need to be confident that they can make a difference in their own socio-cultural context, their counterparts', and/or a mutually understood interculture based on shared meanings and procedural understandings that are adapted to, but different from, the other contexts.[61]

Creative/Imaginative Capacity

While imagination is now recognized as an important part of everyday life,[62] its potential transnational implications and applications remain undeveloped. It is not surprising, therefore, that participants in the 2006 Asia-Pacific Leaders Forum singled out the prevailing "creativity gap" as a situation that should concern today's educators.[63] We hold that imagination provides essential fuel for transnational action. The freeing up of transboundary imaginative capacities is one of the most powerful forces at work in today's professional world.

Four closely related skills promote transnational creative/imaginative competence. The first involves the catalytic ability to foresee and mobilize the synergistic relevance of diverse group perspectives in collective transboundary problem solving.[64] In a deterritorialized world, "the new power of the imagination ... is inescapably tied up with images, ideas, and opportunities that come from elsewhere...."[65] Diversity provides a "proven way to increase the randomness of concept combinations."[66] After playing Brazilian music and exploring instruments such as the Mongolian *morin khuur*, Yo-Yo Ma's musical performances have become broader and richer, demonstrating the inventive "edge effect" attributable to transboundary encounters.[67] Because variegated perspectives create novel connections, the participation of diverse stakeholders in a common project "often triggers a new way to look at and contend with" problems.[68] By expanding the pool of available alternatives, diversity enables teams to move beyond blockages or "sticking points."[69] Transnationally co-creative actors learn to reframe problems, to envision alternative resolutions, to advance the envisioning process,[70] and to leverage the rich potential inherent in multiple-perspective endeavors.[71] The successful mixing and merging of dissimilar backgrounds and viewpoints can produce collective accomplishments that exceed the sum total of the separate contributions.[72]

Another creative/imaginative skill is the ability to articulate novel transnational syntheses and resyntheses of multisource knowledge and aspirations[73] that can be shared among professional colleagues. Creative nation-state transcenders are able to inspire and collaborate with counterparts of diverse identities, disciplines, and locations in the design and nurturing of previously unimagined, but contextually appropriate, approaches to interdependence challenges.

A closely related capacity is the continuous ability to (co-)envision new paradigms, unmet needs, viable alternative futures, processes, and roles that are mutually acceptable among collaborators who possess diverse identities. TC envisioning skills include maintaining a future orientation, recreating and enriching personal and organizational visions,[74] finding creative accommodations, and perceiving opportunities for transboundary resource mobilization. Both people and their roles count.[75] What has already been imagined must be translated into contextually viable action plans.[76] The special challenge facing the transnationally active professional is to create one's own transformative role when existing role definitions are loosely defined and/or unstable. Creating new professional role definitions "demands both imagination and an orientation toward the future."[77]

Associates with the ability to tap into diverse socio-cultural and technical sources for inspiration—the fourth creative/imaginative skill—will strengthen and/or reinforce the other dimensions of transboundary imagination. By frequenting boundaries where concepts from different fields clash, combine, and intersect with diverse human perspectives, professionals will be more likely to perceive synergistic potentials, to envision transnationally acceptable alternatives, and to identify innovative and shared syntheses. Frans Johansson calls this place the "Intersection" and refers to the resulting "explosion of remarkable innovations" as "the Medici Effect."[78]

Communicative Facility

Among professionals from different walks of life who hold diverse perspectives and value preferences, understanding, empathy, synergy, and collaboration are influenced by the ability to engage in meaningful conversations. As the world shrinks and the stakes expand, the philosopher Kwame Appiah foresees, "conversations across boundaries can be delightful, or just vexing; what they mainly are, though, is inevitable."[79]

Based primarily on the extensive literature dealing with intercultural communication, six skills are identified in the transnational communicative-competence domain. First is facility in the spoken and written language used by one's counterparts. This skill, which opens otherwise closed doors along the road to achieving analytic, emotional, and imaginative competency, is most completely actualized by verbal fluency in the others' first language—coupled with "willingness to use it"[80] with emotional power.[81]

Beyond English, academic researchers and global leaders differ over the necessity of language competence in contemporary transnational interactions.[82] Out of 19 skills rated important for professional success in an international organization, the 135 high-level respondents in the 2003 RAND study ranked "written and oral English language skills" eighth and "foreign language fluency" nineteenth.[83] While personal linguistic fluency in another language can be an immense behavioral asset, achieving it is impractical in transnational situations involving multiple and revolving first languages. Such interactions call for skill in interpretation and in using an interpreter.

Transnationally skillful actors also develop proficiency in nonverbal communicative behavior[84] and in interpreting facial expressions, gestures, posturing, use of space, body movement, pace, and other cues.[85] This vital skill in dealing with different communication styles often is overlooked in transboundary training and education.[86] An actor proficient in intercultural nonverbal communication typically responds in a relaxed and spontaneous manner that is situationally appropriate to the cues and codes embedded in counterpart behavior. When mistakes are made, s/he is able to recognize signals indicating inappropriate behavior and adjust accordingly.[87]

Effective transnational communication further requires skill in listening and understanding. Barbara Crosby suggests that global leaders need to "listen carefully for team members' feelings and ideas about the three main aspects of team life: the individual members' needs, the group's cohesion, and the task to be accomplished."[88] The level of communicative capacity achieved by professionals depends, in part, on the extent to which particular individuals discover common "points of entry to cross-cultural conversations"[89] and situationally specific transboundary rules and messages are discerned.

A final transnational communication skill bears directly on collaborative interactions across influence arenas. The public conversations initiated by transnationally competent professionals consist of ongoing reflective dialogues rather than "frozen snapshots."[90] The ability to engage in meaningful dialogue, to facilitate mutual self-disclosure, and to resolve communication misunderstandings across diverse communication styles promotes the initiation and sustenance of positive interpersonal relations. Among professionals, authentic and revealing transnational communication is advanced by welcoming feedback from laypersons (including young people) and communities "regardless of its validity or the eloquence with which it is phrased."[91]

Functional (Project/Task) Adroitness

Possession of the four previously mentioned skill sets does not ensure transnational competence. One "can have the necessary information, be motivated by the appropriate feelings and intentions, and still lack the behavioral skills necessary to achieve competence."[92] Successful professional careers in today's interconnected world also require transnational functional expertise.[93]

Transnationally competent professionals are active agents who contribute to and shape operations and outcomes across multiple boundaries and governance systems. In general, their actions must be perceived by counterparts with diverse identities as appropriate and valuable for "achieving mutual goals or satisfying the requirements of particular tasks" in specific situations.[94] This behavioral challenge requires a final set of five transferrable operational skills that underlie effective social and technical problem solving and project/task performance in transboundary situations.

Successful transnational professionals are adept at nurturing instrumental transboundary relationships, networks, alliances, and partnerships. They are "connectors" who fashion and maintain an exceptionally large number of interpersonal links across diverse systems.[95] Thus, the first of the requisite TC functional skills involves the ability to relate to stakeholders and to develop and maintain positive interpersonal relationships grounded in the mutual discovery of common aspirations and shared humanity.

One key to success in building rapport and common ground is the capacity to behave in ways that demonstrate interest in and awareness of the ways different people understand the world and interpret events and experiences.[96] It is important to recognize that rapport building does not require common value perspectives or preclude the expression of divergent opinions, behavioral differences, and even critical assessment of aspects of the counterpart's lifeworld. Other valuable expressions of the transnational relationship-building skill are "a willingness to treat local counterparts as equals and to share work with them, a willingness to spend time on the job and off with local counterparts and to make an effort to get to know the locals and their families, an interest in the local culture, a willingness to learn the local language, an interest in more than just doing the job they came to do, and a lack of concern about differences in race and status."[97] These skill expressions are consistent with the attributes discovered to generate "swift trust" and "deeper trust" by the Emergency Capacity Building project.[98]

The establishment of positive interpersonal relations is particularly valuable for transnational functional performance because "in intercultural encounters, overall goodwill, respect, and enthusiasm allow people to generate 'credit,' and their credit allows mistakes to be ignored and forgiven."[99] Contrariwise, lack of interpersonal rapport erodes other TC skills—including emotional self-confidence and the ability to comprehend contextual constraints and opportunities.

Functional adroitness further involves the ability to apply policy and procedural insights, empathy, imagination, and communicative proficiency in transboundary collective actions. For instance, effective "milieu-moving"[100] actors must accurately identify stakeholders, assess sources and levels of power, read multiple and shifting identities, ascertain common professional objectives, empower lay participants, apply effective communication strategies, and appropriately respond to multidimensional and changing situations. The capacity to "leverage diversity"[101] greatly enhances these functional skills.

Teams and networks whose members possess multiple identifications approach and accomplish tasks in multiple ways. Skillful professionals possess the ability to employ an extensive and sophisticated array of transnationally accommodative organizational strategies—including diverse and satisfying interaction paths and the management of differences between headquarters and project field sites.[102] Skill in navigating complex local and globally networked channels builds on a high level of transnational analytic competence and is most effective when linked with the capacity to demonstrate flexibility and to improvise when interacting with team and project collaborators through selective application from an expansive repertoire of situationally appropriate actions.[103]

In addition, operational competence requires skill in overcoming technical and social problems, conflicts, and uncertainties along with ability to ensure the participation of key stakeholders and to achieve collective goals when dealing with transnational challenges and tensions among globalization and localization pressures.[104] Skill in attaining desired network and project outcomes builds on high levels of transnational emotional, creative, and communicative competence. It encompasses the capacity to manage conflict and forge compromises through cross-boundary negotiation and skill in transterritorial interorganizational coordination and cross-functional operations.[105]

Finally, in the interest of advancing equity of opportunity and social justice, transnational functional skills necessitate rigor and vigor in ethics and advocacy.[106] Foremost within the advocacy skill subset is the ability to act in ways that advance changes in those domestic and international economic, social, institutional, and legal/policy conditions that produce systematic disparities that constrain individual well-being. Along with skill in issue bundling and policy framing,[107] TC graduates learn to build and activate professional and societal resources that mitigate socio-economic inequities, power differentials, exclusionary policies, and other institutionalized constraints. Skill in connecting previously unconnected innovators and advocates across sectors and borders is emphasized in TC professional education.

Limitations and Relative Strengths of Transnational Competency

Competency—particularly the extensive portfolio of demanding skills required for TC—is relative, never completely realized, and contextual in that successful application is contingent on "both a specific relational context and a particular situational context."[108] Although the components of transnational-competence preparation aim to facilitate effective functioning in a wide variety of transboundary situations, graduates at all levels of education will possess different combinations of analytic, emotional, creative/imaginative, communicative, and functional skills. Like emotional intelligence,[109] no one will master all of the skill domains that comprise TC. Many different paths and TC skill combinations lead to excellence in role performance and the degree of transnational competence required will "vary by the nature of the task."[110] To ensure an impressive outcome in each transboundary interaction, however, the professional's profile of strengths should be spread across all five TC domains and typically include at least two specific skills in each domain.

Although professionals increasingly are expected to serve in different and often unanticipated foreign settings over the course of their careers, they cannot assume that their skill strengths are transferable from one transboundary context and interdependence challenge to another.[111] Thus, one can be minimally competent in an initial set of transboundary interactions and highly competent in the next (and vice versa).[112] Moreover, each TC skill set is always subject to change, and one's competence profile can expand through learning and adaptation or implode over time due to lack of use and/or faulty direction. Thus, aspirations to become transnationally competent require commitment to a lifelong learning process sprinkled with a heavy dose of humility.[113]

Because TC preparation addresses the multiple skills required to collaborate with diverse partners and clients in an era when daily life and work activities increasingly are shaped by networks that transcend nation-state boundaries,[114] we expect that graduated professionals will find transnational-competence applications more powerful and rewarding than intercultural-competence applications are when challenged by practical transboundary interfaces and interdependence issues. The TC framework is particularly inclusive in that it addresses conditions brought about by population movement, multiple identities, porous boundaries, transdisciplinary connections, fluid multinational corporate loyalties,[115] frequent job transfers, and socio-economic divides. TC preparation also resolves the culture-centered conundrum that has entangled intercultural and CC education by emphasizing diverse and flexible approaches that are transferable to interactions involving people who possess a multiplicity of cultural, political, and social identities. And TC education is distinguished by its emphasis on advocacy—a critical, if often overlooked, dimension of professional service.[116]

Chapter 3

Transnational Competence
and Professional Education

*Many, many tasks are required to make the world a better place. Our engagement
is likely to be more effective if we use our energy where it is naturally inclined
to go. When we engage in ways that are aligned with our personal vision and
values and where we already have talent or passion, our activity is also likely to
be sustained for a longer time.*

—Wendy Sarkissian[1]

TRANSNATIONAL COMPETENCE is acquired both experientially and through
formal learning. Certainly, preparation for participation in an interconnected
world is "a matter for the concern not simply of graduate students, but of the
youngest elementary-school children as well, whether enrolled in conventional
schools or in experimental centers."[2] Are students skilled in TC when they
commence professional education? While some students enter professional
degree programs with language facility, authentic overseas learning and service
experiences,[3] knowledge gained through required general-education courses,
or even, on rare occasions, emotional skills developed through links between
indigenous and global education at the primary-school[4] or secondary-school
level, most arrive with a limited TC skill base.[5] Higher educators in professional schools generally must assume that matriculating students will need to
prepare all five TC skill domains.[6]

Professional Higher Education
and Emerging Global Challenges:
Leap Forward or Left Behind?

More than 30 years ago, Alvin Toffler edited a provocative anthology that carried the title *Learning for Tomorrow: The Role of the Future in Education*. In his introduction, Toffler explains that the book's contributors "agree that technological and social change is outracing the educational system, and that social reality is transforming itself more rapidly than our educational images of that reality."[7] Do we find comparable lags in professional higher education today?

If Toffler and his associates were ahead of their time in recognizing that "schools and universities are too past- and present-bound,"[8] their future-peering efforts devoted scant attention to the social and professional transformations that *transnational* interactions would usher in within a few decades. Globally, we now find that professional-education programs are particularly deficient in preparing graduates with the skills needed to work in teams of specialists from many countries and fields.[9] Today, the future of professional education in most fields is tied to institutional and faculty capacity to anticipate and prepare graduates for boundary-spanning challenges; for effective participation on and leadership of multinational and multidisciplinary teams; for creativity, synergy, and initiative in the face of cascading change and uncertainty;[10] for shifting employers' demands for technical/technological expertise and practical training;[11] for lifelong learning; and for humanity's need for equitable and sustainable transnational responses and directions.[12]

To a variable extent, higher-education leaders in all professions and most countries have begun to address the present and future transnational imperative. However, curriculum-renewal efforts "have been limited in perspective and reach"[13] because these initiatives, while innovative and promising, suffer from two common limitations. First, professional higher-education initiatives tend to be partial and uneven, both in curriculum and pedagogy. Second, and particularly disquieting given that the relevant learning processes are fundamentally similar and that comparable obstacles to curriculum transformation prevail,[14] they tend to move in isolation, without awareness and sharing of parallel developments and breakthroughs occurring in other professional fields and locations. In the words of Sheri Sheppard of the Carnegie Foundation for the Advancement of Teaching, "professional preparation tends to be insular, with no mechanism for learning from other fields to develop strategies for tackling common challenges of professional preparation."[15] One notable exception is the 2008 report and recommendations of the International Commission on Education for Sustainable Development Practice supported by the John D. and Catherine T. MacArthur Foundation and based at Columbia University's Earth Institute.[16]

Addressing the Transnational Imperative
Through Transprofessional Enhancements

In the chapters that follow, we address both limitations. In contrast to the prevailing profession-by-profession approach,[17] we devote this book to transprofessional enhancements. By reviewing under the same cover the path-breaking developments and academic challenges that are emerging in diverse specializations where educators rarely converse with one another, we want to encourage U.S. engineering educators to learn about transnational developments in medicine, and to encourage Nigerian educators who prepare tomorrow's public administrators for the sustainable-development challenges that governments at all levels will face to consider the relevance of capacity-building curricular transformation in both engineering and social work. These, of course, are only two of the multiple cross-fertilizations we envision.

Our second objective is even more ambitious. By integrating insights from the transnational-competence conceptual framework presented in Chapter 2 with the most promising programmatic developments and insights identified in our review of selected specialized fields of study, we seek to unveil core elements of a TC professional curriculum and accompanying pedagogy. Our core curriculum suggestions for each professional field of study are provocative and bound to be controversial. Their transnational utility should lie in at least three outcomes.

First, our TC suggestions are meant to provide an initial transnational education framework that will spark multidisciplinary and multisited conversations about competency preparation for interdependent futures among academic leaders in all professional fields. We envision that these conversations will frame core interdisciplinary TC curriculum elements and assessment standards and enlighten the flexible components included in the service-specific approach pursued by each professional program and school.

Second, our presentation is intended to lead educators in multiple countries to engage in focused forward-looking discussions regarding the wisdom of incorporating and adapting some or all of the suggested core elements of TC curriculum and pedagogy as well as fruitful profession-specific considerations of ways to enrich and move beyond these suggestions. In these pages, readers can expect to find not a blueprint for transnational professional education, but a host of ideas and suggestions that can be adopted or adjusted in the creation of variable TC programs that fit the national and local contexts and academic culture of one's own university. Thus, our approach is consistent with Sheila Biddle's conclusion that universities are far more likely to select what works for their particular context than to adopt transferable international-education templates.[18] For most universities, forging and strengthening external links through transnational partnerships offer added dimensions of a synergetic forward-looking TC strategy.

Third, and perhaps most important, to the extent that TC preparation is perceived to enhance one's professional opportunities and performance in terms of the ability to contribute, prosper, and grow, it is likely to promote student motivation to learn. We cast a wide net around the learning-motivation outcome. In addition to mainstream professional education, we envision the TC framework as central to preparation for encore-profession careers. We applaud Harvard University's recent Advanced Leadership Initiative model of collaboration among five professional schools and its societal-impact emphasis.[19] Incorporating TC in "third-stage" educational initiatives would offer experienced professionals engaged in encore-career programs an exciting opportunity to develop new skills that are especially useful in addressing emerging transnational challenges.

Progression and Methods

To prepare graduating professionals for the challenges that will emerge in an interdependent world of chasms and bridges, educators need to keep focused on the horizon. In Chapter 4, we look to the horizon, mainly through the eyes of persons concerned with the future of education in each selected profession. What possible and probable transboundary challenges and "preferable futures"[20] do they envision? Chapter 4 presents selected visions of interconnected futures provided by international-relations scholars and disciplinary specialists, and offers suggestions concerning ways to discern horizon-rising challenges that will impact professional action around the world.

The next six chapters progress along a common path. Through a combination of literature searches, curricular reports, user experience, and extensive interviews with leaders in professional education, we explore ways that the teacher-education, business, engineering, social work, sustainable-development, and health/medicine professions are endeavoring to empower students to address transnational horizon-rising challenges through higher education. With support from the National Association of State Universities and Land Grant Colleges, one of us (Koehn) conducted telephonic and in-person interviews in late 2007 and early 2008 with twenty-one academic leaders at the forefront of international-education initiatives in the fields examined in this volume.[21] The voices of these and other educational innovators figure prominently in the chapters that follow.

Chapter 11 focuses on how professional TC learning can be enhanced. Through the lens of transnational-competence education, we critically review the multiple and innovative initiatives encountered today—from the introduction of new dedicated skill-based courses that are linked to and reinforced by across-the-curriculum learning[22] and overseas immersion experiences to participation in virtual transnational-team projects. Readers will find a rich resource for identifying TC learning approaches that can be adapted usefully across professional-education programs in this transdisciplinary review. Chapter 12 presents practical suggestions for mobilizing resources, institutional support, faculty buy-in, and student interest behind moving professional programs in the TC direction. Throughout *Transnational Competence,* far-sighted contributions, gaps, and ways to overcome obstacles to program innovation are identified with a view toward building tomorrow's professional curriculum today.

Chapter 4

Eyes on the Horizon
Discerning Transnational Challenges

In societies that have more memories than dreams, too many people are spending too many days looking backward.

—Thomas L. Friedman[1]

The possible future is not singular, but plural, subject to the choices we make among innumerable arrayed options. Moreover, the tools we have for identifying possible and probable futures are still very primitive. Yet some lines of development are more likely than others, and it is only by making explicit our assumptions about where we seem to be going that we can formulate sensible goals. Only in this way can we deduce the kinds of human abilities, skills and growth patterns that need to be encouraged.

—Alvin Toffler[2]

THOSE RESPONSIBLE for educating future generations of professionals must keep focused on the dawning horizon. In addition to encouraging inquiry about what is unfolding, an emergence focus is valuable because it alerts us to unfinished contemporary endeavors and the potential of informed and timely interventions.[3] Most essentially, "educators are futurists; they must anticipate tomorrow's needs and equip today's students with the necessary skills to meet those needs."[4]

How future challenges are envisioned largely shapes the kinds of skills that educators nurture. Higher-education institutions prepare learners to advance preferred futures. Among persons working along the edge of intersecting boundaries, the envisioning process carries special meaning because "when visions vividly describe a desired future, they have the magnetic power to draw us toward them and galvanize action."[5] For professionals, the *common future* is that tomorrow's roles will require spanning boundaries of place, field of expertise, socio-cultural context, and identity. Interdependence challenges cannot be treated in lonely silos that stretch precariously upward. The *variable future* rises from the specific form of the constantly evolving transnational challenges and the alternative approaches that unfold along the strands of time.

In this chapter, we bring two perspectives to bear as illuminating guides in unmasking the murky and morphing future transnational challenges that frame demand for the next generation of professional skills. The first is the lens of international relations (IR). Our idealized vision of the IR scholar is a woman or man who has mastered the nimble balancing act of keeping an eye on the horizon and an ear to the ground. For future peering, distant developments need to be juxtaposed with proximate voices. Because the integration of knowledge and experience across disciplines often generates farsighted perception,[6] this book frequently works with crossovers among IR insights and envisioned professional futures.

The second future-discerning perspective embellishes the first with richness of detail. What specific transnational challenges need occupy the attention of educators responsible for preparing the next generations of practitioners? Here, we look for insight to bold specialists who work at the cutting-edge of the professional fields attracting our attention. What urgent challenges that require transnational competence will confront the world's graduates from specialized programs in teacher education, business management, engineering, social-justice work, sustainable development, and health? We expect that many of these challenges will involve "wicked issues" that "bridge and permeate jurisdictional, organizational, functional, professional and generational boundaries" and often become "entangled in a web of other problems creating a kind of dense and complicated policy swamp."[7] The mitigation of wicked horizon-rising transnational challenges will require coordinated and holistic efforts on the part of diverse professionals, networks, and partnerships.

International-Relations Perspectives

A number of the rising generic challenges of the 21st century are at least partially visible today. The challenges are huge, messy, and wicked. By focusing on the interaction of conditions, people, and events far and wide, IR scholars are positioned to identify "overlapping collective fortunes"[8] and to illuminate future directions that will intensify movement toward acceptable levels of peace and prosperity. Four IR insights that bear directly on professional education for the future are briefly considered here.

Porosity and Density

Future generations of professionals will be challenged by a world that is simultaneously becoming increasingly porous and dense. Although they will not entirely disappear, physical borders will be less authoritative and intangible boundaries will be continually breached. At the same time, networks, especially virtual ones, will intensify in density as more participants, rich and poor, professional and lay,[9] aggressive and peaceful, become (further) engaged within them.[10] With an inordinate number of actors operating in each professional-issue environment, and such an extensive degree of interdependence among them, density will often be so great as to enable any event to give rise to turbulence that reverberates in fast-paced ways throughout the environment and the network's components.

From breached boundaries to thickened networks, the future will be one in which mobility rules. One continuing dimension of mobility will be population flows, particularly from poor to rich areas both within and among countries.[11] Another manifestation of mobility will be the penetration, reinforcement, and restructuring of borders in cyberspace. In the words of Moisis Namm, editor of *Foreign Policy*, "these borders cannot be protected by motion sensors or National Guard troops."[12]

As the global governance stage becomes more diverse and crowded, sheer numbers will limit the capacity of all participants, including professionals, to influence the course of events. The virtues of transnational transnetwork cooperation will be heightened as domestic alliances of professionals are hemmed in by other rule systems and steering mechanisms.

Fragmentation and Integration

Future-oriented professionals will be challenged by a world filled with contradictions. At every level of interaction, they will encounter unfolding centralizing and decentralizing pressures, forces advancing globalization and localization, and fragmenting and integrating dynamics.[13] Professional learning, individual and collective creativity, and social-ecological resiliency will be enveloped in both coherence and volatility.

Professionals will need to be extraordinarily nimble as they engage diverse circumstances and complex issues transnationally and locally. They also will need to bear in mind that cross-border challenges often initially have local origins. Thus, it would be erroneous to treat the local as simply the close-at-hand consequences of the global.

The shifting push and pull of fragmenting and integrating forces and processes ensure that transnational outcomes cannot be attributed to global Westernization. The "direction, intensity, and effects" of particular transnational flows are empirical questions.[14] Specialists operating across nation-state borders and professional boundaries must be prepared for South-North and East-West flows as well as for the circular and mutually transforming interface of ideas, norms, roles, and practices.

Linked Destinies and Proliferating Interdependence Dramas

Increasingly, professionals and nonprofessionals around the world will confront "common local, regional, national, and international problems."[15] Interconnectedness in financial markets, for instance, produced spillover effects around the world, even in countries with robust domestic economic growth such as China and India, following the U.S. mortgage and banking crisis.[16] The coordinated efforts needed to address proliferating "transsovereign"[17] challenges that inherently and inescapably transgress nation-state borders require that people develop skills that promote cooperative interaction across boundaries. For instance, Vivien Stewart, Vice President of the Asia Society, foresees that "changing opportunities—such as increasing access to education and health services for all—and changing threats to human security—ranging from environmental degradation and climate change to global diseases, terrorism, and weapons proliferation—are driving international cooperation across a wider range of occupations than ever before."[18]

Using a Cultural Futures Delphi technique, a panel of 182 scholars and practitioners from nine countries reached consensus on a dominant trend for the first quarter of the 21st century that embodies the interdependence theme. The international panel agreed that the dominant undesirable, but highly probable, development is increasing inequality within and among countries coupled with greater resource scarcity. In an outcome of transprofessional concern, they specifically predicted that "conflict of interest between developing and developed nations will increase due to environmental deterioration."[19]

A global context of interconnectedness presents professionals with special challenges. Extensive involvement in transnational and boundary-spanning affairs infuses far greater ambiguity, uncertainty, change,[20] and complexity into professional work. Responding to and shaping interdependent processes requires effective networking and alliance building with counterparts in foreign places that must be rooted in productive links to one's spatial origins, technical expertise, and passionate concerns.[21] For nations in the Global South, the transnational flow of knowledge and skills offers timely opportunities to leap into a brighter horizon. Moving in this direction, Calestous Juma argues, requires (among other initiatives) jettisoning the "old-fashioned metaphor of the 'brain drain.'" The forward-centered challenge for developing countries "is figuring out how to tap the expertise of those who migrate and upgrade their skills while in the diaspora, not engage in futile efforts to stall international migration."[22] In other words, facilitating the transnational migration of transnationally competent academics and professionals offers low-income countries one promising path along the road to sustainable development. [23]

Nonstate Initiatives

In a system of global governance replete with spheres of authority that are deterritorialized and nonhierarchical, densely networked nonstate actors will perform increasingly decisive roles.[24] Many of these initiatives will be exclusively generated by individuals and organizations that are not associated with government entities;[25] others will involve public-private partnerships. In the public-health arena, for instance, "the Global Fund to Fight HIV/AIDS, Tuberculosis, and Malaria emerged in 2001 as a new site of global governance where public and private sector organizations participate in the distribution of aid through country-specific mechanisms."[26] In a forward-looking partnership that bears more directly on the professional higher-education curriculums of concern in this book, APLU, the Partnership to Cut Hunger and Poverty in Africa, the Forum for Agricultural Research in Africa (FARA), Higher Education for Development (HED), and the American Distance Education Consortium (ADEC) came together in 2007 to form the Africa-U.S. Higher Education Initiative.[27] With a $100,000 grant from the Bill & Melinda Gates Foundation and a $1 million commitment from the U.S. Agency for International Development, the Initiative has produced, among other capacity-building priorities, curriculum development in agriculture, environment and natural sciences, engineering, science and technology, health, education and teacher training, business, management, and economics.[28]

Specialist Perspectives

All professionals will need to deal with the general developments that IR scholars detect for the coming decades. In addition, each professional field of study will encounter specific interdependence challenges of varying complexity and urgency. Some of their issues will be unique; others will overlap. Although transboundary transformations will continue to defy full comprehension, the sections that follow explore current thinking about future challenges among specialists in the professional fields selected for attention in this book.[29] The challenges identified provide an important backdrop for the discussion of specific transnational skill preparations we present in Chapters 5 through 10.

Teacher Education

Are today's school teachers preparing their students for the future challenges of a changing world? Scholars have suggested a diverse set of issues and specific approaches as vehicles for effectively addressing the challenges associated with internationalization that will continue to confront secondary and primary education in the coming decades. Merry Merryfield and Angene Wilson's 2005 chapter on "Teaching Global Issues" provides a useful starting point for insights regarding how teacher-education specialists perceive future interconnected issues. The authors begin by asking, "What are global issues that are important for our students to understand?" Their chapter then lists seven broad potential issues that were cited most frequently by educators from fifty-two countries in a cross-national study: ecology and the environment, international development, intercultural relations, peace and conflict, technology, human rights, and social justice.[30]

In 1997, William Cummings, Professor of Education at George Washington University (GWU), foresaw that "whereas programs have traditionally been spoken of as advancing international education, there will be need in the future to give more attention to transnational education."[31] Cummings specifically advocated that teacher-education programs focus on issues that "crosscut national boundaries," such as peace and conflict resolution, free trade, human rights, and environmental protection.[32] In a similar vein, David Bloom posits that "children need to develop the knowledge and skills to deal with issues that go beyond their countries' borders," such as "environmental degradation, international migration, and international security."[33] Additionally, in a 2007 interview that drew on his experience in Japan, Indonesia, and Sri Lanka as well as at GWU, Cummings noted rising interest among U.S. university education majors in international development and diplomacy.[34]

Using change and interdependence as core considerations, Thomas Collins, Frederick Czarra, and Andrew Smith identified ten transnational challenges "as the basis for improved teaching and learning about the international dimension in K–12 schools."[35] Their ten interdependent issue categories are conflict management (violence, terrorism, war); international trade, aid, and investment; belief systems; human rights, social justice, and quality of life; resources, energy, and environment; international political systems and actors; demographic trends and movements; human diversity and commonality; technocratic revolution (science, technology, and communications); and sustainable development.[36] All nations are urged to integrate sustainable-development concepts in their teaching programs under the "Decade of Education for Sustainable Development" launched by the United Nations on January 1, 2005.[37]

For Wilma Longstreet, "alternative futures are at the heart of issues-centered social studies education."[38] She regrets that teachers tend to devote little attention to the future and the possible alternatives. Instead of systematic connection-building "between history, the realities of daily life, and the futures that loom ahead," teachers "seem to veer mindlessly first in one direction, then in another."[39] To improve social studies education at higher levels, Longstreet believes that teachers should be prepared to insert futures units into their curriculum. Such units would productively combine research techniques such as *trends analysis, cross-impact analyses* of multiple changes, and *environmental scanning* of interconnected developments for new trends with *developing scenarios* of probable futures.[40]

As Longstreet recognizes, future issues often overlap. For instance, teachers need to be prepared to guide student analyses of the potential implications of population projections on greenhouse-gas emissions, services such as water supplies and school facilities, housing and transportation, communicable diseases, political agendas, and so on.[41] Alternative futures should be explored by K–12 students from multiple national, regional, and transnational perspectives and preferred futures considered in terms of the entire planet as well as various indigenous, European, Asian, African, North American, corporate, species, and other priorities.[42]

Finally, some of our teacher-education experts emphasized professional challenges and opportunities that need to be addressed to facilitate the unmasking of future interconnectivities. A professor of multicultural education in Finland pointed to the increased need for teachers to engage in "transnational collaboration."[43] As professional spaces expand in education, teachers will be expected to succeed in interconnected transnational working environments.[44] Craig Kissock, Professor of Teacher Education at the University of Minnesota, Morris, with extensive experience in Nigeria, Zimbabwe, and the United Kingdom, foresees that teachers will need to be prepared to move across territorial borders and to instruct in classrooms that will not be monocultural.[45] He is concerned by the entrenched parochialism that prevails in U.S. teacher-education programs,[46] noting (in just one of many instances that could be cited) that there is little curriculum recognition of the Somali immigrants who now work on Minnesota farms or of the thirty-three first languages spoken in Minneapolis–Saint Paul suburban schools.[47] While the future U.S. teaching force will remain predominantly white European American,[48] nonnative speakers of English already account for about 10 percent of all students enrolled in primary and secondary schools, and their share of school enrollment is expected to continue to increase.[49] As more teachers, families, and kids move around the world, Kissock laments the lagging recognition of the value of international education in teacher preparation for the changing classroom[50] and of the potentially richer learning environment that multinational diversity provides for all students.[51]

Craig Kissock's concerns underscore the importance of preparing teachers to make transboundary connections that integrate global and multicultural education.[52] Merry Merryfield reminds teacher educators that linking human commonalities with diversity and "making and sustaining local and global connections with diverse peoples, particularly those marginalized within a national or global system, is a significant part of building the dialogue and community that can lead to conflict management and social justice."[53] And William Cummings foresees that "the big challenge is to move international experiences down to a younger stage in development."[54]

Business Management

In broad terms, interdependent commerce and prosperity in a fragile world economy constitute the future touchstones of business management. Increasingly, "foreign" investments will penetrate political jurisdictions. As one dimension of this emerging phenomenon, the rapidly expanding investment funds that hold vast sums of foreign currency established by the governments of China, Singapore, and the United Arab Emirates, among others, will acquire and divest in assets around the world. These "sovereign wealth funds" already control nearly $3 trillion in investments and "their wealth is expected to grow exponentially in the next five years."[55] Capital mobility ensures that more and more professional positions will be deterritorialized and that management will need to take multinational political interests into account.[56]

Another vision of the future holds that dramatic shifts in trade rules and boundaries are likely to emerge from World Trade Organization (WTO) headquarters in Geneva.[57] In new and often unexpected ways, the WTO will be engaged in governance as much as trade. Domestic higher-education subsidies, hiring practices, accreditation standards, and licensing requirements are likely to be challenged as "barriers to free trade" in the critical educational-services industry.[58] In the future, Lori Wallach, Director of Public Citizens' Global Trade Watch, suggests, business professionals also will be focusing on trade refugees and the global health-services industry.[59]

For today's business students, green technology potentially constitutes "the most important industry of the 21st century."[60] The senior policy makers and stakeholders from fifteen countries who participated in the Pew Center on Global Climate Change–

convened "Climate Dialogue at Pocantico" agreed that climate protection in the post-2012 period should be framed and achieved "in ways consistent with economic development."[61] Among the promising noncarbon-based economic-development pathways that would mitigate GHG emissions and promote sustainable economic objectives are fuel cells and hydrogen storage and refueling stations, zero-pollution zinc-air-battery-powered bicycles and enhanced pedal-power options,[62] plug-in hybrid vehicles, and wind and other renewable energy ventures.[63] Officials in California, for instance, have "consistently linked concern about climate protection with economic development opportunities," and policy makers in Texas have successfully cultivated support for wind farms by emphasizing "entrepreneurial opportunities for renewable energy developers...."[64]

Transnational networks built around capital, management, and technology figure prominently in visions of the profit-taking future. For instance, Ronald Deibert argues that changes associated with the "emerging hypermedia environment" are supporting "the complex diffusion of production across territorial/political boundaries by facilitating multilocational flexibility, transnational joint-ventures, and both global localization and 'local' globalization...."[65] In the service sector, Robert Moran, Philip Harris, and Sarah Moran foresee a continuation of the "twenty-first century trend toward economies of scale favoring large, multi-disciplinary and multinational ... organizations."[66] Christopher Bartlett and colleagues foresee an emerging need to transition from international, multinational, and global management to a worldwide approach to business management that they term "the *transnational* strategic mentality."[67] Transnational strategic management is responsive to local conditions and entrepreneurial at the national level at the same time that it remains focused on global efficiency through an integrated network of distributed and specialized, but interdependent, worldwide operations that capitalize on "comparative advantages, scale economies, and scope economies simultaneously."[68]

In a future of integrated trade but fragmented production across national borders, firms in industrialized and low-income countries that develop specialized small components and/or build on seams and segments of multinational corporate activity will enjoy the prospect of penetrating transnational niche markets.[69] In the face of rapid innovation by competitors, small and medium-sized businesses will find it advantageous to communicate directly with foreign suppliers and customers.[70] Manuel Castells foresees opportunities for enterprises of this size to forge innovative and adaptive transnational connections among themselves or with large corporations and corporate networks.[71]

In the emerging web-like arrangements, the center of operational attention will be the specific business activity established by transborder production, transport, service, and marketing networks.[72] Information-driven networks that respond rapidly to changing political and economic conditions, potential problems, and demands for new services and products will possess a competitive edge. The most useful networks will be integrated, but decentralized and fluid. They will engage multiple producers, suppliers, distributors, and customers.[73] Consequently, they will encompass regionally and nationally diverse management philosophies and practices.[74]

Furthermore, many future business activities will be interindustrial and undertaken by ad hoc multinational teams deployed from multiple headquarters that must demonstrate combinative and transnationally coordinative capabilities.[75] For Michael Marquardt and Lisa Horvath, building unified transnational teams that function effectively in contexts of diversity and distance will be "*the* business challenge of the twenty-first century."[76] As the U.S. Committee for Economic Development acknowledged in 2006, "global business challenges are too complex, occur too quickly, and involve too many resources for *local* teams or leaders to handle on their own."[77] To date, however, multinational teams working "across cultures and time zones" on highly complex projects of considerable importance to business objectives "fail far more often than they succeed"[78] in the absence of transnational competence. They are particularly handicapped when confronted by the unpredictable extreme events that arise from large-scale, complex, dynamic, and interdependent systems—such as global capital markets.[79]

The interwoven future of business management can be discerned in China's developing economy.[80] While China currently is the preferred final assembly station for a vast array of products, many of which are marketed in the United States, most components are manufactured in distant locations and predominant control over product design and profits remains overseas.[81] Today's complex cross-national production chains are powered by multilateral, multisectoral, multilevel, and multicultural strategic alliances and networks. China's future resource-needs outlook ensures that its entrepreneurs and officials will be required "to develop far more intimate relationships with many developing countries than have existed before."[82] In the interdependent yet still highly competitive trade, finance, technological-innovation, and resource-limited environment that will prevail, Chinese managers affiliated with government agencies, state enterprises, and joint ventures will require expertise in collaborating with, negotiating with, and transforming agents of multinational capital and other influential external actors—including overseas investors, business partners, foreign diplomats, representatives of international finance, multilateral and international NGO personnel,[83] government policy makers, business-media representatives, and technology experts in the diaspora. On a daily basis, a growing proportion of China's business managers will perform critical transnational roles associated with infrastructure provision, labor mobilization, product integration, cross-national network maintenance,[84] product licenses, permission to operate locally, and concessions and/or favors.

In our transcontinentally interdependent financial system, "a crisis that began with a bubble in Florida condos and California McMansions caused monetary catastrophe in Iceland" and other countries in 2008.[85] In a future where executives are challenged by cascading crises that constrain sustainable development,[86] TC preparation will be at the cutting edge of professional education for strategic business management.[87] In particular, enhancing human capital needs to accompany institutional and policy reforms if political economies in transition are to attain world-class standards.[88]

With increasing integration into a global economy conditioned by volatile and diminishing natural resources and mergers that cross industries and disparate corporate cultures,[89] transnational competence will become an expected standard of employment for indigenous entrepreneurs and negotiators in the Global South.[90] In order to establish the planning and decision-making processes required to compete successfully in the global marketplace and to advance sustainable development in an age of rapid technological change and exploding linkages, economic and environmental interdependencies, and heightened vulnerability to external strategic manipulation, executives and managers must be skilled at anticipating network effects[91] and negotiating with and learning from people outside their own cultural boundaries.[92] While the financial outcomes sought by domestic partners in international joint ventures typically include investing in future capacity and increasing foreign-exchange reserves, foreign partners concentrate on repatriating maximum profits. If the competence demonstrated in transnational negotiations by the representatives of external business and government interests and the agents of multinational capital far exceeds that demonstrated by domestic actors, then hegemonic rather than mutually influenced hybrid forms of management are likely to prevail and the long-term dimensions of technological and economic development (in particular, the interests of future generations) are likely to be ignored or downplayed.

Engineering

As a profession, engineering is confronted by challenges that span geographical borders, involve interdisciplinary collaboration, necessitate a mobile workforce,[93] shrink time from initial scientific breakthroughs that are emerging at an accelerating pace to the adoption stage,[94] and demand grand and not-so-grand thinking. It is essential that tertiary-level leaders position engineering education for developments that lie on the horizon.[95] Looking ahead, engineering educators will need to build sustainable competencies that are contextually adaptable to challenges that rise across boundaries.[96] Engineering challenges cover a broad range of human concerns, but have in common attention to improving quality of life, joy of living, and commitment to the pursuit of sustainability.[97]

On the grand scale, an international group of leading technological thinkers has identified 14 challenges for engineering in the 21st century. No challenge is limited to a particular territory, and all require cooperation with specialists in other fields. The identified grand challenges awaiting tomorrow's engineers relate to environmentally friendly power, nuclear fusion, capturing and sequestering carbon dioxide, countering nitrogen-cycle problems in ways that enable agriculture to produce adequate supplies of food crops, expanding water quantity and enhancing its quality, contributing to personalized medicine by "reverse-engineering" the brain and cataloging specific dimensions of human genetic endowment that shape individual wellness and illness, computerizing health information in ways that advance tracking of the spread of disease and the relative effectiveness of preventative approaches and therapies, assisting in the development of new medications for emerging diseases, developing technologies for the early detection of terrorist threats, attacks on cyberspace, and natural disasters and for the rapid deployment of effective countermeasures, renewing aging urban infrastructure and services while preserving ecological balance, tailoring the mind's growth to individual propensities and abilities, improving methods of instruction and learning through computer-created virtual realities, and providing new tools that will enhance exploration at the frontiers of insight.[98]

In addressing many of these grand challenges, engineers will confront cutting-edge developments in nanotechnology.[99] The United Nations Non-Governmental Liaison Service (NGLS) foresees that "technological convergence at the nano-scale is poised to become the strategic platform for global control of manufacturing, food, agriculture and health in the immediate years ahead."[100] Growing attention to nanotechnology raises a number of urgent concerns:

> Who will control nanotech? Who will benefit from it? Who will lose? Will it introduce new risks for human health, safety and the environment?[101]

Charles Vest at the Massachusetts Institute of Technology (MIT) arranges engineering's challenges in two frontiers. The first frontier of engineering involves "smaller and smaller spatial scales and faster and faster time scales, the world of so-called bio/nano/info." The second frontier deals with "larger and larger systems of great complexity and, generally, of great importance to society." Vest foresees that the paramount second-frontier challenge that will face engineers of 2020 is "sustainable development of human societies on this system of ultimate complexity and fragility we call Earth."[102] Whether the two frontiers will converge or even merge in the future is uncertain; for now, rapidity is the shared feature and size is what distinguishes them.

Overlaid on these grand visions lies an even more demanding transnational engineering challenge: universal accessibility. Reflecting on the fourteen future challenges identified by its technological thinkers, the National Academy of Engineering concludes that "to disperse the fruits of engineering widely around the globe, to rich and poor alike" constitutes "perhaps the most difficult challenge of all."[103] A major part of the future path for preparing professional engineers, therefore, must include a transition vision that emphasizes practical engineering innovations that will have an impact on the lives of those with the greatest needs.

The design-revolution approach launched at MIT by Amy Smith, recipient of a 2004 MacArthur Foundation "genius" award, is an effort to move engineering education in this direction. At MIT's summer 2007 International Development Design Summit, learners from Brazil, Ghana, Tibet, and other countries focused on developing prototypes of machines that simplify village work. Such transitioning-to-the-future creations must utilize local materials and tools that are cheap enough to be purchased by the world's poorest people, can be bought and sold in increments, are easily fixable, and "fit ways of living that have deep-seated rhythms."[104]

Dan Hirleman has infused a similar vision as director of the global engineering program at Purdue University. Hirleman expects that the future challenges confronting engineers will involve logistics, information, and the design process. He envisions further changes in the types of projects engineers in the United States will be working on, how they will fit within global teams, and how work tasks will be divided among team members:

I think at some point there will be a global equilibration, but as you run systems uncoupled and then you break down the barriers with information technology it takes a while for the system to equilibrate globally.... I think the major challenge for the profession is how do we really add value in proportion to the standard of living.... We are going to have to do ... some different things and do what we do differently in a much more productive way. I would hope that ... the developed world can continue to grow their economies at the same rate and the developing world can grow at a faster rate.... I think innovation is a key here.... There are certain things you can manufacture at a distance and ship from a distance and it works. But, there are some things you can't....[105]

Another promising way of doing engineering differently, productively, and in a cost-effective manner in low-income countries involves bundling information and communication technology infrastructure alongside other critical infrastructure "such as oil and gas pipelines, sewers, drinking water pipes, railroads, electricity power grids, sewer pipes, and roads."[106] This approach, which builds on existing technologies and adaptable engineering skills, will enable populations in developing areas to lower initial investment costs, improve livelihoods, and continue to reap the benefits of spatially and functionally interconnected and interdependent infrastructure systems into the future.[107] By incorporating central learning components in bundled infrastructure projects, engineers will simultaneously contribute to capacity development and technological progress in low-income contexts.[108]

Yating Chang, assistant director of the Purdue program, believes that educators and learners need to consider that "the whole platform of engineering is changing." "Now when you talk about engineering as a platform," she continues, "you know the car is actually designed in Germany, the parts are manufactured in China, they get assembled probably in India and shipped to the United States, and marketing plans are drafted in Japan."[109] Given that the shift in engineering work from the G-8 countries to other locations "is, for the most part, permanent and irreversible," employers will continue to be eager to recruit talented and transnationally skilled engineers who graduate from programs around the world, including those in the South.[110]

In the future, freelance engineers drawn from a global professional-services market will fill an increasing number of permanent and temporary engineering positions.[111] The next generation of engineering students must prepare for professional careers that unavoidably will be transnational in content and practice. The additional 100,000 U.S. engineers and scientists that President Barack Obama proposes to train over the next four years[112] would certainly benefit from a TC engineering education. Future engineering graduates who will be working along the emerging globalized platform will be challenged to respond to the amplifying voice of the social imperative with "social responsibility."[113]

Social-Justice Work

Social responsibility also figures prominently in the future thinking of social-work educators. In the coming decades, social-work professionals can expect to be challenged by growing economic and social inequities and injustices that wash over oceans and territorial borders and involve transnational actors.[114] In *Just Practice*, Janet Finn and Maxine Jacobson challenge social-work students to reflect on the question "can one make meaningful claims for social justice in the United States if those claims are premised on the exploitation of people outside U.S. borders?"[115]

Janet Finn directs the Masters of Social Work program at the University of Montana. Her perspective on what she and Jacobson prefer to characterize as the "social-justice-work" profession has been informed by a joint doctoral degree in social work and anthropology from the University of Michigan and by frequent academic interactions in Chile since 1992. Finn expects social-justice-work professionals to be increasingly challenged in the future by situations that connect environmental concerns and sustainable human communities. In addition, they must be prepared to deal with taxing human, political, and environmental consequences associated with armed-conflict situations and mass migrations.[116] A future filled with "huge amounts of loss, grief, and bereavement" is anticipated by Lynne Koester, Director of the Peace Corps Internationalist masters degree program in Youth and Family Development at the University of Montana.[117] "I think another part of the future," Finn reminds us, "is to look at these challenges, not as something that happens out there, but that we are all intimately connected in these contradictions, inequalities, challenges. They are in the most intimate spaces of our local lives."[118]

Increasingly, social-work professionals throughout the world confront common problems and challenges that spill over national borders. Lynne Healy situates social work as a force for global change and development in an interdependent era. Her conceptualization of the future direction of the profession includes multiculturalism, human rights, and sustainability. The transnational challenges that Healy envisions will engage social-justice workers in the future will demand changes in practice and increased cross-boundary collaboration.[119] Ironically, the AIDS-scarred landscape in many countries necessitates that professionals working with children and youth be trained in gerontology because many of the remaining caregivers are grandparents with limited strength and resources.[120] For the foreseeable future, social workers can expect to face complex practice situations that invoke issues generated by poverty, ethnic conflict, prolonging life, transnational adoptions/abductions and families, the influx of refugees and other migrants, human trafficking, and primary-earner migration.[121]

Finn believes that training for future practice will be well served by a return to the roots of the social-work profession. Rather than emphasizing preparation for one-on-one individual, or clinically-oriented, practice, Finn is convinced that "we could be much more effective if we put our energies into systems like we did in the old days of social work at the turn of the last century, when there was a real movement around community building in response to industrialization, immigration, and urbanization in the United States."[122] What she has in mind is preparing social-justice-work professionals for work as members of interdisciplinary teams of professionals and community participants that address local social development[123] by focusing more on root causes than on consequences. "I don't want to diminish [the importance of] human pain and suffering," Finn acknowledges, "but until we get more proactive in our focus, we are just going to continue to employ ourselves—basically for people who have some level of resources to get individual help."[124]

In a horizon-focused vision that could be applied by all of the professional fields considered in this book, Finn and Jacobson advance "possibility" as a key concept for social-justice-work education. By engaging graduating practitioners in reflection about different alternatives and drawing attention to the power of human agency, "a sense of possibility enables us to look at what has been done, what can be done, and what can exist."[125]

Sustainable Development

Following the World Commission on Environment and Development's 1987 definition,[126] sustainable development has been widely considered to involve meeting the needs and aspirations of the present without compromising the ability of future generations to meet their needs. Thus, "sustainability implies maintaining the capacity of ecological systems to support social and economic systems."[127] While "ill-defined, politically contentious, manipulable, and at times contradictory,"[128] sustainable development carries weight as a guiding principal for collaborative South-North action. At the core of global sustainable development are the fields of agricultural sciences, public administration (government policies and interventions), and environmental (including natural-resource-conservation and climatic-stabilization) studies.[129] Each of these professional fields of study contributes valuable insights on challenges and pathways to improved and sustained quality of life.

Dave Acker, Associate Dean, College of Agriculture and Life Sciences, Iowa State University, has extensive experience working in Tanzania, Malawi, and Greece. From Acker's perspective, the major challenge facing agricultural education in the coming decades will be addressing "the global dimension of problems that used to be quite local; ... such as water scarcity, climate change, human population migration, plant diseases, pests, etc."[130] One example is the emerging connection of livestock methane emissions to climatic change. Worldwide, according to U.N. Food and Agriculture Organization estimates, livestock generates 18 percent of all GHG emissions, a figure that rises to more than 50 percent of total emissions in major meat-producing countries such as Brazil, Australia, and New Zealand.[131]

Earl Kellogg's career includes agricultural-economics research in Thailand and executive-management roles in the Consortium for International Development, Winrock International (a global nonprofit organization focused on rural development and sustainable resource management), and as the University of Illinois' chief international officer. He foresees that the future of agricultural sciences includes a whole set of questions that will focus on energy issues. According to Kellogg, "bioenergy is just one example of what is going to be happening; ... agriculture's engagement in the energy challenges of the future is going to be extraordinarily important globally."[132] World food demands will present concomitant future challenges for sustainable development.[133] "Should we use grain to fuel cars or to feed people?" Lester Brown asks. The use of crops for fuel already is driving up world food prices and the "grain required to fill an SUV's 25-gallon tank with ethanol just once will feed one person for a whole year."[134]

In 2007, NASULGC asked Kellogg to guide its Africa-U.S. Higher Education Initiative. In this role, he has focused on future institutional capacity building and emphasized the importance of linking agricultural areas and disciplines to other parts of the economy and to transnational opportunities. Kellogg is convinced that another challenge for agricultural professionals is that "we are going to be working a lot more across national boundaries and so are going to have to be more creative in thinking about institutional forms as well as your own personal career development that engages with the international and the global.... "[135] These challenges are likely to include "institution-building kind of work" and to require that we "learn how to deal more with other perspectives and the contributions that people in other countries and institutions make."[136] Kellogg's perspective is enhanced by incorporating the professional "team-building" vision advanced by George Wilson, Professor of Agricultural Sciences at North Carolina State University and senior advisor for University Relations and Agricultural Research at USAID.[137] In a similar vein, USAID Administrator Henrietta Fore envisioned a Global Development Commons, defined as "a community of continuous and real-time exchange, of collaboration and partnership and action between public and private donors, agencies, NGOs, host governments, and civil society—all operating as equals."[138]

Based in part on his review of concerns that are attracting rising attention at international public administration conferences, Harvey White, president of the American Society of Public Administration (ASPA), emphasizes the importance of responding to challenges of human security, global health,[139] conflict resolution, global warming,[140] workforce preparation (in response to underemployment and unemployment trends), and infrastructure development. White foresees that effectively addressing these challenges will require "a collective effort on a global scale" and "a framework that facilitates transnational collaboration."[141] The collaborative pathway to sustainable development must include the devolution of authority to levels close to the people coupled with community capacity building, Koehn has argued.[142] Devolution "offers the prospect that energized and dedicated public servants will find it in their interest to utilize their knowledge and skills in the service of active and committed local residents who are aware of the need to conserve natural resources and to maintain valuable infrastructure."[143]

Philip Morgan, Professor in the Graduate School of International Policy Studies at the Monterey Institute since 1997, has extensive experience as a consultant on public administration and development in Africa, particularly in Malawi and Botswana. Morgan also foresees that challenges of security and development, climate stabilization, and societal reconstruction will occupy development practitioners in the future. However, his future outlook places issues of international trade and finance at the center of "everything" that affects sustainable development.[144]

Krishna Tummala is Director of the Masters of Public Administration (MPA) program at Kansas State University. Tummala, who has long held leadership positions within the Comparative and Development Administration Group of ASPA, views "understanding the administrative culture of the other nation(s)" as the principal future skill that graduates in development management will need to master. In particular, he contends, public-administration professionals will need to guard against "the urge to advocate what one knows from experience at home as universally applicable or, worse, the only way to go."[145] Morgan makes a similar case for penetrating beyond "the illusion created by technology that there is far more homogeneity in the world than there is." When people can get to places like Bishkent and Vladivostok "tomorrow" and notice that the new buildings going up look like those in U.S. cities, "they assume all kinds of similarities that are not there."[146]

In addition to overcoming cultural barriers to understanding, Ali Farazmand, Professor of Public Administration at Florida Atlantic University and editor of several academic handbooks that focus on development administration, foresees a pressing need to develop extraordinary skills and capacity in order to prepare public administrators for unpredictable systemic challenges, for uncertainties and complexities that could be equivalent to experiencing three Katrina-like hurricanes at the same time. Farazmand contends that "we are facing an increasingly unknown world because of hyper complexity and changes worldwide." Many changes "are linear, many are cause-and-effect, but others are … not linear; they can happen faster, they can happen chaotically, and they can have multiple effects."[147] The challenges of crisis management, Farazmand adds, will be further complicated when they occur transnationally.[148]

Natural resource–management scholars working at the intersection of social and ecological systems arrive at Farazmand's concerns from a different, even more compelling, direction. Anthropogenic changes in the Earth's biosphere are occurring at a "faster rate than previously experienced in human history" and the resource and environmental problems generated by these changes increasingly "are proving resistant to solutions."[149] Social-ecological resilience is the key to maintaining current equilibria in the face of rapid and unpredictable changes that carry the potential for costly, catastrophic, and irreversible "flips" into new and less-fulfilling stability domains.[150] Thus, a resilient social-ecological system "is synonymous with ecological, economic, and social sustainability."[151] Conversely, sustainability is threatened when the resilience of institutions and natural systems is undermined. Carl Folke, Johan Colding, and Fikret Berkes conclude that ecological resilience is no longer as strong as it was historically due to "widespread human alteration of ecological interactions and biogeochemical processes, from local to global levels….":

> The paradox is that the processes of economic diversification, liberalization, and globalization ultimately depend upon nature's subsidies, on diversity and resilience of ecosystems, but tend to create increasingly fragile ecosystems, as witnessed in modern food, fiber, and timber production systems. Modern belief systems and associated institutional frameworks often seem to create simplified ecosystems with impoverished diversity, low resilience, and reduced capacity to adapt to environmental change. They create their own vulnerability.[152]

The future envisioned by these authors will entail "increased likelihood of surprises, and unpredictable and enhanced variability in essential resource flows."[153]

Climate stabilization has assumed a special place at the forefront of higher-education initiatives devoted to promoting sustainability. The "Climate Commitment" signed by hundreds of U.S. college and university presidents reads, in part, that "colleges and universities must exercise leadership in their communities and throughout society by modeling ways to minimize global warming emissions, and by providing the knowledge and educated graduates to achieve climate neutrality." Educators at the cutting edge of the fields of public administration, environmental studies, agriculture, and natural-resource management recognize that many of the future situations that will challenge professionals concerned with sustainable development are related to climate-change mitigation and adaptation.[154] In their compelling study, Timmons Roberts and Bradley Parks connect unresolved economic-development and equity issues with the failure to make significant headway on a post-Kyoto climate-stabilization regime.[155] In short, improved South-North relations hold the key to sustainable development throughout the world. Roberts and Parks foresee the need for a "new shared worldview of North-South relations" that involves stronger and more effective policies and actions that address poverty and vulnerability, long-term partnerships, and research on sustainable-development pathways. Ideally, engaging actionable perspectives on mitigation and adaptation "would include a large-scale, multinational and multidisciplinary effort, including engineers, climate scientists, economists, political scientists, sociologists, economic and environmental planners, and policy makers, and it would require the integral participation and guidance of scholars and policy makers [and community/group members] from the global South."[156]

Health and Medicine

The diverse future challenges that will confront medical and public-health professionals arise from a variety of interrelated sources. Using the Delphi technique, the World Health Organization elicited turn-of-the-century judgments of experts from developing and industrialized countries on "essential public-health functions" in the year 2020. Overall, the highest degree of consensus emerged around the view that environmental health and health promotion would increase in importance.[157] Specifically, nearly 80 percent of the Delphi-study respondents strongly agreed or agreed that dealing with atmospheric pollution will increasingly challenge public-health professionals in the future, and 73 percent cited "ensuring that hazardous substances and wastes are adequately controlled."[158] Rounding out the top five consensus future public-health functions were promoting community involvement (73 percent), providing information and education for health and skill enhancement through new technologies (72 percent), and protecting and promoting access to safe water (66 percent).[159]

Many of the predicted future public-health developments are connected to climate-change expectations and consumption behaviors. Actions that reduce anthropogenic CO_2 emissions can simultaneously lower personal stress and dramatically diminish direct and indirect threats to individual, family, and community health.[160] In general, policy and behavioral changes will become increasingly important as noncomunicable diseases overtake the burden of infections in the global South[161] and as ever more complex and surprising syndemics arise.[162] The unhealthy convergence of today's nutrition transition to diets high in sugar and rich in saturated fats, discouraged and diminished physical activity, global marketing campaigns, and the "promotion and rising consumption of tobacco and alcohol, have set the scene for 'lifestyles epidemics' to become the greatest challenge of the twenty-first century."[163] Many of the grand challenges of chronic noncommunicable diseases identified in 2007 using the Delphi method by a panel of 155 geographically and culturally diverse stakeholders from 55 countries relate "primarily to policy interventions, such as reform of professional training...."[164] In preparing for this challenging future, therefore, professional programs must build individual and collective capacities to sustain plausible, healthier paths and to counter forces that push people and societies "in dangerous or risky directions."[165]

For growing numbers of people, illness and treatment will involve transnational considerations.[166] Air-travel patterns among infected human hosts predict the spread of certain pathogens (e.g., the case of SARS), while in other cases (e.g., West Nile virus) the biggest risk of geographic spread stems from mosquitoes that hitchhike rides on jet planes.[167] Increased microbial traffic involving novel zoonotic infections that cross from their natural hosts into the human population, and other already present pathogens afforded an opportunity to infect new hosts by changing conditions, are a potent source of emerging pandemic diseases. Peter Daszak, Executive Director of the Consortium for Conservation Medicine, reports that 61 percent of emerging infectious diseases (EIDs) are caused by zoonoses; three-fourths of these involve transmissions from wildlife to human populations.[168] Animal-to-human viral infections have increased dramatically in the past decade and Daszak concludes that the future risk of EID outbreaks will be highest in areas of substantial biodiversity that are experiencing new anthropogenic interventions.[169]

In an era of accelerated human mobility, both elective and coerced, a health problem "'in a remote corner of the world becomes a world problem overnight. A world problem quickly becomes a local problem, in every corner of the world.'"[170] As more people in spatial transition compress the distance/time transmission of infectious and chronic lifestyle-linked diseases, migrant-health protection and treatment will assume increasing consequence for individual patients, receiving societies, and health-care systems. Displaced and otherwise dislocated people are particularly at risk of being bypassed by potentially beneficial interventions and "irregular" and undocumented population movements will pose special challenges of migration health.[171] In the words of Robert C. Like, Professor and Director of the Center for Healthy Families and Cultural Diversity, Department of Family Medicine, Robert Wood Johnson Medical School, this challenge involves "mistrust, fear, and stigmatization relating to migrants, refugees, and selected minority/ethnic populations as well as their own reactions (pro and con) to host countries and health and mental-health systems that may not be welcoming or accessible."[172]

E-health, the application of information and communication technologies to exchange and manage information that facilitates health-service delivery,[173] and telemedicine, synchronous transnational consultations during the course of active medical procedures and/or interactions, will figure prominently in the world's health-care future. E-health will enable underserved communities to access previously un-available and/or unaffordable expertise and information-processing software.[174] One example is the remote (regional or transnational) "use of personal digital assistants for the management of antiretroviral therapy, patient record keeping, patient tracking, data collection, and knowledge building."[175] Another prospect is using mobile phones to photograph malaria parasites and transmit the photographs to distant laboratories where they can swiftly be blown up and identified.[176] As all patients, including the poor and marginalized, become virtually mobile, health-care providers will need to approach their patient's lived world with transnational appreciation, imagination, and augmentation.[177]

Improved public health is essential for sustainable development and the achieve-ment of most, if not all, of the Millennium Development Goals.[178] "How can public health be advanced, especially when socially organized capacities to deliver preven-tion, care, and treatment lag far behind new developments in biomedical science …?" asked Craig Calhoun, President of the U.S. Social Science Research Council.[179] A key dimension of the required human capacity involves the ability to collaborate across boundaries of ethnicity and nationality,[180] or what Like refers to as the chal-lenge of "caring for an increasingly diverse patient population and working with an increasingly diverse health-professions workforce."[181]

The Institute of Medicine's Committee on the Options for Overseas Placement of U.S. Health Professionals recommends the development of new multidisciplinary curricula and the establishment of a Global Health Service Corps of highly skilled health professionals who would fulfill extended assignments based on the priority needs of countries in the South.[182] The most fundamental horizon-rising challenge facing educators at medical schools and public-health programs around the world involves the need to graduate professionals who will be successful in reducing the ethnic, class, and South-North disparities that currently prevail in health risks, ac-cess to beneficial advice and medical procedures, and treatment outcomes.[183] A future challenge for equity in health care involves building the capacity of physicians and treatment facilities in low-income countries to make use of new health-informatics systems and to fulfill the promise of personalized medicine.[184] To an increasing extent, professional success will require that graduating professionals possess the ability to participate effectively in the evolving global health infrastructure.

Tools for Discerning and Preparing for Horizon-Rising Challenges

Emerging from this horizon-focused exploration are challenges that are common and unique to the professions under consideration. For instance, the need to be prepared for and proactive in mitigating environmental impacts, particularly climatic change, figures prominently among the concerns recognized by specialists in teacher educa-tion, business management, engineering, social-justice work, sustainable development, and public health. The potential and threat of nanotechnology as a powerful enabler at the center of converging technologies is a subject expected to demand increasing attention among students and practitioners engaged in engineering, health care, sustainable development, and business.[185] Cascading crises exacerbated by complexity, issues connected to human migration, global health, human rights, security, social justice, new technologies, resource management, and sustainable development are perceived as future challenges by specialists across the professions. Explicitly or implicitly, multisited (especially South-North) impacts/implications and the rising need for transnational collaboration infuse these future-unveiling perspectives. Thus, among the grand challenges of engineering, enhanced capacity for the early detection of natural disasters and for the rapid deployment of effective countermeasures is framed in terms of the interest of populations in both poor and wealthy countries.

Wicked issues are socially and politically complex, nested in overarching systems, and conflictual. Relationships in economics, ecology, and many other areas are clouded, interconnected, and often nonlinear. Uncertainty is inevitable. Errors are likely; breakdowns are inevitable. Unanticipated interactions catapult complex systems built to unprecedented scale into cascading regional and transnational failures.[186] Transformative outcomes are difficult or impossible to predict. Alternative approaches are not immediate available; they must be discovered.[187] In the face of these daunting hazards, professionals in the six selected fields currently have access to a variety of known and yet-to-be-devised[188] techniques for discerning and preparing for horizon-rising transboundary challenges.

An important recurring theme in the future-scanning interviews conducted for this book concerns the value of transdisciplinary rather than "silo" preparation.[189] In October 2008, the International Commission on Education for Sustainable Development Practice concluded that "in a fragile planet that requires management of countless complex and delicate natural and social systems, future generations will require all the cross-disciplinary expertise that they can muster."[190] Such horizon-scanning insights suggest that "the ability to bridge disciplines and transform specialized knowledge into integrated practice may well become one of the defining competencies of universities in this millennium."[191]

In her penetrating analysis of integration and implementation sciences, Gabriele Bammer covers many tools that have application to unmasking interconnected futures across professional-education boundaries. Future-unmasking methodologies developed by systems theorists for probing complexity, uncertainty, and change by exploring the whole and its relationship to the various parts of an issue include "clustering theory, comparative systems analysis, computer modeling and simulation tools, control theory, critical path methods, decision analysis, divergence mapping, flowcharting, game theory techniques, input-output analysis, lifecycle analysis, linkage proposition analysis, network theory, optimization theory, relational database analysis, scenario building, viable system diagnosis, strategic assumption surfacing and testing, interactive planning, and critical systems heuristics."[192] Since sustainable futures are especially conditioned by the interaction of interconnected systems, complexity theory can aid in their illumination.[193] Paul Williams suggests that "the metaphors of complexity theory—strange attractors, bifurcation, edge of chaos and possibility space—may offer useful ways of exploring and understanding societal problems in the future."[194] To address the dynamic relationships shaping the multiple, interacting problems that lead to reinforcing health crises, Bobby Milstein proposes the orienting vision and change-directing power of social navigation, which adapts the Polynesian concept of wayfinding,[195] coupled with systems-dynamics (feedback) mapping, simulation modeling, and democratic participation.[196]

Participatory methods build on the assumption that all stakeholders contribute to unraveling the multiple dimensions of an issue. Participatory tools with application to discerning and/or addressing probable futures include Delphi techniques, focused problem solving, long-term domain development,[197] and taking into account contextual forces and players at local, national, and international levels.

Finally, knowledge management, exchange, and implementation techniques involve valuing different ways of understanding phenomena, enhanced methods of accessing and navigating today's wealth of information, extrapolating from recent trends, and developing in-depth understanding of how action occurs, policies are changed, and outcomes are influenced. For instance, Ray Kurzweil charts technological trajectories to predict future outcomes across professional fields according to his "law of accelerating returns."[198]

Scanning Ahead

The stirring poem "The Edge," written in 1997 by 15-year-old Indian student Lavanya Krishnan,[199] heightens our appreciation for the importance and urgency of preparing graduating professionals throughout the world with the skills they will need to confront tomorrow's transnational challenges with confidence:

> *Strolling along the stream of Today,*
> *I came upon the Edge ...*
> *The Edge of now,*
> *The start of tomorrow,*
> *The golden boat of possibility*
> *Beckoning to follow.*
>
> *What lies beyond ...*
> *... beyond the Edge ...*
> *What does the future hold?*
> *Alluring but evasive*
> *It dances before me*
> *Unfolding hopes of dreams untold ...*
>
> *Is there a room of darkness*
> *With not a glimpse of hope?*
> *Or ... is there a room*
> *With rainbow coloured triumphs*
> *Waiting ... to be explored? ...*

Professionals and nonprofessionals around the world are living and working at the edge of multiple and interconnected boundaries. Some of tomorrow's futures already are emerging; others are nested along more distant horizons. This chapter has explored future-unmasking voices regarding transboundary challenges offered by specialists from the six professional fields selected for special attention in *Transnational Competence*.

Discerning, and learning how to address, interconnected futures are complex and imperfect undertakings that, nevertheless, must inform professional curriculums. Among others, Robert Klitgaard, President of Claremont Graduate University, has recognized that:

> One of our universities' special callings is to take on the hardest issues, even those that seem insolvable. But we have to do it with others and for others. If we don't, who will? Who else will provide the hard analysis, the breakthrough thinking, and the long-run perspective?[200]

Working with others across boundaries on tomorrow's challenges requires that educators responsible for professional programs develop curricula that address interpersonal skills with as much ardor and rigor as devoted to technical competencies.[201] In the following six chapters, we endeavor to prod professional curriculum development by focusing on the transnational capacities needed for a future that will be loaded with interconnected, transboundary challenges. These chapters are intended to be suggestive, ideal, and illustrative. While our application of the five domains of transnational competence is tailored to the specific profession under consideration and draws heavily upon specialists in that field, the interconnected nature of the future challenges identified here ensures that there will be valuable lessons for medical school (professional field interchangeable) curricula among our suggestions for engineering (professional field interchangeable) curricula and vice versa. In building professional curricula that will prepare graduates for 21st-century challenges, we invite educators working at the edge of tomorrow's rainbow to draw in whole or in part from these TC suggestions.

Chapter 5

A TC Framework for Training
Tomorrow's Teachers Today

A key element in preparing a generation of globally competent citizens is the preparation of globally competent teachers.

—George L. Mehaffy[1]

Rᴇsᴘᴏɴsɪʙɪʟɪᴛʏ ꜰᴏʀ ᴇɴᴀʙʟɪɴɢ the next generations to respond successfully to transboundary dynamics in local and networked contexts rests heavily on teachers.[2] Mehaffy estimates that, assuming they instruct on average 150 secondary students a year for 24 years, one cohort of 30 teacher candidates will guide 180,000 students over the course of their professional careers; one group of 30 primary-school teacher candidates will teach 22,000 students.[3] Thus, inadequate teacher preparation anywhere in the world seriously constrains the ability of a country's population to meet future interdependence challenges.[4] We revive with ringing endorsement the 1997 recommendation of the Task Force for Transnational Competence that the U.S. national government should "add Transnational Competence to the list of national goals for secondary education alongside the worthy objectives of realizing world-class standards in math and science,"[5] while recognizing that success in such undertakings starts with enhanced teacher education.[6]

Life-long transnational-competence learning offers primary and secondary educators the opportunity to live and contribute meaningfully in today's diverse, complex, and changing communities.[7] Teacher educators throughout the world face similar challenges and opportunities for, as Craig Kissock reminds them, "we are a global, not local, profession and all educators and educational policy makers are coping with the same issues ... and can often benefit [from] decision making in other contexts."[8]

44

A comprehensive TC framework for the professional education of tomorrow's teachers integrates analytic, emotional, creative, communicative, and functional skill preparation across the curriculum. The flexible framework developed in this chapter for schools of education is built on the contributions of scholars and practitioners concerned with maximizing teachers' potential during and beyond the United Nations Decade for Sustainable Development, which runs through 2014. While this initial presentation focuses on skills that all prospective teachers should find valuable in an interconnected age, we also recognize that colleagues in Mexico, China, Iran, Ethiopia, and elsewhere in the world who are devoted to educating the most effective K–12 educators will want to fill in its gaps and adapt the framework to suit their students' specific and evolving learning needs.[9] Likewise, the structuring of educational policy and transnational-competence curriculums (special focused course(s), infused throughout the curriculum, experiential opportunities, or a combination of approaches)[10] requires decisions that innovating programs must make by taking into consideration placed-based conditions.

Analytic Competence

Transnational analytic competence is the first learning outcome to be pursued under a TC approach to teacher education. Content building and integrating new knowledge into curricula are skills that typically receive considerable attention in teacher-education programs. Provided that one is able to keep up with changes in world affairs, knowledge acquisition and integration is appealing to pre-service and in-service teachers because it reduces fear of making mistakes. As we shall see, however, the comprehensive TC approach to developing analytic competence is quite demanding.

Most students arrive at school with, at best, surface knowledge about persons who are different. Nevertheless, "their lives are intertwined with these 'unknown others' and will become even more so in the future."[11] "From France to Sweden, Brazil to Bolivia, Indonesia to Malaysia," Marcelo Suarez-Orozco and Desiree Baolian Qin-Hilliard remind us, today's children "are more likely than in any previous generation in human history to face a life of working and networking, loving and living with others from different national, linguistic, religious, and racial backgrounds."[12] If all K–12 students are to develop the ability to understand diverse individuals, relevant political, social, and economic conditions, and transnational processes,[13] professional programs must ensure that pre-service and in-service teachers possess analytic competence.

William Cummings suggests that the first step toward analytic competence often involves building a knowledge base. As teacher candidates move toward analysis, he suggests, it is helpful if they first acquire "a factual base in geography [and] a sense of how economies develop, how polities are structured, and what are some of the major similarities and differences in … [political systems] around the world."[14] Merry Merryfield adds ecological, technological, and global systems to this list. She also finds grounding in world history (antecedents to current issues, accelerated interdependence, evolution of global systems, intercultural contact and borrowing, conflict and conflict resolution over time) to be critical.[15] Cummings further believes it is important that teachers gain facility in general social-science principles and familiarity with the particulars of at least several world leaders, including "their background, their upbringing, and what they believe."[16] And TC professionals who will teach in other countries should be able to discern differences in professional standards and practice and how they are interpreted and applied in the contexts in which they will teach.[17]

As the field of comparative education continues to move away from the study of educational systems,[18] teacher educators increasingly advocate approaching the knowledge-building stage by focusing on core issues through a global portal. Drawing in part on exemplary practice, Merryfield and Connie White find that teachers can select issues that "(1) challenge and concern citizens today and tomorrow, (2) affect the lives of persons in many parts of the world, and (3) cannot be adequately understood or addressed solely in a local or national context."[19] Merryfield's list of critical global issues and problems that support the construction of a helpful knowledge base include employment and meaningful jobs, health, population and family planning, development, human rights, migration and refugees, energy, environmental and natural resource management, hunger and food security, distribution of wealth/technology/resources, peace and security, transportation and communication, and prejudice and discrimination.[20]

Issues surrounding sustainable development[21] provide a trenchant illustration of core knowledge building among pre-service and in-service teachers.[22] For many, the principal need is to be in a position to expand their curriculum on "less taught-about parts of the world."[23] In the United Kingdom, for instance, the "Department for International Development is encouraging education about economic development by disseminating and providing teacher training for a curriculum that focuses on the Millennium Development Goals of the U.N."[24] In the United States, Cummings reports an "enormous growth" over the past decade in the number of students (many with multiple overseas experiences) both in George Washington University's international education program and around the country who are interested in careers that incorporate sustainable-development concerns.[25]

While knowledge is indispensable, the primary transnational analytic objective of a TC curriculum involves ways of learning and knowing rather than memorization. Since a university course or program will not be deep enough to sustain a high level of analytic competence regarding particular dynamic situations or cultures, teacher preparation requires attention to lifelong learning processes and reasoning.[26] Teachers' long-term analytic competence involves being in command of multiple local and global sources,[27] networked learning opportunities, and informal as well as formal educational opportunities.[28] They should be cognizant of multiple perspectives,[29] aware that "no single version of 'truth' is total and permanent,"[30] diligent about eliminating and countering stereotypes encountered in instructional materials,[31] and able to apply conceptual frameworks in the analysis of complex issues, situations, and policy decisions.[32] In the analytic domain, therefore, TC teacher education focuses on developing "abilities to collect, analyze, and evaluate information from different perspectives and worldviews."[33] As one component of analytic competence, evaluation should include "determining what is and what is not important when faced with issues and focusing on those things that matter and that can result in progress...."[34] The comparative method of exploring similarities, unique manifestations, contrasts, and analogies in premises, perspectives, policies, and practices is particularly illuminating in connection with this analytic skill.[35]

TC education also places emphasis on the capacity to identify underlying factors that influence local and global events and outcomes and on unmasking ways in which local decisions affect and are affected by transnational connections and transactions. Learning to develop a primary-, middle-, or secondary-school unit organized around a glocal theme such as food production and distribution constitutes one practical application of this transnational analytic skill.[36] In such multidisciplinary endeavors, it remains important that teachers are "able to bring something to the table that is quite solid in [disciplinary or] professional terms."[37] Their special insights into food-security issues and connections might be based on strengths in economics, business management, science, agricultural production, law, or health. For instance, second graders could "study people both inside the United States and outside (such as in Central America) who grow and supply our food, with an emphasis on interdependence of producers and consumers, processors and distributors."[38] In a secondary-school illustration, Merryfield proposes that teachers of an eleventh-grade biology course present students with "case studies of agricultural diffusion in the Philippines, Kenya, the United States, and Argentina, then debate the global effects of new crop strains developed through genetic engineering to increase production."[39]

In navigating from transnational knowledge to critical analysis, it is useful to adopt the metaphor of the holograph, "which presents all dimensions simultaneously to create an image-in-the-round."[40] The goal is to engage students' perceptual skills concurrently at multiple levels of analysis—personal, community, locality, regional, national, and transnational. The holographic perspective further encompasses differences in history, culture, political systems, and environmental conditions; common problems, aspirations, and strengths; and interconnectedness through ecology, networks, and technology.[41] Abilities to perceive connections and inequities across place and time, to situate community challenges such as hunger and homelessness in their global context, and to convey to students how present choices shape alternative futures lie at the root of transnational analytic skill development among educational professionals.[42] Issues surrounding migration and migrant experiences are particularly suited to a holographic learning perspective.[43] Sonia Nieto recommends that teachers enrich their curricula by developing interdisciplinary lessons built around the migration experiences of students or members of their family.[44]

Emotional Competence

Developing emotional competence is arguably the most challenging aspect of a TC teacher-preparation program. A first step in this direction is building what Mehaffy refers to as "coping competencies."[45] The most important of these are flexibility ("the relaxation of rigidity in perspectives and ideas"), tolerance of ambiguity, and open-mindedness (resistance to stereotyping).[46] Recognizing that a rich variety of multiple and hybrid identities and loyalties are needed to understand, imagine, work, and play across boundaries offers an additional coping competency.[47]

A more advanced educational objective is to help pre-service and in-service teachers seek out and begin to see the world from the perspective of stakeholders with profoundly different cultural, socio-economic, and experiential backgrounds.[48] Comparative perspective taking, Kubow and Fossum contend, "is essential for educators in the 21st century."[49] Skill in perspective taking, or "recognizing and analyzing the complexity of peoples' perspectives, and the effects of conflicting perspectives in human relationships,"[50] advances transnational emotional competence among teachers.

Learning to teach transnational perspectives goes beyond knowledge acquisition. It is grounded, in part, on the teacher's personal outlook on diversity.[51] When teachers view diversity as a student strength and a classroom and instructional asset, they will believe in the value of understanding and appreciating beliefs and behaviors of people who are quite different and will "want their students to *connect themselves* to people, issues, problems, and events around the world...."[52] Moreover, approaching student diversity as an asset allows teachers "to make the best of each of the student's contributions in the classroom."[53]

Cummings links transnational perspective taking to empathy, which he explains as "the ability to understand *why* others take positions or have beliefs that are contrary to your own as well as similar to your own."[54] Placing yourself in the role or mindset of another allows the teacher to gain insights into how others think and to be clearer about their priorities.[55] A lesson plan prepared by teachers with a developed capacity for empathy might challenge students "to think about how the things they buy or the jobs their families hold affect or are affected by people around the world."[56] Learning to be empathic also advances the "humanizing task," so that people from other regions of the world are no longer viewed as "less important, more expendable, and less worthy of concern."[57] The key to developing this aspect of transnational emotional competence in teacher-education programs, Cummings maintains, is conveying the importance of "having respect for others."[58]

In a 2007 interview with editors of the *Chronicle of Higher Education*, Karen Hughes, Undersecretary for Public Diplomacy and Public Affairs in the U.S. State Department, recommended that "teacher training should focus on preparing teachers who will foster an *interest in* global issues, global affairs, global knowledge, and language skills among young people."[59] Student motivation for learning about foreign contexts and diverse perspectives is enhanced when the issues teachers select connect global challenges to interests, problems, and/or experiences in the local community and/or in their own lives.[60] Merryfield and White conclude that "once students see that 'their problem' is indeed part of a larger problem that affects people like themselves in other parts of the world, they begin to think globally."[61]

Empathic bridges and connections offer pre-service and in-service teachers a powerful set of transnational emotional skills when they are joined with motivation and efficacy. The teacher who possesses a strong sense of self-efficacy will embrace challenging transnational learning objectives, including emotional-skill development, and convey high achievement expectations to students with diverse backgrounds. Transnationally confident teachers, moreover, are more likely than those with a low sense of efficacy to "hold themselves and their teaching accountable for the achievement of difficult learners."[62]

Professional educators, Cushner and Trifonovitch assert, must be able to "teach students from diverse backgrounds to interact with confidence in the interdependent world they are certain to inherit."[63] This skill begins with learning how to recognize and validate each student's potential contributions to classroom learning and how to teach students to honor their own and others' backgrounds.[64] In a transnational skill-based teacher-education curriculum, graduates (and, ultimately, the K–12 students that they teach) develop a realistic sense of transboundary efficacy for "an increasingly interconnected world."[65] TC teachers empower students by enhancing their personal confidence and courage, expecting and nurturing academic success, instilling the achievement ethic, and celebrating their accomplishments.[66] While a single teacher "cannot save the world ... we can all have a positive impact and leave the world a better place than when we arrived."[67] In short, teachers count!

Creative Competence

Educational efforts to cultivate transnational creative and imaginative competence among teachers are informed by the contemplation and construction of present and future alternatives or possibilities.[68] Thus, one challenge facing teacher-education programs is building capacity to "tap into" rich and diverse sources for inspiration.[69] Fortunately, "putting local issues in a global perspective usually reveals a wealth of new insights and alternatives."[70] Such insights often are useful in helping teachers and students envision desirable changes in an interconnected world.[71] Transboundary syntheses also emerge when teachers effectively employ comparisons to elicit perspective clashes and as a guide to discovering promising synergies.

Connecting different fields of concentration (e.g., art and social studies) with local ethnic heritages can be especially rewarding in terms of enhancing transnational creative competence. At the University of Vermont, for instance, one graduate foundations course "focusing on the aesthetics of education draws on socially conscious art like murals to explore global themes of empowerment and justice."[72] In the many places around the globe where they are available, "indigenous cultures are especially rich learning grounds."[73]

Alongside the discovery of how people in other places have approached dilemmas, the generation of possible alternatives, and consideration of the consequences of alternative approaches,[74] teachers need to develop awareness of the multiple levels available for creative action—personal, community, organizational, regional, national, transnational, international.[75] Skill in creatively employing technology to connect students with diverse peoples, issues, and perspectives will be an immense asset for future teachers at all levels of education.[76]

Creative teacher competence further involves the ability to unleash the untapped innovative potential of one's ethnically and socially diverse students.[77] TC teachers appreciate that "it takes innovation every day in order to meet diverse needs."[78] Preparation for nurturing creativity among a multicultural/multinational and hybrid student body involves learning to recognize different kinds of intelligences, to elicit academic and social insights, to turn resistance into dialogue and alternative suggestions into classroom contributions, to facilitate dynamic interactions and adaptations,[79] and to arrange innovative and risk-accepting teams. TC teachers at all grade levels enable their students to imagine preferred futures and to think audaciously about their roles in constructing them.[80]

Adapting 2,000-year-old insights from the Chinese martial strategist Sun Tzu, Yin Cheng proposes several key elements that are relevant for developing creative competence through teacher education. The principal creative skills to focus on are "doing the right things in the right time and in the right direction," meeting future needs (long-term relevance), "creating and materializing opportunities" from internal and external school environments, encouraging initiative and creativity in learning, teaching, and school development, and promoting human synergy and social harmony.[81] Kissock further emphasizes the importance of focusing on the ability to find creative approaches to dilemmas that "result in long-term/institutionalized processes/actions that continue beyond any particular person ... [or] change in leadership."[82]

Communicative Competence

Transboundary communicative skills are critical for teachers for at least two major reasons. First, they are essential if teachers are to advance learning in today's diverse classroom settings. Second, teachers increasingly need to communicate across cultures, borders, and socio-economic boundaries in the preparation and execution of lesson plans/learning strategies and in interacting with parents and other educational stakeholders who are different from themselves. However, teachers often fail to think carefully about their intercultural-communication approaches. Generally speaking, communication skills "are not in teachers' consciousness; they are not something teachers have been exposed to in their education ... or in their reading."[83]

Language lies at the core of all teaching tasks and the successful performance of the teaching function depends upon effective verbal and nonverbal communication.[84] Thus, developing transboundary communication skills constitutes a prominent feature in a TC-oriented teacher-education program. Learning and using another language is encouraged.[85] Learning a language other than one's first language opens teachers to a "different vision of the world" and to "diversity in communication patterns."[86] One goal of teacher language-learning is to encourage the incorporation at early-childhood and primary-school levels of a "developmental language program" that "allows students to develop a meaningful language sense."[87] Another goal is to ensure that nearly all secondary-school students complete two years of study of a language other than their first language.[88] At most, one-third of U.S. seventh to twelfth grade students study a foreign language.[89] Throughout the Asia-Pacific region, where the compulsory study of English commences at ages 6–12, the English language skills of public-school teachers remain inadequate.[90] In such contexts, the English-language training component of teacher-education programs needs to be strengthened.

In today's multinational classrooms, teachers will encounter students whose first language is different from the language of instruction. The TC teacher treats linguistic diversity as an asset rather than views it as a deficit. To reinforce the message that language diversity is valued, the different languages and dialects that students speak "should be made an explicit part of the curriculum."[91] Nieto suggests several ways that teacher-education programs can provide guidance in building this transnational communicative skill. First, teachers should be encouraged to learn how to say each student's name authentically. By not making "Marisol *Marcy* or Vinh *Vinny*," teachers are taking an important first step "in affirming who students are rather than who we may want them to become."[92] Second, Nieto recommends that teachers learn not to overcorrect student language.[93] Rather than engage in immediate correction, for instance, "teachers can model standard English in their responses or statements."[94] Other language-valuing activities include asking students to teach the teacher and other students some words in their first language that then are used in all-class assignments and to share poems, stories, or songs in their first language.[95]

To promote generic communicative-skill development for teaching effectiveness in the diverse classroom and for transnational collaborations, the TC curriculum envisions intercultural communication as a foundation course for all prospective primary and secondary teachers.[96] Craig Kissock identifies three particularly valuable transnational communicative skills that teachers will need in an interconnected world. First, he recommends that they learn "listening and truly hearing—the ability to step outside the dialog(s)/relationships(s) that one is involved in and view them as if a third party looking on."[97] Hearing what a person means, he adds, requires the ability to attend to what they are communicating nonverbally as well as verbally. In this regard, teachers need to develop sensitivities about potential areas of miscommunication—for instance, in the use of silence and in direct versus indirect communication styles.[98] Second, Kissock recommends that teachers learn vocabulary, tone, and a speech pattern that can be understood across boundaries.[99] His third recommendation involves "thinking from the other person's point of view"; that is, "what they are thinking as well as what they are saying" and "what do they need in order to understand me?"[100] This transnational communicative skill is important because "students may know much more than they are able to communicate, or they may be communicating much more than their teachers are able to discern."[101]

In a related vein, Michael Byram, Adam Nichols, and David Stevens contend that comparing, interpreting, and relating skills are crucial if teachers are to avoid misunderstanding what is said or written in intercultural communications. Transnational communication in the classroom and beyond is advanced when teachers are able to place comments and documents side by side, interpret how they are viewed from different perspectives, and relate the results to the situation at hand.[102] These scholars also emphasize the *discovery*-skill dimension of intercultural communication.[103] In order to acquire valuable knowledge, teachers need to learn how to inquire of their students and others with different backgrounds about beliefs, values, and practices.

William Cummings also contributes helpful suggestions regarding communication skills that transnationally competent teachers would want to learn. First, he cites "the tactful ability to pick up on what someone has tried to say, but hasn't quite articulated in a way other people understand, and to help get that set of ideas and beliefs fully communicated to those who are at the table."[104] This is particularly important when the first language (or the spoken English) of the person one is working with differs from one's own.[105] In a related vein, teachers should develop the communicative ability "to steer conversations away from dead ends and from deadlocks."[106] In transnational communication situations, moreover, teachers are challenged to articulate and elaborate interesting examples that are meaningful to students from diverse backgrounds.[107] Finally, Cummings warns against the U.S. communication tendency to "want to say the most." Many American communicators, he contends, feel that they have "won" if they have "commanded the floor for the longest period of time." A far more productive transnational communicative style for teachers, Cummings suggests, "is to let others have an equal role in the dialogue."[108]

Functional Competence

In teacher education, transnational functional competence involves both interpersonal skills and teaching outcomes. At the interpersonal level, Kissock notes the importance of developing close personal and professional relationships, while keeping the two in balance.[109] Gay emphasizes the importance of consistent and genuine caring about all students' academic, physical, economic, interpersonal, and emotional conditions, establishing positive personal relationships with students, and maintaining high performance expectations.[110] In professional interactions, teachers are called upon to treat people of means and those mired in poverty with equal respect.[111] In Cummings words, educators must "truly believe that everyone that you are working with has something to offer."[112]

Teachers need to be prepared to build school-based partnerships with diverse groups of parents, community members, and resource persons.[113] Partnership building requires an elaborate repertoire of functional skills, including political acumen,[114] collaboration in transboundary groups,[115] negotiation, the "ability to manipulate systems to achieve goals,"[116] problem solving, and measuring the achievement of diverse students.[117] One specific strategic partnership, recommended by the Task Force for Transnational Competence in 1997, would involve higher-education programs in joint work with local school districts on planning new K–12 initiatives "for strengthening transnational competence."[118]

TC preparation culminates in learning how to be active local and transnational participants, decision makers,[119] and problem solvers[120] based on analytic, emotional, creative, and communicative skills. Along with the knowledge and skills needed to participate effectively, teachers "must also develop a commitment to personal, social, and civic action."[121] Active pursuit of social justice is a valid and essential outcome of TC education.[122]

In a world that is "increasingly transnational, ethical practitioners need to avoid reproducing inequalities [among nonmainstream students] and instead steward educational experiences that can aid social mobility."[123] It is incumbent upon teachers, therefore, to develop sufficient functional competence "to help the children of people who have little political power or economic resources or people who are suffering from discrimination or oppression...."[124] At the University of Wisconsin, Madison, for instance, "a film of schooling in rural Peru helps students understand the pivotal role of teachers in ensuring that poor students gain access to health care."[125]

Transnational functional-competency objectives for teachers are aligned with the new wave of advocacy initiatives focused on the objective of "education for all."[126] The nonstate actors involved in transnational education-advocacy initiatives "work at both international and national levels, attempting to build strong national coalitions of NGOs and civil society actors that are capable of bringing grassroots demands home to Southern governments while also generating the international support capable of altering the policies and resource allocations made to education by international organizations and the Northern governments who dominate them."[127] For instance, the nongovernmental Global Campaign for Education initiative supported by Oxfam, ActionAid (which promotes South-South collaboration on education for life), Education International (an advocacy initiative launched through cooperation among international teachers unions), and Southern groups "mobilizes public pressure on governments and the international community to fulfill their promises to provide free, compulsory public education for all people."[128]

A capping dimension of functional competency involves curriculum development. The practical curriculum challenge for teachers committed to nurturing the transnational functional competence of their students is a demanding one. First, teachers will need to ask if "inclusion of the curriculum or springboard ... [will] be likely to result in some plan of action?"[129] The next curriculum challenge is to help students find ways to employ their transnational skills effectively in an advocacy capacity.[130] This includes learning techniques that help develop student political efficacy.[131] For instance, Steve Shapiro in the Social Studies and Global Education Department at Ohio State University nurtured a student teacher's ability to empower his students to address racial conflicts in their school "through interdisciplinary planning of a six-week unit on conflict management and racial conflict in South Africa."[132]

Chapter 6

Business Management

Educating MBAs Who Are Ready to Take On the World

> *Last week at a forum in Chicago, CEOs from four large corporations, including Caterpillar, all said that they want graduates with technical skills and some international competence (awareness, sensitivity, language).*
> —William Brustein, Associate Provost for International Affairs,
> University of Illinois[1]

> *If I wanted to recruit people who are both technically skilled and culturally aware, I wouldn't even waste time looking for them on U.S. college campuses.*
> —Anonymous global corporation respondent,
> RAND Corporation survey[2]

> *[T]he challenge of managing across borders is the ideal way to develop the skills required for managing across boundaries of all kinds in the modern corporation.*
> —Christopher A. Bartlett, Sumantra Ghoshal,
> and Julian Birkinshaw[3]

ARE YOU READY to take on the *World*?" reads the title of Duke University's 1997–1998 Fuqua School of Business bulletin.[4] A dozen years later, it is time to revisit the Fuqua School's question in a new and expanded light. Are Master of Business Administration (MBA) programs around the world preparing sufficient numbers of graduates who are competent to engage in effective transnational business management? What curricular enhancements are likely to enable today's graduating business professionals to excel in an interconnected global economy?

Consideration of the issues raised by these questions is important because corporate executives are more involved in global affairs in comparison with professionals who are not located in the world of business.[5] They have considerable clout within their firms, within domestic and foreign markets, and within national and global governance systems. Business managers are conspicuous among the global elite. In short, business executives count internationally.

Because men and women at all levels interact across borders with colleagues and customers in today's corporate environment, transnational competence is essential among new recruits who fill entry-level positions.[6] One can identify MBA programs, such as those offered by U.S. Centers for International Business Education and Research (CIBER) universities[7] or by the Asian Institute of Management (AIM),[8] that are specifically devoted to teaching international business strategy and/or providing instruction in useful foreign languages. New university centers for sustainable enterprise link transnational business management with respect for the environment.[9] However, corporate human-resource managers continue to rue the chronic supply shortage of top-level and middle-level managerial personnel qualified to engage responsibility and effectively on cross-boundary assignments by employing transnational competence.[10] In a 2002 survey of large U.S. corporations, for instance, roughly 30 percent of the respondents indicated that their company had failed to take full advantage of business opportunities "due to insufficient personnel with international skills."[11] The Task Force for Transnational Competence specifically advised Japanese corporations to devote greater attention to the transnational competence of managers selected for overseas assignments.[12] More recent research revealed that only a small proportion of surveyed Chinese executives based in Shanghai recognized the growing importance for China of a transnationally competent workforce.[13]

Many U.S. university graduates are not ready to take on an increasingly boundaryless world, the Association of American Colleges and Universities (AACU) warned in 2007.[14] While U.S. tertiary institutions lag behind Europe and Asia in preparing businesspeople to work on global teams,[15] even graduates of Japan's business schools are prone to adjustment difficulties when assigned overseas.[16] A similar dearth of transnationally competent business managers are graduating in low-income and transition countries.[17] Without increased attention among tertiary-education institutions to enhancing the TC of the managers of private domestic firms, joint ventures, and state-enterprise, China's remarkable development will be difficult to sustain given the demands of multinational production chains, volatile interdependent financial systems, global resource constraints, and the challenges involved in managing multilateral, multisectoral, and multilevel relations in China's long-term economic interests.[18]

To meet the growing worldwide need for transpatriate[19] recruits who possess the skills called for by global business leaders,[20] extensive curriculum changes will be required in most MBA programs.[21] For instance, business-school faculties at CIBER institutions have recommended major analytic, cross-cultural, and foreign-language curricular improvements in university programs.[22] Business management programs must ensure that the development of skills emphasized in the actual curriculum matches the soaring rhetoric that often accompanies use of the "international" and "global" descriptors.[23]

Building on the concerns and suggestions contributed by scholars and practitioners involved with transnational business, this chapter presents a generic, but flexible, TC framework for the professional education of tomorrow's business managers. We focus here on useful analytic, emotional, creative, communicative, and functional skills, recognizing that curriculum reformers throughout the world will want to adapt the flexible framework provided to suit their students' particular contextual learning needs.[24]

Analytic Competence

The analytic focus of MBA programs that strive to enhance transnational competence must be informed by contemporary and likely future employment trends. In the face of growth in foreign acquisitions, international mergers, foreign joint ventures, and strategic alliances involving foreign partners as well as increased competition arising from economic globalization, companies are valuing transnational experience even over cost-cutting skills.[25] With 294 offices in 48 countries, Intel (one multinational corporate example) regularly deploys teams consisting of employees with diverse national backgrounds to different locations around the world.[26]

Firms are adopting multiple strategies for moving transnational expertise.[27] Long-term expatriate assignments are less common today than in the past. They are being replaced by short-term and project-based experiences lasting less than one year. Some employees engaged in project work move up to four times in a year.[28] Managers and consultants also undertake short business visits.[29] Short-term transmigration allows little time for learning about each place of assignment. Meanwhile, new graduates from multiple overseas locations are being positioned at corporate headquarters early in their careers.[30] Employees based in their home offices are required to secure and interpret international data; ensure that foreign sites are supplied with information, goods, and services; and review and evaluate overseas opportunities.[31] To meet home-based needs for transnational analytic competence, firms also are "moving the mind without the body" through virtual networking.[32]

In professional business-education programs, the key to preparing students for such diverse and changing analytic responsibilities is learning how to learn[33] and to appreciate the value of continuous learning.[34] Managers are expected to be familiar with headquarters' operating style and key decision makers and to understand over-seas business contexts and the product lines, operations, and overall competitiveness of foreign subsidiaries.[35] In international business, therefore, transnational learning requires skill in accessing information face to face[36] as well as remotely. Graduates must possess the ability to tap into relevant economic-trend data, to engage in risk analysis,[37] to locate useful resources and human talent,[38] and to recognize promising technological and product innovations occurring elsewhere.[39] At the same time, they will need to be skilled at cultivating helpful information sources inside and outside project teams—including foreign nationals who contribute "understanding of workers and customers from their part of the world."[40] Determining the utility of gathered information requires "understanding the forces, events, and dynamics that influence the evolving performance expectations of a team."[41]

Among business-management students, transnational analytic competence includes technical skills, forward thinking about critical global challenges, the ability to engage in interdisciplinary analysis of complex relationships[42] and interconnected risks of cascading failures,[43] and cultural knowledge–building capacity. Valuable technical knowledge and skills are acquired through coursework in micro-finance and international finance, international accounting, international marketing, international human-resource management, international operations, comparative politics and international relations, international political economy, and international strategy.[44] A TC-focused analytic education emphasizes developing students' abilities to assess critically the forces that condition international business,[45] to draw insights from shifting value-chain linkages,[46] to frame management challenges and objectives in a transnational context, to identify valuable networks and define effective strategic alliances, and to "recognize and connect global market trends, technological innovation, and business strategy."[47] The capacity to maintain a thorough and current understanding of a firm's overseas markets and capabilities, as well as the organization's own culture(s)[48] and the cultures encountered at strategic-alliance and structural-support partner organizations, interfacing government organizations, and international and nongovernmental organizations, refines and strengthens managerial TC in the analytic domain.[49] Honing awareness of the changing connections that link multiple dimensions of sustainability and risk reduction constitutes another critical component in a far-sighted transnational analytic framework. Learning to conceptualize problems and to define approaches to problem resolution in sustainable terms are of particular value for managing "green" business ventures.[50]

The utility of cultural learning as a transnational analytic skill is demonstrated by the published results of a survey of MBA alumni of Thunderbird's Garvin School of International Management. About 90 percent of the respondents reported that their ability to acquire cultural knowledge has given them "significant" or "some" competitive advantage in their professional work.[51] Multicultural management has become universal.[52] Cultural knowledge is vital both for parent-company employees who must work with the personnel, customers, and regulators of varying ethnicity affiliated with overseas subsidiaries[53] and for international employees assigned to increasingly diverse corporate headquarters.[54]

In the TC curriculum, national and subnational cultural variations provide a starting point for more refined analysis.[55] In the multinational business context, for instance, it is important to recognize national and subnational variations in problem statements and procedures,[56] and to comprehend the culturally informed principles applied in cost-benefit analysis.[57] The TC approach to analysis moves beyond simplistic binary and static cultural abstractions, however. It also avoids the cultural-attribution error by explicitly rejecting the notion that all employees of a particular nation will behave in accordance with stereotypes based on national culture traits.[58]

As an analytic tool, nuanced cultural-knowledge building includes ethnographic understanding of different (and common)[59] perspectives, approaches to decision making, and management styles that prevail among Eastern, Western, Southern, and diasporic partners and competitors.[60] Enhancing the transnational analytic precision of business-management students involves a dynamic and complex view of culture. The TC learner appreciates that cognitive frames, schemas, and scripts can "change over time as a function of experience and situational influence ..." and that cultural obstacles to collaboration can be overcome.[61]

In short, other (social, economic, and political) variables must be considered alongside culture as important influences on behavior in business organizations, and students need to develop the discriminating ability to distinguish the extent to which culture matters. Determining the impact of national culture is largely a function of identifying moderating or amplifying conditions and untangling the extent to which they are present in isolation or in concert in each unique situation. For instance, national culture has a greater effect in situations where participants strongly identify as a member of their culture of origin and interpret the task at hand primarily in cultural terms; it is a less potent predictor among those for whom educational or professional identification play a stronger role in self-identifications and in situations where participants perceive cultural considerations to have limited relevance.[62]

Emotional Competence

Acknowledging emotions in business transactions is not a sign of weakness. Indeed, acting with emotional competence constitutes sound business practice. Developing *transnational* emotional competence for business situations presents a unique set of challenges for educators in professional schools of business.

In a working environment characterized by socio-cultural diversity, maintaining respect for different values, traditions, practices, and perspectives pays dividends. In the emotional domain, transnational-competence education reaches beyond acceptance of diversity; it demonstrates how respecting and embracing differences enriches interactions and enhances performance in multinational operations.[63] A starting point is recognition that all cultures merit equal respect.[64]

Respecting multiple perspectives requires proactive learning. The TC curriculum encourages students to connect emotionally with people of diverse ethnic, class, and disciplinary backgrounds who reside in abutting and far-flung locations. Realization that the outcomes of emotional connectedness include personal acceptance and improved decision making enhances student motivation to experience dramatically different situations and student interest in transnational empathy.[65] The ability to read emotional messages conveyed by persons with vastly different backgrounds provides the business manager with otherwise inscrutable, and at times unsolicited, insights concerning "current and evolving" employee and end-user needs and aspirations, competitor dispositions, potentially rewarding interfaces, and local social and political conditions.[66] Robert Moran and colleagues are convinced that the business leader "who is unable or unwilling to view reality from the many different perspectives involved is bound to make gross errors in judgments."[67]

Emotional competence requires attentive activation of all of one's senses.[68] Through the TC curriculum, the business student learns to be comfortable in transboundary situations, to seek out new cultural experiences, to be "open and flexible in approaching others," and to be "willing to reexamine and alter personal attitudes and perceptions."[69] Students also develop the ability to perceive the strengths and possibilities inherent in different perspectives.[70] By learning to avoid ethnocentrism and to manage multiple identities, ambiguity, role shifts, and unfamiliar living and working conditions, the emotionally skilled graduate opens the door to fruitful transnational exchanges and adaptation.[71]

Creative Competence

Innovations arise from the unique ideas contributed individually and synergistically by people working in organizations. In the business environment, transnational creative competence promotes innovative attitudes, products, strategies, procedures, and processes.[72] Creative TC is highly valued in transnational and overseas operations because managers are called upon "to respond imaginatively to diverse and fast-changing operating environments."[73]

The TC framework prepares students to think beyond political, cultural, disciplinary, and historical boundaries.[74] Marc Tucker, head of the National Center on Education and the Economy, reports that creativity "'typically occurs when people who have mastered two or more quite different fields use the framework in one to think afresh about the other.'"[75] TC educators further understand that creativity is liberated by "a vision unfettered by national definition...."[76]

TC learners seek genuine syntheses of distinct influences rather than predominantly one-sided impositions on foreign subsidiaries by managers associated with a more powerful parent company.[77] TC educators aim to stimulate positive, peaceful imaginations that celebrate interdependence.[78] They encourage students to recognize and be able to promote opportunities for productive transnational and cross-industry intersections and synergies in the global business environment.[79]

Transnational innovation arises from successful scanning, pooling, and integrating of widely dispersed assets, ideas, and capacities.[80] Thus, the ability to enhance development of a transnationally inspired organizational environment involves attention to implementing selection and evaluation criteria that are not nationally biased and adopting incentive schemes that promise to appeal to persons "from many nations ... who are capable of creating cultural synergy."[81] TC business students learn to pursue innovative processes that are locally leveraged and transnationally linked. Graduates need to possess the ability to identify local innovations that have applications in another, often distant, location and "to take market intelligence developed in one part of the organization, perhaps link it to specialized expertise [centers of excellence] located in a second entity and a scarce resource in a third, before eventually diffusing the new product or proposal worldwide."[82]

Facility in collaborating at the intersection of specialized boundaries will provide the key to unfolding the next layers of innovation.[83] A wealth of empirical data indicates that "the most innovative companies are diverse."[84] The TC business-management curriculum emphasizes developing students' ability to realize and take advantage of the synergistic potential inherent in transnational diversity and transboundary interfaces. Integrating the strengths of divergent cultural influences, for instance, expands the bases for continuous idea creation and innovative problem solving, and enhances prospects for mutual benefit.[85] Transnational interfaces typically initially involve considerable uncertainty. In the interest of encouraging the spontaneous emergence of transboundary synergy, students learn to embrace ambiguity:

> Become comfortable with the sense of not knowing what to do. Allow possibilities to arise. Open yourself to inspiration and tap your infinite creativity for constructing appropriate responses.[86]

To promote transnational creative competence, educators also guide students to cultivate "a sharp eye for spotting potential synergies where no one else sees them...."[87] With foreign students occupying 40 percent of the seats in many business-school classes, U.S. MBA programs have access to an incredibly valuable reservoir of entrepreneurial insights to draw upon in building transnational creative competence.[88]

Transnational creative skills are particularly valuable for contemporary business managers because the 21st century will be packed with massive "adaptive problems." Adaptive problems admit no ready solutions, require a new effort for which "no satisfactory response has yet been developed," and cannot be fully resolved by available technical expertise.[89] The global credit crisis of 2008 offered an introduction to the type of massive transnational adaptive problems likely to confront the business world throughout the current century. One worldwide TC curricular challenge, therefore, is to prepare business students for the kind of transnational networking and collaboration that will enable tomorrow's managers to "learn their way into the creation of something that does not yet exist."[90]

Communicative Competence

A critical challenge facing contemporary corporations and transnational business teams is "maintaining communication richness over distances."[91] Communication richness in business transactions and negotiations depends upon language proficiency and appropriate communicative behavior. To address the global need for enhanced capacity "for effective communication across cultural and linguistic boundaries,"[92] the TC curriculum incorporates both language training and valuable communication-behavior skills.

The first question to be addressed in building the TC communicative-competence curriculum involves the extent to which language training should be emphasized. Powerful arguments are advanced on both sides of the foreign-language-preparation issue, which we will consider in this section. The degree to which foreign-language competence is emphasized in the TC curriculum is a matter for individual program determination.

In most, but not all, cases, transnational business transactions are now conducted in English. Even multinationals with headquarters outside of English-speaking countries increasingly carry out business in English.[93] Because English is a language of wider communication among individuals from one country as well as among those from different countries, it serves as the "international language *par excellence* ... in both a global and a local sense."[94] According to Yves Meny, President of the European University Institute, "'the more the EU expands, the more English as a lingua franca is a necessity.'"[95] This situation requires that competence in oral and written English be guaranteed in MBA curriculums around the world. In places where English is not an official language, at present it must be offered as an essential foreign language.[96] Although English has served as the prevailing language of international commerce for some time,[97] William Brustein cautions "that may not be the case in twenty or thirty years; it may be Mandarin, it may be Hindi."[98] Given the number of Mandarin and Hindi speakers in the world and the dynamic economies of China and India, far-sighted programs will encourage students to be prepared in one or both.[99]

The value of language proficiency when participating on transnational teams or negotiating with overseas partners and clients is indisputable. In the Thunderbird study, 82 percent of the responding alumni reported that they had experienced a competitive edge in business due to their foreign-language skills. The respondents used their foreign-language proficiency for conversations (81 percent), meetings (62 percent), email (59 percent), presentations (52 percent), negotiations (47 percent), and reports (37 percent). Graduates with higher levels of proficiency were particularly likely to have realized a competitive advantage in their work.[100] There is a further reason why additional language competency advantages business professionals. If you can speak the first language of the person you are interacting with, Brustein explains, "you can reach a depth in terms of the conversation that you can't reach if you are just speaking a second tongue to them."[101] Thus, foreign-language ability facilitates transnational understanding and relationship-building. Nancy Lockwood, a human-resources specialist at the Society for Human Resource Management, found that speaking a counterpart's first language demonstrates respect, promotes rapport, and quickens the development of trust.[102]

Evidence that foreign-language proficiency is an important business asset has prompted some national leaders and scholars to support foreign-language requirements in business-school curriculums.[103] Nevertheless, many multinational corporations do not view foreign-language competency with the same urgency. One reason for the divergent practitioner viewpoint is the ubiquitous status of English as the language of commerce. According to Chris Van Someren, president of global markets at Korn/Ferry, "there's very little commercial application for foreign-language skills.

Because of that, the need to help expatriates learn local languages is not high on the corporate agenda."[104]

Edwin Miller, Director of International Development at the University of Michigan's Business School, asks, "will language training be the best allocation of a student's time, and will it lead to the development of a global competence?"[105] When graduates are expected to become mobile transpatriates rather than expatriates assigned to a single overseas location,[106] investing in learning a particular language—with the exception of the predominant language used at the parent company's headquarters—makes little sense. Moreover, Kenneth Lieberthal, China expert and professor of international business at the University of Michigan, suggests that the rewards and expertise/career sacrifices associated with learning a language such as Chinese, which can take three years of study just to reach the conversational level, are not worth the time investment. Occupying future executives with vocabulary memorization at the expense of other competencies is costly and might not produce substantial returns for the individual or his/her firm.[107] Given the variable returns associated with developing and maintaining proficiency and the vast number of existing world languages, the TC curriculum emphasizes (1) skill in locating and using a trained interpreter as a communication bridge, and (2) functional competence in collaborating with colleagues who return to home countries where they are fluent in one or more of the host-country languages.[108]

Beyond language proficiency, transnational communicative competence also involves skill in understanding common barriers to effective information sharing,[109] in listening and observing,[110] and in attention to nonverbal behavior. Transnationally competent listeners do not rely exclusively on electronic or other forms of long-distance communication, which increase the potential for misinterpretations. Face-to-face communication is "much richer."[111]

Although nonverbal-communication skills are crucial dimensions of transnational-communication competence,[112] they often are overlooked in business curriculums. Up to 80 percent of the messages people communicate are "nonverbal and implicit," and, in many cultures, nonverbal cues are more important and revealing than verbal statements are.[113] TC graduates will be poised to avoid "gaffes resulting from ignorance of nonverbal behaviors"[114] that damage business relationships and diminish the effectiveness of transnational negotiations.[115] Students will learn to demonstrate themes, to restate ideas visually, to encourage nonverbal participation, and to interpret silence accurately.[116]

The TC curriculum prepares students for the complexities of transnational communication by combining skill in the consistent application of established principles of intercultural communication across business networks with facility in adapting one's communicative approach to the local context and to individual relationships.[117] Thus, additional key communication skills in the transnational business context include sensitivity to the extra effort, stress, and fatigue experienced by team members who are working in a language that is not their first-learned (e.g., holding shorter meetings), the ability to discuss cultural and other differences openly, and the ability to elicit indications that "things are going wrong."[118]

Functional Competence

Transnational functional competence involves the ability to apply one's insights and skills effectively in a variety of performance-influencing settings that call for professional action and interactions that cross boundaries of place and culture. In 21st-century business careers, all managers will "need sound functional skills"[119] on a daily basis.[120] To succeed in transnational operations, functional competence requires more than technical and cognitive abilities in areas such as marketing, accounting, finance, human-resource management, and management-information systems. Two critical transnational functional skills for business managers are the capacity to engage in positive interpersonal relationships with people from diverse backgrounds simultaneously[121] and the ability to build and leverage mutually beneficial internal and external strategic alliances and partnerships.[122]

Employers increasingly expect graduates of MBA programs to participate on and lead transnational business teams.[123] Yet, critics contend that U.S. business-school graduates "have difficulty with even the most elemental issues of international business and intercultural functionally."[124] A 2007 survey of 305 U.S. company executives identified rarely available "teamwork skills" as one the top three qualifications sought among graduating job candidates.[125] The TC curriculum aims to graduate business managers who are "able to operate cross-functionally, cross-divisionally, and cross-culturally around the world."[126] A key transitional learning step toward successful transnational networking and collaboration is to focus on skill in developing social and professional relationships with persons who are different.[127]

Transnational business leaders rely on influence rather than authority. To be successful, therefore, they "need to establish mutual trust with a host of other people."[128] Lewicki, McAllister, and Bies define trust in terms of *"confident positive expectations regarding another's conduct."*[129] In transnational relationships reinforced by trust, all parties are positioned to transcend the risks associated with social and cultural complexity.[130]

To compound the challenges involved, the members of transnational business teams often are total strangers from distant geographic areas with different perspectives who "must focus quickly on critical tasks and have little time for building relationships or even for in-person contact."[131] Learning how to develop and express trust quickly in a context of simultaneous interaction with multiple and diverse colleagues is an important objective of transnational functional-competence education.[132] First, the ability to demonstrate sincere interest in a counterpart's life world facilitates the establishment and maintenance of interpersonal trust and good will.[133] In addition, emphasizing interdependencies and common objectives, and readily verbalizing positive feelings about trusted parties as well as appreciation and support, promotes and sustains bonding and bridging social capital.[134]

The ability to link disparate and dispersed stakeholders constitutes another important 21st-century functional capacity.[135] Some key relationships are intra-organizational; others are interorganizational and customer-oriented.[136] Functional ability to establish networks and build mutually beneficial internal and external alliances is nurtured by effective preparation in professional business programs. Today's challenges for TC educators in MBA programs are clear-cut. Graduates will be called upon to develop rewarding strategic transnational economic and political alliances,[137] and to enhance the local functional competence of partner firms responsible for specific components of the overall business activity.[138]

MBA students are aware that transnational functional skills are valuable for field-office assignments,[139] headquarters interactions, and top-management positions in today's global business environment. Japanese parent companies, for instance, hire non-Japanese and place the new graduates directly in positions at headquarters in Japan for two to four years. Early-career assignment at headquarters offers transnationally competent graduates opportunities to establish helpful "relationships with mentors and key managers, persons who can provide the necessary guidance and support once the foreigner is sent overseas."[140] European firms have led the way in breaking down the glass ceiling that has reserved top-management positions for locals. In mid 2008, for instance, 34 of the 100 companies on the UK FTSE 100 index were led by non-British chief executives—including 3 Frenchmen, a Spaniard, an Indian, a Kazakh, and a Swede.[141] The largest U.S. corporations also are hiring foreign-born CEOs.[142] Moreover, nonnationals are filling management jobs below the chief executive, and corporate boards increasingly are transnational in composition.[143]

These developments indicate that transnational competence rather than nationality provides the key to advancement in today's corporate world. Among the functional skills in a TC curriculum that enhance transnational role performance in local, headquarters, and top-management capacities are coordinating cross-border linkages,[144] demonstrating responsiveness to the interests of local units and higher organizational echelons, advocating for and securing resources and support, managing diversity,[145] handling distance and dispersion, arranging and facilitating the work of transboundary crisis-management teams,[146] and facilitating team operations.[147] Specific transnational-team-related functional skills include assessing members' strengths and limitations without cultural bias, motivating members and building confidence in their abilities to attain challenging goals, developing common expectations and commitments,[148] negotiating acceptable working relationships and equitable rewards, facilitating positive interactions, integrating team-member skills, and meshing different role perspectives.[149]

In the TC curriculum, functional-competence learning also encompasses ethical considerations. Specifically, TC's advocacy approach to corporate social responsibility integrates sustainable strategic management from an environmental perspective with the firm's long-term interests.[150] As Rick Crandall and Edwin Mensah explain, "sustainable development is not just focused on firms reducing emissions and ensuring the reuse of renewable and recyclable resource stocks, but also on the preservation of natural resources...."[151] In addition, MBA graduates are encouraged to view their responsibilities to include involvement in shaping the global economy so that equity as well as prosperity prevails. This aspect of a TC business-management education dovetails with the social-entrepreneurship curriculum already introduced by nearly thirty business schools around the world. Social-entrepreneurship programs address societal problems rather than merely focusing on business profitability.[152]

Chapter 7

Engineering Education for Interdependent Connections
Technology and Society

[G]lobalization of the engineering profession ... is forcing us to reconsider the role of future engineering graduates and the education required to meet that goal.
—Larry Shuman, Mary Besterfield-Sacre, and Jack McGourty[1]

Somehow we have to integrate global competency into the engineering curriculum so that it improves all our skill sets.
—E. Daniel Hirleman, Interim Director,
Purdue University's Global Engineering Program[2]

THE TRADITIONAL "RIGIDLY CONSTRUCTED CURRICULA" that have characterized engineering education are devoted entirely to developing technical expertise.[3] When engineering education is exclusively concerned with the technical dimensions of a problem, "it leaves out the important human dimensions, defining these as extraneous and irrelevant and inhibiting engineers from learning how to address them."[4] There is a pressing need to align the engineering curriculum more closely with "the challenges and opportunities graduates will face in the workplace...."[5]

One finds growing recognition among engineering educators around the world that preparation for a successful professional career now requires skill in collaborating with diverse colleagues on transnational teams and projects.[6] John Grandin, director of the highly regarded International Engineering Program at the University of Rhode Island, notes that "I tell students that they will be working with transnational

65

teams, ... collaborating with engineers ... in multiple locations around the world, ... although that won't necessarily mean that they will be working someplace else in the world."[7] Building transnational capacity among engineering graduates requires new and innovative higher-education programs.[8]

Although farsighted professionals urge engineering educators to facilitate transnational mobility by learning how to develop student multicultural competencies, the gap between desired and prevailing outcomes remains vast. In the United States, the National Academy of Engineering has expressed "concern that engineering students of today may not be appropriately educated to meet the demands that will be placed on the engineer of 2020...."[9] The specific challenge facing U.S. higher education is "how to enrich and broaden engineering education so that those technically grounded graduates will be better prepared to work in a constantly changing global economy."[10] Furthermore, existing Northern "systems of mutual recognition do not guarantee that a graduate possesses the necessary attributes to work effectively in a global/international environment."[11]

Transnational educational shortcomings also exist in the global South. Although enrollment in engineering programs has declined precipitously in some industrialized countries,[12] India now graduates some 400,000 engineers per year. However, a 2006 study concluded that only one-fourth are employable; the rest are deficient in communication skills and/or in the ability to work on a team.[13] Similarly, the mass production of engineering graduates in Egypt does not allow for the development of interpersonal competence.[14] At many Southern universities, curricula fail to invoke cross-disciplinary approaches or to address problems of national/local relevance.[15]

While one encounters substantial differences in engineering education across Europe, a key commonality across and within countries is "commitment to and felt responsibility for technological development." In contrast to the TC approach, however, the vast majority of existing engineering curricula in Europe lack a consistent and integrated framework for presenting the human dimensions of engineering work.[16]

This chapter addresses the question "What capacities will best prepare engineering students for transnational mobility and success as members of transboundary work teams?" In exploring this timely question, we find considerable guidance in the thoughtful and tested curricular and pedagogical contributions of Gary L. Downey and colleagues. Their learning objective for engineering professionals is consistent with the educational outcome envisioned by the TC approach: "*Through course instruction and interactions, students will acquire the knowledge, ability, and predisposition to work effectively with people who define problems differently than they do.*"[17]

Although we draw frequently upon the insights and suggestions for the "other (human) half" of engineering work presented by Downey and colleagues in three of the following sections (analytic, emotional, and functional), we find it conceptually helpful, of practical career-directed value, and interprofessionally consistent to place their contributions, along with the contributions of others who are concerned with re-envisioning engineering programs,[18] within the transnational-competence framework. The guiding and encouraging framework for engineering education that we present affirms engineering at the same time that it infuses transnational learning.

The TC framework developed in this chapter affirms engineering by consistently treating technological problem definition and problem solving as core dimensions of each skill domain.

Analytic Competence

In the TC engineering curriculum, multisited analytic competence is championed by integrating core technical and "professional" skills.[19] Given that the half-life of cutting-edge technical knowledge is "on the order of a few years"[20] and that global economic, political, and environmental conditions and trends, along with human interconnections, are subject to rapid and dramatic changes, learning how to learn over the course of one's career is emphasized in TC analytic education. To prepare engineering graduates for the still unknown problems and technological developments they will confront, TC educators concentrate on developing self-initiated efforts to acquire, replenish, and update knowledge, on thinking analytically,[21] and on potential applications of what one has learned.[22]

Technical analytic skills include the ability to identify and formulate a wide range of engineering problems and the ability "to design a system, component, or process to meet desired needs *within realistic constraints such as economic, environmental, social, political, ethical, health and safety, manufacturability, and sustainability.*"[23] Learning to accommodate "changes demanded by evolving technologies"[24] is a critical aspect of the technical curriculum. Reducing size, complexity, and "choke points" is a concomitant emphasis.[25]

Downey argues for preparing engineers to engage early on—"before the problem has been defined clearly."[26] The TC approach to technical analysis makes clear to students that "they can solve problems in more than one way."[27] The focus is on problem-solving methods, on identifying connections and patterns among complex data drawn from multiple sources, and on holistic thinking rather than on prede-signed solutions.[28]

Alternative solutions carry different implications for various stakeholders.[29] *Professional* analytic expertise includes knowledge of contemporary issues, awareness of global, regional, and local economic, environmental, and societal factors, and ability to assess the cross-border impacts and unintended consequences of alternative engineering approaches.[30] Among other analytic skills, engineering graduates must be prepared to "recognize and deal with the political dimensions of their work..."[31] that often determine outcomes.[32] Work at the interface of science, technology, and international relations, for instance, facilitates "progress on otherwise intractable transboundary conflicts."[33]

As technological developments increasingly become intertwined with political decisions, moreover, engineering students need to "develop a stronger sense of how technology and public policy interact."[34] Particularly relevant are policies that condition the design of appropriate, affordable, accessible, and sustainable transportation, water-supply, energy, sanitation, telecommunications, and waste-management systems.[35] The TC analytic foundation encourages students to pursue engineering practices built upon global, socio-political, historical, multicultural, business, and sustainable-development understandings[36] without abandoning rigor in argument and evidence and practical reasoning.[37]

Dan Hirleman does not think that "whether you make pieces in different parts of your plan in one place or around the globe changes much of the analytic process." However, complicated logistical, information, and process challenges arise when one strives to ensure that "the system stays integrated when it is being designed and done at a distance."[38] In skill-based TC programs, educators must possess in-depth understanding of how to nurture contextual analytic competence that discerns the effects on integrated design processes of ethnicity, nationality, class, poverty and underdevelopment, ethics, distance, and language. The objective is to graduate contextually reflective engineering practitioners[39] who are prepared to address the technical, socio-economic, and transboundary dimensions of engineering processes simultaneously.[40]

Thus, transnational analytic competence focuses on developing students' ability to apply technical expertise in a specific, often culturally complex, transdisciplinary, and/or rapidly changing, project context.[41] Professional preparation for transnational contexts requires the capacity to take into consideration the determinants of diverse approaches to work when planning, designing, and generating engineering services and products.[42] To help students build these skills, engineering educators must be capable of applying theory, methodologies, and case studies in ways that enhance transnational analytic competence.[43] "I teach basic engineering principles and apply them to different countries in the world," Tammo Steenhuis at Cornell University explains.[44]

In TC-informed engineering education, students learn that the effects of culture are "idiosyncratic."[45] In light of increases in population mobility across national borders and the high level of diversity that exists within contemporary nation-states, "individual cases become quite complicated"—particularly when "people spend substantial periods of their lives in countries outside their country of birth."[46] Thus, collaborators who "are raised, educated, and living in other countries are likely to define technical problems in different ways even if their own identities are multinational in some significant sense."[47] Rather than cultural attribution, the key TC learning objective is the ability to engage and understand ways of thinking about engineering work that differ from one's own.[48]

When engineering challenges involve multisited process- and product-development collaborations, skill in transnational analysis is indispensable. TC preparation for transnational teamwork includes learning to assess and take into account the competencies and life experiences of ethnically, socially, and academically diverse project participants.[49] In this connection, student progress often is made by learning from mistakes.[50]

In addition, the ability to participate in interdisciplinary analysis is emphasized in the TC curriculum.[51] The interdisciplinary emphasis is critical because "global competency for engineers necessarily involves knowledge domains at a far reach from the physical sciences and mathematics that constitute the core of technical knowledge."[52]

Increasingly, for instance, product-defining and technology-developing teamwork "puts engineers at the table with business managers, marketing and salespeople, researchers, labour representatives, information technology specialists, and so on."[53] Indeed, nearly half of the U.S. graduates with engineering degrees are not principally employed in engineering occupations.[54]

Emotional Competence

Preparation in transnational emotional competence recognizes the role of motivation and commitment in engineering. Among engineering professionals, motivation arises from "passion for designing systems, structures, and devices to solve problems" and conviction that engineering work "offers rich rewards for serving the interests of society."[55] In the inspiring words of the NGO's founder, Bernard Amadei, professor of civil engineering at the University of Colorado, Boulder, "you cannot do Engineers Without Borders if you don't bring your heart into it."[56]

People raised and trained in other countries and systems are "likely to draw boundaries around problems in different ways and to judge problems to have different sorts of implications...."[57] Collaborating with engineers who perceive and define problems differently "has become a regular condition of engineering work."[58] The emotional-competence dimension of TC learning addresses needs that arise in engineering contexts that are permeated with diversity.

TC emotional preparation for transnational project work involves the ability to anticipate and discern individual differences in orientations toward value, time, and space and in expectations regarding decision making and other work-related practices. For instance, it matters "if mathematics is highly valued, if low cost is essential, or if precision is a defining value."[59] Students learn the valuable lesson that their own perspective constitutes only one point of view among many that bear upon the processes of problem definition and technology development.[60]

Downey and colleagues provide valuable guidance for gaining insight into transnational, transdisciplinary, and transorganizational perspectives. They suggest that engineers learn to explore underlying dimensions of *location* and *knowledge*:

> *Location*: Who is defining the problem? Where are they located or how are they positioned?... Where are the key boundaries among different types of groups, and where are the alliances?
> *Knowledge*: What forms of knowledge do the representatives of each perspective have? How do they understand the problem at hand? What are their assumptions? From what sources did they gain their knowledge? How did their knowledge evolve?[61]

The next step in TC emotional-competence preparation involves mapping how and why different stakeholders understand and define the problem, their responsibilities, and the implications for their future roles and identities.[62] Mapping what alternative problem definitions mean to stakeholders (their motives and objectives) "requires stepping outside of one's own perspective and attempting to understand the problem in terms of different perspectives."[63] Put differently, emotionally competent engineers "show empathy with all diverse communities and individuals affected by engineering decisions taken in any given situation or environment."[64] This step is likely to yield essential insights regarding the constraints and opportunities that drive design choice.[65]

Dan Hirleman, head of mechanical engineering at Purdue University, maintains that "you are not a global engineer until you have sat around a table, face to face, and had to make decisions based on other people's different cultural views either on what problem we should be working on, or how we define the problem, or how we solve it."[66] The ability to identify the general concerns, fears, aspirations, and opportunity perceptions[67] of team members is a useful TC emotional skill in such contexts. Moreover, multinational situations often require the ability to accept, process, and thrive on ambiguity.[68]

By striving to discern technical issues from diverse points of view, the TC-educated engineer learns to recognize the limitations of his/her own perspective[69] and to respect and appreciate other nation's values and engineering practices.[70] Transnational humility and the predisposition to treat coworkers from different backgrounds as people who possess insights of value[71] are effective precursors for the collective energy that propels transboundary efficacy. One valuable advantage of developing respect for different perspectives is enhanced emotional ability to "assess how and when to apply the engineering method to the problems" one encounters.[72]

Perhaps the culminating transnational-emotional skill for engineers involves adapting one's own problem definition in ways that accommodate the perspectives of other stakeholders.[73] Learning these emotional skills is particularly important for U.S. engineering graduates who are "going to be in a minority on design teams in the future."[74] Skill in perspective accommodation also promotes transnational-creative competence.

Creative Competence

One defining component of educational preparation for engineering careers is technological innovation.[75] Technological innovation involves "the *application of invention*—the fusion of new developments and new approaches to solve real problems."[76] The TC creative-competence curriculum encourages engineering students to identify and explore opportunities to harness creative synergies that incorporate, but extend beyond, technological innovation. For instance, Allert and colleagues include the boundary-spanning ability to "synthesize engineering, business, and societal perspectives" as a key attribute of the global engineering professional.[77]

In our new interdependent context, Yating Chang foresees that "the number-one issue our students are going to have to work out is the balance between competition and synergy among countries."[78] Tomorrow's engineers will need to be prepared to think outside the box, beyond their nation's interests, beyond their country's resources.[79] They will need to be able to adapt to rapid changes in the global environment of constraints and opportunities.[80] One common creative challenge is to transform innovative ideas and scientific breakthroughs into transnationally valuable solutions quickly and with minimal expense.[81]

TC educators approach creative skill development in a synergistic way, teaching "the fundamentals of engineering materials better by including a transnational component."[82] Openness to and respect for diversity in perspectives and interpersonal interactions generate creativity in collaborative problem definition.[83] One of the leading engineering programs in transnational creative skill development is offered by Worchester Polytechnic Institute (WPI). For their senior project at WPI, about 35 percent of the electrical and computer engineering students address a real-world technical problem through design and synthesis carried out at an overseas project center.[84] At MIT, Design that Matters (DtM) offers engineering students "the opportunities and resources to work on projects for underserved communities in developing countries as independent projects."[85] DtM students have "developed numerous innovative strategies for solving problems in health, water testing and treatment, and rural education, among others."[86]

To cultivate transnational creative competence in Purdue's Global Engineering Program, Dan Hirleman challenges all students working on design projects. Consider, for instance, his solar oven project:

> I essentially had them working on the world's most expensive high-tech possible solar oven that would weigh nothing. You could carry it to the top of all of Colorado's fourteeners in a weekend or something and you don't care what it costs. Then, I had them designing one that only costs 30 bucks for Tanzania … , [where they] can't get Plexiglas.[87]

Implicit in Hirleman's teaching approach is confidence that contrasts in conditions, constraints, and value inspire and/or promote curiosity, imagination, and transnational creativity in engineering. In such exercises, mixing domestic with foreign students prepares a fertile learning environment for imagining new and different approaches to engineering problem solving.

Communicative Competence

The ability to communicate effectively across boundaries is widely recognized as an essential professional skill for engineers who work on transnational design projects.[88] More than twenty years ago, with a Fund for the Improvement of Postsecondary Education (FIPSE) grant, John Grandin initiated the University of Rhode Island's communication-laced international engineering program. Through the five-year URI program, students complete both a BA in a major foreign language and a BS in any of the engineering specialties. Originally, the program only offered the BA in German; today, it has expanded to include French, Spanish, and Chinese. Students spend one semester studying at a partner university and complete a six-month internship with a company overseas.[89]

Grandin concedes that globe-ish (stripped down, metaphorically free English) currently prevails in most multinational engineering team situations. Nevertheless, he contends, the benefits to graduates of becoming bilingual are "enormous." The benefits range from becoming sensitive to the nuances that distinguish native from nonnative speakers (of English) to deep exposure and understanding.[90] Grandin's position is that "bilingualism, if not trilingualism, is a basic qualification for the global workforce today."[91] He notes that European and Chinese graduates are expected to be trilingual "if they are going to be put on the fast track or a rising position in a company."[92] When group overseas experiential opportunities can be identified in advance, therefore, TC educators will find it advantageous to collaborate with colleagues who teach the foreign language that prevails at the assignment's location in preparing students for multinational team design work, academic study, and/or internships and work experiences.[93]

The TC communicative-competence curriculum for engineers extends beyond language training. Other key elements of effective transnational communication include nonverbal proficiency[94] as well as skill in working with interpreters and translators. Allan and Chisholm note that "no matter how good an understanding an engineer has of engineering technology, its implementation and successful development are directly related to competence in multicultural communication."[95] Transnational communication is advanced by helping engineering students develop the ability to listen sensitively, to disclose their limitations, and to discern "what they do not know."[96]

Engineering students need to develop the ability to "communicate with people from across the border or across the ocean … ; with people from different cultural backgrounds"[97] both face to face and via communication technology.[98] One aim of a TC education is to develop skill in articulating one's design, approach, or device with a diverse group of engineering and nonengineering team members, with customers around the world, and with policy makers.[99] Learning to communicate clearly and concisely by electronic means (email, data transmission, teleconferencing) is valuable preparation for transnational collaboration.[100] Enabling engineering students to recognize, understand, and respond appropriately to diverse audiences for their work[101] is another helpful TC communicative-skill contribution.

Functional Competence

Hirleman's goal for Purdue's Global Engineering Program is "100 percent impact." While he does not expect that every student will attain the highest level of performance, this ambitious objective does mean that "100 percent of our students have to move up that transnational competency scale."[102] Developing functional competence offers educators an avenue for ensuring that students progress along the TC continuum. For engineering students, transnational functional competence involves learning how to apply technical, interpersonal, management, and policy skills productively when interacting and negotiating with a diverse community of practice in different environmental contexts that remain unknown at the time of one's studies. The ultimate functional accomplishment one prepares for is the delivery of culturally and socio-economically appropriate products that meet societal needs.[103]

Increasingly, engineers are expected to demonstrate these process skills as team members working on transnational problem-definition, product-design, process-improvement, and manufacturing projects.[104] Allan and Chisholm recently concluded that "teamwork, regardless of race, ethnicity or culture, is a key driver in seeking effective engineering solutions."[105] In response to professional practice, "where teamwork has become the prevalent mode" of operation from idea conception to implementation, TC educators design problem-focused and work-centered courses that help students learn to be effective collaborators in and inclusive leaders of shifting multinational teams, projects, and sites.[106]

Yating Chang reminds engineering students that "if you are collaborating with other people, there is always negotiating involved."[107] In the first place, engineers are centrally involved in negotiating and renegotiating the contours of technological problems. Although the functional skill of transnational negotiation and the concomitant ability to overcome conflicts are essential in learning to "work effectively with people who define problems differently than oneself, including both engineers and nonengineers ... , the traditional engineering method, which is still regularly taught in engineering science courses, offers no method or mechanism for working with people who draw boundaries around problems in different manners."[108] TC education prepares engineering graduates to address and reconcile differences in problem definition, initial individually developed designs, and final collective solutions through the application of open-mindedness and sensitivity regarding the perspectives of diverse stakeholders during transnational negotiations.[109] Preparation for technical mediation is particularly valuable in this connection. Transnational technical mediation involves reconciling differences among diverse stakeholders, "alternative definitions of the problem, and alternative perspectives about what is taking place, including ... [one's] own" by introducing tradeoffs that meet technical and societal needs.[110]

Since the outcome of collaboration rests on intensely social exercises, TC engineering educators also emphasize the importance of personal relationship–building for successful transnational and transdisciplinary alliances, partnerships, and teams.[111] Improved ability to engage in interpersonal interactions that traverse boundaries and time zones allows students to amplify the application of their acquired technical skills and to overcome challenging political and logistical obstacles.[112] This aspect of TC functional engineering education is enhanced through the construction of strong transnational partnerships built on mutual learning.[113]

In engineering education, transnational functional-skill preparation also involves learning how to resolve ethical dilemmas[114] and how to act on social concerns. TC educators face head-on the ethical and social-impact issues raised by complex new engineering systems that engineers, for the most part, have "not been thinking about."[115] Specifically, they include "moral imagination" in engineering ethics education. Moral imagination involves "learning to critically assess one's own point of view and evaluate alternative courses of action."[116] TC educators also encourage engineering students to plan for the equitable distribution of essential resources.[117]

Across professions, there is growing student interest in meaningful action. However, teaching skills of social decision making has not been a priority among engineering educators.[118] A central focus of TC engineering education is on "tools that will improve the quality of life."[119] TC functional-skill education promotes professional commitment among engineering graduates to address the implications of their work through the lens of socio-economic inequities and power disparities.[120] For engineers of the future, Linda Katehi maintains, "accepting social responsibility" is an issue of survival, not philanthropy.[121] Certainly, considerations of sustainable development must be a major component in the transnationally competent engineer's functional portfolio. As Charles Vest of MIT asserts, "sustainable development must be on our agenda as we prepare the engineers of 2020."[122]

In pursuing sustainable development, the transnationally skilled engineer must be functionally prepared for "service in community-based environments which are racially, culturally, ethnically and linguistically different from their own."[123] TC educators nurture student interest in the humanitarian dimensions of engineering.[124] The service commitment directs student attention to low-income and otherwise disadvantaged communities and countries. When engaged in sustainable-development activity, the engineer's ability to apply certain tools contributed by nanotechnology and to utilize low-cost building materials is likely to be increasingly valuable.[125]

With some 250 small-scale engineering projects in 43 countries, the NGO Engineers Without Borders (EWB) is out in front in terms of practical initiatives that address self-identified community needs.[126] EWB "partners with disadvantaged communities to improve their quality of life through implementation of sustainable engineering projects, while involving and training internationally responsible engineering professionals and students."[127] The founding president of EWB-USA and co-founder of EWB-International, Bernard Amadei, simultaneously directs a parallel program in Engineering for Developing Communities (EDC) at the University of Colorado (CU) in Boulder (where EWB-USA is based).[128] By approaching low-income countries as "the classroom of the twenty-first century," the EDC program at Colorado enables engineering students to develop functional skills in mitigating socio-economic inequities through water purification, small-scale infrastructure, shelter, energy-production, communication, and other community-based projects.[129] In one recent EDC project, for instance, CU graduate student Marco Kuhlmann helped connect the remote village of Yanamano in Peru with a solar-powered wireless network that extends basic educational services.[130]

Chapter 8

Educating for Social–Justice Work in a Disparate World

Certainly it is hard to imagine a social work career in the twenty-first century that does not involve practice or problem situations with a global dimension.
—Katherine A. Kendall, Honorary President, IASSW[1]

In this age of transnational movements of people, power, and information, we need an approach to social justice work that crosses national, geographic, cultural, organizational, and professional boundaries and expands our thinking along the way.
—Janet Finn and Maxine Jacobson[2]

Across the globe, 21st-century social-justice workers will be engaged with cases or issues within their usual practice at schools, welfare centers, hospitals, and community settings that transcend national borders and involve transparent and clouded cross-boundary interconnections.[3] Regrettably, "many professionals are unprepared to provide informed and skilled assistance to individuals and families from other countries and cultures."[4] In much of the world, therefore, social-work educators are challenged to provide graduating practitioners with "new knowledge and competencies to cope with the social problems and conditions emerging from interdependence."[5] Although specific task content will vary by site, social-justice workers require transferable transnational skills to carry out their roles successfully.[6]

To paraphrase Katherine Kendall, social-work programs must become transnational if they are to be relevant in the 21st century.[7] While elements of a transnational perspective can be found in Canadian, New Zealand, Australian, and some EU professional programs,[8] few social-work programs in the United States and Japan have explicitly recognized the interdependence of conditioning factors and practice challenges or incorporated a transnational focus that will enable new practitioners to engage diversity competently across boundaries and distance.[9] Likewise, the transformative potential of a social-development perspective is insufficiently appreciated in U.S. programs;[10] social-work educators in the Global South are more likely to incorporate development concepts and objectives.[11] With few exceptions, however, the international dimensions of social-work curricula everywhere remain underdeveloped and uneven, and learning goals that involve developing transnational competence have not been addressed in a comprehensive and integrated manner.[12] This chapter elaborates a framework for introducing the five dimensions of transnational competence in professional social-work preparation.

Analytic Competence

The TC approach to analytic competence emphasizes lifelong *learning* skills; it concentrates on penetrating analyses of important social problems, approaches social justice and social exclusion from a global perspective,[13] and moves beyond the amassing of information about different social policies that has characterized international social-work education. In place of mastery of a limited and impermanent knowledge base, graduates will possess lifelong ability to access "the major sources of global and cross-national data on social work" along with helpful sources that deal with ways to improve one's practice.[14] This learning process includes developing the capacity to exchange relevant information and experiences with professionals in other countries, participating in international meetings and web-based courses, teleconferencing, and consulting foreign books, periodicals, reports, and news accounts.[15] It further involves cultivating the ability to engage in co-learning, where "the social worker and other participants in the process recognize their wisdom and the limits of their knowledge, consider the knowledge they need to inform action, identify ways to gather data, and draw upon their collective wisdom in rendering the data meaningful in the context of their work."[16]

TC analytic learning involves critical reflection on the social construction of knowledge and systems in light of power relations, developing the ability to deconstruct prevailing ideas, and becoming skilled at discerning *what is at stake*.[17] In a TC program, social-work students learn to question taken-for-granted assumptions and to assess the relative importance of various circumstances. Through critical-question posing, learners "make connections among seemingly disparate issues or events ... [contexts, and experiences, and] discover the underlying themes that resonate or have a pervasive influence for an individual, group, organization, or community."[18] In other words, a TC analytic education points students to the "need to grapple with the relationships between individual, family, and community struggles and broader political, social, and economic arrangements."[19] Graduating social-justice practitioners develop and refine personal critical frameworks for policy and political analysis and for recognizing and assessing the multiple and mutually influencing contextual influence of different values and ethics, hierarchies, and socio-economic relations[20]—including the influence over domestic social policy exerted by global economic institutions such as the International Monetary Fund, the World Bank, and the World Trade Organization.[21]

Transnational analytic competence is built on awareness of the dynamic interplay "that we are part of the construction of institutions and policies that have effects and constraints on human actions, but [we] never lose mindfulness of the possibility of human agency to change those structures."[22] Through the TC approach, students learn to discern emerging multisited "possibilities" that arise from the interaction of lessons drawn from policy and practice in vastly different social-work settings.[23] They discover how processes of macro, meso, and micro empowerment are connected to possibilities for social change. TC graduates also are technically equipped for participatory community-needs assessments, promoting neighborhood and household welfare,[24] grassroots outcomes research, and program evaluations.[25]

Economic and cultural analyses constitute additional foundational skills.[26] Social-work educators have long recognized the influence of culture on behavior. Thus, social-work graduates are likely to be ahead of many other professionals in cultural knowledge.[27] However, educators still face the constant challenge of unfreezing comfortable "assumptions of common ground as opposed to difference."[28] In a TC program, new social-justice practitioners learn to appreciate the role and limits of culture in shaping behavior.[29] Under the TC analytic framework, social-justice workers also consider the contextual influence on individual situations of economic, social, and political relationships.[30] In moving beyond strictly cultural explanations of diversity and appreciation for the sameness of our underlying humanity, they learn to recognize "ways in which unjust structural arrangements and histories of exclusion and oppression shape the meaning and power of difference"[31] and the contemporary social and psychological manifestations of poverty.[32]

The TC analytic focus is on interdependence. Through a systems perspective, students develop a "sense of the interconnectedness and ripple effects of one's actions."[33] In place of narrow specialization, TC emphasizes holistic understanding of the multiple and interlocking wicked problems (e.g., "drug misuse, abusive relationships, low skills, poor housing, street crime, poor health and unemployment") that confront front-line social-justice workers.[34] In social-policy courses, students devote special attention to the interacting multisectoral and glocal forces that condition wicked social problems.[35] In TC analytic learning, students in U.S. social-work programs constantly consider the question: *"Can one make meaningful claims for social justice in the United States if those claims are premised on the exploitation of people outside U.S. borders?"*[36]

To assist a foreign-born family or individual, the social-justice worker must be able to gather reliable information about particular stresses and losses encountered at five stages of the migration experience: premigration, departure, transit, resettlement(s), and temporary or permanent return to one's place of origin.[37] Take, for example, the social worker assigned to assist a newly arrived refugee ("Mussa") from Somalia in a U.S. middle school. This case required ethnographic skills.[38] The social-justice

professional needed to learn about Mussa's trauma and losses in Somalia, his extended family, his migration experiences, his ties to the Somali community, and any
continued physical or virtual interaction with persons in Somalia, Somaliland, or
Puntland.[39] "'Without an understanding of his background and his life,'" the case
worker reflected later, "'I was unable to comprehend Mussa's struggles. I would have
risked retraumatizing Mussa.'"[40] In the case of adult undocumented migrants, who
are ineligible for most public services, graduates also need to be prepared to search
for informal sources of support and to be informed about the legal and ethical implications of current reporting requirements.[41]

Social workers in countries of emigration face different challenges, including
children abandoned to inadequate care situations and the loss of breadwinners.[42]
In transnationally divided family situations, practitioners on both sides struggle
with complex child-custody and abduction issues.[43] Throughout the world, today's
professional social-justice workers need to be versed in immigration law, the effects
of different immigration statuses, and custody rights and expectations. In a number
of complex situations, "dialogue between social workers from sending and receiving
countries would be useful in resolving challenging issues...."[44]

Emotional Competence

Developing transnational emotional competence requires opening oneself to deep
learning about different outlooks and practices. Social-work students begin the
opening-up process "from a place of not knowing and uncertainty and allow ...
[themselves] to wonder."[45] The first step in opening up is to avoid assuming that
one knows another's experience and orientations. This requires the ability to "feel
and be present for another story," to open oneself to "another experience, another
learning moment," and to find ways that one "really accompanies another person
on their journey or a group or a community by really being present ... to hear the
story."[46] The student's inherent motivations to become emotionally competent and
to improve living conditions for vulnerable groups, particularly the poor,[47] are enhanced when personal openings are rewarded by new insights from and about others
that advance social-justice practice. Advancing social justice, in turn, generates joy
in work processes and successful transnational outcomes and diminishes prospects
for burnout among social workers.[48]

In building the transnational emotional competence that is required for social-
work practice in 21st-century contexts that are replete with diversity and multiple ways
of seeing and understanding, educators are challenged to assist learners comprehend
"how others make sense of their world...."[49] In connection with empathy-building,
it is helpful to remind students of the partiality of one's own understanding, help
them become aware of and overcome the roots of their own biases,[50] and encourage
them to sense and explore different ways people express emotions[51] as well as meanings that lie behind surface content.[52] Finn and Jacobson recommend that students
of social work learn to prepare for practice situations by engaging in "anticipatory

empathy"—a process of reflecting on the possible vulnerabilities, concerns, struggles, and interests of other participants.[53] At the same time, the empathic social worker is prepared to recognize individual and community capabilities, creativity, resilience, and readiness for change, and can discern untapped "social, emotional, and material resources that may be outside of ... [her/his] own experience."[54] In short, anticipatory empathy puts one "in touch with both pain and possibility."[55]

The transnationally emotionally competent social justice–work student learns to respect different values and experiences, including resilience, personal connectedness with family and/or community, environmental appreciation, and societal well-being.[56] Learning to identify and nurture strengths rather than concentrating on deficit-focused interventions will enable social-justice workers to promote individual, group, and community empowerment.[57] In the words of Michael Running Wolf, "empowerment not crafted by one's own strength is an illusion."[58]

At times, being transnationally respectful requires that social-work professionals learn to suspend judgment about unfamiliar practices (e.g., co-sleeping with babies). However, students need to learn where to draw the line in order to prevent irreparable damage to individuals and clear violations of human rights.[59]

An important part of transnational emotional competence is the social worker's sense of self-efficacy in transboundary situations. Demonstrations of the dimensions of emotional competence discussed earlier strengthens the new practitioner's confidence to act. Students gain confidence in their transnational skills through classroom case-study analyses and role plays, and through overseas field experiences—educational methods that are discussed in detail in the Chapter 11 of this book.

Creative Competence

In TC programs, social-work graduates will be "constantly challenged to engage with the circumstances and resources at hand, be inventive, and expand the spaces of hope."[60] The challenges will be especially acute in transnational situations marked by scarce resources. To prepare for their innovative roles, Finn and Jacobson suggest that social workers strive to become *bricoleurs*, "cultural beings with the wherewithal and imagination and sense of discovery and possibility needed to adapt and transform human and material resources in response to new challenges."[61]

In building capacity for sustained transnational creative actions,[62] TC educators emphasize creating a climate that is conducive to co-learning. Social-justice workers focus on becoming skilled animators, facilitators, and researchers who recognize that learning in partnership with persons who possess insights based on lived experience and a sense of place enables creativity in collective problem solving.[63] Janet Finn has found integrating Paulo Freire's strategies of popular education and street theater/dramatic performances into the social-justice learning context useful in connection with moving students out of their comfort zones and into truly creative spaces.[64]

To advance co-learning, the transnational approach to professional education also directs learners to exchanges of innovative thinking and acting with counterparts around the globe.[65] Hidden adaptive potential often is revealed by exploring the component parts of diverse perspectives.[66] Awareness of alternative forms of practice often stimulates creative applications that prove to be powerful in one's own social justice–work context.[67] Developing a transnational perspective is particularly valuable in this connection because "it is as likely that practice innovations and potential problem solutions will be generated in places previously labeled less developed, as in the industrial nations."[68] Given the speed at which social-work situations can change, students also need to be skilled at creative Internet searching and at generating novel transnational syntheses through teleconferences that involve dispersed colleagues who can share lessons from successful, but disparate, field experiences.[69]

Communicative Competence

TC social-work education emphasizes the development of strong interpersonal-communication skills. Where appropriate (e.g., for work among Spanish-speaking communities in the United States), graduates will be expected to possess language facility.[70] Some social-work educators believe that learning more than one language brings additional benefits, including enhanced appreciation for the challenges involved in the communicative piece of transnational competence. Janet Finn, for instance, contends that knowing "at least one language beyond English opens up that sense of appreciation [for] the nontranslatability of many concepts, the idea that we are always, at best, partially understanding."[71]

To prepare for most transnational practice situations, social-work students need to learn how to work effectively with professional interpreters (rather than family members). It is particularly important that students learn "not to use children to interpret for their parents, as this exacerbates already problematic generational conflicts in role and respect."[72] Double checking, ensuring that the interpreter asks your questions and reports full responses, realizing that something will inevitably be lost in translation, and carefully attending to what might have been lost are important dimensions of transnational-communicative competence in situations that require interpretation.

The TC approach to communicative education also recognizes that nonverbal-communication skills will be useful in most transnational social-work roles. Active listening relies, in part, on effective nonverbal gestures that demonstrate attentiveness. Listening intently to silence[73] as well as speech is a powerful skill for social-justice professionals. The communicative skill of active listening "gives voice, affirmation, and confidence to those individuals and groups who have been typically ignored, marginalized, and oppressed."[74]

Dialogues that promote information exchange (an analytic skill), perspective sharing (an emotional skill), and the identification of synergistic alternatives (a creative skill) all rely on transnational communicative competence.[75] Exploring "telesocial-work" opportunities can be useful in advancing these dialogues. By utilizing available ICT tools, "social workers in one country can access appropriate expertise from around the world, adapt the knowledge to the local context, and, then, through ongoing exchange, broaden the knowledge base of others."[76]

Functional Competence

Functional competence is a key asset for social workers who increasingly face trans-boundary challenges. Preparing future professionals with transnational functional skills involves three major educational objectives: (1) the capacity to build positive interpersonal relationships; (2) the ability to overcome conflicts[77] and successfully assist those in need; and (3) the ability to promote social justice.

Transnational Relationships

The ability to develop and maintain positive interpersonal relationships with persons of different backgrounds is an essential component in transnational functional competence. For all professionals, the existence of strong interpersonal relationships opens doors for successful task performance. Person-to-person relations are arguably even more fundamental for social-justice workers than for other professionals because they cut across all facets of their practice.[78]

Educators have long urged social-work students to draw close to the people they work with—both professionally and personally.[79] Interpersonal closeness implies not treating "clients" in demeaning top-down fashion, ensuring that all voices are at the table,[80] respecting those one interacts with as equals, and appreciating people for more than their problems and needs.[81] As Dennis Saleebey explains, "in the end, clients want to know that you actually care about them, that how they fare makes a difference to you...."[82] A TC program takes this educational commitment to constructing interpersonal relationships that have value in themselves and are not merely sought for instrumental purposes to the more complex level of transnational diversity. Although transnational contexts differ and can be more demanding, many of the basic relationship-building and partnership-building skills that students need to cultivate already are embedded in social justice–work programs. They include building trust through dialogue and demonstrated caring, humility, and commitment.[83]

Transnational Performance

To ascertain the functional skills required of tomorrow's social workers, we first need to have an idea of what "transnational performance" will involve. Social workers need to be prepared for a rich variety of cross-border and overseas professional roles.[84] As illustrated in the introduction to this chapter, they will encounter foreign site–connected case and community issues in their daily practice.[85]

Drawing on three core purposes of social work articulated by the Council on Social Work Education,[86] we suggest that TC preparation for functional performance would focus on alleviating and preventing individual, family, group, and community distress, exclusion, and disempowerment; on meeting basic human needs, building human capacities, creating social capital, and developing economic opportunities that promote improvements in people's welfare;[87] and on advocating for resources and policies that promote and sustain social and economic justice. In TC education, these domestic purposes are "scaled up" so that all social workers are prepared to engage them when transnational diversity appears on their doorstep and/or when they physically or virtually practice professionally in foreign settings.

Transnational Social Justice

Social work stands out as a profession that explicitly views challenging social injustice and promoting human rights as a primary mission.[88] "For more than a century," Finn and Jacobson remind us, "social workers have dedicated themselves to improving life conditions for vulnerable and marginalized individuals and groups and advocating for social policies."[89] To prepare students with the functional competence they will need to confront injustices that, increasingly, are locally and globally interconnected, however, educators will need to take this action commitment to a new level where borders are removed from their thinking about social action and policy.[90] Among other transnational social-justice roles, social-work students need to be prepared to "contribute to mutual problem solving on global social problems" and to "monitor the impact of their own nation's policies on other countries' and peoples' well-being."[91] Social justice–work learners in the United States "can usefully learn from the experience of other countries as they seek to identify developmental forms of practice that transcend the profession's conventional remedial interventions."[92]

New social-work practitioners need to be prepared to transform the inequities and injustices that burden individuals, communities, societies, and the world through reflective, proactive practice and through advocacy for the people with whom they work as well as others who are disadvantaged. Addressing transnational injustice is aided by competence in challenging negative discrimination and unjust policies and practices,[93] particularly when such are directed against persons from other lands or perpetuate global economic and environmental inequities, and by skill in negotiating on behalf of those who are dispossessed and disadvantaged.[94] Another key functional skill involves empowering diverse individuals and groups for full societal inclusion and participation,[95] and enjoyment of their legal and human rights.

The organizational dimension of transnational functional competence includes the ability to facilitate processes that determine the most effective spokespersons for the group and appropriately target specific actions.[96] Ideally, students prepared for empowerment practice will be able to raise consciousness; identify and reinforce individual and community strengths; encourage micro-enterprise activity;[97] engage in social-policy research, analysis, and interpretation, legislative advocacy, litigation, and social action; teach organizing, communicating, advocating, conflict-managing/transforming, risk-taking, and power-building/applying skills; frame public appeals in persuasive fashion; and motivate service users who are in need to participate in the collective change process.[98] To support and enhance empowerment gains made through transformative action, moreover, TC functional education emphasizes the value of sustained "accompaniment"[99] via genuine collaborative partnerships built on mutual trust that span diverse borders.

For social-justice practitioners in industrialized countries, tilting "internationally related national policies [toward social justice] is a particularly important role."[100] To confront transnational injustices, including those conditioned by foreign and domestic (e.g., immigration and persecution) policies[101] and global economic institutions,[102] TC-prepared social workers will be able to mobilize societal and professional resources and to act in solidarity across national borders. Transformative policy and social action requires skill in creating transnational organizations, networks,[103] coalitions,[104] alliances,[105] and partnerships,[106] in activating multisited resources, in applying ICT, in collaborating with allies and partners (including international and indigenous social-justice NGOs), in expanding transnational opportunities, and in integrating, sustaining, and building upon gains.[107] To advance sustainability, TC social-work education advises that external change agents "plan their exit strategies at the outset" of projects.[108]

Completion of a TC-based professional education has the advantage of preparing social-work graduates for international development assignments at multiple jurisdictional levels. As Healy points out, "real change and action on global problems are possible when professionals engage in mutual work across national and cultural boundaries."[109] The time is right for the social-work profession worldwide, including its foremost teachers, to "turn to efforts to strengthen its role in international action as a force for humane social change."[110]

Chapter 9

Preparing for Sustainable
International–Development
Practice

[T]he challenges of sustainable development require a new and more systematic approach to teaching, learning and problem solving for development practitioners.

—International Commission on Education
for Sustainable Development Practice (2008)[1]

What concerns me is the young city manager in a smaller municipality who may have to broker trade deals, manage immigration, or deal with such unsavory problems as drug trafficking across borders or pollution spilling in from a neighboring country on the border. The challenge for us as academics educating that next generation is to enrich our curriculum and our research with global perspectives.

—Astrid E. Merget, ASPA Stone Lecture[2]

RECENTLY, ARIZONA STATE UNIVERSITY inaugurated its Global Institute of Sustainability. The University of Tennessee created the Institute for a Secure and Sustainable Environment. Rochester Institute of Technology established the Golisano Institute for Sustainability.[3] Sustainability is rapidly becoming *the* buzzword governing post-millennium higher-education initiatives.[4]

Sustainability connects disciplines, continents, and generations. Our focus in this chapter is on international sustainable-development practice, a key component of transnational professional education. While all of the professions considered in this book embrace sustainable-development objectives, the emphasis here is on three fields of study that place sustainability at the core of their cross-border academic enterprise: agricultural sciences, natural-resource and environmental management, and development administration/management.[5] Mainstreaming sustainable development in these professional fields of study across the globe is consistent with the thrust of the U.N. Decade of Education for Sustainable Development.[6] For the most part, we treat professional-education programs in these fields collectively, since there is considerable overlap in the interwoven challenges they confront[7] and the transnational skills their graduates require. Our decision to consider these fields collectively was reinforced when the October 2008 report of the International Commission on Education for Sustainable Development Practice identified a pressing worldwide need to educate a "new generation of development practitioners" who possess the core competencies needed to secure positions and work fluidly at the intersection of these professional disciplines as well as across national borders.[8]

Our interest in identifying a core TC curriculum for sustainable-development practice runs parallel in many respects to the Commission's proposal for the establishment of Master's in Development Practice (MDP) degrees based on integrated cross-disciplinary preparation.[9] However, as universities such as Columbia and Georgetown in the United States, Tsinghua in China, Ibadan in Nigeria, Makerere in Uganda, Internacional del Ecuador, and the UK's Institute of Development Studies in Sussex, move in the direction of introducing generalist MDP degrees,[10] we suggest that they (along with others active in the related professional fields of study) would be well-served to bear in mind that cross-disciplinary education that connects learning across development-related fields of study will be insufficient preparation for the challenges that face current and future practitioners. Lacking in the Commission's recommended core curriculum, and central in the transnational-competence framework we elaborate in this chapter, is attention to development of transboundary emotional, creative, and relationship-building skills.[11] While the Commission's transdisciplinary connections are compelling, especially in terms of analytic-skill preparation in understanding specialist insights and the interactions among them, they alone are not enough. We hold that building interpersonal-interaction skills merits at least equal attention if separate or consolidated professional-education programs are to graduate transnationally competent women and men who will be well-positioned for sustainable-development teamwork as transnational, diasporic,[12] regional, national, and subnational development planners and budgeters, community organizers, grant writers, project directors, forest-resource managers, sustainable-farming consultants, eco-tourist developers, international-trade officers, financial analysts, climate-adaptation and green-policy advisors (among other opportunities) with U.N. agencies, bilateral donors, foundations, multilateral financial institutions, national ministries, provincial and local governments, state enterprises, international and indigenous NGOs, and academic/research bodies.[13] The future occupants of these positions will need to be as skilled in collaborating with one another on projects that cross borders as they will need to be adept at integrating sustainable advances in science and technology with domestic- and foreign-policy decisions.[14]

Analytic Competence

Since sustainable-development professionals work at analytic intersections, graduating practitioners need to nurture the capacity to gather and diagnose sufficient technical information and to extract critical insights regarding the key drivers and obstacles of a situation from multiple fields, including their own.[15] As in the other professions considered in this book, specialized knowledge about sustainable development rapidly becomes obsolete and, therefore, must be secured continuously. In the words of the authors of the RAND study on challenges for developing international leadership, "being able to learn and to solve problems is in the long run more important than any present-day knowledge."[16]

The transnational/transdisciplinary TC framework for analyzing sustainable-development processes incorporates insights from social sciences, natural (and health) sciences, and management studies, and directs attention to the complex interactions and interdependencies among the natural and social processes illuminated by these fields.[17] The TC curriculum would include rigorous analysis of social-ecological linkages that cross disciplinary boundaries and challenge sustainable development. Each course would be grounded in contemporary policy issues. Through the knowledge-sharing[18] and analytic core of the TC curriculum, sustainable-development graduates develop ability to discern the dynamics of distant life-support ecosystems,[19] to perceive ways in which relief, development, and peace-building work can fruitfully be connected,[20] to appreciate the interplay between developing and sustaining,[21] to recognize local and external threats to sustainability,[22] to map the intensity of domestic and transnational connections, to identify available assets[23] and vulnerabilities, to assess the strengths and weaknesses of diverse organizational structures, to understand budgeting processes and activity plans, and to grasp how specific credit and microfinancing systems work.[24]

We can illustrate the multidisciplinary basis of sustainable-development analysis by reference to the challenge of chronic hunger in Sub-Saharan Africa.[25] Applications of agricultural science are useful for understanding biophysical influences on crop yields and for identifying technical approaches and access to inputs that could boost secure food production over the long term. Environmental science contributes to understanding land and water conditions and interactions with climate change. Engineering illuminates infrastructure requirements, gaps, and potential. Economic analysis works with household-income data, market opportunities and risks, capital needs, international trade and monetary policies, and sustainable and equitable paths to breaking the grip of poverty. Anthropology reveals local priorities, indigenous and adapted innovations, and fertility trends. Public health engages nutrition, infectious and chronic disease, and health issues that condition sustainable-development processes. Political science highlights local, national, and international governance constraints on sustainable development, explores political-economic conflict and migration, and identifies policy options. Public administration equips for financial management, facilitates understanding of local and national long-term institutional capacity, including project-management skills and NGO/population strengths, and addresses stakeholder participation in contextual-mapping, needs-assessment, planning, monitoring, maintenance, and (short- and long-run) evaluation processes. The student of sustainable approaches to the challenge of chronic hunger is not expected to master the specialized knowledge and tools that distinguish each of these fields. The aim of a TC education is to prepare practitioners who "understand the essential questions that must be answered in order to move forward," can think laterally and span critical knowledge boundaries,[26] and are in a position "to identify strengths and weaknesses within a proposed policy."[27]

Alongside the generic transnational and transdisciplinary skills that generate breadth and depth of technical knowledge and insight, TC analytic-skill preparation involves awareness of political processes and divisions.[28] Process competence includes the ability to acquire "familiarity with the complex formal rules and routines of government [at national and subnational levels], as well as more tacit knowledge regarding the contours of partisan and ethnic alliances and the history of rivalries among individuals and organizations."[29] Understanding how policies are made and implemented, and why some fail, are essential components of a TC-analytic education for learners who will be expected to navigate among institutions responsible for sustainable development.[30] The TC program also strives to prepare graduating sustainable-development practitioners who can compare and critically evaluate the effects of external expert-driven versus local community-based approaches.[31]

The TC analytic framework highlights the importance of assessing the sociocultural context in which sustainable-development processes are embedded. Different beliefs, value orientations, and motivations shape individual and collective action. A TC approach strives to "remove barriers to seeing how others live."[32] By comparing similar phenomena across multiple national perspectives, underlying processes (rather than just events) associated with sustainable development become apparent.

In TC programs, students learn to analyze the lay public's problem awareness, value orientations, and motivational pathways in assessing prospects for behavioral change—for instance, durable shifts to sustainable-consumption practices.[33] TC-prepared graduates from conservation programs will be positioned to discern "the spiritual, cultural, and utilitarian connections" that exist among "natural resources, protected areas, and communities."[34] According to the Associate Dean of Iowa State University's College of Agriculture and Life Sciences, moreover, students should be able to understand "the socio-cultural implications of change within each setting that is touched by a complex transnational problem."[35] This understanding should guide identification of the specific sustainable-development activities that citizens are encouraged to train for.[36]

Emotional Competence

For students of sustainable-development practice, the ability to open up to diverse transnational experiences and perspectives is an especially valuable component of an emotional skill set. Krishna Tummala suggests that students of sustainable development should "start with an open mind. It is natural to be insular, either because of one's current state or because of fear of the new and unknown. One needs to transcend these limitations and acquire an appreciation of the 'outside.'"[37] Tummala adds that this emotional skill cannot be mastered in a short time, but "ought to be a life-time preoccupation."[38]

Developing self-awareness is an important part of emotional-intelligence management. Activating awareness of personal commitments and objectives can help students and practitioners maintain motivation in the face of complex transnational and transboundary challenges and in the wake of disappointments.[39] "If people don't have the motivation to learn or the interest in transnational challenges and opportunities," Steve McCool observes, "none of the other skills will be put to use."[40] TC educators encourage students of sustainable development to find "increasing the life chances of people in misery more satisfying than simply improving the material wealth of people"[41] (including themselves). Motivation arises from a sense of equality, a belief that, in our independent world, we sink or swim together.[42] The TC emotional-educational objective is not value inculcation, but teaching ways to remain intellectually challenged and personally focused. The emotionally competent transnational-boundary spanner derives satisfaction and confidence from participating in the local culture.[43]

Motivation to help, absent "arrogance that we are right or that others are dependent on us," helps to promote empathy.[44] Students of sustainable development must pay close attention to a multiplicity of transnational and transboundary perspectives.[45] Learning to grasp the perspectives of others quickly,[46] while retaining some identity distance,[47] is a further step toward developing empathic capacity. In the context of sustainable-development work, empathy involves identifying and respecting differences in value orientations, needs, pains, and aspirations.[48] Empathy, in turn, enhances the sustainable-development practitioner's ability to appreciate and reinforce individual and community resilience.

Creative Competence

Personal creative competence is built on persistent openness to new and alternative approaches and vigilance in exploring emerging tensions and interconnections. Creativity is particularly important in development practice because "sustainability requires the ability to cope with, adapt to, and shape change without losing options for future adaptability."[49] A valuable TC synergy-generating skill for the sustainable-development professional is the ability to tap into, reflect upon, and integrate diverse sources of inspiration and promising connections across communities of expertise and experience.[50] Working in teams and with community groups that embrace heterogeneity and social distance engages complementary skills and knowledge, and enhances the likelihood that fruitful synergies will ensue.[51]

The Internet and cell-phone technology provide students and practitioners with one set of opportunities to access and exchange new ideas.[52] Mobile-phone opportunities are particularly promising in Africa.[53] TC educators work to set up transnational learning platforms that facilitate the exchange of sustainable-development insights among stakeholders[54] and promote the establishment of promising transnational and transdisciplinary partnerships.[55]

Local and traditional knowledge also offer "a rich source of lessons for social-ecological adaptations."[56] Although the long time-series of observations preserved in local experiential-knowledge systems are not sufficient to maintain sustainable development in our globally interdependent world, it is crucial for adaptive learning that innovation-seekers avoid homogenizing, diluting, or diminishing the diversity of indigenous insights.[57] Combining multiple sources of knowledge to draw out sustainable-development lessons nested in social and ecological diversity and disturbance facilitates the discovery of adaptive innovations that help build resilience, increase flexibility and opportunities, and avoid flips into undesirable stability domains.[58] Nurturing diversity and redundancy is especially important for sustainable creativity because they provide the social and ecological components of historical memory that make "development and innovation following disturbance and crisis possible...."[59]

Dave Acker suggests several strategies that enhance learners' ability to envision mutually acceptable alternatives. A TC creative-skill-building effort should encourage students of sustainable-development to give "full consideration to potential solutions that may at first appear to be outliers."[60] In searching for transnationally acceptable alternatives, Acker also advises, it is helpful to explore the contextual strengths and limitations of various technologies that have been applied around the world, and to construct and apply "tests of potential solutions that will identify vulnerabilities or unintended consequences."[61]

Bob Charlick's recommended learning strategies for developing transnational creative competence focus on developing mutually acceptable win-win solutions. The first step in his approach is to gain a clear understanding of the other sides' core interests. That understanding enables one to imagine mutually beneficial syntheses that will satisfy everyone without necessitating merger. The multiplication of rewards is useful throughout the creative process; that is, without negating one's own interests, one should constantly work on increasing the number of potential material and nonmaterial payoffs so that all parties in the transnational interaction exchange ideas and emerge as winners.[62]

In preparing for transnational creative competence, students need to bear in mind that, in most sustainable-development situations they will encounter, "the kind of creativity we are talking about is identifying opportunities to alter conditions with imagination rather than [with] large amounts of resources."[63] In such resource-limited contexts, Philip Morgan maintains, one key to creativity is entrepreneurial ability to envision a variety of uses for small amounts of capital that will create productive opportunities for people.[64] Others emphasize lateral thinking, catalytic roles, mobilizing sustainable-resource packages,[65] focusing on flexible (and rapid-risk-responsive) local institutions,[66] and the value of policy entrepreneurship.[67] In any event, one can expect that a critical part of the search for innovative sustainable-development approaches will concentrate on "visions of smaller-scale, more environmentally sound and more democratic and nested resource management systems that are self-organizing, adaptive, and resilient."[68] A creativity-inspiring project for a team of sustainable-development students would involve proposing a holistic and durable climate-change adaptation and mitigation strategy for a specific small-scale geographic or political unit.[69]

Communicative Competence

For students preparing to be boundary-spanning sustainable-development professionals, "the value of basic and effective oral, written, and presentational communication skills cannot be overestimated."[70] Along with professional communicative competence, the capacity to express genuine passion for the message one conveys constitute "an extraordinarily powerful package."[71] TC-prepared professionals around the world who seek to access information or support for sustainable-development activities need to be proficient using English in these communication capacities. For instance, "English is often necessary for securing funds for development either through international organizations or private funding sources."[72]

The sustainable-development experts interviewed for this book generally appreciate the value of spoken second-language proficiency.[73] In Philip Morgan's words, for instance, "anyone who has the ability to operate in a second or third language is going to be much more effective than someone who is constantly operating in English."[74] Most agreed with Charlick's observation that learning a language can be advantageous "because it gives one windows into how people think ... insights into the way people approach issues by the way they express things."[75]

The sticky issue for sustainable-development students, as for the other transpatriate professionals-in-training considered in this book who are likely to serve in unpredictable countries and even different regions over the course of their career, is: which language? Morgan recommends investing in a language that "lots of people speak" or "is spoken in lots of countries."[76] McCool's recommendation is "most likely Chinese."[77] Tummala offers the most practical suggestion. "Even a smattering of the local language" where one is currently working, he opines, "serves as a confidence builder and opens up some doors that might otherwise not open."[78]

Respondents in the RAND study ranked foreign-language fluency nineteenth out of nineteen skills that define a successful professional career in an international organization, and the authors of this study caution that "serious negotiations will always require professional translators."[79] However, Charlick contends that is difficult to work with an interpreter without some knowledge of the language being spoken because "interpreters completely miss subtleties and give you what you want to hear."[80] These prospects underscore the vital role played by advance training in working with an interpreter and double-checking translations as part of TC communicative education. Charlick's final piece of advice is likely to be the most useful: always insist on including a person familiar with the local language on the project team.[81]

ICT provides a tool that can enhance transnational communicative competence in interesting ways. One promising use of ICT in sustainable development involves linking skilled and committed diaspora members with homeland information and capacity-building needs, either directly with local governments or communities or in cooperation with international/indigenous NGOs. For instance, Somalinet, a large digital diaspora, functions, in part, as a platform for discussion regarding how to rebuild Somalia.[82] Sustainable-development practitioners also can use communication networks to email documents to telecommuters who possess specific foreign-language proficiency for overnight translation.[83]

Sustainable-development practitioners can expect to be constantly challenged to function in meetings and on teams where multiple languages are spoken.[84] TC communicative-skill preparation emphasizes the value of attentive listening[85] and the importance of attending to nonverbal cues. Kellogg points to the special insights that accrue to the sustainable-development professional from active listening for the contributions of people who do not speak one's "disciplinary language," have not amassed scholarly publications, or do not possess advanced degrees.[86] Transnationally competent sustainable-development professionals employ all four dimensions of deep listening in their work with disadvantaged communities: "your ears, your eyes, your undivided attention, and your heart."[87]

Functional Competence

Transnational functional preparation aims to prepare graduating sustainable-development practitioners to function smoothly and be successful in transferring knowledge and expertise in multiple overseas living and working contexts.[88] Success in both contexts largely depends upon the graduate's "interaction management" skills.[89] Competent boundary spanners are distinguished by "their ability to engage with others and deploy effective relational and interpersonal competencies."[90]

The classic study conducted by the Canadian International Development Agency (CIDA) concerning the overseas ineffectiveness of Canadian technical advisers (particularly in transferring skills) revealed the importance of developing positive social as well as professional interpersonal relationships with counterparts. Interviews with 136 nationals from eighteen countries revealed common frustration with the treatment received from the Canadian advisors. Nationals objected to the lack of social contact initiated by the foreign advisors, to the advisors' failure to acknowledge counterpart abilities, to treatment as subordinates rather than as equals, and to being excluded from decision making.[91] We continue to observe this kind of disrespectful treatment in too many development situations.[92] Philip Morgan reports, with particular reference to "sharp-elbowed World Bank people," that the project atmosphere is often so disrespectful that "the indigenous management cannot wait for their visiting fireman from Washington to get out of town."[93]

The TC functional-education curriculum builds on the lessons from the CIDA study. The first functional skills to be developed are long-term transnational networking and interpersonal relationship cultivating. Students initially focus on enhancing their ability to "build and maintain friendly, cooperative, trusting relationships"[94] across nationality and other defining lines.[95] Gaining trust is the pivotal ingredient in successful transnational relationship building and mutual learning.[96] In this connection, the importance of spending time socially with one's professional counterpart and getting to know his/her family, interests, and aspirations[97] is often underestimated. Eventually, "if it passes the tests of reliability, delivering on promises, not being underhanded and being honest, the relationship moves on to a possibly more enduring state of 'deep trust.'"[98]

In TC programs, graduating sustainable-development practitioners learn to interact with community leaders, colleagues, partners, and other stakeholders from diverse backgrounds and disciplines. Kellogg emphasizes the importance of competence in working with NGOs because "they provide a service that the public sector used to [provide], they're extraordinarily powerful in terms of policy impacts, [and] they are often creative and imaginative in terms of new solutions and ideas."[99] We would add increasingly active diasporic organizations to the mix of transnational actors that are engaged in important ways in sustainable-development processes.[100]

The capacity to interact effectively with indigenous people, to mobilize resources, and to gather reliable allies is essential for success on virtually all projects.[101] According to Morgan, "no matter where you are in the food chain—policies, programs, projects, some would say even smaller than projects (operations)—you really do need to be looking for allies" not just for resource purposes, but for the basic "legitimacy of being able to conduct the work."[102] TC educators prepare students for the interpersonal challenges involved in gaining allies, establishing legitimacy, and building long-term partnerships by emphasizing respectful and trusting social relationships, along with tact and skill in coordinating diverse political, economic, cultural, and ecological resources and applying participatory methodologies.[103]

The ability to build and participate productively on teams with multiple partners who "span sectors as well as national borders" is an increasing expectation of graduating sustainable-development practitioners.[104] TC-prepared professionals are skilled at introducing participatory budget-planning processes.[105] Additional valuable participatory-process skills include agenda setting; facilitating and negotiating agreements on visions, objectives, priorities, resource allocation, logistical and procurement operations, funding proposals, outcome measures, and accountability; credit sharing; capacity building; and managing conflict-laden situations.[106] Paul Williams notes that "the acid test of a robust relationship is considered to be the ability to manage conflict and criticism—the potential to disagree and fallout, but a willingness to move on without harming the relationship."[107]

Generic skills in public and nonprofit management are valuable assets for all development professionals. In light of the social-ecological core of sustainable-development challenges, TC graduates also need to be functionally prepared to formulate and employ an extensive range of transdisciplinary problem-solving strategies and policies. For instance, practitioners should be able to apply GIS findings in needs-assessment, risk-analysis, and monitoring and evaluation processes.[108] Policy and management considerations should be an integral part of each course in the TC curriculum.[109] In connection with formulating policy options and engaging in strategic management, TC-prepared students learn to apply analytic insights regarding the social-ecological and cultural context and political, economic, and logistical constraints and opportunities.[110] Managing for sustainability involves learning (1) how to maintain and enhance diversity, adaptability, and renewal capacity, (2) means of incorporating and retaining redundancy, and (3) ways to retain flexibility and spread risks.[111]

TC functional capacity to advance sustainable development also requires advocacy skills.[112] In the interest of fostering sustainable development, universities in South America, Africa, and Asia explicitly strive to educate "graduates who serve as agents of socioeconomic change...."[113] Ghana's Institute for Development Studies, for instance, ensures that students study subjects that cultivate skill in addressing poverty.[114]

The capacity to shape policy change for sustainability and resilience is enhanced by "framing skills."[115] In a resource-challenged future, human welfare will be dependent on forward-looking managers who are capable of promoting "social-ecological resilience for adaptive capacity and sustainability."[116] Transnational functional competence is essential for success in such professional advocacy initiatives because "local solutions in an increasingly globalized world cannot work by themselves."[117]

Chapter 10

Guiding the Transnational Flow of Health Expertise[1]

What is no longer sustainable is to educate students in such a way that their perspectives are limited to medical practices in the context of their own country.
—Ronald M. Harden, General Secretary,
Association of Medical Education in Europe[2]

American medical students have become increasingly more interested and active in global health, but medical schools have been slow to respond.
—Paul Drain (National Institutes of Health
Fogarty/Ellison Clinical Research fellow) and colleagues[3]

MORE THAN 800 MILLION PEOPLE (including visitors on business or personal/family trips) traverse nation-state borders annually,[4] and at least one million per week move between the global South and the global North.[5] Demographic dynamics in our mobility-upheaval era are introducing major health-care challenges. Nearly half of Toronto's residents were born outside of Canada.[6] In many German hospitals, migrant patients and their offspring occupy a majority of the beds in maternity and pediatrics wards. Since 2000, six of every ten babies born in New York City have at least one foreign-born parent.[7] Increasingly, hospitals are challenged to provide emergency care for undocumented migrants.[8]

Preparing for Careers in Medicine and Public Health in an Era of Mobility and Mixing

Worldwide migration and trade "are mixing people and microorganisms on an unprecedented scale"[9] at breakneck speed.[10] People on the move either can "introduce

94

new or previously eradicated diseases to the region of destination, or contract diseases unknown to the migrants' region of origin."[11] As more people in spatial transition compress the distance/time transmission of infectious and chronic lifestyle-linked diseases, health protection and treatment assume increasing consequence for individual patients, sending and receiving societies and health-care systems,[12] and global futures.[13] In a shrinking world, it is in the interests of all health specialists to contribute to the treatment and control of diseases only a swift journey from one's own place.[14]

Human migration is more than a transporter and mixer of pathogens and genetic material. Migrants often leave behind safe social settings to congregate in particularly vulnerable spatial surroundings.[15] Individuals and families on the move frequently confront new and additional health risks associated with "health-compromising working and living conditions" along with inequities in health-care access and medical treatment.[16] Mobility simultaneously facilitates cumulative social-change processes (including isolation, marginalization, segregation, concentration in unhealthy environments, and discrimination) and risk-taking behaviors that are associated with increased susceptibility to and spread of noncommunicable as well as communicable diseases.[17]

Downstream Interactions, Upstream Forces, and Midstream Mediating Conditions

Downstream from many of the sources of infectious disease and the onset of chronic illness, care-seekers and health professionals come together in medical and health-promotion encounters. In a context of increasing population mobility, many health outcomes are shaped by transnational interactions among care-providers and recipients who meet in settings where nationality/ethnic match is a diminishing option.

In transnational consultations, clinicians and patients often must deal with a wide variety of unfamiliar health threats and behaviors. Growing numbers of students enrolled in medical schools and health-related professional programs are recognizing the importance of developing skills that can be used when working with foreign-born and foreign-connected populations.[18]

Educators increasingly appreciate that health is a global public good. The distribution of this good remains vastly unequal, however. Individual health-care constraints and opportunities are not independent of upstream forces linked to globalization—including economic pressures, political actions, and military incursions that result in displacement and migration, and the "fatal flow" of health expertise from low-income to industrialized countries.[19] In large measure, life-threatening disparities in health status reflect coping practices that are mediated by one's advantageous/disadvantageous socio-economic position and ability to access/use health-care opportunities.[20] Among the world's poor, the most common social and economic determinants of health disparities are undernourishment, lack of access to safe water, absent or deficient sanitation, and unhygienic housing conditions.[21] The proliferation of stovepipe initiatives focused on particular communicable diseases has resulted in insufficient attention to fundamental sectorwide weaknesses "such as lack of a cold chain, shortages of skilled personnel, insufficient resources for operating vehicles, etc."[22]

The Need for Curricular Redirection

In general, however, "medical school faculty[ies] rarely recognize or teach that public health issues are important factors in virtually all clinical encounters."[23] Furthermore, "the possibility of physicians working to improve contextual sources of distress" has been "overlooked" in medical education.[24] Addressing intraprofessional status and power blinders[25] as well as social and political barriers to greater equity in access to health care falls outside the scope of most medical-school curriculums.[26] In the absence of curriculum redirection, then, advocacy on behalf of one's patient will continue to be viewed as peripheral, optional, and/or beyond one's capacity by future generations of physicians. The exigencies of the current century's transnational milieu underscore the need to develop curricula that "interweave medicine and public health into a single, complementary program of study."[27]

Educating transnationally competent health-care professionals for challenging and changing roles is vitally important at a time when people and pathogens move and mix in unexpected surges for at least two reasons. First, loss of health forces individuals and families everywhere onto a pathway that circles viciously toward poverty and despair.[28] Physicians, mental-health-care providers, nurses, public-health specialists, along with their faculty, form the backbone of the health-protection sector throughout the world, and their education holds out the promise of contributing to the observable reduction of health handicaps. Second, TC education offers a change strategy that is proactive and encompasses the creation of health gain in a world characterized by continued population exchanges rather than a strategy that is primarily reactive and preoccupied with eliminating disease.[29] The prevailing shortage of adequately trained health workers, especially in low-income countries, underscores the critical importance of introducing higher-education programs that will enhance the competence of the global health workforce.[30] Here we have in mind strengthening curricula in poor countries as well as expanding the pool of graduating health professionals who are prepared for and committed to transnational service.

Many domestically focused medical-school curriculums, residency programs, and continuing-education initiatives have not kept up with the transformative transnational health challenges that are emerging in our era of global mobility. Throughout the global North and the global South, health workers are encountering care users in spatial transition from a multitude of dissimilar nation states or ethnic communities. Practitioners graduating from some culture-centered programs are prone to stereotyping, to making inaccurate assumptions,[31] and to missing the diversity of perspectives and behaviors that exists *within* groups due to different social origins, unique and mixed experiences and identities, and extent of sustained transnational participation. In individual encounters, health professionals need to be cognizant of the dynamic interplay with culture of gender, socio-economic status, power position, discrimination, persecution, and transborder connections. In a globalizing world, one outcome of health and medical education must be skill in identifying and addressing the special circumstances that surround and define the individual care recipient.

This chapter focuses on the preparation of students who will be involved in providing professional health care. It elaborates a framework for the education of physicians, nurses, dentists, physical therapists, occupational-health workers, pharmacists, psychologists and psychiatrists, public-health specialists, and allied health professionals.[32] The unifying teaching framework presented is designed to be applied in undergraduate medical education and across all specialized post-graduate programs, including "emergency medicine and surgery, in which diagnostic accuracy and the obtaining of informed consent are paramount."[33] In all fields of health and medical practice, educators around the world need to ask, "Are we doing enough to prepare our students to succeed in a globalized world? Are we giving them the skills necessary to practice as clinicians and doctors within the 21st-century global village in which we live?"[34] In our increasingly borderless era, health-care initiatives and interactions need to be informed and supported by enhanced transnational educational capacity.[35]

In the 1990s, most medical schools began incorporating cultural competency somewhere in their four-year curriculums. By 2004, slightly more than half of 8,000-odd surveyed U.S. graduate medical programs offered some cultural-competence training.[36] There is little uniformity in scope or content among these undergraduate and graduate programs, however.[37] It is not surprising, therefore, that the cultural-competence experts from academic medicine interviewed in a 2002 study confirmed the "need for a unified conceptual teaching framework."[38]

Although the cultural-competence (CC) approach to medical and health education is incomplete and inconsistent, researchers and educators within this tradition have identified many skills that are usefully adopted and adapted in the TC curriculum.[39] One of the major drivers for curriculum change in U.S. medical schools and residency programs is the AAMC's Tool for Assessing Cultural Competence Training (TACCT).[40] The five TACCT domains incorporate a number of cultural competencies that overlap with transnational competencies. This chapter will create a crosswalk between TACCT's CC skills and transnational competence in the health professions, embedding the former in the TC framework of five mutually enhancing skill sets[41] while concomitantly expanding preparation for cross-border, transboundary, and multilocational practice over the more narrowly and domestically focused CC approach.

Surging Student Interest

Lifted by enhanced transnational connectedness, the world is witnessing a surge in student interest in global health.[42] For instance, by 2006, 27 percent of graduating medical students in the United States had elected to participate in an overseas professional experience (compared with just 6 percent in 1984).[43] However, many of these experiences remain to be integrated into a comprehensive, transnational skill–based curriculum.[44] In addition, a number of outstanding medical school programs have launched new (often multidisciplinary) global-health initiatives.[45] At the same time, universities are developing new Masters of Public Health (MPH) programs that encompass global health.[46]

The TC Approach and Objectives

The comprehensive set of practical skills that form the core of a TC curriculum promises to reinforce new initiatives and redirect traditional medical school and health education in ways that specifically and effectively work with connections among poverty, displacement, discrimination, and health disparities. TC approaches transnational medical and health encounters as micro-level interpersonal interactions that occur in a social/power context and are shaped by macro-level (global, regional, national, and local) structural factors. Advocacy is a conceptually integral skill component in TC preparation. In the TC curriculum, students are expected to address the social and power context, and to promote the health rights, of underserved populations through specific recommendations that are discussed and evaluated by faculty, preceptors, and care receivers.

Across its five skill domains, the TC curriculum remains focused on two primary and interconnected objectives: improved health outcomes, and reduced health inequities for dislocated men, women, and children as well as for disadvantaged individuals and communities. Both objectives lie at the core of the People's Charter for Health that emerged from the People's Health Assembly held at Savar, Bangladesh, in 2000.[47] And the foundational TC curriculum elaborated here would provide valuable preparation for professional assignments with the U.S. Global Health Service Corps and similar programs in other countries.

Preparation for Transnational Practice

Global mobility also means that foreign-trained health-care professionals play a growing role in many nations.[48] Among migrant professionals and their coworkers, transnational skills are needed for interacting with colleagues as well as with service users. Our vision is that TC-infused curriculums will be available on a worldwide basis.[49] Ideally, all graduating practitioners will be prepared for domestic, foreign, and transnational roles. We find value in Ronald Harden's vision for advancing the spread of transnational education through transborder collaboration among a consortia of programs that share learning outcomes. Harden maintains that "the future lies in a transnational curriculum with international teachers and international students."[50] He envisions students completing a curriculum that is not rooted in one physical location, is infused with challenges set in transnational contexts, and integrates (often virtual) international learning experiences and study under teachers from multiple countries.[51] The common global and local challenges confronting medical and other health-care providers would form an integral part of the transnational learning experience.[52]

Analytic Competence

Expectations for biomedical knowledge are constantly changing, and much of the information that medical and other health-related professionals are exposed to during their university education will be outdated at some point in their career.[53] Rather than relying on stored knowledge, the analytic domain of the cross-national TC curriculum focuses on developing the abilities to gather, integrate, and analyze evidence related to interconnected[54] and supraterritorial impacts on health, transborder patterns of disease,[55] and care-seeker conditions.[56] The TC curriculum is designed to foster skill in context-based analysis of health and health-care issues in diverse settings that involve local groups, communities of migrants, and individual care recipients.

Utilizing analytic techniques transnationally requires special preparation. First, TC educators emphasize eliciting comprehensive narratives and biopsychosocial explanatory frameworks by moving beyond the prevalent "brief and perfunctory social history."[57] They also teach strategies to avoid stereotyping.[58] As Like reminds us, "within-group diversity is often greater than between-group diversity."[59] Students learn to gather and utilize relevant evidence about the care seeker's homeland, migration experiences, ethnicity, cultural and spiritual practices, economic situation, degree of societal incorporation, support systems, population-specific disease incidence/prevalence/outcomes, new and emerging diseases, and antimicrobile resistance as a starting point for physical/mental-health inquiry, confirmation, disconfirmation, enriched and refined analysis, and recommended therapies/referrals.[60] They further learn to identify and access reliable secondary sources (including the Internet[61] and telemedicine along with the published and current research findings of knowledgeable social and behavioral scientists); to locate and learn from proximate and highly regarded ethnic- and diaspora-community leaders, ethnic-health specialists, extended-family members, and other care providers;[62] and to search out and integrate information concerning the pharmacological properties of the user's ethnocultural preparations (ethnopharmacology).[63]

The TC curriculum recognizes the necessity to probe beyond ethnicity/culture. As Moustafa Bayoumi observes, "by obsessively focusing on culture, we avoid talking about history, economics and politics."[64] An exclusively ethnic/cultural focus "obscures the social and structural basis of the need...."[65] TC-prepared students gain "understanding of the limitations of cultural analysis and [of] the role played by other historical, political, economic, technologic, and environmental forces...."[66] They learn that both ethnocultural and socio-political analysis are required of health professionals. They are able to identify the full range of professional and institutional actors, including transnational networks of state and nonstate elites, who are positioned to shape local and distant policies affecting health care in particular and heterogeneous settings.[67]

To avoid misconstruing explanations and to identify congruent and incongruent provider-receiver understandings,[68] medical students, residents, and others preparing to be health professionals must develop expanded receptors for discerning political and socio-economic determinants of individual health;[69] that is, the ability to perceive health situations through what Mary Duffy refers to as the care receiver's "global lens."[70] Care providers who possess transnational analytic skill are able to comprehend critically the interconnected forces that affect health by expanding the frame of reference to encompass linked macro-structural and micro "origins of personal suffering"[71]— including war(s), global manipulations of national and subnational economies,[72] corporate contributions to the nutrition transition,[73] foreign-policy interventions,[74] persecution, and the type, combination, and frequency of trauma experiences.[75]

Concepts from waste and consumption studies[76] strengthen the theoretical base for analyzing the particular transnational socio-economic and political factors that influence individual and community health. The notion of a *chain,* with individual decision nodes that increasingly tend to be severed from contextualized understanding of shaping and constraining upstream and downstream social forces and power relations that invoke hidden costs, is the first useful concept. Chain identification is usefully coupled with analysis of the process of *distancing;* that is, stretching of the chain (geographically, culturally, and mentally). Mental distance includes gulfs of information, awareness, and responsibility. TC-prepared students learn that by moving upstream and downstream along the health chain, they can reconstitute shattered process understandings. They uncover contextual stakeholders, discover relations of influence, and develop the ability to recognize the presence and impact of prejudice, discrimination, and bias.[77] These discoveries promote the realization that individual care alone cannot be sufficient to sustain practices that will maximize a person's health potential.

TC analytic preparation also connects concepts of class, identity, power, and distancing to efforts to discern and analyze critically specific proximate and distant political, economic, social, and environmental determinants of physical and mental health "variability, vulnerability, and strength"[78] and of health-care disparities.[79] Consistent with the core-teaching recommendations of the Society of General Internal Medicine Health Disparities Task Force, the TC curriculum encourages analysis of "the existence and magnitude of health disparities, including the multifactorial causes of health disparities and the many solutions required to eliminate them."[80]

The development of transnational analytic skills can be promoted by focusing on the theme of "migration and health."[81] In preparing to care for migrants, for instance, students learn to consider key distant and proximate factors, including dislocation and migration experiences, altered nutrition practices, and the extent (and positive and negative effects) of adaptation.[82] Transnational analytic skill facilitates unraveling links with post-migration constraints and stressors associated with local reception practices.[83] For instance, an individual's capacity for self-care may be limited by ongoing "cultural and linguistic isolation, fragmentation of the family, deformation of social relationships, chronic absence of adequate support systems, poverty, prejudice, and unemployment."[84] A TC program emphasizes skill in discerning lifestyle and health consequences of the patient's changing class profile—often characterized by radical downward mobility in the case of involuntary (politically dislocated) migrants and upward mobility for voluntary (economic) migrants (accompanied by exposure to new risks and the adoption of detrimental health behaviors in the North). Furthermore, events and conditions in the sending country often continue to affect the mental health and physical well-being of service users who possess transnational ties and identities. It is particularly important that health practitioners elicit and explore the longitudinal dimensions of transnational mobility, as persons in spatial transition often are dealing with "unfinished endings" that preceded their arrival in the current locale[85] and continue to shape their lives.

Recognition that a multiplicity of interconnected factors determines health status and health care both in relatively wealthy and low-income situations leads TC educators to emphasize analytic techniques that expand one's frames of reference by choosing spatial context as the initial referent. A place-based orientation "acknowledges more of the plurality that exists throughout the health system (in terms of people, problems, and policies)."[86] The TC place-based analytic approach encourages students to pursue connections by gathering proximate and navigational data that reveal "what links to what."[87] Mapping connections among clusters of afflictions and transnational disease processes "provides a more complete picture of the health challenge that people face."[88] By applying a wide-angle, transnationally linked perspective, students learn to avoid the fundamental attribution error of "blaming or scapegoating individuals for seemingly unproductive actions, recognizing that if other people were put in the same position and exposed to the same pressures, they too might behave in similar ways."[89]

Another useful transnational analytic skill is the ability to ascertain the role of ethnocultural and other nonmainstream health-related beliefs, values, practices, and paradoxes in the decision-making processes of individual care-seekers and/or families. The TC analytic-education program aims to develop the ability of graduating health professionals to discern the care seeker's ethnocultural identification(s) and his/her specific (including nonbiomedical) beliefs and practices regarding the causes, treatment, and prevention of illness.[90] The TC-prepared practitioner inquires regarding whom else the care seeker has seen, what other explanations s/he has received, and what other treatments s/he is using or has used.[91] Furthermore, the rarely treated *multiplace* and *multiprovider* context of contemporary health-care needs to be discerned, respected, and addressed by students.[92] Increasingly, for instance, transmigrant health-care practices include actual and virtual return to the country of origin for physical- and mental-health advice, traditional remedies and nutritional supplements, and treatments.

TC health and medical education emphasizes patient-centered learning. Students approach consultations as partnerships among informed stakeholders, with the care recipient participating as teacher as well as learner and the student valuing the learning and mentoring dimensions of his/her role. Rather than ignoring the perspectives of the least advantaged, the service-petitioner's voice is treated as an indispensable source of expertise and experiential insight.[93] In addition, the care provider learns to consult the "centrality of patient voice" in ascertaining the applicant's relationship with his/ her community. As Melanie Tervalon and Jann Murray-Garcia point out, "only the patient is uniquely qualified to help the physician understand the intersection of race, ethnicity, religion, class, and so on in forming his (the patient's) identity and to clarify the relevance and impact of this intersection on the present illness or wellness experience"; that is, "how little or how much culture has to do with that particular clinical encounter."[94] The TC learner anticipates, therefore, that health-care outcomes are advantaged when care seekers also possess transnational competence.[95]

When health-care providers work with diverse service seekers, a "bottom-up" approach to information gathering that emphasizes contextual insights derived from proximate and current sources—the patient himself/herself and family, friends, and community members—is most reliable. Thus, the predominantly inductive TC approach to skill development focuses on the patient as the starting point for discovery. In light of the existence of national subcultures and the presence of intracultural (and changing) variations that occur due to "age, gender, income, education, acculturation, individual differences, and multiple other factors," general epidemiological evidence about the patient's country and its endemic diseases, ethnic group, or religious affiliation is "regarded as having some bearing but requires further validation to be considered immediately useful."[96]

A central component of TC analytic skill, therefore, is the ability to construct a "mini ethnography" of health, illness, and migration/adaptation experiences.[97] In the transnational health encounter, the care petitioner's narrative of lived experience—including stressful social and environmental situations, networks of transnational social relations, fluid and emerging identities[98]—is particularly valuable and should be highly valued by care providers.[99] In her case study of Lia Lee's treatment by U.S. doctors, Anne Fadiman reports that Lia's medical chart "grew longer and longer, until it contained more than 400,000 words. . . . [Yet] not a single one dealt with the Lees' perception of their daughter's illness."[100] The mini-ethnography approach reduces prospects that decisions will be based on stereotypic oversimplifications and/or insufficient information and helps practitioners avoid the tendency to perceive and treat all migrants as somatized and/or traumatized victims.[101]

Emotional Competence

Transnational emotional competence builds on the ability to express interest in new cultural patterns—language, family life, dietary practices, customs, and so on. Developing emotional TC includes gaining, maintaining, and demonstrating sensitivity and genuine respect for a multiplicity of values, beliefs, traditions, experiences, and feelings of satisfaction or emotional distress stemming from social circumstances.[102] Learning to acknowledge and validate ethnocultural and other nonbiomedical health beliefs can be especially valuable in this connection.

Among students preparing for encounters with health-care seekers of multiple nationalities and diverse identities, the emotional skill domain is engaged through "willingness to try" to understand and empathize with the user's perspective.[103] Whereas empathic skills generally are underemphasized in current health-care curriculums,[104] TC-prepared graduating practitioners develop the capacity to realize health-care insights through transnational empathy. This emotional skill is supported by treating other perspectives as distinctive rather than inferior or deviant, by taking seriously lay beliefs regarding the mediating effect of "luck, chance, randomness and personal destiny" on healthy lifestyles,[105] and by generating an appropriate emotional response to care seekers' feelings and problems.[106] Javier Escobar suggests that if students are able to surmount the empathic gap, developing the other dimensions of TC will come more readily.[107]

Emotionally skillful participants appreciate that every medical encounter is a multidimensional interaction among the cultures of the patient, the physician, the support professional(s), and the health-care contexts/systems that surround them.[108] TC-prepared professionals learn to discern, rather than stereotypically assume, the relative weight and preference assigned to biomedical, alternative, and complementary approaches.[109] Simultaneously, students are able to avoid the "cultural blind spot syndrome," where the practitioner presumes no distinctive health-care beliefs/practices exist because the care seeker looks and behaves much the same way s/he does.[110]

The emotional-competence domain of the TC curriculum further emphasizes appreciation for people's strengths[111] and resilience.[112] Studies show that a sense of personal, family, and/or group efficacy constitutes a powerful determinant of the adoption and maintenance of health-promoting actions and is associated with a host of health-enhancement and illness-prevention outcomes.[113] Under the vulnerable and stressful environmental conditions that migrants face as the result of formidable language and cultural constraints, discrimination, the threat of long-term unemployment, and/or lack of social support, provider appreciation for patient/family health-care assets/capabilities and for manageable self-care responsibilities reinforces individual and collective perceptions of transnational efficacy and strengthens confidence and perseverance to sustain new and/or demanding psychological and physiological health-enhancing behaviors. Students reinforce/restore efficacy by demonstrating appreciation for resilience and achievements and successes in overcoming dislocation challenges and/or disparities in treatment, and by conveying an optimistic outlook on prospects that the health-care seeker's needs can be addressed.

When working transnationally, "the *ability to identify assets* in a family beset by overwhelming liabilities" and vulnerabilities "often produces the turning point toward successful interventions."[114] The bases for resilience vary among patients and are subject to change over time.[115] Possibilities for students to explore include hopeful vision for the future; religious faith; self-reliance; personal history of overcoming adversity; roots; finding meaning/purpose in life; and community assistance and support. TC education also aims to provide the graduating health-care practitioner with a toolkit of ways of *reinforcing* and expanding resilience, *reversing* devaluation and disempowerment by providing opportunities to demonstrate and develop role competence and increased control over one's life both in and beyond health-care situations, and enabling migrants to *resist* the adoption of health-adverse behaviors practiced by members of the receiving society.

The motivation skill domain of TC emotional competence involves lifelong commitment to promoting personal growth in transnational competence and to cultivating and maintaining reflection, critical self-appraisal and stereotyping/bias remediation,[116] and cultural humility.[117] In addition to generating and sustaining enthusiasm and passion for engaging in transnational activities and for rectifying disparities in health and health care,[118] students develop and refine stress-coping strategies.[119] TC-educated professionals also learn to inspire health improvements through transnational sociophysiologic feedback.[120] The ability to motivate others is important because many people from non-Western contexts look for help in dealing with the emotional aspects of chronic or other illness and are shocked when care providers approach their case only in terms of technical efficiency.[121]

Creative Competence

Professionals cannot pursue healthier directions if they cannot perceive them. The freeing up of imaginative capacities is a powerful force for positive health outcomes in transnational encounters.

Skillful transnational health practitioners are creative synthesizers who are able to inspire collaborators of diverse identities in the co-design and nurturing of innovative and contextually appropriate action plans. They are constantly searching transborder trajectories for plausible futures that could unfold,[122] ever vigilant for unanticipated and serendipitous possibilities. They forge synergetic and congruent linkages between what the care recipient believes and what the professional believes.[123] They learn to articulate health plans that are based on shared transnational synthesis—a complementary blend of biomedical and personal ethnocultural/mixed cultural health-care beliefs, practices, and strengths that is neither clinically nor culturally contraindicated.[124]

TC creative-skill education encourages learning to work across boundaries and barriers. Some students integrate spatial data obtained from GIS technology with data collected through ethnographic inquiry.[125] Others seek innovative ways to utilize telemedicine tools productively in providing transnational care.[126]

Creative approaches to managing demands for medical treatment and health protection include complementary integrations of biomedical, alternative, and ethnocultural explanatory frameworks and health-related practices. Ability to co-create informal transnational paths is particularly valuable because a substantial proportion of all health care is provided "outside the perimeter of the formal health care system."[127]

A key TC innovative skill is the ability to initiate fruitful new connections among distant and proximate parts of the care seeker's experience. In a TC creative-skill curriculum, students learn to integrate the service user's unique life context (physical and emotional experiences and institutional forces) and current place-specific environment (housing, social disorganization, transportation, and so on) in a tailored health-action plan. The petitioner's own ideas, suggestions, resources, and ingenuity feature prominently in the mutually agreed-upon health plan.

Practitioners must be prepared to relate transnational physical and emotional experiences both to approaches that effectively address people's current health-promotion needs and to promising social changes and policy alternatives.[128] Such creative approaches incorporate multilevel and multilocational linkages of individual, socio-political, and ecological considerations. TC-prepared health professionals aim to become "master synthesizers" of local meanings and transnational processes.[129] In TC creative-skill preparation, students further develop the ability to construct a health-promotion action plan that includes societal reinforcement of linked physical/mental-health interventions.

Communicative Competence

Effective provider-user communication is widely perceived as "a core competency in the health care profession."[130] What is at stake is the ability to elicit critical information and to convey health-care options and recommendations across technical, literacy, linguistic, socio-cultural, and national boundaries.[131] Increasingly, moreover, transnational communicative competence is valuable in interactions with a linguistically diverse body of health-care professionals and staff.[132] Transnationally sensitive communication promises to contribute to substantial improvements in the health status of vulnerable populations.[133]

While personal linguistic fluency in the care recipient's first language is an immense behavioral asset, language-concordant practitioners seldom are available[134] and striving to prepare graduating physicians and other health-care professionals who are able to practice in the receiver's first language is impractical when the health-care situations providers face involve multiple and changing first languages.[135] In New York City, for instance, care seekers might speak one of 150 different languages.[136]

Thus, the TC curriculum emphasizes skill in using an interpreter and the importance of employing professional interpreters.[137] TC educators emphasize the best practices associated with the participation of interpreters in health consultations[138] and facility in speech-simplification strategies.[139]

Transnationally skillful actors also develop proficiency in discerning nonverbal-communication messages and responding in a contextually appropriate manner.[140] In health-related encounters, "nonverbal communication skills ... are as important as verbal skills, if not more so."[141] In transnational medical interactions, interview pace is particularly important in order to ensure that participants are not rushed, prematurely interrupted, ignored, or incompletely understood. The TC-prepared health professional learns to discern ways people experience illness through their expressions in the form of literature, poetry, art, music, and theater.[142] In addition, communication-recovery skills, such as humor, apology, and admission that one does not know everything, "reinforce confidence as well as competence because, when it is known that there is something to fall back on, one is less likely to avoid interactions that may prove difficult."[143]

The capacity to facilitate mutual self-disclosure via questioning and to engage in meaningful dialogue about options is particularly important in transnational health-care situations characterized by vast social distance. The TC communicative curriculum emphasizes learning how to elicit relevant background information, questions, preferences, and treatment refinements across socio-cultural boundaries rather than working off of assumptions.[144] This skill is enriched by active listening.[145]

TC communicative-skill preparation opens the door for the negotiation of appropriate treatment plans and for reinforced commitment to health-care agreements by developing the ability to create a collaborative atmosphere where encounter participants are comfortable expressing serious doubts, concerns, and disagreements.[146] TC-prepared graduates also are ready to provide thorough contextually comprehensible and appropriate explanations to care seekers directly and via tailored health-promotion campaigns that employ trusted media.[147]

Functional Competence

Functional competence involves the interpersonal as well as technical ability to accomplish tasks and achieve objectives. In transnational encounters, the functional skills of both care providers and care receivers affect illness management and wellness promotion. Effective functional interventions take into account both the individual's condition and the social context affecting health behavior. TC efforts incorporate "health protection strategies that address unique problems uniquely, as well as complementary strategies that focus on assuring safer, healthier living conditions for all."[148] In functionally effective roles, health professionals apply transnational analytic, emotional, creative, and communicative skills toward mobilizing specific resources and support that will empower users in addressing institutional barriers and societal challenges to positive health outcomes.[149]

While there is consensus among major professional associations that addressing health-care inequities "is a fundamental principle of physician professionalism," this learning objective remains to be translated into critical components of the medical-education curriculum.[150] Transnational functional competence is explicitly concerned with addressing disparities in health and health care. The reasons for disparities in screening, medical treatments, morbidity, and mortality among persons who lack "voice" in biomedical institutions are multiple and complex.[151] Displaced and otherwise dislocated people are particularly at risk of being bypassed by potentially beneficial health interventions. An African war-zone study carried out by Physicians for Human Rights concluded that the "first killer is flight" for desperately poor persons driven by conflict from a fragile existence into a hostile and personally threatening environment where health services are nonexistent or not functioning.[152]

"Irregular" and undocumented population movements pose special health and health-care challenges. During all stages of migration (transportation, transit places, and final destination), irregular migrants (including persons smuggled and trafficked) "are particularly exposed to contracting or transmitting diseases, to injuries or even death."[153] The vulnerability of irregular migrants is exacerbated by poverty, powerlessness, the absence of social, legal, and insurance protection, and lack of access to reliable health-care services. This situation often obliges them to seek medical attention through unofficial and unsafe means.[154]

Skill in establishing positive and meaningful interpersonal relations is particularly valuable for the functional domain of transnational health care.[155] Learning to relate to diverse care seekers in ways that build mutual trust is a prerequisite for TC functional-skill development. Keys to success in building trusted and fruitful transnational relationships include demonstrating sustained personal as well as professional interest in the care recipient as an individual (that is, showing that one genuinely is interested in and cares about the care seeker's current situation,[156] quality of life,[157] and aspirations, and not just his/her physical health),[158] attention to social inclusion,[159] and the ability to resolve conflicts to mutual satisfaction.

The functional dimension of transnational competence also is promoted by establishing provider/recipient partnerships. For many vulnerable care seekers, sustainable care agreements necessitate involvement by (extended) family- and/or community-support networks.[160] TC-functional education aims to develop the practitioner's ability to negotiate a mutually agreed upon and situationally tailored health/treatment plan with diverse care seekers and their families.[161] This includes learning how to resolve differences between the practitioner's professional agenda and expectations, and the personal agenda and expectations of diverse care receivers.[162]

TC educators also devote attention to preparing for transnational collaboration with unfamiliar partners in crisis situations, such as those involving new and emerging infectious diseases. Training in medical economics, health systems, and business and risk management can enhance the graduating professional's functional ability to address partnership building and joint care planning with confidence in novel transnational situations.[163]

The TC curriculum recognizes that cultural sensitivity alone is insufficient to remedy health and health-care disparities.[164] A passionate commitment to reducing inequities[165] and skill in advocating for the health of patients and communities also are needed.[166] TC educators emphasize that, in the case of persons who lack voice in the socio-political context they find themselves in, concern for the well-being of care petitioners is demonstrated by individual and collective actions that address the institutionalized sources responsible for personal suffering.[167] Students learn to build and activate community, professional, and societal resources that are likely to enhance the health situation of vulnerable care seekers by mitigating the site-specific environmental constraints they confront.[168]

Valuable TC-provider interventions include facilitating access to traditional healers, medicine, and nutrition; promoting ties to community-support systems (including lay health workers and intercultural mediators);[169] helping with transportation to health-care appointments; connecting with other professional-service providers;[170] and providing support for the development of mainstream-language proficiency. Other supportive actions on behalf of disenfranchised and disadvantaged patients are promoting further education and credential (re)certification; facilitating employment; promoting the maintenance of children's healthy practices;[171] challenging prejudice, bias, and discrimination whenever encountered in health-care settings or society;[172] encouraging legal/policy coalition building with professional colleagues, stakeholder organizations,[173] and transnational NGOs; and acting as the patient's advocate within the medical/health establishment and with government agencies and community associations.

In the interest of promoting equitable health opportunities, transnational functional adroitness necessitates advocacy competence; that is, recommendations and actions that will generate upstream and downstream changes in domestic and international economic, social, institutional, and policy conditions that produce the systemic disparities that constrain individual health and preclude the realization of health gains.[174] TC students learn to navigate networks of global governance, and to enhance the vulnerable care seeker's health situation by mitigating the socio-economic inequities, power differentials, exclusionary policies, and other institutionalized constraints they confront.[175] There are abundant opportunities for collective action, ranging from Physicians for Social Responsibility ("the medical and public health voice working to prevent the use or spread of nuclear weapons and to slow, stop and reverse global warming and the toxic degradation of the environment")[176] to Missoula Medical Aid (collaborative health work in Honduras);[177] from the Unite for Diabetes

Campaign (place diabetes on the global agenda and address poverty as an obstacle to health care)[178] to the Oxford Health Alliance (addressing risk factors in chronic disease cross-nationally through health education, community coalition building, and policy change).[179]

In TC professional education, emphasis is placed on building multisector transborder networks, coalitions, and teams that include counterparts and institutions in low-income countries and other settings where one finds the greatest disparities in health and health care. It is likely to be particularly rewarding for effective functional-skill development to focus advocacy attention on "hot spots" and to guide students to develop specific interventions that address context- and site-specific conditions that are conducive to elevated risk-taking behavior.[180] TC-prepared health-care professionals recognize that "multisited ethnography must beget multilevel advocacy."[181]

Concluding Reflection

It is time for a fresh, proactive, and mobility-grounded redirection of medical and health education on a global scale. Our framework provides a competency-based curriculum that is comprehensive in scope, links medical and public-health perspectives, adaptable to a wide variety of service users and worldwide practice sites, and of utility in addressing both the quality of personal care and social constraints on population health. Conceptually, the TC health-care curriculum (1) provides a comprehensive set of core competencies involving five ongoing skill-acquisition challenges; (2) accepts that acquired mastery of the "multiplicity of cultures that comprise the patient populations of today"[182] is neither feasible nor necessary for quality assurance and cost containment and, instead, focuses on discerning each care seeker's multiple and complex (rather than single-source) identities and distinctive health perspectives and personal needs; (3) places the physical- and mental-health consequences of economic disparities and underlying global/local structural contributors front and center; (4) aims to equip both service users and service providers with parallel skills; (5) recognizes that empowering the multinational therapeutic alliance to deal with social-context challenges results in improved health outcomes and disparity reductions; and (6) applies to health-care professionals in all countries who work with diverse patients. Consequently, a TC education equips learners for transnational and not just local practice—an important qualification in our era of population and professional exchanges.

Chapter 11

Learning Processes for Enriching the TC Professional Curriculum

Achieving advanced levels of transnational competence requires a combination of real-life experience and classroom learning.
—William K. Cummings[1]

I N THIS CHAPTER, we present pedagogical suggestions that can enrich professional TC curriculums. Some of the ideas encountered here have origins and/or applications outside transnationally focused higher-education initiatives; others are drawn directly from experience with international or global education. We have organized these promising learning processes first by setting (in-class and out-of-class) and next according to professional specialization. We deliberately place the separate professional-program discussions in a single chapter to encourage and facilitate transdisciplinary borrowing and adaptations.

We begin this discussion with a caveat. Students cannot be expected to master all required TC skills over the course of a short professional course of study. Therefore, selecting degree candidates on the basis of preprofessional preparation is a critical complementary component. The learning processes incorporated in TC professional programs need to build on first-degree and secondary-school attainments, particularly in the realm of communicative (additional-language) proficiency.[2] In our interdependent age characterized by rapid changes in conditions, knowledge, technologies, and required expertise, TC educators concomitantly are constantly challenged to innovate and redefine "ways in which we can better prepare young people for diversity, equity, and interconnectedness in their own community and the world."[3] Thus, TC professional programs must be designed in ways that initiate, encourage, and facilitate processes of lifelong learning.[4]

Common Threads

The modest objective of TC transboundary learning processes is to generate profession-specific practitioner strengths within a common core of analytic, emotional, creative, communicative, and functional skills. TC educators recognize that this objective cannot be served by adding an elective or required course on diversity, international affairs, or area studies.[5] TC skills are nurtured by appropriate in-class and out-of-class methods and activities that are infused across the professional curriculum.

TC learning processes share several common threads that cross disciplines. They often start with interconnected and transdisciplinary issues that challenge students to apply the five TC skills.[6] They link foundational local insights and experiences to wider transregional social-ecological contexts and tie conditions and concerns that transcend place back to local specificities.[7] Aside from English, no one language or combination of languages is required in the preparation of transnational specialists.[8]

The precise nature and sequence of TC in-class activities, team projects, and immersion experiences will vary from higher-education institution to institution and from professional program to program. In selecting and arranging teaching processes, the main common consideration is developing competencies that will be readily transferable from "the world of learning to the world of work."[9] Transformation and transferability are advanced by "unpacking" skills in rewarding transboundary experiential-learning opportunities.[10] Whether in-class or beyond, TC methods are designed to de-center perspectives that are locked on the familiar and to engage students' interest, imagination, and creativity.

In-Class TC Learning

The in-class TC teaching approach combines lecture/discussion and experiential learning, with emphasis on the latter. The principal role of the teacher is to guide and facilitate independent and collaborative learning. TC teachers design, arrange, simulate, and monitor stimulating, complex, and professionally tailored transboundary learning environments.[11]

Across the professional curriculum, lectures and seminar discussions approach topics that are infused with transnational content utilizing a holistic and interdisciplinary perspective.[12] Research assignments include non-Western sources and sites. Students critique the prevailing perspective on an approach to a problem from an alternative perspective, debate current topics in their field employing diverse orientations, and demonstrate ways to utilize their privileged situation to effect change.[13]

Future TC practitioners are paired on group projects with their peers from diverse socio-economic and cultural backgrounds,[14] listen and respond to presentations by invited community representatives, alumni of learning-abroad programs, and exchange faculty,[15] are linked in electronic interactions surrounding interconnected issues with students at overseas universities,[16] develop creative multimedia presentations,[17] and are encouraged to complete additional language modules.[18]

TC educators reinforce and enhance the application of analytic, emotional, creative, communicative, and functional skills through practical in-class exercises. Valuable in-class activities include case-study analysis, role playing, dramatizations, group projects, trends analysis and scenario building,[19] professional policy workshops,[20] and simulations coupled with coaching and feedback.[21] These active-learning methods often generate the level of excitement associated with playing, and "playing becomes the key factor in fostering a commitment to life-long learning...."[22] Carefully planned active-learning exercises focus on the development of specific skills for particular transnational professional contexts. Illustrations are provided in the profession-centered sections of this chapter.

The case-study method engages learners in the analysis and development of recommendations based on reports of others' experiences presented from the perspective of central figures in actual incidents and events.[23] Case discussion, "the defining classroom manifestation of this method," involves "a collaborative exercise in wrestling with the dilemmas, issues, and implications of a compelling story."[24] In the TC course, cases typically reflect different value orientations, alternative ethical systems, and unexpected professional responses.[25] Educators present students with a range of professionally relevant case studies drawn from diverse country, socio-economic, and transnational contexts and, acting as facilitators, guide individual reflection, group discussion, and the collective construction of creative TC approaches.

Role plays occur in a context of adequate situational background and conceptual preparation for each TC skill to be demonstrated. Students engage in interpersonal interactions among themselves based on their assigned character. One type of role play asks students to act out professional behaviors that violate the expectations of their dominant culture.[26] In the critical-incidents format, problematic and unfamiliar transboundary interaction situations that closely reflect professional reality are presented to the student, who must think through and then (sometimes repeatedly) play out his/her role.[27] Other formative role-play exercises "allow students to practice and experience both giving and receiving help."[28] Another (virtual) role-play possibility is the Diversity Opportunity Tool (DOT) developed under a FIPSE grant by Alma Clayton-Pedersen. DOT uses video to simulate critical incidents of intolerance. Users' selection of a response to a common incident triggers a research-based vignette depicting the likely outcome of that choice and information about helpful resources for dealing with situations of that type.[29] In all role-play exercises, TC educators encourage empathy,[30] allow ample time for critical reflection on and internalization of lessons learned,[31] and provide detailed feedback regarding alternative and augmentative approaches, demonstrated skill strengths, and needed skill enhancements/acquisitions.[32]

Off-Campus Learning

Off-campus TC-skill learning includes professional-contact building, student exchanges,[33] overseas and interethnic internships and work opportunities, and action training. When arranged to be liberating rather than threatening, to build confidence rather than inflict suffering, and to promote advancement to increased complexity of identity, off-campus experiential learning can be transformative in terms of TC skill development. There is considerable evidence that work in another country both strengthens transnational competencies and enhances employment prospects for graduating professionals.[34] In short, offering the transboundary problem-based and skill-focused curriculum transnationally is a powerful educational strategy.[35] Moreover, as Holly Carter reminds us, "students can have valuable 'international' study abroad experiences at home in the ethnic communities surrounding all of our campuses."[36] TC service-learning experiences go one step beyond internships in that they integrate structured reflection regarding skills that are applied and acquired.[37]

Action learning offers a particularly efficient opportunity for TC skill development and application. In TC professional education, the action-learning process engages a diverse team of students in addressing an actual problem (or problems) that confronts a cooperating organization. Students simultaneously focus "on what they are learning and how their learning can benefit each group member, the group itself, and the organization...."[38] Action learning[39] is built around a transnational challenge, project, or task that is important to the organization and provides an opportunity for TC skill development. Action learning first investigates and clarifies the precise nature of the problem and its underlying contributors. Then, possible solutions are identified, an approach selected and proposed,[40] and, if approved, implemented in stages. Reframings and refinements are adopted throughout the learning process as the "synergy of diverse groups asking fresh questions generates creativity."[41]

Assessment

Professional programs have lofty expectations of themselves and are held to high standards by university authorities and external oversight agencies. In today's outcomes-occupied academic world,[42] educators already are experienced measuring key competencies. Here, we briefly address the rising interest in identifying and assessing global or transnational competencies.[43]

As a predominantly skill-based initiative, authentic TC-competency assessment focuses on *behavioral demonstrations of skill-development expectations* rather than on internal facilitators such as personal knowledge acquisition and attitudinal change. Useful TC outcome statements identify what graduating practitioners are and are not able to do, are reported in "result-focused, observable, measurable, or inferable terms," are developmental, are "comprehensive and broad enough to be interdisciplinary," and involve both formative and summative expectations, allowing the graduate continuously to build capacity and improve upon his/her performance.[44]

Graduates of professional programs throughout the world should be able to demonstrate individual and team achievements consistently across all five transnational-competency domains and when confronted by differing circumstances.[45] In the analytic realm, for instance, graduating practitioners should recognize and be able to explain transboundary interconnections, demonstrate ability to describe short-term and long-term tradeoffs among interdependent factors, and be able to explain how distant events and trends connect to their profession and community and how local actions contribute to or ameliorate distant conditions.[46] As a further illustration, Downey and colleagues suggest specific analytic-learning expectations for today's engineering students that are relevant for other TC programs:

1. Students will demonstrate substantial knowledge of the similarities and differences among engineers and nonengineers from different countries.
2. Students will demonstrate an ability to analyze how people's lives and experiences in other countries may shape or affect what they consider to be at stake in engineering work.
3. Students will demonstrate an ability to analyze how national differences are important in engineering work.[47]

These authors also propose, as a TC functional-learning expectation for engineering programs, that students display the ability "to treat co-workers from other countries as people who have both knowledge and value" and are "likely to bring these different perspectives to bear in processes of problem definition and problem solution" along with the ability to "accommodate their own perspectives to those of other engineering problem solvers."[48] In short, functionally skilled graduating professionals are able to demonstrate ability "to work with people who define problems differently than they do."[49]

As part of the assessment process, educators across the curriculum design transboundary challenges that fall within the technical, interpersonal, and advocacy capacities of a graduating professional. In TC professional programs, it is critical that students manifest multidimensional skills through their interactions in *multiple* socio-culturally diverse situations. Individual programs and professional accrediting bodies will determine levels of desired proficiency,[50] leaving room for future skill development, lifelong learning, and long-term follow-up assessments.[51]

Since in-class exercises and off-campus learning situations challenge students to demonstrate acquired skill-proficiency levels, such performance opportunities will play a major part in TC assessments. Overseas student teaching, for instance, offers the chance to assess "competence and potential for growth as a teacher."[52] Students' ability to apply TC skills also can be noninvasively observed via in-class and teamwork exercises that mirror plausible real-life professional challenges and through practice demonstrations, performance, and presentations in out-of-class experiential-learning situations.[53] Two illustrative TC-skill-demonstration tasks for teacher-education programs are: (1) "choose an important current controversial international issue; identify primary sources that portray at least three different perspectives on that issue. Design, teach, and reflect upon a lesson plan in which fifth-grade students will use the materials you have compiled to better understand and evaluate these perspectives. (2) Create and teach a 1- to 3-day lesson [for secondary-school students] that uses a simulation to teach the concept of global interdependence."[54] Student portfolios that describe transnational issue-oriented work, incorporate policy analysis, and demonstrate the application of each TC-skill expectation in diverse contexts over time provide another performance-assessment format.[55]

In programs designed to prepare transnationally competent professionals, "assessment is used diagnostically to discover the [variable] strengths and weaknesses of students and to provide appropriate support to improve student performance."[56] Whenever possible, pretraining and post-training demonstrations should be documented by video for purposes of assessing skill gains, determining levels of goal attainment and transnational task effectiveness, and analyzing and addressing weaknesses through performance repetitions. Multisource feedback[57] promotes comprehensive skill assessment and enables the graduating professional to grasp "both his or her personal strengths and areas in need of development."[58] In all cases, evaluators emphasize recognizing learners who demonstrate specific TC skills and supporting those who need to improve.[59] TC educators also refer to skill gaps revealed by critical assessments when determining new competencies that need to be developed in a particular professional program.[60]

In TC assessments, the linked technical and interpersonal performance of graduating practitioners should be evaluated from multiple perspectives by socio-culturally diverse observers and participants.[61] In addition, TC programs themselves are exposed to periodic review.[62] Internal and independent external program evaluations should incorporate a variety of transnational skill-expectation indicators,[63] utilize multiple assessment methods,[64] and include ongoing module, format, and pedagogy assessments.[65] Downey recommends that review teams be "trained to expect diversity" so that schools and departments can "develop and defend alternative ways in which their programmes meet outcomes criteria."[66]

Pedagogical Tools for Preparing TC Teachers

TC teacher-education programs start from the premise that "positive recognition of and attitudes toward ethnic and cultural diversity are necessary but not sufficient for dealing effectively with the educational needs and potentialities of ethnically diverse students."[67] Moving far beyond tolerance, the transformative TC curriculum models pedagogies that reinforce those to be employed as practicing teachers.[68] TC modeling includes "developing a classroom atmosphere that is inclusive and supportive of diversity" and living the lifestyle of "a person committed to equity, diversity, and interconnectedness."[69]

Helpful learning processes[70] include:

- infusing TC-skill preparation across the curriculum (in teacher-education courses and at all grade levels);[71]
- ensuring that the transnational *characterizes* learning opportunities, cases, and experiences at all times (including in-service professional development);

- simultaneously addressing analytic, emotional, creative, communicative, and functional skills in preparation for multiple manifestations of diversity;
- cultivating an ethos of academic progress and technical-skill development within a context of interpersonal reciprocal learning and collaborative work in diverse groups;[72]
- initiating paired dialog poems;[73]
- carefully designing and selecting transnational cases, role plays, and simulations;[74]
- providing "forums for voices from the margins";[75]
- creating and maintaining a reinforcing combination of curriculum content, academic climate, instructional strategies, diverse interpersonal interactions, and interactive virtual and actual transnational experiences;[76]
- placing prospective teachers in practice situations with expert TC educators;[77]
- building bridges that connect transnationally focused content and skill learning with active and effective participation in glocal service learning[78] and social-justice advocacy initiatives.[79]

Among TC educators and the future teachers they are preparing, "personal awareness and empathic feelings about ethnic and cultural diversity without accompanying pedagogical actions do not lead to instructional improvements" for mainstream or marginalized students.[80] Mastery of effective interconnected issue-based pedagogies requires attention, energy, and, especially, immersion experiences.[81] The most effective methods of enhancing the abilities of preservice teachers to interact productively with diverse stakeholders, to teach and learn across cultures and socio-economic divides, and to develop inclusive instructional materials and approaches involve well-designed, authentic, extensive, and repeated transboundary encounters.[82] For this reason, Mehaffy argues that "a powerful, well-crafted, experiential, cultural component, designed to foster global competence, ought to be a critical, indeed central, element in teacher preparation programming."[83]

Pedagogical Tools for Preparing TC Business Managers

The preparation of TC business managers also emphasizes the integration of transnational skill-development elements across the academic and extra curriculum.[84] The focus is on nurturing competency in interpersonal business interactions that cross boundaries. In preparing students for participation on transnational business teams, in-class facilitators design role-play exercises that advance conflict-resolution and consensus-building skills, and invite overseas representatives to reflect and comment on student performance.[85] Business faculty in TC programs also prepare and lead analyses of case studies that address actual transnational management challenges.[86]

TC educators recognize that graduates who have successfully completed an internship or other substantial practical experience in an unfamiliar low-income (or industrialized) country will be advantaged in the eyes of business recruiters who generally are not impressed with study-abroad programs that primarily involve interaction with one's compatriots or with the completion of language studies that emphasize literature.[87] Distance learning will be an especially valuable component in the education of management practitioners who are unable to take advantage of overseas experiential learning opportunities.[88] In this connection, TC programs around the world will endeavor to tap into the International Finance Commission's emerging e-learning platform.[89]

The flexible TC business curriculum might include a capstone experience that enables the coherent demonstration of the five skill domains.[90] For graduating business managers intent on demonstrating TC, the capstone challenge is likely to involve a major paper, a reflective overseas experience, collaborating with faculty/business executives on an overseas research project,[91] undertaking a transnational consulting assignment for a firm,[92] participating as a team member on an actual transnational business endeavor,[93] or engaging in a transnational service-learning/advocacy activity with an internationally oriented NGO or community group.[94]

Pedagogical Tools for Preparing TC Engineers

A number of global engineering programs have developed learning activities designed to "prepare engineering students to work with people who define problems differently"[95] that can be adopted or readily adapted in TC education. This section draws upon these initiatives to suggest a set of pedagogical tools that would amplify the TC engineering curriculum highlighted in Chapter 7. Our discussion begins with in-class methods and, then, turns to external learning formats.

As in other professional TC programs, analytic, emotional, creative, communicative, and functional skills will be infused throughout the full range of the engineering curriculum. Required courses might include *Global Engineering and Project Management, Communication in Transnational Design Teams, Earth's Resources: Engineering for Sustainable Development,* and *Global Governance and Engineering Outcomes.*[96] In these and all other courses, TC instructors would employ pedagogies that "help engineers understand and engage diverse technical perspectives" and enable students to translate fundamental forms of knowledge and modes of analysis into practical transboundary problem definition and solving.[97]

TC skills are fruitfully advanced through student participation in transnationally interactive learning spaces.[98] TC engineering educators utilize case studies and in-class exercises that connect technical designs, ethical decisions, intercultural considerations, and policy proposals to real-world transnational challenges.[99] In TC cases, students encounter situations involving interconnected open-ended problems "with multiple possible answers, key decision points, and trade-offs" that require critical analysis, perspective taking, brainstorming, and independent judgment and decision making.[100] According to Hirleman, relevant cases offer one analytic approach with the potential to "change the thermodynamics course in a way that infuses global perspectives."[101] Other TC-applicable learning activities include role plays,[102] game simulations, and participation on product-design projects with transnational and humanitarian dimensions.[103]

TC in-class learning activities aim to maximize "fidelity," or "the similarity of the training situation to the students' present and future working conditions."[104] Higher fidelity and complexity enhance TC-skill transferability to authentic workplace situations. While the exact working environment for graduating practitioners will be unpredictable and dynamic, and conditions can never be perfectly replicated, factors such as time limits and deadlines, material and human resources, prevailing technological context, and transnational team diversity can be closely matched.[105]

In the interest of promoting TC-skill development among graduating engineers, pedagogical emphasis should be placed on multidisciplinary and multinational (and shifting) team experiences that energize synergizes throughout the curriculum.[106] Teamwork-learning activities typically involve applications of technical knowledge through interpersonal interactions. In TC engineering education, teams address both grand challenges of the 21st century[107] and the need for small-scale community-based innovations.[108]

Multidisciplinary and multinational teams formed around common professional interests can be classroom-based (involving participation by international students and faculty),[109] virtual,[110] or multilocational. With support from the National Science Foundation, Dan Hirleman established an engineering virtual community, called Global-HUB, that uses the Internet to facilitate transnational collaboration on team-design projects. He estimates that, through Global-HUB, twice as many U.S. engineering students will participate in a transnational collaboration experience by 2010.[111] Hirleman also has had success blending short overseas student visits to a site in Puerto Rico with semester-long distance work on a community water project.[112]

While preparatory classroom and distance teamwork can offer engineering students a valuable knowledge and TC-skill bridge to overseas learning activities,[113] "there is no real substitute for the face-to-face"[114] in the ideal TC professional program. International enrollment lifts students out of their comfort zones and engages them in first-hand experiences with people who "think differently about engineering work...."[115] The GEARE program at Purdue offers an exemplary model of a credit-bearing engineering experience abroad.[116] GEARE participants "spend a semester in Germany or China doing a design project taught by the German or Chinese professor. Then, the entire group comes back to Purdue for the build.... You are never the same after you've sat in China next to a guy who's way smarter than you making ten dollars a day and you are saying 'I could have stayed in Detroit.'"[117] Enhanced transnational-communicative skill and the ability to function effectively with diverse populations are gains that engineering students who elect overseas enrollment can expect from TC programs.[118]

Venturing overseas to participate in a collaborative research project or an internship offers another valuable TC-learning activity. Hirleman, who is working to arrange transnational student teams on research projects large enough to support two Master's theses ("double-size master's projects"), notes that "you could say I did a global Ph. D. in that the research rig I needed was in Denmark."[119] NSF's International Research Experiences for Students (IRES) program awards institutional grants up to $50,000 per year for three years in support of teams of students engaged in intensively mentored research abroad.[120] Lengthy (six-month) internships are a distinguishing featuring of the University of Rhode Island's international engineering program. Its director, John Grandin, reports that overseas internships help in the recruitment of outstanding students and provide a motivational focus for those enrolled in the program.[121]

Finally, TC preparation strives to arrange transboundary work-based-learning and service-learning placements for graduating engineers.[122] In developing such apprentice-like opportunities in conjunction with employers and communities,[123] educators need to consider "the extent to which the particular environment is capable of delivering the required competencies" and should ensure that students are assigned to committed workplace mentors who are skilled at facilitating the development of transnational competence.[124] Transnational work and service-learning placements afford students the opportunity "to test directly how they will respond to the demands of engineering work in foreign contexts."[125] Yating Chang at Purdue is a strong advocate of transnational service learning because the experience enhances social responsibility among tomorrow's engineers. She believes that service learning helps students internalize that engineering challenges are not just an individual's problem and not just a country's problem, but "everyone's problem" and, then, to go from there to create designs that "make this world better."[126]

Pedagogical Tools for TC Social-Justice Workers

In the TC social-work program, all courses would incorporate learning activities that enhance the five dimensions of transnational competence. In social-work courses, "there is a high expectation for participatory engagement and talking about what that means in terms of power relations and who speaks and how we build a sense of community of learners, what we then bring to the table, and how we share that responsibility and look at a collaborative approach to learning."[127] Since the participatory model is a central component of social-work pedagogy, the primary challenge for TC educators involves selecting and expanding on existing approaches.

Case studies are a particularly helpful TC pedagogical tool when they provide a detailed historical, social, and political context for social-work students to operate within. Lively and challenging transnational case material engages graduating practitioners working in diverse teams with novel perspectives, stimulates the analysis of possible outcomes and directions, and encourages taking responsibility for aspects of problem solving.[128] Reflective one-on-one and group role plays with peer and facilitator feedback also will feature prominently as a TC-learning activity. Use of transnational case studies and role plays should incorporate instruction in modeling these learning processes so that graduating social workers can effectively engage in training trainers.[129]

Fortunately, community problem solving already constitutes an important part of social-justice-work education. Incorporating video is likely to be especially valuable in generating helpful formative feedback on students' transnational-communication skills.[130] TC educators strive to arrange rewarding overseas fieldwork experiences for graduating social workers who have completed core coursework. Internships, social-development-practicum placements,[131] and research collaborations abroad are preferred to study tours.[132] Projects that focus on mutual challenges, such as issues that link source and receiving areas of migration, are particularly valuable for TC-skill development.[133] Well-designed transnational collaborations build long-term social capital that can be called upon in support of advocacy regarding international, national, or local policy.[134] For a novel learning activity that enhances transnational-functional competence, Janet Finn suggests coupling action research with the "reverse missionary" approach, whereby social-work students discover indigenous knowledge and return having accepted responsibility for "engaging policies here at home."[135]

Overseas work placements are powerful, often life-altering, tools for preparing students for future transnational social-work practice.[136] One model calls for students to shadow one or more overseas practitioners, recording their observations and impressions for reflection and discussion upon return to the home university. A second, more demanding, immersion model aims at developing TC skills in the student's specialized area of study, "such as administration, casework, community organization, or medical social work, child and family, etc.," through actual practice coupled with transnational analysis and innovation.[137]

Service learning, a third placement model, is particularly valuable in promoting TC functional-skill preparation. Arranging useful service-learning positions abroad is challenging, however. Careful planning and flexibility on the part of both faculty and students is essential for successful service-learning placements. Assignments in pairs are likely to result in the most positive and easily supervised service-learning experiences.[138] TC educators need to ensure that service learning does not turn a transnational social-justice opportunity into a patronizing, top-down, charity model ("something that you can do for *them*, whomever they are").[139]

Pedagogical Tools for Preparing
TC Sustainable-Development Professionals

An integrated TC curriculum for sustainable-development practitioners would draw upon several interconnected disciplines. Adopting institutions around the world would seriously consider the range of rigorous multidisciplinary course work recommended in 2008 for the Master's in Development Practice (MDP) by the International Commission on Education for Sustainable Development Practice. The ideal sustainable-development curriculum proposed for the MDP includes courses in economic and policy analysis, tropical agriculture, global health, energy and the environment, managing multisectoral development projects, and science and technology, and culminates in a transdisciplinary practical exercise.[140] Hub TC programs focused on a distinct sustainable-development challenge could be established as regional centers of expertise.[141] Specialized TC programs can be linked in cyberspace by distance courses, online learning,[142] web-based collaborative activities, and communication portals.[143]

TC programs for sustainable-development practitioners find utility in interactive learning through skill-focused practical exercises. Case studies involving bounded narratives of actual development challenges and related policy issues are incorporated into most courses. TC educators guide students who have limited prior overseas experience in learning to select relevant data for decision making and to provide and justify creative and feasible transboundary approaches to resolving a variety of empirically grounded case problems that can be mitigated in multiple ways.[144] Peer role-play activities enable graduating practitioners to nurture empathy, motivation, and other TC-emotional skills.[145] Sustainable-development practitioners further learn how to engage lay publics in performances (skits, story telling, artwork, dance, song) that join indigenous visualization with imagining sustainable futures and innovative approaches to glocal challenges.[146] In addition, students work in teams whose members possess diverse backgrounds and interests on class-based or action-research projects that address specific, usually micro-level, challenges to poverty reduction and sustainable development.[147] These types of TC exercises enhance competencies that will be of value to sustainable-development practitioners in such areas as problem analysis, transnational communication and negotiation, teamwork, project design, planning and budgeting, and project management.[148]

The acquisition of TC skills by sustainable-development professionals is advanced by practical experience through overseas study, internship, research, and fieldwork programs. Earl Kellogg anticipates considerable skill development (especially in the emotional, creative, and communicative domains) from placing students of sustainable development in unfamiliar overseas learning locations. "It's important to have someone sitting next to them from another country; it's important to get them into … [communities and institutions] where they are out of their element," Kellogg maintains, because "you never learn faster than when you are in a situation that you don't [initially] understand."[149] Therefore, TC educators arrange professionally and personally rewarding year-long overseas immersion programs, including South-South exchanges, at partner universities in development-challenged locations.[150] They also build overseas internship and research opportunities.[151] The ideal TC fieldwork program would be hosted by a committed partner (often an NGO),[152] involve hands-on professional training and individual work assignments guided by an experienced mentor, and culminate in a comprehensive field-experience[153] reflection.

Universities in some Southern countries already have initiated programs in sustainable development that incorporate many TC curriculum objectives and learning activities. For instance, Costa Rica's EARTH University offers a comprehensive sustainable-development education that emphasizes "practical learning, entrepreneurial capabilities, ethics and values, teamwork, group problem-solving, communication skills, vertical and horizontal integration of the curriculum, and fostering of social sensitivity through the acquisition of community development skills."[154] After one year of study, masters and Ph.D. students at TERI University in India participate in semester-long projects that address problems of poverty and environmental degradation.[155] The pedagogical approach followed at Ghana's University for Development Studies emphasizes "practice-oriented, community-based, problem-solving, gender-sensitive and interactive learning. It aims to address deep-seated socio-economic imbalances through well-focused education, research and service."[156] This program arranges for all students to live for extended periods in rural communities, where they work on designing development projects in collaboration with local people and private entrepreneurs.[157]

Pedagogical Tools for Preparing TC Health-Care Practitioners

In TC-grounded medical and health education, tools for practical skill-based learning are longitudinally integrated throughout the curriculum[158]—including all graduate medical education.[159] This discussion focuses on preclinical and clinical medical education. Many of the most useful pedagogical tools for the preparation of public-health workers have been treated already in the sections on social-justice-work and sustainable-development education.

Attention to pedagogy is important in generating student interest in TC medical education.[160] Highly regarded and experienced TC educators[161] endeavor to infuse reinforcing formal and informal TC learning activities into coursework, small-group seminars, named lectures, role plays and simulated patients,[162] Balint groups,[163] preceptorships,[164] clinical clerkships, morning reports, case conferences, grand rounds, morbidity and mortality conferences, community fieldwork experiences, and continuing medical education.[165] Initial didactic and Socratic teaching is complemented by case-based group discussions, observed and filmed doctor-patient interactions with formative feedback,[166] and ongoing personal and peer reflection on issues that arise.[167] Reinforcing discussions and shared reflections often take place in informal settings—immediately following a class, "in the hallways after rounds, in the anatomy lab locker room, at lunch in the hospital cafeteria...."[168] TC faculty role models transform the hidden curriculum that encourages and rewards technological interventions in lieu of ethnographic inquiry, interpersonal interaction, compassion, and advocacy.[169]

In systematic, context-specific case analysis, the discussion leader covers "the specifics of the clinical [or policy] problem, the precise nature of the ethical dilemma or professional issue, and the existing knowledge base (in medicine, law or other fields) that relates to the ... situation."[170] TC learning is enhanced when cases present considerable clinical and interpersonal detail and integrate technical and transnational challenges.[171] In some medical schools, such as the Centre for Medical Education at the University of Dundee (where students from seventy countries are enrolled), group discussions will be enriched by the presence of participants from different parts of the world.[172]

In online instructional connections, teachers and learners are not constrained by spatial distance.[173] Robert Like recommends "the development of live and web-based courses interfacing various transnational competencies and different clinical and public health problems."[174] Virtual classrooms open new spaces for TC conversations and reflections among peers and experienced mentors.[175] Further, e-learning offers considerable potential for maintaining one's TC skills through continuing medical education over the course of a career.

Under the TC curriculum, learning is expected to be especially robust during the student's clinical-clerkship experience(s). Clinical clerkships simultaneously present students with a variety of medical challenges influenced by compelling cultural perspectives and diverse social backgrounds and provide opportunities for engaging in guided individual and group reflection,[176] initiating useful recommendations, and testing new behaviors that utilize one's TC strengths and improve upon one's deficiencies.[177] TC clerkships emphasize the validation and promotion of protective factors that are positive and facilitative for health recovery/maintenance, transnational adaptation, and survival. Furthermore, TC clerkships confirm that the extra time spent on caring behavior (estimated at an additional five to seven minutes per encounter until the caring relationship is established) results in multiple benefits for both practitioner and patient.[178] The TC residency experience also is informed by interaction with role models who are capable mentors and skilled at providing transnational care.[179]

TC educators are active in partnering with diverse domestic and foreign community organizations to arrange mutually beneficial skill-refinement experiences. In-country experiential learning opportunities for future physicians, nurses, mental-health practitioners, lab technicians, and medical-record keepers include reflective, socially relevant service-learning placements and community-service projects among diverse underserved populations.[180] Graduating physicians and other medical professionals are often challenged by the absence or shortfall of health-system supports[181] and the discovery of health-care disparities to "engage their commitment to social justice"[182] and to sharpen their patient- and policy-advocacy skills.[183] A valuable team project[184] would involve advancing a set of recommendations aimed at building institutional and community support for pro-health and disparity-eliminating approaches that recognize the effects of social context on ethnically and economically diverse patients and incorporate patients' assets. High-achieving individuals and teams will be honored in high-profile venues while recognizing that, with sufficient effort, all TC learners can attain similar excellence and achievement in working with the underserved.[185]

Overseas immersion experiences help medical students hone skills that are valuable in serving diverse and underserved populations.[186] Through partnerships with committed medical institutions abroad, TC educators encourage (and support) students to complete a rotation in a low-income country. Overseas practice experiences in resource-scarce contexts enable graduating medical professionals to deepen their understanding of global health issues and become more transnationally proficient[187] at the same time that they "learn to practice medicine with limited access to laboratory tests and expensive diagnostic procedures, relying on strengthened physical examination skills...."[188] that later can come in handy in rural practice in industrialized countries.[189]

Chapter 12

Conclusion

Preparing Transnationally Competent Professionals

> *We need a curriculum for our border-crossing, migration-prone, multiple-identity-taking planet, not one that relies on old-fashioned, essentialist, historically lifeless categories that only deter students from tackling the marvelous complexities of current affairs and the human past.*
>
> —Ross Dunn[1]

FROM VAST DISPARITIES in health and health care to a sinking global economy, daunting transboundary and borderless challenges await graduating professionals. The pages we authored in the preceding chapters document our conviction that transnational competence offers an emerging educational platform that promises to prepare men and women who opt for careers in education, engineering, business, social-justice work, sustainable development, and health/medicine to navigate the complex and interdependent technical and interpersonal challenges of the 21st century. Students who aspire to professional competency will be attracted to TC learning because it is stimulating, practical, useful, and relevant to the challenges they will face in their work.[2]

In the near future, contextually relevant forms of transnational-competence preparation will be embedded in professional programs around the world. This chapter is devoted to guiding that transition. Shaping, and reshaping, professional programs that are positioned to graduate TC-skilled practitioners is a transformative task that requires gaps analysis, curricular reform, pedagogical modification, and institutional commitment. While comprehensive TC professional programs remain to be organized and delivered, many of the curriculum and pedagogical pieces exist at universities around the world. Existing components remain to be connected, adapted transprofessionally, aligned with faculty teaching skills and student career aspirations, and integrated into unique and enriched program initiatives.

Transitioning to transnational capacity building for a new century of professional practice is both a historical necessity[3] and a leadership responsibility. We recognize, however, that higher-education advances do not come easily. Programmatic change presents profound challenges for those committed to advancing TC education. University communities tend to view new initiatives with suspicion.[4] Professional schools are notoriously resistant to extensive rehabilitations of established academic programs; the difficulty of "moving cemeteries" is an apt analogy.

We would be remiss in concluding this book without directly addressing the challenge of curricular reform that educational leaders committed to preparing transnationally competent professionals will face. In this final chapter, therefore, we identify and address the principal obstacles to embracing a TC approach designed to enhance the competence profile of graduating professionals. Fortunately, for every major impediment, one can find pivotal and feasible barrier busters. Since most of the obstacles encountered are common across professional schools and programs, and since the most promising ways to address them can be applied (or adapted and applied) across disciplinary boundaries as well as geographic borders, we present this discussion generically.

Obstacles and Initiatives

Our aim in this section is to identify critical obstacles to introducing the TC professional curriculum and accompanying pedagogy and to link each obstacle to a feasible offsetting initiative. Before we go there, it is important to acknowledge that variable sources are likely to provide the foresight and transformative leadership[5] required to revamp a professional program. In the United States, the impetus for moving in the TC direction is most likely to "emerge from efforts of faculty members or administrators working in isolation or in small-scale collaborations."[6] In Europe, the European Commission and various EU grant initiatives are likely to be in the lead.[7] In much of the global South, transnational partnerships[8] supported by foundation funding are likely to provide the impetus for transforming professional programs in order that their graduates are equipped with the TC skills and savvy required to meet current and emerging transnational challenges.

Innovative TC curriculum suggestions are not likely by themselves to overcome entrenched barriers to change in professional programs and institutional arrangements.[9] Fundamental academic-program transformations also require resource infusions, administrative support, faculty buy-in, and student demand. With specific reference to TC preparation and common concerns encountered across the professional fields we considered, we explore each of these contributing factors as obstacles and opportunities in the sections that follow.

Resources

Professional programs cannot be transformed by unfunded mandates. As we shall see, overt or covert resistance to change on the part of administrators, faculty, staff, and students often is linked to resource issues. Without new resources, primarily financial support, that are specifically matched with curriculum and pedagogical initiatives, TC professional preparation will not progress in any substantial way.[10]

With strategic planning based on the identification of internal and external sources of power, the resource barrier can be largely overcome.[11] Part of the answer lies in internal transfers and incentives, but most universities will need to find external sources of funding to support the bulk of their resource needs.[12] Foundation initiatives, capital campaigns, entrepreneurial endeavors,[13] government grant programs,[14] professional associations,[15] and prosperous alums are leading external prospects given the interest of these stakeholders in ensuring that tomorrow's graduates are prepared for emerging technical and societal challenges. We reaffirm the Task Force for Transnational Competence's call for a review of all U.S. national government programs that support international education with the aim of "fortifying those that strengthen" transnational competence.[16] Education ministries throughout the North and South should undertake similar initiatives.

Administrative Support

The successful introduction of TC preparation in professional programs rests on top-down and bottom-up leadership. This section focuses on overcoming the institutional-leadership barrier.[17] Without buy-in, enthusiastic support, and participation from top administrators responsible for the program itself (including deans) and for articulating the university-wide perspective (presidents, vice chancellors, rectors, provosts, chief international officers, and research vice presidents), the transition to TC learning will not be forthcoming and sustained.[18] Sheila Biddle's study of internationalization efforts at five U.S. universities (Columbia, Duke, Iowa, Michigan, and Washington) supports this assessment. She concludes that without "commitment, starting at the top levels of administration, there is not much hope that deans and department chairs, who are the key actors, will find it worth their while to develop and support international initiatives."[19]

Limited vision, multiple demands for additional resource allocations, and traditional accreditation pressures pose administrative barriers to moving professional programs in the TC direction.[20] The misperception encountered among some high-level administrators, faculty, and program review–team members that developing interpersonal and transnational skills is not fundamental for professional preparation especially constrains programmatic innovation and change.[21]

Recruiting a program director committed to TC professional learning[22] and securing buy-in at the deanship level constitute powerful first steps toward overcoming softness in institutional support. Then, the issue of resources becomes less one of total amounts than "the strategy used to dispense them."[23] Higher-education leaders will find compelling resource needs among competing initiatives. Nevertheless, TC's pan-profession skill-based emphasis on preparing for future transnational challenges and effectively addressing contextual contributors to ethnic and economic disparities in sustainable fashion certainly must be a central part of the forward-looking university's strategic agenda.[24] At the University of Pittsburgh, for instance, the provost, acting in response to NASULGC's 2004 "Call to Leadership," "required that all deans incorporate into future strategic plans the steps they are taking to integrate global competence into their schools."[25]

Restructuring and enriching curricular visions to encompass transnational-competence preparation becomes an easier task once a supportive dean and an inspirational senior program director are in place and the transborder perspective is sewn into the fabric of the higher-education institution.[26] The next step is to recruit strong and credible faculty advocates who can convince their colleagues of the relevance, utility, and viability of TC education.[27] Transnationally experienced role models and mentors understand that "we would not pursue scientific and technological advances so fervently if we did not value human life and our common humanity so passionately"[28] and are able to transmit this core TC passion among colleagues and students. Sustained administrative commitment and encouragement, therefore, enables faculty buy-in.

Faculty Buy-In

Professional programs in the fields addressed in this book will not be transformed unless faculty[29] also commit to the TC initiative.[30] In all fields of study, engaging faculty, who hold the keys to curricular transformation and are responsible for course development, "is essential to expanding their global competence and internationalizing the campus."[31]

In the initial stages of professional-program transformation, TC champions are likely to encounter professors who are *disinterested* in the skill-based curriculum framework, *unprepared* to adopt its novel and heavily interactive learning activities,[32] and/or *unwilling* to include transnational components among the professional competencies they teach.[33] When Duke's Fuqua School of Business decided to infuse international components in all its courses, for instance, "a significant number of faculty were not happy with the decision; they felt they had enough to do without taking on the additional burden of internationalizing their courses...."[34] It is safe to conclude, therefore, that if there is no faculty discussion about and participation in the TC initiative, they will be more reluctant to accept ownership of the proposed program.[35]

Fortunately, it is within the reach of committed TC program initiators to address each of these faculty-related constraints. The rest of our "faculty-buy-in" discussion is devoted to suggesting feasible approaches to overcoming faculty disinterest, incapacity, and unwillingness to change.

Addressing Disinterest. One place to begin raising faculty interest in the TC framework is with collegial assessment of the skills that will be needed by graduating practitioners over the next half century. Discussing and reaching collective agreement on the importance of introducing TC skill preparation in light of horizon-rising professional challenges will go a long way toward generating and enhancing faculty enthusiasm for curriculum transformation and pedagogical innovation.[36] Faculty interest can be further stimulated by considering lessons drawn from parallel TC initiatives in the same field or another profession.

The next step following discussion and agreement regarding student-skill expectations involves active faculty participation in designing a contextually informed TC curriculum for their unique professional program. Involvement in constructing the specific details of the TC curriculum design and associated learning activities encourages the emergence of program champions and gives all participating faculty a vested interest in the professional success of its graduates. Faculty members are most likely to take ownership of the TC transformation process when it engages them at the heart of their intellectual interests. In arranging TC program responsibilities, therefore, every effort should be made to tap the academic passions of collaborating faculty.[37] Identifying TC as a curriculum-policy priority also often paves the way for securing the additional resources needed to inspire leading faculty to undertake retooling where needed.[38]

Addressing Perceived Incapacity. A fundamental requirement for curriculum transformation is the availability of core faculty members who are confident and enthusiastic about their ability to prepare graduating professionals with TC skills.[39] The need for qualified faculty is addressed, in part, through judicious hiring[40] and partnership exchanges. The community of TC faculty will be far more capable, engaging, and productive to the extent that it becomes transnational.

In most professional programs, the successful adoption and sustained delivery of TC skill-development components highlighted in this book also will require attention to faculty development.[41] "'I tell presidents if they have any money at all for internationalization,'" Madeleine F. Green, vice president for international initiatives at the American Council on Education reports, "'faculty development is the place to put it.'"[42] The most promising TC faculty-development efforts concentrate on relevant and dynamic transnational challenges, on connections across boundaries of expertise, and on dimensions of student training that are of personal and professional interest and "learnable" and "updateable" within a reasonable period of time.[43]

TC faculty development should focus on improved ability to teach some combination of analytic, emotional, creative, communicative, and functional skills. Many valuable mechanisms are available for enhancing the capacity of faculty to participate effectively in a TC professional program. These include participating in workshops on how to provide future practitioners with TC skills,[44] joining South-South peer-support networks for case writing and teaching,[45] and developing productive learning networks and long-term insight-sharing relationships with fellow educators around the world.[46] For most faculty members preparing to participate in a TC program, gaining new and/or additional overseas experience would be especially worthwhile. This objective is served by sabbaticals and professional leaves in another country,[47] short-term assignments in low-income countries,[48] participation on multinational and transboundary project teams, and support for overseas research.

Addressing Unwillingness to Change. We do not expect, nor does successful implementation require, that all faculty members fully embrace TC education overnight. Inevitably, some professors will not "*need* global education personally or professionally"[49] or be convinced it should be a priority.[50] However, a critical mass of faculty advocates is required if professional-program transformation is to occur. As faculty members ourselves, we recognize and value the autonomy that professors exercise over what they choose to teach and how they elect to teach it. Rather than mandate particular courses or instructional approaches, we advise emerging TC programs to emphasize sustained opportunities and inducements.[51]

We observed earlier that a major factor blocking faculty willingness to move in a TC direction will be the drag of competing demands on their time. This obstacle can be overcome, but success requires compelling emotional and material incentives.[52] For some faculty, buy-in will require travel grants,[53] compensation, or released time that support engagement in research and/or course development/revision.[54] In some cases, the allocation of teaching assistants to support TC-skill development would bring in initially hesitant faculty.[55] For hard-pressed faculty, infusing TC-skill development across existing courses might have considerably greater appeal than would developing new courses.[56]

In addition, personal intellectual rewards and financial incentives usually are motivating.[57] Linking curriculum transformation to a faculty member's research interests and inherent desire to excel as a teacher offers a particularly promising approach.[58] Participating faculty can be expected to discover that long-term transnational partnerships and transboundary stretching are intellectually exciting, and that making an important difference in students' careers and lives and a sustained contribution in multiple societal contexts, are emotionally rewarding.[59] In a clear signal of institutional transformation, the willingness of program faculty members to incorporate the TC approach in their teaching would constitute a major positive consideration in tenure, promotion, special recognition, and merit-award decisions.[60] In all professional and transprofession programs committed to introducing the TC framework, the dedication of additional resources and the creation of an enriched skill-development environment will help generate faculty support.[61]

Student Demand

We anticipate that future generations of students will favor higher-education institutions that elect to incorporate TC skills in their professional-degree programs. Nevertheless, we expect that many students would be constrained from insisting on curriculum-transforming TC initiatives by issues that resemble the obstacles initially

confronting program faculty. Foremost among these are "maxed-out" course requirements, perceptions that TC skills are nonessential,[62] and limited financial support
for transnational learning.

Professional curriculums are notoriously crowded with subjects that educational
authorities believe must be covered,[63] and few students want to extend the time to
graduation.[64] The prevailing emphasis on traditional subjects, coupled with lack of
awareness of the educational and professional advantages that accrue from learning
TC skills, can generate student disinterest. Some students also are concerned about
the added costs and dislocation from family, friends, and employment places that
overseas learning normally involves.[65]

Infusing TC skills in existing courses is likely to resolve the full-load issue for most
students involved in professional programs.[66] Relevancy is a critical consideration
for professionally oriented students.[67] The TC framework has a decided advantage
in this regard; the emphasis on practical skill development distinguishes graduating
practitioners from both Southern and Northern TC programs. University and external
financial support for students to engage in off-campus TC-learning activities will
encourage participation.[68] In addition, students themselves will invest enthusiastically
in transformative experiential learning that prepares them well for the transnational
challenges that teachers, engineers, business managers, social workers, sustainable-
development professionals, or physicians and other health professionals will face
following graduation.

Conclusion

Higher-education institutions in the North and South contribute in decisive ways to
advancing the transnational-competence dimension of the global skill revolution. At
the same time, workplaces and societies greet university graduates with ever-higher
expectations and reward those who have learned to generate innovative approaches
to emerging transnational challenges and to navigate nimbly and collaboratively
when implementing them across multiple boundaries and barriers. In *Transnational
Competence*, we have endeavored to show how, by introducing comprehensive TC-
informed curriculums and learning activities, professional programs can prepare
graduating practitioners who are equipped with the analytic, emotional, creative,
communicative, and functional skills needed to tackle horizon-rising challenges.

In professional higher education, student demand is influenced by the perceived
quality and long-term utility of an academic course of study. In our interconnected
world, informed and committed incoming students will seek out professional programs that link technical expertise with relevant transnational skills in an experiential
learning environment that is both stimulating and richly rewarding. We look forward
to the blossoming of contextually inspired, uniquely carved, and extraordinarily at-
tractive TC-influenced professional programs that are infused with faculty passion,
rewarding in terms of student aspirations, and responsive to the transboundary,
sea-spanning, and marvelously interconnected challenges of our time.

Notes

Notes for Introduction

1. Philip Werdell, "Futurism and the Reform of Higher Education," in *Learning for Tomorrow: The Role of the Future in Education,* edited by Alvin Toffler (New York: Vintage Books, 1974), p. 286.

2. See James N. Rosenau, *Along the Domestic-Foreign Frontier: Exploring Governance in a Turbulent World* (Cambridge: Cambridge University Press, 1997); Peter H. Koehn, "Sustainable Development Frontiers and Divides: Transnational Actors and US/China Greenhouse Gas Emissions," *International Journal of Sustainable Development and World Ecology* 11, No. 4 (December 2004): 380.

3. James N. Rosenau, *People Count! Networked Individuals in Global Politics* (Boulder: Paradigm Publishers, 2008).

4. Interview with Earl Kellogg conducted by Peter Koehn in Washington, DC, December 5, 2007.

5. See Beth Peoc'h (ed.), *Downsizing Development: An Introduction to Nano-Scale Technologies and the Implications for the Global South* (New York: U.N. Non-Governmental Liaison Service, ETC Group, 2008).

6. With reference to U.S. university students, William Cummings, Professor of International Education and International Affairs at the George Washington University, observed in autumn 2007 that "there is a feeling that we as a nation are not handling ourselves very well, so there is a feeling that I've got to try to take some of the world in my own hands and do good in a small way, perhaps to correct for some other mistakes." Interview conducted by Peter Koehn in Washington, DC, November 29, 2007.

7. Wendy Sarkissian, *Kitchen Table Sustainability: Practical Recipes for Community Engagement with Sustainability* (London: Earthscan, 2009), p. 252.

8. NASULGC, *Expanding the International Scope of Universities* (Washington, DC: NASULGC, 2000), p. 9. In early 2009, NASULGC changed its name to the Association of Public and Land-Grant Universities (APLU). An "active skills" emphasis also characterized Richard Lambert's earlier notion of global competence. Richard D. Lambert, "Summary and Prospectus," in *Educational Exchange and Global Competence,* edited by Richard D. Lambert (Portland, ME: Council on International Educational Exchange, 1994), p. 286.

9. William B. DeLauder, *et al., A Call to Leadership: The Presidential Role in Internationalizing the University* (Washington, DC: NASULGC Task Force on International Education, 2004), p. vii.

10. Karin Fischer, "Community-College Educators Focus on Globalization," *Chronicle of Higher Education,* March 7, 2008, p. A24.

11. Marcelo M. Suarez-Orozco and Desiree B. Qin-Hilliard, "Globalization: Culture and Education in the New Millennium," in *Globalization: Culture and Education in the New Millennium,* edited by Marcelo M. Suarez-Orozco and Desiree B. Qin-Hilliard (Berkeley: University of California Press, 2004), p. 6 [emphasis in original].

12. Unpublished results of the 2007 "Changing Academic Professions" survey of faculty in seventeen

countries summarized in Karin Fischer, "U.S. Faculty Members Lag on Global Engagement," *Chronicle of Higher Education*, February 13, 2009, p. A37.

13. For a concise statement of early milestone studies and initiatives, see Seth Spaulding, James Mauch, and Lin Lin, "The Internationalization of Higher Education: Policy and Program Issues," in *Changing Perspectives on International Education*, edited by Patrick O'Meara, Howard D. Mehlinger, and Roxanna Ma Newman (Bloomington: Indiana University Press, 2001), p. 205.

14. Sheila Biddle, *Internationalization: Rhetoric or Reality?* (New York: American Council of Learned Societies, 2002), pp. 8, 119.

15. George M. Dennison, "Review of Derek Bok's *Our Underachieving Colleges*," *Montana Professor* 17, No. 2 (2007): 47. Senior international officers at the Big 10 universities (plus the University of Chicago) have confronted a similar dilemma in their interinstitutional deliberations (Kellogg interview).

16. Tora K. Bikson, Gregory F. Treverton, Joy Moini, and Gustav Lindstrom, *New Challenges for International Leadership: Lessons from Organizations with Global Missions* (Santa Monica: RAND, 2003), p. xxi.

17. Biddle, *Internationalization*, p. 54.

18. Ulrich Teichler, *The Requirements of the World of Work*, Volume IV of the World Conference on Higher Education (Paris: UNESCO, 1999), ED.99/HEP/WCHE/Vol. IV-1, p. 22.

19. See, for instance, the American Council on Education's report on *Educating for Global Competence* (Washington, DC: American Council on Education, Commission on International Education, 1997).

20. NASULGC, "Summary of Proceedings from the Africa Region Post-Summit Workshop held at Howard University, 1 May 2008" (Washington, DC: NASULGC, 2008), p. 2.

21. Universities in Africa, Ramphele continues, confront the steepest human capacity–building challenges. Mamphela Ramphele, "The University As an Actor in Development: New Perspectives and Demands," in *African Higher Education: Implications for Development*, edited by Cheryl R. Doss, Robert E. Evanson, and Nancy L. Ruther (New Haven: Yale Center for International and Area Studies, 2003), p. 1.

22. Damtew Teferra and Philip G. Altbach, "African Higher Education: Challenges for the 21st Century," *Higher Education* 47 (2004): 22.

23. Joel S. Migdal, "Mental Maps and Virtual Checkpoints: Struggles to Construct and Maintain State and Social Boundaries," in *Boundaries and Belonging: States and Societies in the Struggle to Shape Identities and Local Practices*, edited by Joel S. Migdal (Cambridge: Cambridge University Press, 2004), p. 5.

24. Migdal, "Mental Maps," pp. 6, 23.

25. Darla Deardorff's research with international education administrators revealed "no consensus on terms." Panel on "Intercultural Competence," 25th Annual Meeting of the Association of International Education Administrators, Washington, DC, 20 February 2008.

26. We reserve "global" for references that include the entire world, use "international" to refer to a particular form of organization and to relations among nations, and prefer "transnational" as a descriptor for the wide range of person-to-person and collectivity relations that transcend nation-state, ethnic-identity, and professional-activity boundaries.

27. NASULGC Commission on International Programs, *A National Action Agenda for Internationalizing Higher Education* (Washington, DC: NASULGC, 2007), p. 6.

28. Richard D. Lambert, "Parsing the Concept of Global Competence," in *Educational Exchange and Global Competence*, edited by Richard D. Lambert (Portland, ME: Council on International Educational Exchange, 1994), p. 11.

29. Stefanie Rathje, "Intercultural Competence: The Status and Future of a Controversial Concept," *Language and Intercultural Communication* 7, No. 4 (2007): 255, 257; Darla K. Deardorff, "Identification and Assessment of Intercultural Competence as a Student Outcome of Internationalization," *Journal of Studies in International Education* 10, No. 3 (Fall 2006): 242.

30. In 2008, about 250,000 U.S. students studied abroad annually. The Commission's goal is to reach one million within ten years. Legislation authorizing the Paul Simon Study Abroad Foundation passed the full House of Representatives and the Senate Foreign Relations Committee unanimously in 2008, but "was hung up at the last minute on the Senate floor." Supporters are seeking $50 million for

the Foundation in the State Department's budget request. Letter from Peter McPherson, APLU President, to President-elect Barack Obama's State Department transition advisors dated December 15, 2008.

31. Commission, *Internationalizing Higher Education*, p. 5.

32. Andrew Abbott, *The System of Professions: An Essay on the Division of Expert Labor* (Chicago: University of Chicago Press, 1988), pp. 8–9.

33. Eliot Freidson, *Professionalism: The Third Logic* (Cambridge, UK: Polity Press, 2001), p. 17.

34. Robert T. Moran, Philip R. Harris, and Sarah V. Moran, *Managing Cultural Differences: Global Leadership Strategies for the 21st Century* (Amsterdam: Elsevier, 2007), p. 251.

35. One recent study found that 86 percent of U.S. "cutting-edgers" (and only 43 percent of other leaders) closely or somewhat identified with professional associates abroad. Cutting-edgers also were more than twice as likely to consider "home" to be wherever their professional colleagues might be situated. James N. Rosenau, David C. Earnest, Yale H. Ferguson, and Ole R. Holsti, *On the Cutting Edge of Globalization: An Inquiry into American Elites* (Lanham: Rowman & Littlefield, 2006), pp. 29, 51.

36. Abbott, *The System of Professions*, p. 30.

37. Aihwa Ong, "Higher Learning: Educational Availability and Flexible Citizenship in Global Space," in *Diversity and Citizenship Education: Global Perspectives*, edited by James A. Banks (New York: Jossey-Bass, 2004), p. 67.

38. Freidson, *Professionalism*, pp. 29, 84, 95, 127. In Europe, a profession's "ties with government are generally stronger and those with the universities correspondingly weaker." Abbott, *The System of Professions*, p. 80.

39. Freidson, *Professionalism*, p. 144.

40. Abbott, *The System of Professions*, p. 84.

41. Chathapuram S. Ramanathan and Rosemary J. Link, "Future Visions for Global Studies in Social Work," in *All Our Futures: Principles and Resources for Social Work Practice in a Global Era*, edited by Chathapuram S. Ramanathan and Rosemary J. Link (Albany: Brooks/Cole, Wadsworth, 1999), p. 234. Within the European Union, *harmonization* of national credential requirements has opened the door for increased labor mobility among professionals. Freidson, *Professionalism*, p. 194.The 26-member-country European Federation of National Engineering Associations (FEANI) has granted the EUR ING professional title to about 30,000 registered engineers. This recognition is intended to "facilitate mobility by assigning a 'guarantee of competence' to engineers who wish to practice outside their own countries." Other transnational mobility–enhancing efforts are the Register of International Engineers maintained by the Engineers Mobility Forum, the International Register of Professional Engineers, and the Asia-Pacific Economic Cooperation Engineer register. Kevin Sweeney, "International Recognition of Engineering Degrees, Programs, and Accreditation Systems," in National Academy of Engineering, *Educating the Engineer of 2020: Adapting Engineering Education to the New Century* (Washington, DC: National Academies Press, 2005), pp. 136–138, 140–142.

42. Biddle, *Internationalization*, p. 51. In some U.S. states, policy makers have pressed for professional cultural-competence preparation. New Jersey's 2005 law mandates that practicing physicians, residents, and medical students take "cultural-competency training" in order to secure a license from, or be relicensed by, the State Board of Medical Examiners. Sue Pelletier, "N.J. Mandates Cultural-Competency Training" (June 1, 2005, at meetingsnet.com; accessed November 27, 2007). Additionally, the New Jersey law requires that all medical schools in the state provide coursework in cultural competence. Subsequently, California and Washington required cultural-competence training "as part of health education and/or licensure and accreditation." Darci Graves, Robert Like, Nataly Kelly, and Alexa Hohensee, "Legislation as Intervention: A Survey of Cultural Competence Policy in Health Care," *Journal of Health Care Law & Policy* 10 (2007): 353, 349.

43. Merry M. Merryfield, "A Framework for Teacher Education in Global Perspectives," in *Preparing Teachers to Teach Global Perspectives: A Handbook for Teacher Educators*, edited by Merry M. Merryfield, Elaine Jarchow, and Sarah Pickert (Thousand Oaks, CA: Corwin Press, 1997), p. 1. Since 1981, NCATE's accreditation standards for all teacher-preparation programs have mandated evidence that *multicultural* content and perspectives have been included in the curriculum. Marilyn Cochran-Smith, "Standing at the Crossroads: Multicultural Teacher Education at the Beginning of the 21st Century," *Multicultural Perspectives* 5, No. 3 (2003): 3.

44. See Lynne M. Healy, *International Social Work: Professional Action in an Interdependent World*,

2nd edition (Oxford: Oxford University Press, 2008), p. 353. On the variable recognition historically granted to international considerations by CSWE, see Lynne Healy, "International Social Work Curriculum in Historical Perspective," in *All Our Futures: Principles and Resources for Social Work Practice in a Global Era*, edited by Chathapuram S. Ramanathan and Rosemary J. Link (Albany: Brooks/Cole, Wadsworth, 1999), pp. 19–21.

45. Healy, *International Social Work*, p. 201. The National [U.S.] Association of Social Workers also "supports and encourages the development of standards for culturally competent social work practice ...." National Association of Social Workers, *NASW Standards for Cultural Competence in Social Work Practice* (2001), http://www.socialworkers.org/sections/credentials/cultural_comp.asp. Schools of social work in Africa and Asia typically are connected to international professional associations and adopt similar accrediting standards. Rosemary J. Link and Chathapuram S. Ramanathan, "Introduction," in *All Our Futures: Principles and Resources for Social Work Practice in a Global Era*, edited by Chathapuram S. Ramanathan and Rosemary J. Link (Albany: Brooks/Cole, 1999), p. 3.

46. ACBSP, "Accreditation Standards and Criteria for Demonstrating Excellence in Baccalaureate/ Graduate Degree Schools and Programs" (Overland Park, KS: ACBSP, revision F, May 2008), p. 41. See also Association to Advance Collegiate Schools of Business (AACSB), *Eligibility Procedures and Accreditation Standards for Business Accreditation* (Tampa, FL: AACSB, 2005), p. 69.

47. Cited in Scott Carlson, "A Global Approach to Engineering," *Chronicle of Higher Education*, June 1, 2007, p. A33. The FEANI-affiliated European Standing Observatory for the Engineering Profession and Education aims to become "*the* European body dealing with accreditation." Sweeney, "International Recognition," p. 138.

48. Liaison Committee on Medical Education, *Functions and Structure of a Medical School: Standards for Accreditation of Medical Education Programs Leading to the M.D. Degree*, at http://www.lcme.org/ functions2006june.pdf, p. 13. Support for intercultural-competence education also has been expressed by professional associations of physicians, mental-health professionals, nurses, pharmacists, physician assistants, and physical therapists. Graves, *et al.*, "Legislation As Intervention," pp. 354–358.

49. Biddle, *Internationalization*, p. 52. One partial exception is the AAMC's Tool for Assessing Cultural Competency Training (TACCT). Association of American Medical Colleges, *Tool for Assessing Cultural Competence Training* (TACCT) at http://www.aamc.org/meded/tacct/start.htm.

50. Thus, gains in individual transnational competence promote advances in the TC of the nation as a whole. See Gilbert W. Merkx, "Foreign Area Studies in U.S. Global Competence," in *Educational Exchange and Global Competence*, edited by Richard D. Lambert (Portland, ME: Council on International Educational Exchange, 1994), p. 151.

51. On the dark side, criminals engaged in trafficking drugs and human beings across borders and persons planning terrorist acts around the world also benefit from enhanced TC. See Thomas L. Friedman, *The World Is Flat: A Brief Introduction of the Twenty-First Century* (New York: Farrar, Straus and Giroux, 2006), pp. 546–547; Jenna S. Demir, "The Trafficking of Women for Sexual Exploitation: A Gender-Based and Well-Founded Fear of Persecution?" New Issues in Refugee Research Working Paper No. 80 (Geneva: UNHCR, Evaluation and Policy Analysis Unit, March 2003), p. 9; James N. Rosenau, "Turbulence and Terrorism: Reframing or Readjusting the Model?" in *Globalization, Security, and the Nation-State: Paradigms in Transition*, edited by Ersel Aydinli and James N. Rosenau (Albany: State University of New York Press, 2005), p. 225. Also see Wolfgang H. Reinicke, *Global Public Policy: Governing Without Government?* (Washington, DC: Brookings Institution, 1998), pp. 135–137. In short, the acquisition of TC does not guarantee that professionals or other people will employ their new skills in morally desirable and socially progressive ways. However, we have elected to focus in this book on professional actors who employ their skills in the interest of improving the human condition. Thus, we envision TC as "a potential platform to advance the interests and aspirations of the oppressed and less well to do." Mitchell A. Orenstein and Hans P. Schmitz, "The New Transnationalism and Comparative Politics," *Comparative Politics* 38, No. 4 (July 2006): 493.

52. Sidney Tarrow, *The New Transnational Activism* (Cambridge: Cambridge University Press, 2005), pp. 42–43.

53. Albert-Laszlo Barabasi demonstrates that, due to the highly interconnected nature of contemporary networks, "our ability to reach people has less and less to do with the physical distance between us. Discovering common acquaintances with perfect strangers on worldwide trips repeatedly reminds

us that some people on the other side of the planet are often closer along the social network than people living next door." Albert-Laszlo Barabasi, *Linked: The New Science of Networks* (Cambridge, MA: Perseus Publishing, 2002), pp. 40, 34.

54. Tarrow, *New Transnational Activism*, p. 2.

55. Arjun Appadurai, *Modernity at Large: Cultural Dimensions of Globalization* (Minneapolis: University of Minnesota Press, 1996), pp. 4, 53.

56. See Michel S. Laguerre, "The Globalization of a Panethnopolis: Richmond District As the New Chinatown in San Francisco," *GeoJournal* 64 (2005): 48.

57. Peter H. Koehn, *Refugees from Revolution: U.S. Policy and Third-World Migration* (Boulder: Westview Press, 1991), pp. 312–336.

58. Steven Vertovec and Alisdair Rogers, "Introduction," in *Muslim European Youth: Reproducing Ethnicity, Religion, Culture* (Aldershot: Ashgate, 1998), pp. 6–9; Peter H. Koehn and Phyllis B. Ngai, "Citizenship Education for an Age of Population Mobility and Glocally Interconnected Destinies," *Finnish Journal of Ethnicity and Migration* 1, No. 1 (2006): 31.

59. Ronnie D. Lipschutz, "Networks of Knowledge and Practice: Global Civil Society and Protection of the Global Environment," in *Saving the Seas: Values, Scientists, and International Governance,* edited by L. Anathea Brooks and Stacey D. VanDeveer (College Park: University of Maryland, 1997), pp. 434–437.

60. In boundary-overlay situations, specialized experts possess no inherent competence advantage over lay publics. Bobby Milstein, *Hygeia's Constellation: Navigating Health Futures in a Dynamic and Democratic World* (Atlanta, GA: Centers for Disease Control and Prevention, 2008), pp. 62, 45.

61. Peter Willetts, "Who Cares about the Environment?" in *The Environment and International Relations,* edited by John Vogler and Mark F. Imber (London: Routledge, 1996), p. 134. One manifestation of this development is the increase in the number of uninsured and underinsured U.S. citizens seeking quality medical treatment abroad at affordable rates. An estimated half million persons from Europe and the United States traveled to India for health-care treatment in 2007. Robert K. Crone, "Flat Medicine? Exploring Trends in the Globalization of Health Care," *Academic Medicine* 83, No. 2 (2008): 118–119, 120.

62. Peter H. Koehn, "Improving Transnational Health-Care Encounters and Outcomes: The Challenge of Enhanced Transnational Competence for Migrants and Health Professionals." In *Proceedings of the Hospitals in a Culturally Diverse Europe Conference on Quality-Assured Health Care and Health Promotion for Migrants and Ethnic Minorities, Amsterdam, 9–11 December 2004.* www.mfh-eu.net/conf/results/ (2005).

63. See Eric J. Cassell, *The Healer's Art* (Cambridge: MIT Press, 1976), p. 138.

64. Bikson, Treverton, Moini, and Lindstrom, *New Challenges for International Leadership,* p. xviii.

65. Commission, *Internationalizing Higher Education,* p. 35.

Notes for Chapter 1

1. Fernando Reimers, "'Global Competency' Is Imperative for Global Success," *Chronicle of Higher Education,* January 30, 2009, p. A29.

2. Freidson, *Professionalism,* p. 33.

3. See James N. Rosenau, *Distant Proximities: Dynamics Beyond Globalization* (Princeton: Princeton University Press, 2003), pp. 232–255.

4. Friedman, *The World Is Flat,* p. 11.

5. Rosenau, *Distant Proximities,* p. 251.

6. Paul Williams, "The Competent Boundary Spanner," *Public Administration* 80, No. 1 (2002):103, 106.

7. See Rosenau, *People Count!* p. 106.

8. Joseph Shaules, *Deep Culture: The Hidden Challenges of Global Living* (Clevedon, UK: Multilingual Matters, 2007), p. 14. Shaules further cautions (p. 18) that "superficial contact and technological convergence across borders can mask the deeper and more subtle cultural differences that often create

intercultural misunderstanding." Even increased interpersonal contact, when not facilitated by adequate preparation for transboundary encounters, will not result in harmonious and mutually rewarding working experiences.

9. Ann Marie Kimball, *et al.*, "The Asian Pacific Economic Cooperation Emerging Infections Network," *American Journal of Preventive Medicine* 17, 2 (1999): 157–158.

10. Williams, "Competent Boundary Spanner," p. 106.

11. See Ulf Hannerz, *Transnational Connections: Culture, People, Places* (London: Routledge, 1996), p. 27; Tarrow, *New Transnational Activism*, p. 212.

12. Kenneth Cushner, "Intercultural Education from an International Perspective: Commonalities and Future Prospects," in *International Perspectives on Intercultural Education*, edited by Kenneth Cushner (Mahwah, NJ: Lawrence Erlbaum Associates, 1998), p. 369.

13. See James N. Rosenau, "Governance in the 21st Century," *Global Governance* 1 (1995): 13-43.

14. James N. Rosenau, "Governance in a New Global Order," in *Governing Globalization: Power, Authority and Global Governance*, edited by David Held and Anthony McGrew (Oxford: Blackwell, 2002), p. 80; Reinicke, *Global Public Policy*, p. 220; Thomas Risse, "Transnational Actors and World Politics," in *Handbook of International Relations*, edited by Walter Carlsnaes, Thomas Risse, and Beth A. Simmons (Thousand Oaks, CA: Sage, 2001), p. 269. Gilles Paquet submits that "all modern effective systems have tended to become more decentralized and distributed, organizationally or spatially, or both." Gilles Paquet, *The New Geo-Governance: A Baroque Approach* (Toronto: University of Ottawa Press, 2005), pp. xi–xii, 2–3, 9. On global public-private partnerships, see Kent Buse and Gill Walt, "Globalisation and Multilateral Public-Private Health Partnerships: Issues for Health Policy," in *Health Policy in a Globalising World*, edited by Kelley Lee, Kent Buse, and Suzanne Fustukian (Cambridge: Cambridge University Press, 2002), pp. 42–44.

15. For an elaboration of some of the arguments set forth in this paragraph, see Tanja A. Borzel, "Organizing Babylon: On the Different Conceptions of Policy Networks," *Public Administration* 76, 2 (Summer 1998): 259–266.

16. Steering mechanisms include raising issues and articulating their implications, setting standards, mobilizing concerned groups and individuals, direct lobbying, and monitoring compliance. Srilatha Batliwala and L. David Brown, "Introduction: Why Transnational Civil Society Matters," in *Transnational Civil Society: An Introduction*, edited by Srilatha Batliwala and L. David Brown (Bloomfield, CT: Kumarian, 2006), p. 5.

17. See Tarrow, *New Transnational Activism*. For instance, flourishing cross-border citizen networks now "infiltrate nearly every major international political issue-area. ..." Ronald J. Deibert, "International Plug 'n Play: Citizen Activism, the Internet, and Global Public Policy," *International Studies Perspectives* 1 (2000): 255–256, 271.

18. Peter M. Haas, "Scientific Communities and Multiple Paths to Environmental Management," in *Saving the Seas: Values, Scientists, and International Governance*, edited by L. Anathea Brooks and Stacy D. VanDeveer (College Park: University of Maryland Press, 1997), pp. 193–228.

19. Some students of civic transnationalism estimate that professional associations esteemed for technical and scientific expertise "constitute the largest proportion of cross-border nonprofit, nongovernmental organizations in the world." Sanjeev Khagram and Sarah Alvord, "The Rise of Civic Transnationalism," in *Transnational Civil Society: An Introduction*, edited by Srilatha Batliwala and L. David Brown (Bloomfield, CT: Kumarian, 2006), p. 73.

20. Risse, "Transnational Actors and World Politics," p. 269.

21. Joe Wallis and Brian Dollery, "Government Failure, Social Capital and the Appropriateness of the New Zealand Model for Public Sector Reform in Developing Countries," *World Development* 29, No. 2 (February 2001): 249, 260.

22. Mary B. McDonnell, "Introducing the Human Capital Initiative." *Items* 52, Nos. 2/3 (1998): 30.

23. Susan B. Sutton, "Making Partnerships the Driving Force of Campus Internationalization," *IIE Networker* Supplement (Spring 2007).

24. Buse and Walt, "Multilateral Public-Private Health Partnerships," p. 44.

25. Tarrow, *New Transnational Activism*, pp. 163–164.

26. Coalitions typically "form around short-term threats and opportunities...." *Ibid.*, pp. 164–165.

27. Hubs are able to dominate network structures because they offer short paths between nodes in the network. Barabasi, *Linked,* p. 64.

28. See Peter H. Koehn, Montague Demment, and Anne-Claire Hervy, "Enhancing Higher Education's Engagement in International Development: Africa-U.S. Partnerships," *Journal of the World Universities Forum* 1, 6 (2008): 127–140.

29. According to Elizabeth E. Lyons, NSF's Regional Program Coordinator for Africa, Near East and South Asia Program in the Office of International Science and Engineering (personal email communication to Peter Koehn, November 19, 2007), "the international activity must be closely related to the original objectives of the award and the disciplinary program officer must concur that the supplemental funding is meritorious. We strongly encourage that U.S. students [also] be involved."

30. The roughly 800 international research and development project profiles submitted by NASULGC member institutions by March of 2009 are posted at http://www.nasulgc.org/NetCommunity/Page.apx?pid=776&srcid=776.

31. Tarrow, *New Transnational Activism,* pp. 163–165.

Notes for Chapter 2

1. NASULGC Commission, *Internationalizing Higher Education,* p. 5.

2. See Jane Knight, "Internationalisation of Higher Education," in *Quality and Internationalisation in Higher Education,* edited by Jane Knight and Hans de Wit (Paris: Organisation for Economic Co-operation and Development, 1999), pp. 15–16.

3. Khagram and Alvord, "Civic Transnationalism,"pp. 65–66.

4. See Merry M. Merryfield and Angene Wilson, *Social Studies and the World: Teaching Global Perspectives* (Silver Spring, MD: National Council for the Social Studies, 2005), pp. 20–21; Holly M. Carter, "Multiculturalism, Diversity, and Global Competence," in *Educational Exchange and Global Competence,* edited by Richard D. Lambert (Portland, ME: Council on International Educational Exchange, 1994), pp. 53, 56.

5. Ann Florini and P.J. Simmons also opt for "transnational" rather than "global" in their discussion of border-crossing civil society in recognition of "the fact that rarely are these ties truly global, in the sense of involving groups and individuals from every part of the world." Ann M. Florini and P.J. Simmons, "What the World Needs Now?" in *The Third Force: The Rise of Transnational Civil Society,* edited by Ann M. Florini (Washington, DC: Carnegie Endowment for International Peace, 2000), p. 7. Even "campaigns, organizations, networks, and/or movements that claim to be global do not ... reach all corners of the planet." Khagram and Alvord, "Civic Transnationalism," p. 66.

6. This discussion draws upon Peter H. Koehn and Herbert Swick, "Medical Education for a Changing World: Moving Beyond Cultural Competence into Transnational Competence," *Academic Medicine* 81, No. 6 (June 2006): 548–556.

7. J. Zweifler and A.M. Gonzalez, "Teaching Residents to Care for Culturally Diverse Populations," *Academic Medicine* 73, No. 10 (1998): 1058; Janelle S. Taylor, "Confronting 'Culture' in Medicine's 'Culture of No Culture,'" *Academic Medicine* 78, No. 6 (June 2003): 555; Delese Wear, "Respect for Patients: A Case Study of the Formal and Hidden Curriculum," in *Professionalism in Medicine: Critical Perspectives,* edited by Delese Wear and Julie M. Aultman (New York: Springer, 2006), pp. 92–93. In its concentration on U.S. content, the CC approach resembles multicultural education in scope. See Merryfield and Wilson, *Social Studies and the World,* pp. 21–22.

8. Mary E. Duffy, "A Critique of Cultural Education in Nursing," *Journal of Advanced Nursing* 36, No. 4 (2001): 487–491. On the potency of social class as a force affecting health and longevity in the United States, see Janny Scott, "Life at the Top in America Isn't Just Better, It's Longer," *New York Times,* May 16, 2005, pp. A1, A18.

9. Jennifer S. Hirsch, "Anthropologists, Migrants, and Health Research: Confronting Cultural Appropriateness," in *American Arrivals: Anthropology Engages the New Immigration,* edited by Nancy Foner (Oxford: James Currey, 2003), p. 239.

10. Delese Wear, "Insurgent Multiculturalism: Rethinking How and Why We Teach Culture in Medical Education," *Academic Medicine* 78, No. 6 (June 2003): 550–551. In short, "essentialism is a technique

of oversimplification leading to false conclusions ..." Kathleen Fuller, "Eradicating Essentialism from Cultural Competency Education," *Academic Medicine* 77, No. 3 (March, 2002): 199.

11. On the latter point, see, for instance, Peter H. Koehn and Marja Tiilikainen, "Migration and Transnational Health Care: Connecting Finland and Somaliland," *Siirtolaisuus—Migration* 34, No. 1 (2007): 2–9.

12. Janet L. Finn and Maxine Jacobson, *Just Practice: A Social Justice Approach to Social Work,* 2nd edition (Peosta, IA: Eddie Bowers Publishing, 2008), pp. 220–221.

13. Jennifer Hirsch ("Confronting Cultural Appropriateness," p. 242) maintains that "the most problematic aspect of the cultural competence paradigm is that it reifies racial and ethnic differences as the key explanatory variables to which we must attend and reduces the salience of social class factors." Also see Fuller, "Eradicating Essentialism," 200; Merryfield and Wilson, *Social Studies and the World,* p. 61.

14. Hirsch, "Confronting Cultural Appropriateness," p. 238; Wear, "Respect for Patients," p. 95.

15. David Thom and colleagues studied the effects of the training they provided to physicians for cross-cultural knowledge and communication-skill development. The results of this CC-focused and short-duration intervention showed no significant differences in patient-reported cultural competence scores or in patient trust, satisfaction, weight, systolic blood pressure, and glycosylated haemoglobin among the trained and untrained physicians. David H. Thom, Miguel D. Tirado, Tommy L. Woon, and Melen R. McBride, "Development and Evaluation of a Cultural Competency Training Curriculum," *BMC Medical Education* 6 (July 2006): 38.

16. Scott, "Life at the Top in America," pp. A1, A18–19.

17. B.D. Smedley, A.Y. Stith, and A.R. Nelson (eds.), *Unequal Treatment: Confronting Racial and Ethnic Disparities in Health Care* (Washington, DC: National Academy Press, 2003), p. 35; Lincoln C. Chen, Timothy G. Evans, and R.A. Cash, "Health As a Global Public Good," in *Global Public Goods: International Cooperation in the 21st Century,* edited by Inge Kaul, Isabelle Grunberg, and Marc A. Stern (Oxford: Oxford University Press, 1999), pp. 284–287, 294.

18. Wear, "Insurgent Multiculturalism," pp. 551–552. Lynne Healy (*International Social Work,* p. 362) cites the same insufficiency of the cultural-competence approach in social work education. A framework is needed that incorporates preparing graduates to serve a diverse set of care receivers *and* to engage the action agenda that is integral to the social-justice mission of the social work profession.

19. Rhian F. Loudon, Pauline M. Anderson, Paramjit S. Gill, and Sheila M. Greenfield, "Educating Medical Students for Work in Culturally Diverse Societies," *Journal of the American Medical Association* 282, No. 9 (1999): 877.

20. See Peter H. Koehn, "Globalization, Migration Health, and Educational Preparation for Transnational Medical Encounters," *Globalization and Health* 2, No. 2 (30 January 2006): 1-43.

21. Kenneth Cushner, "Intercultural Education from an International Perspective: An Introduction," in *International Perspectives on Intercultural Education,* edited by Kenneth Cushner (Mahwah, NJ: Lawrence Erlbaum Associates, 1998), p. 4.

22. *Ibid.*

23. Deardorff, 25th Annual AIEA Meeting, 2008.

24. Derek Bok, *Our Underachieving Colleges: A Candid Look at How Much Students Learn and Why They Should Be Learning More* (Princeton: Princeton University Press, 2006), p. 76.

25. *Ibid.* [emphasis ours]; Bok also emphasizes the importance of interpersonal competence. See pp. 221–224.

26. John N. Hawkins and William K. Cummings (eds.), *Transnational Competence: Rethinking the U.S.-Japan Educational Relationship* (Albany: State University of New York Press, 2000).

27. Task Force for Transnational Competence, *Towards Transnational Competence: Rethinking International Education (A U.S.-Japan Case Study),* IIE Research Report 28 (New York: Institute of International Education, 1997), p. 9.

28. In their 1997 book, the authors refer to transnational competence with the acronym TNC. We prefer TC to avoid confusion with the already widely used TNC in reference to "transnational corporations."

29. Task Force for Transnational Competence, *Towards Transnational Competence,* pp. 5–6; William K. Cummings, "Transnationalism and Transnational Competence," in *Transnational Competence:*

Rethinking the U.S.-Japan Educational Relationship, edited by John N. Hawkins and William K. Cummings (Albany: State University of New York Press, 2000), p. 8. This interesting initiative was short-lived. The Task Force Coordinator, education professor William Cummings at The George Washington University, explained that he moved on to other projects (personal interview with Koehn, November 29, 2007).

30. For details regarding the initial construction of the conceptual framework, which we have subsequently refined, see Peter H. Koehn and James N. Rosenau, "Transnational Competence in an Emergent Epoch," *International Studies Perspectives* 3 (May 2002): 105–127.

31. See Freidson, *Professionalism,* p. 25; Charles Ping, "Educational Imperatives for a New Era: The University Must Actively Encourage Mobility" (Paris: UNESCO, 2003) http://portal.unesco.org/education/en/ev.php-URL_ID=7687%26URL_DO=.

32. Jessica Gregg and Somnath Saha, "Losing Culture on the Way to Competence: The Use and Misuse of Culture in Medical Education," *Academic Medicine* 81, 6 (June 2006): 546.

33. Kimberly A. Maynard, *Healing Communities in Conflict: International Assistance in Complex Emergencies* (New York: Columbia University Press, 1999), p. 164.

34. Michael J. Marquardt and Nancy O. Berger, *Global Leaders for the Twenty-First Century* (Albany: State University of New York Press, 2000), p. 19; Christa Olson, Rhodri Evans, and Robert E. Shoenberg, *At Home in the World: Bridging the Gap Between Internationalization and Multicultural Education* (Washington, DC: American Council on Education, 2007). In this connection, professionals are well-served by skill in "[multiple] perspective taking, the ability to look at an event or issue through the eyes" of counterparts who are different from oneself. Merry M. Merryfield, "Pedagogy for Global Perspectives in Education: Studies of Teachers' Thinking and Practice," in *Changing Perspectives on International Education,* edited by Patrick O'Meara, Howard D. Mehlinger, and Roxanna Ma Newman (Bloomington: Indiana University Press, 2001), p. 266. This dimension of analytic TC encompasses the five awareness components of Robert Hanvey's "global perspective": perspective consciousness, state-of-the planet awareness, cross-cultural awareness, knowledge of global dynamics, and awareness of human choices. See Robert G. Hanvey, "An Attainable Global Perspective," in *Changing Perspectives on International Education,* edited by Patrick O'Meara, Howard D. Mehlinger, and Roxanna Ma Newman (Bloomington: Indiana University Press, 2001), pp. 218–224.

35. See Rosenau, *Distant Proximities,* Chapter 3.

36. James A. Banks, *et al., Democracy and Diversity: Principles and Concepts for Educating Citizens in a Global Age* (Seattle: Center for Multicultural Education, College of Education, 2005), pp. 5, 12.

37. Biddle, *Internationalization,* p. 5.

38. Merry M. Merryfield, "The Difference a Global Educator Can Make," *Educational Leadership* 90, 2 (October 2002): 19. Also see Maynard's valuable discussion of "contextualization." Maynard, *Healing Communities,* pp. 163–165.

39. Cummings, "Transnationalism and Transnational Competence," p. 8.

40. Norman Dinges, "Intercultural Competence," in *Handbook of Intercultural Training.* Vol. II, edited by Dan Landis and Richard W. Brislin (New York: Pergamon, 1983), p. 178.

41. Maynard, *Healing Communities,* p. 164; Daniel Goleman, *Working with Emotional Intelligence* (New York: Bantam Books, 1998), p. 162.

42. John Vogler, "The Environment in International Relations: Legacies and Contentions," in *The Environment and International Relations,* edited by John Vogler and Mark F. Imber (London: Routledge, 1996), p. 7.

43. Philip C. Salzman, *The Anthropology of Real Life: Events in Human Experience* (Prospect Heights, IL: Waveland, 1999), p. 10.

44. Kevin Connolly and Jerome Bruner, "Competence: Its Nature and Nurture," in *The Growth of Competence,* edited by Kevin Connolly and Jerome Bruner (London: Academic Press, 1974), p. 3.

45. Less skillful individuals will evaluate fewer paths in constructing their scenarios and will rely more on "either-or" or "mine-yours" choices. James N. Rosenau and W. Michael Fagen, "A New Dynamism in World Politics: Increasingly Skillful Individuals?" *International Studies Quarterly* 41, No. 4 (December 1997): 662.

46. Out of 19 skills rated important for professional success in an international organization, the 135 high-level respondents in the 2003 RAND study ranked "general cognitive skills (e.g., problem solving, analytic ability)" first overall, "ability to think in policy and strategy terms" seventh, "substantive

knowledge in a technical or professional field" twelfth, "multidisciplinary orientation" thirteenth, and "knowledge of international affairs, geographic area studies" fourteenth. Bikson, Treverton, Moini, and Lindstrom, *New Challenges for International Leadership,* p. 25.

47. Carlos E. Cortes and Louise C. Wilkinson, "Developing and Implementing A Multicultural Vision," in *Contemporary Leadership and Intercultural Competence: Exploring the Cross-Cultural Dynamics Within Organizations,* edited by Michael A. Moodian (Los Angeles, CA: Sage, 2009), p. 21.

48. Linda E. Anderson, "A New Look at an Old Construct: Cross-Cultural Adaptation," *International Journal of Intercultural Relations* 18, No. 3 (1994): 313; M.W. Lustig and J. Koester, *Intercultural Competence: Interpersonal Communication across Cultures,* 2nd edition (New York: HarperCollins, 1996), p. 63; Cary Cherniss, "Emotional Intelligence and the Good Community," *American Journal of Community Psychology* 30, 1 (February 2002): 5; Daniel Goleman, *Emotional Intelligence* (New York: Bantam Books, 1995), pp. xii, 34.

49. Dov Seidman, *How: Why HOW We Do Anything Means Everything ... in Business (and in Life)* (New York: John Wiley & Sons, 2007), pp. 295, 287.

50. David Held, "Culture and Political Community: National, Global, and Cosmopolitan," in *Conceiving Cosmopolitanism: Theory, Context, and Practice,* edited by Steven Vertovec and Robin Cohen (Oxford: Oxford University Press, 2002), p. 58; Cortes and Wilkinson, "A Multicultural Vision," p. 23.

51. Kwame A. Appiah, *Cosmopolitanism: Ethics in a World of Strangers* (New York: W.W. Norton, 2006), p. 144.

52. Goleman, *Working with Emotional Intelligence,* pp. 18, 24, 27, 135.

53. That is, "to construct the world as they do and to experience the action tendencies and emotions that they do." Ronald Taft, "The Role and Personality of the Mediator," in *The Mediating Person: Bridges Between Cultures,* edited by Stephen Bochner (Boston: G.K. Hall, 1981), p. 82. Although compassion might (or might not) result from empathetic understanding, empathy "is not an emotional state of feeling sympathetic or sorry for someone." John L. Coulehan and Marian R. Block, *The Medical Interview: Mastering Skills for Clinical Practice,* 3rd edition (Philadelphia: FA Davis, 1997), p. 27. Similarly, while value change might be an outcome of empathetic understanding, empathy does not require agreement on values or beliefs. Appiah, *Cosmopolitanism,* p. 78.

54. Cortes and Wilkinson, "A Multicultural Vision," p. 23.

55. Cushner, "Commonalities," p. 369. Also see Thomas Homer-Dixon, *The Ingenuity Gap* (New York: Alfred A. Knopf, 2000), pp. 395–396.

56. Held, "National, Global, and Cosmopolitan," p. 58. Out of 19 skills rated important for professional success in an international organization, the 135 high-level respondents in the 2003 RAND study ranked "ambiguity tolerance, adaptivity" third, "minority sensitivity" ninth, and "empathy, nonjudgmental perspective" eleventh. Bikson, Treverton, Moini, and Lindstrom, *New Challenges for International Leadership,* p. 25.

57. Michael L. Hecht, Mary J. Collie, and Sidney Ribeau, *African American Communication* (Newbury Park, CA: Sage, 1993).

58. Since "compassionless capability can be dangerous," Matthew Hirshberg persuasively argues, "capability must be balanced with a strong dose of compassion to yield citizens [one could readily substitute "professionals"] who will make the world a better place." Matthew Hirshberg, "Teaching Compassionate Social Studies," in *Values Education for Citizens in the New Century,* edited by Roger H.M. Cheng, John C.K. Lee, and Leslie N.K. Lo (Hong Kong: Chinese University Press, 2006), pp. 165, 173, 175.

59. Connolly and Bruner, "Competence," p. 5.

60. Goleman, *Emotional Intelligence,* pp. 89–90.

61. Susanne Weber, "A Framework for Teaching and Learning 'Intercultural Competence,'" in *Intercultural Experience and Education,* edited by Geof Alred, Michael Bynam, and Mike Fleming (Clevedon, UK: Mutlilingual Matters, 2003), p. 200; Terence P. Hannigan, "Traits, Attitudes, and Skills That Are Related to Intercultural Effectiveness and their Implications for Cross-Cultural Training: A Review of the Literature," *International Journal of Intercultural Effectiveness* 14, No. 1 (1990): 96.

62. Appadurai, *Modernity at Large,* pp. 5, 7.

63. Edward B. Fiske, *Learning in a Global Age: Knowledge and Skills for a Flat World* (New York: Asia Society, 2007), p. 28.

64. Goleman, *Working with Emotional Intelligence,* p. 27.

65. Appadurai, *Modernity at Large,* p. 54.

66. Frans Johansson, *The Medici Effect* (Cambridge, MA: Harvard Business School Press, 2004), p. 79.

67. Johanna Keller, "Yo-Yo Ma's Edge Effect," *Chronicle of Higher Education,* 23 March 2007, pp. B10–B13. For examples of other South to North innovation diffusions, see Sanjeev Khagram and Peggy Levitt, "Constructing Transnational Studies," in *Rethinking Transnationalism: The Meso-Link of Organisations,* edited by Ludger Pries (London: Routledge, 2008), p. 33.

68. Gabriele Bammer, "Integration and Implementation Sciences: Building a New Specialization," *Ecology and Society* 10, No. 2 (2005): 6.

69. Scott E. Page, *The Difference: How the Power of Diversity Creates Better Groups, Firms, Schools, and Societies* (Princeton: Princeton University Press, 2007), pp. 9–10, 16; Claudia Dreifus, "In Professor's Model, Diversity = Productivity; A Conversation with Scott E. Page," *New York Times,* January 8, 2008, p. D2.

70. Cortes and Wilkinson, "A Multicultural Vision," p. 29.

71. Cummings, "Transnationalism and Transnational Competence," p. 8.

72. Moran, Harris, and Moran, *Managing Cultural Differences,* p. 229.

73. Cortes and Wilkinson, "A Multicultural Vision," pp. 18, 23.

74. *Ibid.,* p. 18.

75. See Rosenau, *People Count!,* pp. 9–12.

76. Mira Kamdar, keynote address, 25th Annual Meeting of the Association of International Education Administrators, Washington, D.C., February 20, 2008; Seidman, *How,* p. x.

77. Werdell, "Futurism," p. 290.

78. Johansson, *The Medici Effect,* pp. 2, 16–17, 20, 22–23, 46-47. Out of 19 skills rated important for professional success in an international organization, the 135 high-level respondents in the 2003 RAND study ranked "innovative, able to take risks" tenth. Bikson, Treverton, Moini, and Lindstrom, *New Challenges for International Leadership,* p. 25.

79. Appiah, *Cosmopolitanism,* p. xxi.

80. Richard Brislin, *Understanding Culture's Influence on Behavior* (Fort Worth: Harcourt Brace Jovanovich, 1993), p. 215.

81. Goleman, *Working with Emotional Intelligence,* p. 24.

82. Panel on "Intercultural Competence," 25th Annual Meeting of the Association of International Education Administrators, Washington, DC, February 20, 2008.

83. Bikson, Treverton, Moini, and Lindstrom, *New Challenges for International Leadership,* p. 25.

84. Nonverbally conveying empathic awareness is a particularly useful transnational-communicative skill. See Geof Alred, "Becoming a 'Better Stranger': A Therapeutic Perspective on Intercultural Experience and/As Education," in *Intercultural Experience and Education,* edited by Geof Alred, Michael Bynam, and Mike Fleming (Clevedon, UK: Mutlilingual Matters, 2003), pp. 20–21.

85. Phyllis B. Ngai, "Nonverbal Communication Behavior in Intercultural Negotiations: Insights and Applications Based on Findings from Ethiopia, Tanzania, Hong Kong, and the China Mainland," *World Communication* 29, No. 4 (2001): 3–35; Cheryl Lausch, Loretta Heuer, Charlene Guasasco, and Marlene Bengiamin, "The Experiences of Migrant Health Nurses Employed in Seasonal Satellite Nurse-Managed Centers: A Qualitative Study," *Journal of Community Health Nursing* 20, 2 (2003): 75–76.

86. Hannigan, "Traits, Attitudes, and Skills," p. 103.

87. Taft, "Role and Personality of the Mediator," pp. 76–77.

88. Barbara C. Crosby, *Leadership for Global Citizenship: Building Transnational Community* (Thousand Oaks, CA: Sage, 1999), p. 65.

89. Appiah, *Cosmopolitanism,* p. 97.

90. Tina Wang, "Intercultural Dialogue and Understanding: Implications for Teachers," in *Teaching in Transnational Higher Education: Enhancing Learning for Offshore International Students,* edited by Lee Dunn and Michelle Wallace (New York: Routledge, 2008), p. 59.

91. Sarkissian, *Kitchen Table Sustainability,* pp. 172, 207.

92. Lustig and Koester, *Intercultural Competence,* p. 63.

93. Louis W. Goodman, "Foreword," in *Preparing Global Professionals for the New Century: Issues,*

Curricula and Strategies for International Affairs Education, edited by Michele C. Titi (Washington, DC: Association of Professional Schools of International Affairs, 1998), p. vii.

94. Dinges, "Intercultural Competence," p. 193.

95. Barabasi, *Linked,* pp. 43, 55-56.

96. Lustig and Koester, *Intercultural Competence,* p. 330–331.

97. Karen Schneider, "Transpatriate Success Factors: A Concurrent Validation Study in China," (unpublished Ph.D. dissertation, University of Houston, 1997), p. 11; Goleman, *Working with Emotional Intelligence,* pp. 209–210.

98. Bimla Ojelay-Surtees, *Building Trust in Diverse Teams: The Toolkit for Emergency Response* (Dorset, UK: Oxfam GB, 2007), pp. 7–105.

99. Brislin, *Culture's Influence on Behavior,* p. 215; Goleman, *Working with Emotional Intelligence,* p. 209.

100. Vertovec and Rogers, "Introduction," p. 8.

101. Goleman, *Working with Emotional Intelligence,* p. 27.

102. Hossein Dadfar and Peter Gustavsson, "Competition by Effective Management of Cultural Diversity: The Case of International Construction Projects," *International Studies of Management and Organization* 22, No. 4 (1992): 90–91.

103. Out of 19 skills rated important for professional success in an international organization, the 135 high-level respondents in the 2003 RAND study ranked "interpersonal and relationship skills" second, "the ability to work well in different cultures and with people of different origins" fifth, and "ability to work in teams" sixth. Bikson, Treverton, Moini, and Lindstrom, *New Challenges for International Leadership,* p. 25.

104. Allen J. Morrison, "Developing a Global Leadership Model," *Human Resource Management* 39, Nos. 2 and 3 (2000): 125.

105. Marquardt and Berger, *Global Leaders,* p. 19.

106. Also see Reimers, "'Global Competency,'" p. A29.

107. See, for instance, Peter H. Koehn, "Underneath Kyoto: Emerging Subnational Government Initiatives and Incipient Issue-Bundling Opportunities in China and the United States," *Global Environmental Politics* 8, No. 1 (Fall 2008): 62–72.

108. Lustig and Koester, *Intercultural Competence,* pp. 57–58; Rathje, "Intercultural Competence," p. 257.

109. Goleman, *Working with Emotional Intelligence,* p. 25.

110. Lambert, "Summary and Prospectus," p. 288.

111. Lambert ("Summary and Prospectus," p. 286) makes a similar point.

112. In Robert Hanvey's terms, "any given individual may be rich in certain elements and relatively lacking in others." Hanvey, "An Attainable Global Perspective," p. 217.

113. Melanie Tervalon and J. Murray-Garcia, "Cultural Humility Versus Cultural Competence: A Critical Distinction in Defining Physician Training Outcomes in Multicultural Education," *Journal of Health Care for the Poor and Underserved* 9, No. 2 (1998): 117–125.

114. Task Force for Transnational Competence, *Towards Transnational Competence,* pp. 16, 18.

115. Kenichi Ohmae, *The Borderless World: Management Lessons in the New Logic of the Global Market Place* (London: Collins, 1990).

116. The emphasis of TC preparation on functional skill in addressing institutional and policy inequities rooted in local, national, and international conditions incorporates and extends the historic contributions of the multicultural-education field. See Merryfield and Wilson, *Social Studies and the World,* pp. 20–21; Merry M. Merryfield (ed.), *Making Connections Between Multicultural and Global Education: Teacher Educators and Teacher Education Programs* (Washington, DC: American Association of Colleges for Teacher Education, 1996), pp. 48, 189, 230, 239.

Notes for Chapter 3

1. Sarkissian, *Kitchen Table Sustainability,* p. 252.

2. Alvin Toffler, "Introduction," in *Learning for Tomorrow: The Role of the Future in Education,*

edited by Alvin Toffler (New York: Vintage Books, 1974), p. xxv; also Alvin Toffler, "The Psychology of the Future," in *Learning for Tomorrow: The Role of the Future in Education*, edited by Alvin Toffler (New York: Vintage Books, 1974), p. 14.

3. See Glauco De Vita, "Taking Stock: An Appraisal of the Literature on Internationalising HE Learning," in *Internationalising Higher Education*, edited by Elspeth Jones and Sally Brown (London: Routledge, 2007), p. 165.

4. See Phyllis B. Ngai, "Community-Based Indigenous Education for Global Competence," *International Journal of Diversity in Organizations, Communities and Nations* 7, No. 2 (2007), online.

5. This is particularly likely in four-year undergraduate programs, such as most engineering programs. In 2005, the National Academy of Engineering recommended that engineering schools "create accredited 'professional' master's degree programs intended to expand and improve the skills and enhance the ability of an engineer to practice engineering." National Academy of Engineering, *Educating the Engineer of 2020: Adapting Engineering Education to the New Century* (Washington, DC: National Academies Press, 2005), pp. 52, 22.

6. There are some exceptions, such as well-prepared international students, first-generation migrants and their offspring, and graduates of international schools.

7. Toffler, "Introduction," p. xxiv.

8. *Ibid.*

9. Amy Shaw and Jae Kim, *Report from the International Commission on Education for Sustainable Development Practice* (Brooklyn, NY: A.J. Bart, 2008), p. iii.

10. Williams, "Competent Boundary Spanner," p. 106.

11. Freidson, *Professionalism*, p. 211.

12. Many of these transprofessional skill needs were identified at UNESCO's 1998 World Conference on Higher Education in the Twenty-First Century: Vision and Action. Teichler, *The Requirements of the World of Work*, pp. 22–23.

13. Walter C. Parker, Akira Ninomiya, and John Cogan, "Educating World Citizens: Toward Multinational Curriculum Development," *American Educational Research Journal* 36, No. 2 (Summer 1999): 119.

14. We treat transferable learning processes and common barriers to academic-program change in Chapters 11 and 12.

15. Sheri Sheppard, "Preparation for the Professions Program: Engineering Education in the United States," in National Academy of Engineering, *Educating the Engineer of 2020: Adapting Engineering Education to the New Century* (Washington, DC: National Academies Press, 2005), p. 131.

16. We treat the Commission's findings and recommendations in depth in Chapter 9.

17. Abbott, *System of Professions*, p. 18.

18. Biddle, *Internationalization*, pp. 10, 113.

19. See Steve Lohr, "Starting Over, with a Second Career Goal of Changing Society," *New York Times*, December 13, 2008, pp. B1, B8.

20. Sheppard, *Educating the Engineer of 2020*, p. xxv.

21. These individuals are identified, and their perspectives explored, in the chapters that follow.

22. See Wally R. Smith, Joseph R. Betancourt, Matthew K. Wynia, Jada Bussey-Jones, Valerie E. Stone, Christopher O. Phillips, Alicia Fernandez, Elizabeth Jacobs, and Jacqueline Bowles, "Recommendations for Teaching about Racial and Ethnic Disparities in Health and Health Care," *Annals of Internal Medicine* 147 (2007): 660.

Notes for Chapter 4

1. Friedman, *The World Is Flat*, p. 553.

2. Toffler, "The Psychology of the Future," p. 5.

3. Gary L. Downey and Joseph Dumit, "Locating and Intervening: An Introduction," in *Cyborgs & Citadels: Anthropological Interventions in Emerging Sciences and Technologies*, edited by Gary L. Downey and Joseph Dumit (Santa Fe, NM: School of American Research Press, 1997), p. 10.

4. Kenneth Cushner and Gregory Trifonovitch, "Understanding Misunderstanding: Barriers

to Dealing with Diversity," in *Multicultural Education: A Global Approach*, edited by Don Bragaw and W. Scott Thomson (New York: American Forum for Global Education, 1992), p. 300.

5. Cortes and Wilkinson, "A Multicultural Vision," p. 18.

6. Bammer, "Integration and Implementation Sciences," 6.

7. Williams, "Competent Boundary Spanner," 104.

8. Held, "National, Global, and Cosmopolitan," p. 58.

9. Deibert, "Citizen Activism," p. 262.

10. The density of the multicentric world has been promoted by the rise of interdependence issues. See Rosenau, *Along the Domestic-Foreign Frontier*, p. 72.

11. Parker, Ninomiya, and Cogan, "Multinational Curriculum Development," p. 124; Stephen Castles, *Ethnicity and Globalization: From Migrant Worker to Transnational Citizen* (Thousand Oaks, CA: Sage, 2000), pp. 206–207.

12. Moisis Namm, "It's Not about Maps: We Must Rethink Where America's Borders Really Are," *Missoulian*, May 30, 2006, p. A6.

13. Rosenau has labeled these transformative tensions holistically as "fragmegration." See Rosenau, *Distant Proximities*, pp. 11–12.

14. Khagram and Levitt, "Constructing Transnational Studies," p. 33.

15. Cushner, "Intercultural Education," p. 368.

16. Shefali Anand, "An Ugly Market's Lessons for Investors," *Wall Street Journal*, October 5, 2008.

17. See Maryann K. Cusimano, *Beyond Sovereignty: Issues for a Global Agenda* (Boston: Bedford/ St. Martins, 2000), p. 3.

18. Vivien Stewart, "A World Transformed: How Other Countries Are Preparing Students for the Interconnected World of the 21st Century," *Phi Delta Kappan* 87, No. 3 (November 2005): 229. Also see Rosenau, *Distant Proximities*, p. 77; Claudia H. Deutsch, "A Threat so Big, Academics Try Collaboration: Disciplines Cross Lines to Fight Global Warming," *New York Times*, December 25, 2007, pp. C1–C2.

19. Parker, Ninomiya, and Cogan, "Multinational Curriculum Development," pp. 120–124, 137.

20. Bammer cautions that "unknowns are compounded by constant *change*—occurring on many fronts, including biological evolution...; scientific, technological, and economic developments; international relations; and manifold intended and unintended consequences of local, national, and international policy and programs." Bammer, "Integration and Implementation Sciences," p. 6.

21. See Rosenau, Earnest, Ferguson, and Holsti, *Cutting Edge of Globalization*, pp. 30–31, 49; Deibert, "Citizen Activists," 264.

22. Calestous Juma, "Reinventing Growth," in *Going for Growth: Science, Technology and Innovation in Africa*, edited by Calestous Juma (London: Smith Institute, 2005), pp. 18–19.

23. See Philip G. Altbach, "Globalisation and the University: Myths and Realities in an Unequal World," *Tertiary Education and Management* 10 (2004): 14-15. China has been particularly successful in recruiting academic "sea turtles" (returnees) to oversee curriculum reform. As Dean of Peking University's new College of Environmental Sciences, for instance, C.S. Kiang, formerly of the Georgia Institute of Technology, introduced academic programs built around "internationalization, interdisciplinarity, integration, and innovation." Mara Hvistendahl, "China Entices Its Scholars to Come Home: U.S.-Educated Academics Are Increasingly Returning to Teach and Spearhead Special Programs," *Chronicle of Higher Education*, December 19, 2008, pp. A20–A21.

24. Manuel Castells foresaw that the networking form of social organization will expand throughout human society. He suggests that the performance of a network will depend on two fundamental attributes: "its *connectedness*, that is its structural ability to facilitate noise-free communication between its components; its *consistency*, that is the extent to which there is sharing of interests between the network's goals and the goals of its components." Manuel Castells, *The Rise of the Networked Society* (Oxford: Blackwell, 1996), pp. 171, 469.

25. Enormous variations exist among nongovernmental organizations in terms of size, financial resources, influence, and competence. See Peter Koehn and Olatunde Ojo, "Nongovernmental Organizations and Government-Organized Nongovernmental Organizations: Management in Africa in the Twenty-First Century," in *Subsaharan Africa in the 1990s: Challenges to Democracy and Development*, edited by Rukhsana A. Siddiqui (Westport, CT: Praeger, 1997), pp. 111–121.

26. Orenstein and Schmitz, "New Transnationalism," p. 492.

27. Transnational higher-education partnerships offer opportunities to link and leap over skill chasms that lie in the way of development. See Damtew and Altbach, "African Higher Education," pp. 22, 38, 41.

28. Earl Kellogg, "Africa-U.S. Higher Education Initiative: Empowering African Higher Education for Africa's Transformation" (unpublished paper, May 2008). Also see Peter Koehn, Montague Demment, and Anne-Claire Hervy, "Partnerships in Africa: Enhancing Higher Education's Engagement in International Development" (virtual paper for the World Education Forum, Davos, Switzerland, January 2008). http://nasulgc.org/NetCommunity/Document.Doc?id=1195.

29. The visions presented are unavoidably selective, and we make no claim that they are comprehensive. Most of the referenced visionaries are based at U.S. higher-education institutions, although their backgrounds are diverse and their professional experiences are multinational.

30. Merryfield and Wilson, *Social Studies and the World*, p. 105. Gagel and Himmelmann's political/democratic education-content list closely parallels these identifications. Cited in Michael Byram, "Developing a Concept of Intercultural Citizenship," in *Education for Intercultural Citizenship: Concepts and Comparisons*, edited by Geof Alred, Mike Byram, and Mike Fleming (Clevedon, UK: Multilingual Matters, 2006), p. 124.

31. Cummings, *Towards Transnational Competence*, p. 45.

32. *Ibid.*, p. 44.

33. David E. Bloom, "Globalization and Education: An Economic Perspective," in *Globalization: Culture and Education in the New Millennium*, edited by Marcelo M. Suarez-Orozco and Desiree B. Qin-Hilliard (Berkeley: University of California Press, 2004), p. 69. The low priority that many U.S. K–12 educators place on transnational perspectives is reflected in curricula that devote "little or no attention to the context, complexity, and linkages of … [course] content to other world regions, global themes, and crosscutting issues." Jane A. Boston, "Professional Development in Global Education," in *Preparing Teachers to Teach Global Perspectives: A Handbook for Teacher Educators*, edited by Merry M. Merryfield, Elaine Jarchow, and Sarah Pickert (Thousand Oaks, CA: Corwin Press, 1997), p. 169.

34. William Cummings, personal interview with Peter Koehn, November 29, 2007.

35. H. Thomas Collins, Frederick R. Czarra, and Andrew F. Smith, "Guidelines for Global and International Studies Education," in *Changing Perspectives on International Education*, edited by Patrick O'Meara, Howard D. Mehlinger, and Roxanna Ma Newman (Bloomington: Indiana University Press, 2001), p. 228.

36. *Ibid.*, pp. 228–232.

37. See http://www.gdrc.org/sustdev/un-desd/intro_un-desd.html (accessed 2 October 2008).

38. Wilma S. Longstreet, "Alternative Futures and the Social Studies," in *Handbook on Teaching Social Issues*, edited by Ronald W. Evans and David W. Saxe (Washington, DC: National Council for the Social Studies, 1996), p. 317.

39. *Ibid.*

40. *Ibid.*, p. 323.

41. See Merry M. Merryfield and Connie S. White, "Issues-Centered Global Education," in *Handbook on Teaching Social Issues*, edited by Ronald W. Evans and David W. Saxe (Washington, DC: National Council for the Social Studies, 1996), p. 178.

42. *Ibid.*, p. 181; Christine Sleeter, "Teaching Globalization," *Multicultural Perspectives* 5, No. 2 (2003): 9.

43. Written response to interview questions, December 2007. On future demand for transnational education, see Allison Doorbar and Christine Bateman, "The Growth of Transnational Higher Education: The UK Perspective," in *Teaching in Transnational Higher Education: Enhancing Learning for Offshore International Students*, edited by Lee Dunn and Michelle Wallace (New York: Routledge, 2008), p. 15.

44. Pirkko Pitkanen and Pauliina Jarvinen-Alenius, "Emergence of Transnational Professional Spaces," in *Transnationalization and Institutional Transformations*, edited by Thomas Faist and Pirkko Pitkanen (forthcoming).

45. Phyllis Ngai, who has taught and conducted professional training sessions in China and Hong Kong, also expects that teachers' ability to communicate well with students *and parents* of diverse backgrounds will constitute their principal future challenge. Personal interview conducted in Washington, DC,

by Peter Koehn with Phyllis B. Ngai, Adjunct Assistant Professor of Communication Studies, University of Montana, November 27, 2007.

46. In 2006, a U.S. Committee for Economic Development (CED) report confirmed that, in general, "teacher education requires few courses on international topics." John Brademas, Charles E.M. Kolb, and Alfred T. Mockett, *Education for Global Leadership: The Importance of International Studies and Foreign Language Education for U.S. Economic and National Security* (Washington, DC: CED, 2006), p. 1.

47. In 2008, 97 countries were represented among the 72,000 residents of Mount Vernon, New York. Fernanda Santos, "A Police Effort to Improve Relations Starts with Language," *New York Times*, April 24, 2008, p. A25.

48. Cochran-Smith, "Standing at the Crossroads," p. 4.

49. Brademas, Kolb, and Mockett, *Education for Global Leadership*, p. 11. It is imperative, therefore, that teacher candidates in all subjects who will "bring language skills that support immigrant students be a recruitment target." Linda Darling-Hammond, "We Need to Invest in Math and Science Teachers," *Chronicle of Higher Education*, December 21, 2007, p. B20.

50. Kissock, who chaired the International Committee of the American Association for Teacher Education for four years, bluntly asserts that "AATE has dumped international for domestic cultural issues." Kissock interview, December 5, 2007.

51. Also Patricia K. Kubow and Paul R. Fossum, *Comparative Education: Exploring Issues in International Context*, 2nd edition (Upper Saddle River, NJ: Pearson, 2007), p. 298.

52. As Merryfield points out, "interconnectedness and interdependence are concepts central to both multicultural and global education." Merry M. Merryfield, "Learning from Current Practice: Looking Across Profiles of Teacher Educators and Teacher Education Programs," in *Making Connections Between Multicultural and Global Education: Teacher Educators and Teacher Education Programs*, edited by Merry M. Merryfield (Washington, DC: American Association of Colleges for Teacher Education, 1996), p. 4. Global and multicultural education share many overlapping concerns. However, multicultural-education concerns that focus on "the domestic dimensions of cross-cultural living" typically fall "outside the realm of global education." See Merryfield, *Making Connections Between Multicultural and Global Education*, p. 14. In contrast, domestic transcultural interactions are ensconced within the TC educational framework. For a promising approach that integrates multicultural learning at the primary-school level with the early development of transferable transnational competencies, see Phyllis B. Ngai, "Grassroots Suggestions for Linking Native-Language Learning, Native American Studies, and Mainstream Education in Reservation Schools with Mixed Indian and White Student Populations," *Language, Culture and Curriculum* 19, No. 2 (2006): 231–235.

53. For instance, students can study ways in which global economic systems and poverty/wealth play out in different classrooms. Merryfield, "Learning from Current Practice," pp. 4–5, 7.

54. William Cummings, interview, November 29, 2007. For a short description of one successful place-based experiential approach to introducing a different worldview among primary-school students, see Phyllis Ngai and Karen Allen, "Indian Education for All in an Urban Public School," *Phi Delta Kappan* 88, No. 3 (November 2006): 211.

55. Steven R. Weisman, "World Bank Calls on Sovereign Funds to Invest in Africa," *New York Times*, April 3, 2008, p. A8; also Steven R. Weisman, "A Fear of Foreign Investments," *New York Times*, August, 21, 2007, pp. C1, C5. Sovereign-wealth funds based in the Persian Gulf are particularly active in investing in the British financial industry and in central London real estate. Julia Werdigier, "From the Gulf, Money for Towers in London," *New York Times*, June 20, 2008, p. C6.

56. Andrew A. Sorkin, "What Money Can Buy: Influence," *New York Times*, January 22, 2008, pp. C1, C10.

57. Namm, "It's Not About Maps," p. A6.

58. "How World Trade Organization Service Sector Negotiations Threaten to Undermine Higher Education in the United States," *Public Citizen* (Washington, DC: Global Trade Watch, n.d.), pp. 1–2; Christopher Ziguras and Grant McBurnie, "The Impact of Trade Liberalization on Transnational Education," in *Teaching in Transnational Higher Education: Enhancing Learning for Offshore International Students*, edited by Lee Dunn and Michelle Wallace (New York: Routledge, 2008), pp. 7–9. Ziguras and McBurnie maintain that "to say, as many critics of trade liberalization do, that education is not a commodity, and therefore cannot be traded, clearly flies in the face of facts.... To say, in the context of GATS,

that education is a complex service that *should not* be treated the same as cars and bananas, is another matter." Also see Altbach, "Globalisation and the University," pp. 22–23.

59. Lori Wallach, opening plenary address, AIEA Annual Conference, Washington, DC, February 18, 2008.

60. Thomas L. Friedman, "China's Little Green Book," *New York Times*, November, 2, 2005, p. A31. Other platform technologies that promise broad business applications in the foreseeable future include nanotechnology, biotechnology, and new materials. Calestous Juma and Lee Yee-Cheong, *Innovation: Applying Knowledge in Development* (London: Earthscan, 2005), p. 47.

61. Eileen Claussen and Ged Davis, *International Climate Efforts Beyond 2012: Report of the Climate Dialogue at Pocantico* (Arlington, VA: Pew Center on Global Climate Change, 2005), p. 10.

62. Peter H. Koehn, "Back to the Future: Bicycles, Human Health, and GHG Emissions in China," *China Environment Series* 9 (2007): 123–126; J. Harry Wray, *Pedal Power: The Quiet Rise of the Bicycle in American Public Life* (Boulder: Paradigm Publishers, 2008); David L. Greene and Andreas Schafer, *Reducing Greenhouse Gas Emissions from U.S. Transportation* (Arlington, VA: Pew Center on Global Climate Change, 2003), p. iv.

63. See Koehn, "Underneath Kyoto," pp. 69–70; Lester R. Brown, *Plan B 3.0: Mobilizing to Save Civilization* (New York: W.W. Norton, 2008), pp. 200–201, 239–252.

64. Barry G. Rabe, Mikael Roman, and Arthur N. Dobelis, "State Competition As a Source Driving Climate Change Mitigation," *New York University Environmental Law Journal* 14 (2005): 9–10, 38.

65. Ronald J. Deibert, *Parchment, Printing, and Hypermedia: Communication in World Order Transformation* (New York: Columbia University Press, 1997), pp. 204–205.

66. Moran, Harris, and Moran, *Global Leadership Strategies*, p. 26.

67. Christopher A. Bartlett, Sumantra Ghoshal, and Julian Birkinshaw, *Transnational Management: Text, Cases, and Readings in Cross-Border Management* (Boston: McGraw Hill, 2004), p. 12 [emphasis in original].

68. *Ibid.*, pp. 12, 103, 458, 669, 763.

69. Juma and Yee-Cheong, *Innovation*, pp. 41, 128–129.

70. Brademas, Kolb, and Mockett, *Education for Global Leadership*, pp. 6–7.

71. Castells, *Rise of the Network Society*, pp. 96, 165.

72. *Ibid.*, p. 165.

73. Such networks of small firms reduce prospects for catastrophic crises because the failure of one component in the overall mix "does not disturb the interdependencies, since other firms in the network can easily expand to absorb the business." Charles Perrow, *The Next Catastrophe: Reducing Our Vulnerabilities to Natural, Industrial, and Terrorist Disasters* (Princeton: Princeton University Press, 2007), pp. 300–303.

74. A. Dwivedi, R.K. Ball, R.N.G. Naguib, and N. Wickramasinghe, "The Importance of Understanding Different Management Paradigms in Today's Global Economy," *International Journal of Innovation and Learning* 5, No. 3 (2008): 319–320; Perrow, *The Next Catastrophe*, p. 334. Ericsson, the Swedish telecommunications firm, transfers large numbers of employees back and forth between headquarters and subsidiaries to achieve "a balanced two-way flow with people coming to the parent company not only to learn but also to bring their expertise." Bartlett, Ghoshal, and Birkinshaw, *Transnational Management*, p. 463.

75. See Jukka Bergman, Ari Jantunen, Satu Viljainen, and Jarmo Partanen, "The Exploration of Future Service Innovations in the Radically Changing Business Environment Within the Electricity Distribution Industry," *International Journal of Entrepreneurship and Innovation Management* 8, No. 2 (2008): 121.

76. Michael J. Marquardt and Lisa Horvath, *Global Teams: How Top Multinationals Span Boundaries and Cultures with High-Speed Teamwork* (Palo Alto, CA: Davies-Black Publishing, 2001), p. ix.

77. Brademas, Kolb, and Mockett, *Education for Global Leadership*, p. 6 (first articulated in Marquardt and Horvath, *Global Teams*, p. 6).

78. Marquardt and Horvath, *Global Teams*, pp. 4–5.

79. James G. Rickards, "Risk, Ugly Rewards," *Missoulian*, October 5, 2008, p. E8. No central node controls the multiple transnational links that comprise dynamic networked systems. Consequently, "the independent actions of millions of nodes and links lead to spectacular emergent behavior." Barabasi, *Linked*, p. 221.

80. See Peter H. Koehn, "Peaceful and Sustainable Development? Middle-Management Entrepreneurship and Transnational Competence in China," *East Asia* 24, No. 3 (Fall, 2007): 251–263.

81. David Barboza, "Some Assembly Needed: China As Asia Factory," *New York Times*, February 9, 2006, pp. C1, C7; Nicholas R. Lardy, *Integrating China into the Global Economy* (Washington, DC: Brookings Institution Press, 2002), pp. 20–21.

82. David Hale, "China's Growing Appetites," *National Interest* 76 (Summer 2004): 146.

83. See Peter H. Koehn, "Sustainable-Development Frontiers and Divides: Transnational Actors and U.S./China Greenhouse-Gas Emissions," *International Journal of Sustainable Development & World Ecology* 11, No. 4 (2004): 380–396.

84. Castells, *Rise of the Network Society*, pp. 188–189.

85. Paul Krugman, "Moment of Truth," *New York Times*, October 10, 2008, p. A29.

86. See Rick Crandall and Edwin C. Mensah, "Crisis Management and Sustainable Development: A Framework and Proposed Research Agenda," *International Journal of Sustainable Strategic Management* 1, No. 1 (2008): 17. The connection of networked economies to cascading failures is treated in Barabasi, *Linked*, pp. 119–122, 211.

87. The "ideal business strategy" secures both market and environmental sustainability. The integration of expertise from diverse fields of study, including those outside the traditional domain of business, such as biology, is imperative for a sustainable approach. John A. Parnell, "Sustainable Strategic Management: Construct, Parameters, Research Directions," *International Journal of Sustainable Strategic Management* 1, No. 1 (2008): 38–40.

88. United Nations, *Unlocking the Human Potential for Public Sector Performance*, World Public Sector Report (New York: United Nations, 2005).

89. Marquardt and Horvath. *Global Teams*, p. 9.

90. Nancy J. Adler and Nakiye Boyacigiller, "Global Management in the 21st Century," in Betty J. Punnet and Oded Shenkar (eds.), *Handbook for International Management Research* (Oxford: Blackwell, 1996), pp. 549–551.

91. Barabasi, *Linked*, pp. 200, 211–213.

92. Nancy J. Adler and Susan Bartholomew, "Managing Globally Competent People," *Academy of Management Executive* 6, No. 3 (1992): 57. Also see Juma and Yee-Cheong, *Innovation*, p. 156; Juma, "Reinventing Growth," pp. 11, 17.

93. Larry J. Shuman, Mary Besterfield-Sacre, and Jack McGourty, "The ABET 'Professional Skills': Can They Be Taught? Can They Be Assessed?" *Journal of Engineering Education* (January 2005): 43; National Academy of Engineering, *Educating the Engineer of 2020, Adapting Engineering Education to the New Century* (Washington, DC: National Academies Press, 2005), p. 10; Linda Katehi, "The Global Engineer," in National Academy of Engineering, *Educating the Engineer of 2020*, p. 152; Martin Fackler, "High-Tech Japanese Running Out of Engineers," *New York Times*, May 17, 2008, pp. A1, B4.

94. Richard Nader, "International Opportunities for Students" (PowerPoint presentation at the American Council on Education meeting, Washington, DC, December 5, 2007); National Academy of Engineering, *Educating the Engineer of 2020*, p. 7. Rapid developments in climate and genetic engineering, nanotechnology, and robotics, for instance, are replete with powerful "unknown unknowns" and involve risks and consequences that often do not emerge and/or are not comprehended until the new technology is "put into widespread use at a scale impossible to turn back...." Cornelia Dean, "Handle with Care: The Ethics of 'Geoengineering,'" *New York Times*, August 12, 2008, pp. D1, D4.

95. See National Academy of Engineering, *Educating the Engineer of 2020*, p. xi.

96. Malcolm Allan and Colin U. Chisholm, "Achieving Engineering Competencies in the Global Information Society Through the Integration of On-Campus and Workplace Environments," *Industry & Higher Education* 22, No. 3 (June 2008): 146, 148.

97. See National Academy of Engineering, "Grand Challenges for Engineering," www.engineeringchallenges.org (accessed 20 June 2008).

98. *Ibid.* Also see National Academy of Engineering, *Educating the Engineer of 2020*, p. 8.

99. Nanotechnology is "the study, design, creation, synthesis, manipulation, and application of functional materials, devices, and systems through control of matter at the atomic and molecular levels and the exploitation of novel phenomena and properties of matter at that scale." Juma and Yee-Cheong, *Innovation*, pp. 69–74.

100. Peoc'h, *Downsizing Development*, pp. 11, 14, 21.

101. The NGLS report adds that "if current trends continue, nanotech threatens to widen the gap between rich and poor and further consolidate economic power in the hands of multinational corporations." Peoc'h, *Downsizing Development*, pp. 11, 17, 55, 58–59. Following its analysis of the research strategy of the National Nanotechnology Initiative (the program that coordinates U.S. efforts in nanotechnology research and development), an expert panel of the National Research Council chaired by Andrew D. Maynard, chief science advisor to the Project on Emerging Nanotechnology at the Woodrow Wilson Institute, reported in December 2008 that the U.S. government "was not doing enough to identify potential health and environmental risks from engineered nanomaterials." Cornelia Dean, "Panel Criticizes U.S. Effort on Nanomaterial Risks," *New York Times*, December 11, 2008, p. A31.

102. Charles M. Vest, "Educating Engineers for 2020 and Beyond," in National Academy of Engineering, *Educating the Engineer of 2020: Adapting Engineering Education to the New Century* (Washington, DC: National Academies Press, 2005), pp. 163–166.

103. National Academy of Engineering, "Grand Challenges for Engineering"; also see Katehi, "Global Engineer," p. 152.

104. Andrew C. Revkin, "Low Technologies, High Aims," *New York Times*, September 11, 2007, pp. D1, D4.

105. Daniel Hirleman, telephonic interview with Peter Koehn, November 30, 2007.

106. Bob W. Bell, Jr., and Calestous Juma, "Bundling Critical Information Infrastructure in Africa: Implications for Science and Innovation Policy," *International Journal of Technology and Globalization* 4, No. 2 (2008): 192.

107. *Ibid.*, p. 188.

108. *Ibid.*, p. 191.

109. Yating Chang, Assistant Director, Global Engineering Program, Purdue University, telephonic interview with Peter Koehn, November 30, 2007.

110. Shuman, *et al.*, "ABET 'Professional Skills,'" p. 43; National Academy of Engineering, *Educating the Engineer of 2020*, p. 4. On the shortage of transnationally skilled and experienced engineers graduating from U.S. universities, see Carlson, "Global Approach to Engineering," p. A33. Brazilian firms are coping with the country's insufficient supply of skilled engineering graduates by employing foreign labor. Andrew Downie, "Wanted: Skilled Workers for a Growing Economy in Brazil," *New York Times*, July 2, 2008, pp. C1, C5.

111. Shuman, *et al.*, "ABET 'Professional Skills,'" p. 46; A.M. Findlay, F.L.N. Li, A.J. Jowett, and R. Skeldon, "Skilled International Migration and the Global City: A Study of Expatriates in Hong Kong," *Transnational Institute of British Geography* 21 (1996): 53. Moreover, many engineering graduates will use their education for careers in business management, medicine, and other fields. Shuman, *et al.*, "ABET 'Professional Skills,'" p. 43.

112. Broad and Dean, "Unleashing Innovation," p. A18.

113. Yating Chang, interview, November 30, 2007.

114. John F. Jones and Asfaw Kumssa, "Professional Growth in the Global Context," in *All Our Futures: Principles and Resources for Social Work Practice in a Global Era*, edited by Chathapuram S. Ramanathan and Rosemary J. Link (Albany: Brooks/Cole, Wadsworth, 1999), pp. 217.

115. Finn and Jacobson, *Just Practice*, p. 31.

116. Janet Finn, interview conducted by Peter Koehn in Missoula, Montana, May 19, 2008. One long-term structural consequence for social-justice workers of the abuse and neglect that accompanies conflict and poverty is that "millions of children are growing up without parental care, living on the streets, and fending for themselves." Finn and Jacobson, *Just Practice*, pp. 414–415.

117. Lynne Koester, interview conducted by Peter Koehn in Missoula, Montana, February 15, 2008. Similarly, Ramanathan and Link ("Future Visions for Global Studies in Social Work," p. 235) anticipate a "period of immense pain and carnage."

118. Janet Finn, interview, May 19, 2008.

119. Healy, *International Social Work*, pp. xiii, 75, 230.

120. Lynne Koester, interview, February 15, 2008. In some parts of the world, child-headed households will present social workers with new challenges. Healy, *International Social Work*, pp. 45, 98.

121. See Healy, *International Social Work*, pp. 41, 43, 46, 80–81, 90, 94–95, 231, 298–305, 314, 361–362;

Ramanathan and Link, "Future Visions for Global Studies in Social Work," p. 235; Katherine A. Kendall, "Foreword," in Lynne M. Healy, *International Social Work: Professional Action in an Interdependent World*, 2nd edition (Oxford: Oxford University Press, 2008), pp. vii–viii. Social workers in some rural parts of Mexico and other countries in the South can expect to encounter communities composed primarily of the very young and the very old as migration persists in the wake of global economic pressures. The elderly will present social workers with an immense challenge as populations age throughout the world. By 2025, more than a billion people will be 65 or older. Finn and Jacobson, *Just Practice*, pp. 224, 416. In low-income countries, most elderly people will live in rural areas. Healy, *International Social Work*, p. 99.

122. Janet Finn, interview, May 19, 2008.

123. A shift to local social development, including emphasis on economics and local government, also is advocated for social-work faculty by Jones and Kumssa ("Professional Growth in the Global Context," pp. 208–209).

124. Janet Finn, interview, May 19, 2008.

125. Finn and Jacobson, *Just Practice*, p. 47.

126. Brundtland Commission, *Our Common Future* (London: Oxford University Press, 1987).

127. Berkes, Colding, and Folke, "Introduction," p. 2.

128. J. Timmons Roberts and Bradley C. Parks, *A Climate of Injustice: Global Inequality, North-South Politics, and Climate Policy* (Cambridge, MA: MIT Press, 2007), pp. 223–224.

129. The 2008–2009 cycle of the U.N.'s Commission on Sustainable Development covered the themes of agriculture, rural development, drought and desertification, and land use, and focused on Africa. Romain Perez and Malika Bhandarkar, *Innovation for Sustainable Development: Local Cases from Africa* (New York: United Nations, Department of Economic and Social Affairs, Division for Sustainable Development, 2007), p. 5.

130. Written response to interview questions submitted by Dave Acker in December 2007. Others expect global agribusiness connections to assume increasing importance in the developing world. Joyce Cacho and Ronald Turko, "Agribusiness Education: Focusing on Human Resources to Support African Agribusiness Market Investment" (flyer in the authors' possession distributed in 2008 by the Corporate Council on Africa).

131. Elisabeth Rosenthal, "From Hoof to Plate, a New Bid to Cut Emissions," *New York Times*, December 4, 2008, pp. A1, A16.

132. Earl Kellogg, interview, December 5, 2007. Also see Vest, "Educating Engineers for 2020," pp. 162–163.

133. Earl Kellogg, interview, December 5, 2007. On prospects for growing artemisia for use in controlling malaria in Africa and Asia, see Peoc'h, *Downsizing Development*, pp. 41–45.

134. Brown, *Plan B 3.0*, pp. 39–42.

135. *Ibid.*

136. *Ibid.*

137. L. George Wilson, telephonic interview conducted by Peter Koehn, November 27, 2007. Wilson has worked professionally in Latin America for eleven years, nine of them in Peru.

138. "Fore Sets Agenda for Change," *Frontlines* [USAID], October 2007, p. 1.

139. See Peter H. Koehn, "Global Health and Human Rights: Challenges for Public-Health Administrators in an Era of Interdependence and Mobility," in *Handbook of Globalization, Governance, and Public Administration*, edited by Ali Farazmand and Jack Pinkowski (Boca Raton, FL: CRC Press, 2007), pp. 1045–1073.

140. See Peter H. Koehn, "Global Climatic Stabilization: Challenges for Public Administration in China and the United States," in *Handbook of Globalization, Governance, and Public Administration*, edited by Ali Farazmand and Jack Pinkowski (Boca Raton, FL: CRC Press, 2007), pp. 1089–1135.

141. Harvey L. White, "Transformation, Internationalization and Globalization of Public Administration," *PA Times International Supplement*, March 2008, p. 3.

142. Peter H. Koehn, "Decentralisation for Sustainable Development," in *Development Management in Africa: Toward Dynamism, Empowerment, and Entrepreneurship*, edited by Sadig Rasheed and David F. Luke (Boulder: Westview Press, 1995), pp. 77–79.

143. *Ibid.*, p. 78.

144. Philip Morgan, interview, December 10, 2007. Here, we would add the ripple effects of multinational corporate restructuring.

145. Written response to interview questions submitted by Krishna Tummala, January 2008.

146. Philip Morgan, interview, December 10, 2007.

147. Ali Farazmand, telephonic interview conducted by Peter Koehn, November 30, 2007. Also see Gustav A. Koehler, Guenther G. Kress, and Randi L. Miller, "What Disaster Response Management Can Learn from Chaos Theory," in *Handbook of Crisis and Emergency Management*, edited by Ali Farazmand (New York: Marcel Dekker, 2001), pp. 293–308.

148. Ali Farazmand, interview, November 30, 2007.

149. Fikret Berkes, Johan Colding, and Carl Folke, "Introduction," in *Navigating Social-Ecological Systems: Building Resilience for Complexity and Change*, edited by Fikret Berkes, Johan Colding, and Carl Folke (Cambridge: Cambridge University Press, 2003), p. 1.

150. One example is "the transformation of productive grasslands in subtropical Africa into thorny shrublands as a consequence of poor cattle management practices." *Ibid.*, pp. 5–6, 14. Malcolm Gladwell popularized "that one dramatic moment ... when everything can change all at once" as "the Tipping Point." Malcolm Gladwell, *The Tipping Point: How Little Things Can Make a Big Difference* (Boston: Little, Brown and Company, 2000), p. 9.

151. Berkes, Colding, and Folke, "Introduction," pp. 14–15.

152. Carl Folke, Johan Colding, and Fikret Berkes, "Synthesis: Building Resilience and Adaptive Capacity in Socio-Ecological Systems," in *Navigating Social-Ecological Systems: Building Resilience for Complexity and Change*, edited by Fikret Berkes, Johan Colding, and Carl Folke (Cambridge: Cambridge University Press, 2003), p. 382.

153. *Ibid.* p. 382.

154. Koichiro Matsuura, "UNESCO Director General's Statement on Climate Change and World Heritage" (Nairobi, Kenya, November 6, 2006) http://whc.unesco.org/en/activities/396; UNESCO, *Climate Change and World Heritage,* World Heritage Reports No. 22 (May 2007) http://whc.unesco .org/en/activities/474; Kemal Dervis, Administrator, UNDP, "Building the Infrastructure for Development and Peace" (presentation at the Johns Hopkins University School of Advanced International Studies, November 2, 2007); Juha I. Uitto and Rajib Shaw, "Adaptation to Changing Climate: Promoting Community-Based Approaches in the Developing Countries," *Sansai* 1 (January 2006): 93–107.

155. Roberts and Parks, *Climate of Injustice.*

156. *Ibid.*, pp. 233, 213, 217–218, 231, 235, 241.

157. Douglas W. Bettcher, Steve Sapirie, and Eric H. Goon, "Essential Public Health Functions: Results of the International Delphi Study," *World Health Statistical Quarterly* 51, No. 1 (1998): 50.

158. *Ibid.* On the negative health effects of e-waste and other hazardous-waste movement and disposal, see Jennifer Clapp, "The Distancing of Waste: Overconsumption in a Global Economy," in *Confronting Consumption*, edited by Thomas Princen, Michael Maniates, and Ken Conca (Cambridge, MA: MIT Press, 2002), pp. 155–176; Jamie Choi, "High Tech's Toxic Legacy in China," *China Environment Series* 9 (2007): 77–81.

159. Bettcher, Sapirie, and Goon, "Essential Public Health Functions," p. 50.

160. See Koehn, "Underneath Kyoto," pp. 66–69.

161. Donald G. McNeil, Jr., "Noninfectious Illnesses Are Expected to Become Top Killers Within 20 Years," *New York Times*, June 3, 2008, p. D6; Derek Yach and Robert Beaglehole, "Globalization of Risks for Chronic Diseases Demands Global Solutions" in Richard L. Harris and Melinda Seid (eds.), *Globalization and Health* (Leiden: Brill, 2004), pp. 213–233; Bettcher, Sapirie, and Goon, "Essential Public Health Functions," p. 50.

162. The CDC defines *syndemics* as "two or more afflictions, interacting synergistically, contributing to excess burden of disease in a population." www.cdc.gov/syndemics. Also see Milstein, *Hygeia's Constellation*, pp. 1, 7.

163. Roger S. Magnusson, "Non-Communicable Diseases and Global Health Governance: Enhancing Global Processes to Improve Health Development," *Globalization and Health* 3, No. 2 (2007); Karen Siegel and K.M. Venkat Narayan, "The Unite for Diabetes Campaign: Overcoming Constraints to Find a Global Policy Solution," *Globalization and Health* 4, No. 3 (2008).

164. Abdallah S. Daar, *et al.*, "Grand Challenges in Chronic Non-Communicable Diseases," *Nature* 450, No. 22 (November 2007): 494–496.

165. Milstein, *Hygeia's Constellation*, pp. 14, 16, 21. Health-depleting forces include armed conflict and failed states.

166. Koehn, "Global Health and Human Rights," pp. 1045–1073.

167. Peter Daszak, "Why Do Emerging Diseases Happen and What Can We Do to Stop Them?" (lecture presented at the University of Montana, November 10, 2008).

168. One example is the *nipah* virus spread by fruit bats via pigs to humans in Malaysia. Daszak, "Why Do Emerging Diseases Happen?"; Rob Chaney, "Speaker: Humans Have Ability to Spread Disease Worldwide," *Missoulian*, November 1, 2008, pp. B1–B2.

169. Daszak, "Why Do Emerging Diseases Happen?"

170. Julie Gerberding, cited in Edward W. Lempinen, "CDC Director Gerberding Cites Avian Flu As 'Very Ominous' Threat," *AAAS News*, February 21, 2005. www.aaas.org/news/releases/2005/0221flu.shtml; also see Jennifer Brower and Peter Chalk, *The Global Threat of New and Reemerging Infectious Diseases: Reconciling U.S. National Security and Public Health Policy* (Santa Monica, CA: Rand Corporation, 2003).

171. See Peter H. Koehn, "Globalization, Migration Health, and Educational Preparation for Transnational Medical Encounters," *Globalization and Health* 2, No. 2 (January 30, 2006): 3. For instance, Taneli Puumalainen of GlaxoSmithKline expects vaccines for chronic diseases (e.g., nicotine addiction) to be on the market by 2018. However, they will be "hugely expensive." Taneli Puumalainen, "Role of New Vaccines in Improving Global Health" (presentation at the 2nd Tampere Symposium on Global Health Research, University of Tampere, September 5, 2008).

172. Robert C. Like, University of Medicine and Dentistry of New Jersey–Robert Wood Johnson Medical School, written response to interview questions submitted in December 2007. Like's long-term personal/professional experience includes work in Portugal/Azores.

173. Fitzhugh Mullan, Claire Panosian, and Patricia Cuff (eds.), *Healers Abroad: Americans Responding to the Human Resource Crisis in HIV/AIDS* (Washington, DC: National Academies Press, 2005), p. 15. The AIDS Treatment Information Center (ATIC) provides a toll-free phone- and Internet-based network that disseminates drug and clinical information to clinicians in thirteen African countries. Merle Sande and Allan Ronald, "The Academic Alliance for AIDS Care and Prevention in Africa," *Academic Medicine*, 83, No. 2 (2008): 182–183.

174. See, for instance, Juma and Yee-Cheong, *Innovation*, pp. 57–58. Although largely unrecognized by Northern health-care providers, self-care among Southern migrants (particularly for mental health and chronic illness) often includes virtual visits to healers in their countries of origin. Marja Tiilikainen, "Transnational Healing Practices: Some Considerations Based on Fieldwork in Northern Somalia" (paper presented at the 4th Biennial Conference of the European Network of Medical Anthropology at Home, Seili, Finland, March 16, 2006).

175. Mullan, *et al.*, *Healers Abroad*, p. 15.

176. Per Ashorn, Professor of International Health, University of Tampere Medical School, and Vinod Diwan, Karolinska Institute, personal communication to Peter Koehn, September 5, 2008. Although there are now more mobile phones in use in Africa than there are fixed-line telephones (and many of these are shared), few published studies have assessed the use of mobile telephones as a health-care intervention for HIV, TB, malaria, or chronic conditions, or have measured clinical outcomes and the cost effectiveness of mobile-phone telemedicine. Warren A. Kaplan, "Can the Ubiquitous Power of Mobile Phones Be Used to Improve Health Outcomes in Developing Countries?" *Globalization and Health* 2 (2006): 9.

177. Peter H. Koehn and Marja Tiilikainen, "Migration and Transnational Health Care: Connecting Finland and Somaliland," *Siirtolaisuus: Migration* 34, No. 1 (2007): 7.

178. Perez and Bhandarkar, *Innovation for Sustainable Development*, p. 39.

179. Craig Calhoun, "Toward a More Public Social Science," *SSRC Items* 5, Nos. 1–2 (2004): 14. On emerging tools of biotechnology that are likely to be helpful in addressing health challenges in low-income settings, see Juma and Yee-Cheong, *Innovation*, pp. 59–69. For the 2003 list of the fourteen fundable scientific and technological innovations for solving a major health problem in low-income countries that comprise the Bill & Melinda Gates Foundation's "Grand Challenges in Global Health," see Juma and Yee-Cheong, *Innovation*, p. 124.

180. Javier I. Escobar, Associate Dean for Global Health, University of Medicine and Dentistry of New Jersey–Robert Wood Johnson Medical School, written response to interview questions submitted in December 2007. Dr. Escobar's long-term professional experience includes work in Columbia, Argentina, and Spain.

181. Like, interview, December 2007.

182. Mullan, *et al.*, *Healers Abroad*, pp. 145, 9.

183. See, for instance, B.D. Smedley, A.Y. Stith, and A.R. Nelson (eds.), *Unequal Treatment: Confronting Racial and Ethnic Disparities in Health Care* (Washington, DC: National Academy Press, 2003); Gary L. Kreps, "Communication and Racial Inequities in Health Care," *American Behavioral Scientist* 49, No. 6 (2006): 1–3.

184. See National Academy of Engineering, "Grand Challenges for Engineering."

185. Peoc'h, *Downsizing Development*, pp. 55, 40–43.

186. Perrow, *Next Catastrophe*, p. 261; Rickards, "Risk," p. E6; Berkes, Colding, and Folke, "Introduction," pp. 5–6, 16.

187. Stephen A. Webb, *Social Work in a Risk Society: Social and Political Perspectives* (New York: Palgrave Macmillan, 2006), pp. 191–193.

188. This notion is drawn from Milstein, *Hygeia's Constellation*, p. 53.

189. Also see Patricia L. Rosenfield, "The Potential of Transdisciplinary Research for Sustaining and Extending Linkages Between the Health and Social Sciences," *Social Science and Medicine* 35, No. 11 (1992): 1343–1357; Webb, *Social Work in a Risk Society*, p. 194.

190. Shaw and Kim, *Education for Sustainable Development Practice*, p. 55.

191. Kathy L. Anderson, "Bridging Disciplines to Bridge Global Divides: Interdisciplinary Approaches to the Millennium's Most Challenging Dilemmas" (paper presented at the World Universities Forum, Davos, Switzerland, January 2008).

192. Bammer, "Integration and Implementation Sciences," p. 6. For instance, the scenario process explores "the simultaneous impact of various uncertainties by changing multiple variables at a time," thereby proactively channeling firms toward new innovations that address future needs in situations of complex and rapid change. Following idea generation and evaluation at brainstorming sessions, innovations can be linked with sustainable capability development utilizing *fit analysis*. Bergman, *et al.*, "Exploration of Future Service Innovations," pp. 125–138. Complex systems thinking that bridges biophysical and social sciences provides the basis for many of the new integrative approaches. Berkes, Colding, and Folke, "Introduction," p. 2. To this list, one might add critical questioning, which seeks "connections among seemingly disparate issues or events." Finn and Jacobson, *Just Practice*, p. 43.

193. Alain Nicolas, Katia Radja, and Patrick Schembri, "Which Professionalizing Education Programmes for Which Sustainable Development?" *Industry & Higher Education* 22, No. 3 (June 2008): 163. Complexity science can be useful, for instance, in mapping and understanding how diseases are transmitted globally and locally. Brian Castellani and Frederic W. Hafferty, "The Complexities of Medical Professionalism," in *Professionalism in Medicine: Critical Perspectives*, edited by Delese Wear and Julie M. Aultman (New York: Springer, 2006), p. 4.

194. Williams, "Competent Boundary Spanner," pp. 104–105.

195. Wayfinding "combines the notion of navigating from place to place with the concepts of moving forward through time while transferring a continually evolving culture from one generation to the next." Milstein, *Hygeia's Constellation*, p. 13. On the effectiveness of Polynesian navigational methods, see David Lewis, *We, the Navigators: The Ancient Art of Landfinding in the Pacific* (Honolulu: University of Hawaii Press, 1972), pp. 11, 308–309.

196. Milstein, *Hygeia's Constellation*, pp. 1, 6, 8, 13–14, 17–18, 38, 40, 45, 52–53, 63, 68, 71. By identifying "high-leverage drivers with system-wide influence," causal mapping facilitates alignment of the efforts of diverse stakeholders (p. 53).

197. Participatory long-term domain development can produce new paradigms that are "particularly useful in providing in-depth analysis over the longer term of poorly understood problems." Bammer, "Integration and Implementation Sciences," p. 6.

198. Based on this technique, Kurzweil predicts that solar energy will be cost-competitive with fossil fuels by 2013. He also foresees, given rapid progress in nanotechnology, gene sequencing, and brain-scan

resolution, that we will be adding computers to our brains in the 2020s. See John Tierney, "The Future Is Now? Pretty Soon, at Least," *New York Times*, June 3, 2008, pp. D1, D3.

199. Cited in Ramanathan and Link, "Future Visions for Global Studies," pp. 235–236.

200. Robert Klitgaard, "Universities Have the Responsibility to Tackle the World's Toughest Problems," *Chronicle of Higher Education* 54, No. 21 (February 1, 2008): A36.

201. Robert Charlick, Professor Emeritus at Cleveland State University, among others, holds that the "vast majority" of advanced students do not possess "useable" interpersonal skills. Robert Charlick, response to interview questions, November 26, 2007. Offering a world-class program and attracting international students and staff do not guarantee the presence of a transnationally useful curriculum. See Donald G. McCloud, "Global Higher Education: An American Perspective," *Malaysian Business*, January 16, 2004, p. 7.

Notes for Chapter 5

1. George L. Mehaffy, "Educating a New Generation of Globally Competent Teachers," in *Educational Exchange and Global Competence*, edited by Richard D. Lambert (Washington, DC: Council on International Educational Exchange, 1994), p. 127.

2. Suarez-Orozco and Qin-Hilliard, "Globalization," p. 3.

3. Mehaffy, "Educating a New Generation of Globally Competent Teachers," p. 128.

4. There is considerable evidence that U.S. teacher-education programs "provide preservice teachers with insufficient guidance in developing knowledge, skills, and dispositions for dealing with diversity issues in the classroom." Phyllis B. Ngai, "A Reinforcing Curriculum and Program Reform Proposal for 21st Century Teacher Education: Vital First Steps for Advancing K–12 Multicultural Education," *Equity & Excellence in Education* 37 (2004): 321. Marilyn Cochran-Smith further asserts that many in-service teachers in the United States "often have difficulty constructing curriculum, instruction, and interactional patterns that are culturally responsive" (Cochran-Smith, "Standing at the Crossroads," pp. 3–4). Ryan Wells argues for "reforming teacher education programs to be more aligned with the globalized world in which they exist…." Ryan Wells, "The Global and the Multicultural: Opportunities, Challenges, and Suggestions for Teacher Education," *Multicultural Perspectives* 10, No. 3 (2008): 148.

5. Task Force for Transnational Competence, *Towards Transnational Competence*, p. 122. Also see Brademas, Kolb, and Mockett, *Education for Global Leadership*, p. 1. This 2006 report of the U.S. Council for Economic Development notes that "state high school graduation requirements often include only minimal course work in international studies … and some states require none at all" (p. 1) and singles out encouraging "upgrades" recently introduced in Delaware, New Jersey, and North Carolina (pp. 22–23). A 2003/2004 K–12 Delaware study found that "less than half of Delaware's students are actually exposed to meaningful and sustained international education." Fran O'Malley, Jeanette Miller, and Shuhan Wang, *Report on the Delaware K–20 International Education Capacity Study* (Newark, DE: Institute for Public Administration, University of Delaware, 2004), p. 1.

6. Ngai, "21st Century Teacher Education," p. 321. To address current weaknesses, the U.S. CED also has recommended, in less specific terms than those developed here, that "teacher education programs in colleges and universities should include a strong international component." Brademas, Kolb, and Mockett, *Education for Global Leadership*, pp. 27, 13–14.

7. Merryfield, "Learning from Current Practice," p. 3. Most teacher candidates hail from mainstream backgrounds and enter tertiary-education programs possessing limited experience with or understanding of individuals from other socioeconomic/ethnic groups. Don Bragaw and W. Scott Thompson, "Future Teachers and Multicultural Education," in *Multicultural Education: A Global Approach*, edited by Don Bragaw and W. Scott Thomson (New York: American Forum for Global Education, 1992), p. 205.

8. Kissock interview.

9. See Yin C. Cheng, "New Education and New Teacher Education: A Paradigm Shift for the Future," in *New Teacher Education for the Future: International Perspectives*, edited by Yin C. Cheng, King W. Chow, and Kwok T. Tsui (Dordrecht, Netherlands: Kluwer Academic, 2001), p. 56.

10. See Chapter 11.

11. Geneva Gay, *Culturally Responsive Teaching: Theory, Research, & Practice* (New York: Teachers College Press, 2000), p. 20.

12. Suarez-Orozco and Qin-Hilliard, "Globalization," p. 4.

13. *Ibid.*, p. 3.

14. Cummings interview.

15. Merryfield, "Framework for Teacher Education," p. 8.

16. Cummings interview. Given their growing role in global governance, it would be valuable for teacher-education curriculums to include content that treats a sampling of different nonstate actors. See Merry M. Merryfield, "Science-Technology-Society and Global Perspectives," in *Multicultural Education: A Global Approach,* edited by Don Bragaw and W. Scott Thomson (New York: American Forum for Global Education, 1992), pp. 181–185.

17. Betty Leask, "Teaching for Learning in the Transnational Classroom," in *Teaching in Transnational Higher Education: Enhancing Learning for Offshore International Students,* edited by Lee Dunn and Michelle Wallace (New York: Routledge, 2008), p. 124.

18. Kubow and Fossum, *Comparative Education,* p. 23.

19. Merryfield and White, "Issues-Centered Global Education," p. 177.

20. Many of these core elements would be covered in courses offered by colleagues outside of education programs. Merryfield, "Framework for Teacher Education," pp. 7–8. For specific examples under most of these broad issue categories, along with suggested classroom applications, see Merryfield, "Science-Technology-Society," pp. 182–185.

21. See Banks, *et al., Democracy and Diversity,* who maintain that "sustainable development should be part of the explicit curriculum of schools" (p. 19).

22. Merryfield and White ("Issues-Centered Global Education," p. 184) point out that "most practicing teachers in today's classrooms did not receive a global education themselves, nor were they taught to teach an issues-centered approach in their preservice teacher education programs." This reality underscores the importance of "extensive in-service education and professional development" regarding core issues along with "ongoing updates ... of global events...."

23. Merryfield, "Pedagogy for Global Perspectives," p. 261.

24. Stewart, "A World Transformed," pp. 230–231. She also reports that schools in Finland, Sweden, and the Netherlands are increasing their emphasis on development issues, that the Asia Education Foundation has helped diffuse the study of Asia into different curriculum areas in Australian schools, and that the People's Republic of China is increasing the international focus of schools in order to "prepare young people to be able to function in an increasingly complex and interconnected world."

25. Cummings interview.

26. In Merryfield's study of classroom practice in global education, "the ability to integrate higher level thinking skills with globally oriented content was one of the few places where teachers said a teacher education program or course had made a positive difference in their teaching." Merryfield, "Pedagogy for Global Perspectives," pp. 259–260.

27. Including primary sources, databases, social-science research findings, first-hand accounts, local case studies, journal articles, biographies, nonfiction, historical fiction, videos, resource organizations and people, music, and critical and ethnic scholarship. Merryfield, "Pedagogy for Global Perspectives," pp. 254, 260; Gay, *Culturally Responsive Teaching,* pp. 35, 142; Leask, "Transnational Classroom," pp. 124–125.

28. Cheng, "New Teacher Education," p. 49.

29. The University of Wisconsin, Madison's "Teach for Diversity" Master's degree with elementary certification program introduces all students to diverse perspectives through integrated courses in literacies and the arts; math, science, and environmental education; and health, physical education, and social studies. Merryfield (ed.), *Making Connections,* p. 239. Teachers also need to be prepared for the multiple perspectives encountered in their classrooms. Mehaffy ("Educating a New Generation," p. 127) notes that "as our classrooms become increasingly heterogeneous, the need to understand student perspectives and respond appropriately becomes increasingly important."

30. Gay, *Culturally Responsive Teaching,* p. 35. TC education encourages teachers to collaborate regularly with community leaders to ensure that curriculum content about local ethnic groups is accurate and up to date.

31. Gay, *Culturally Responsive Teaching*, p. 145.

32. See Don Bragaw, "The Global Imperative and Its Metalanguage," in *Multicultural Education: A Global Approach*, edited by Don Bragaw and W. Scott Thomson (New York: American Forum for Global Education, 1992), p. 193; Gay, *Culturally Responsive Teaching*, p. 142.

33. Merryfield, "Framework for Teacher Education," p. 9; Gay, *Culturally Responsive Teaching*, p. 143; Sleeter, "Teaching Globalization," p. 7. In addition to views that differ from their own, teachers should be prepared to respect perspectives that differ from "'the powers that be'" or their government's perspective. Merryfield, "Pedagogy for Global Perspectives," p. 254.

34. Kissock interview.

35. See Merryfield, "Pedagogy for Global Perspectives," p. 254; Kubow and Fossum, *Comparative Education*, p. 23; Gay, *Culturally Responsive Teaching*, p. 213. In comparative analysis, Byron Massialas suggests addressing the "how is the problem treated in societies elsewhere" question. Byron G. Massialas, "Criteria for Issues-Centered Content Selection," in *Handbook on Teaching Social Studies*, edited by Ronald W. Evans and David W. Saxe (Washington, DC: National Council for the Social Studies, 1996), p. 49.

36. See Merryfield, "Pedagogy for Global Perspectives," pp. 266–267; Banks, *et al.*, *Democracy and Diversity*, p. 19.

37. Cummings interview.

38. Sleeter, "Teaching Globalization," p. 4.

39. Merryfield, "Science-Technology-Society," p. 184.

40. Sharon L. Pugh and Jesus Garcia, "Issues-Centered Education in Multicultural Environments," in *Handbook on Teaching Social Studies*, edited by Ronald W. Evans and David W. Saxe (Washington, DC: National Council for the Social Studies, 1996), p. 122.

41. See Merryfield, "Learning from Current Practice," pp. 1–2; Merryfield, "Framework for Teacher Education," p. 5. Taking a holographic view, moreover, is likely to sharpen the analytic skill of "realizing that the more we know, the more we do not know." Kissock interview.

42. Merryfield, "Pedagogy for Global Perspectives," pp. 256–258; Merryfield and Wilson, *Teaching Global Perspectives*, p. 17; Sleeter, "Teaching Globalization," p. 6.

43. See Banks, *et al.*, *Democracy and Diversity*, p. 22; Merryfield, "Science-Technology-Society," p. 184.

44. Sonia Nieto, *Affirming Diversity: The Sociopolitical Context of Multicultural Education*, 2nd edition (White Plains, NY: Longman, 1996), p. 380. In addition, introducing a holographic perspective among the children of first-generation migrants helps them realize the value of transnational competence. See Anita S. Mak, Marvin J. Westwood, F. Ishu Ishiyama, and Michelle C. Barker, "Optimising Conditions for Learning Sociocultural Competencies for Success," in *Intercultural Communication: A Reader*, 10th edition, edited by Larry A. Samovar and Richard E. Porter (Belmont, CA: Thompson/Wadsworth, 2003), p. 365.

45. Mehaffy, "Educating a New Generation," p. 128.

46. *Ibid.*

47. See Merryfield, "Framework for Teacher Education," p. 9; Howard Gardner, "How Education Changes: Considerations of History, Science, and Values," in *Globalization: Culture and Education in the New Millennium*, edited by Marcelo M. Suarez-Orozco and Desiree B. Qin-Hilliard (Berkeley: University of California Press, 2004), p. 255.

48. Kissock interview; Merryfield and White, "Issues-Centered Global Education," p. 178 ; Hanvey, "Attainable Global Perspective," p. 218.

49. Kubow and Fossum, *Comparative Education*, p. 302.

50. Merryfield, "Pedagogy for Global Perspectives," p. 254.

51. Cochran-Smith ("Standing at the Crossroads," pp. 4–5) maintains that "many White middle-class teachers" in the United States "understand diversity as deficit to be overcome and have low expectations and fears about students who are different from themselves...."

52. Merryfield, "Pedagogy for Global Perspectives," p. 268 [emphasis ours].

53. Mehaffy, "Educating a New Generation," pp. 127–128.

54. Cummings interview.

55. *Ibid.*

56. Merryfield, "Pedagogy for Global Perspectives," p. 258.

57. Jeanne A.K. Hey, "Teaching about the Third World with Cases," in *The New International Studies Classroom: Active Teaching, Active Learning,* edited by Jeffrey S. Lantis, Lynn M. Kuzma, and John Boehrer (Boulder: Lynne Rienner, 2000), pp. 56–57.

58. Cummings interview.

59. "A Q&A with Karen Hughes," *Chronicle of Higher Education,* January 5, 2007, pp. A35–A36.

60. Merryfield and White, "Issues-Centered Global Education," pp. 178, 182–183; Massialas, "Criteria for Issues-Centered Content Selection," p. 49; Merryfield, "Pedagogy for Global Perspectives," pp. 255–256, 263, 268.

61. Merryfield and White, "Issues-Centered Global Education," p. 184.

62. Gay, *Culturally Responsive Teaching,* p. 61.

63. Cushner and Trifonovitch, "Understanding Misunderstanding," p. 300.

64. Gay, *Culturally Responsive Teaching,* pp. 1, 29, 33–34.

65. Merryfield, "Pedagogy for Global Perspectives," p. 269; Bragaw, "Global Imperative," p. 193. Massialas ("Criteria for Issues-Centered Content Selection," p. 49) suggests that critically examining *school-based* issues in comparative perspective enhances the student's sense of social and political efficacy.

66. Gay, *Culturally Responsive Teaching,* pp. 32, 60.

67. Kissock interview.

68. See, for instance, Cynthia B. Dillard, "Following Your Talk with Your Walk: Rethinking Teacher Education in a Multicultural World," in *Multicultural Education: A Global Approach,* edited by Don Bragaw and W. Scott Thomson (New York: American Forum for Global Education, 1992), p. 242.

69. Ngai, "21st Century Teacher Education," p. 324.

70. Merryfield and White, "Issues-Centered Global Education," p. 182.

71. Kubow and Fossum, *Comparative Education,* p. 302.

72. Merryfield (ed.), *Making Connections,* p. 231.

73. Phyllis B. Ngai, "Community-Based Indigenous Education for Global Competence," *International Journal of Diversity in Organisations, Communities and Nations* 7 (2007).

74. Massialas, "Criteria for Issues-Centered Content Selection," p. 49.

75. Merryfield, "Framework for Teacher Education," p. 9.

76. Ngai interview.

77. Gay, *Culturally Responsive Teaching,* p. 20.

78. Ngai interview.

79. Wang, "Intercultural Dialogue," p. 59.

80. Gay, *Culturally Responsive Teaching,* p. 214.

81. Cheng, "New Teacher Education," p. 35.

82. Kissock interview.

83. Ngai interview.

84. Gay, *Culturally Responsive Teaching,* pp. 78–79.

85. Wells ("The Global and the Multicultural," p. 148) advocates increased second/foreign language competence among teacher-education faculty and students and proposes that teacher-education courses be offered in multiple languages.

86. Ngai, "Community-Based Indigenous Education for Global Competence."

87. Bragaw, "Global Imperative," p. 193. For an innovative program where teachers introduced primary-school students to a local indigenous language, see Ngai, "Community-Based Indigenous Education for Global Competence."

88. This recommendation affirms the position taken by the Task Force for Transnational Competence in 1997 (*Towards Transnational Competence,* p. 126). The authors of the Delaware K–20 report assert that proficiency and literacy in one or more additional languages constitute "part of the 'basic skills' that global citizens must possess." O'Malley, Miller, and Wang, *Delaware K–20 International Education Capacity Study,* p. 31.

89. Spanish accounts for about 70 percent of U.S. secondary-school enrollments and even Chinese and Arabic rank among the less commonly taught languages. Brademas, Kolb, and Mockett, *Education for Global Leadership,* pp. 1–2, 13, 22.

90. David Nunan, "The Impact of English as a Global Language on Educational Policies and Practices in the Asia-Pacific Region," *TESOL Quarterly* 37, No. 4 (Winter 2003): 594, 606.

91. Nieto, *Affirming Diversity*, p. 380.

92. *Ibid.*, p. 381.

93. Indeed, if teachers fail to understand or accept a student's communication style, his/her "academic performance may be misdiagnosed or trapped in communication mismatches." Gay, *Culturally Responsive Teaching*, p. 78.

94. Nieto, *Affirming Diversity*, p. 380.

95. *Ibid.*

96. This idea came from Phyllis Ngai (interview). See also Savario J. Mungo, "Training Teachers for Cultural Diversity," in *Multicultural Education: A Global Approach*, edited by Don Bragaw and W. Scott Thomson (New York: American Forum for Global Education, 1992), p. 225; Merryfield (ed.), *Making Connections*, p. 189.

97. Kissock interview; also Cummings interview.

98. Ngai interview.

99. Kissock interview.

100. *Ibid.*

101. Gay, *Culturally Responsive Teaching*, p. 78.

102. Michael Byram, Adam Nichols, and David Stevens, "Introduction," in *Developing Intercultural Competence in Practice: Languages for Intercultural Communication and Education*, edited by Michael Byram, Adam Nichols, and David Stevens (Clevedon, UK: Multilingual Matters, 2001), p. 6.

103. *Ibid.*

104. Cummings interview.

105. Merryfield, "Pedagogy for Global Perspectives," p. 258.

106. Cummings interview.

107. Cummings interview.

108. Cummings interview.

109. Kissock interview.

110. Gay also notes that "teachers who genuinely care about students generate higher levels of all kinds of success than those who do not." Gay, *Culturally Responsive Teaching*, pp. 47–50, 214.

111. Kissock interview.

112. Cummings interview.

113. Ngai interview; Task Force for Transnational Competence, *Towards Transnational Competence*, p. 126; Marcelo M. Suarez-Orozco, "Rethinking Education in the Global Era," *Phi Delta Kappan* 87, No. 3 (November 2005): 212. Kissock (interview) identified partnership building as the most serious transnational skill gap among teachers.

114. Cochran-Smith, "Standing at the Crossroads," p. 9.

115. Merryfield, "Pedagogy for Global Perspectives," p. 258.

116. Kissock interview; Cummings interview.

117. Bragaw, "Global Imperative," p. 193; Giselle O. Martin-Kniep, "Assessing Teachers for Learner-centered Global Education," in *Preparing Teachers to Teach Global Perspectives: A Handbook for Teacher Educators*, edited by Merry M. Merryfield, Elaine Jarchow, and Sarah Picket (Thousand Oaks: Corwin Press, 1997), p. 102.

118. Task Force for Transnational Competence, *Towards Transnational Competence*, p. 125.

119. Merryfield, "Science-Technology-Society," p. 181; Merryfield, "Framework for Teacher Education," p. 9.

120. Pugh and Garcia, "Issues-Centered Education," p. 121.

121. James Banks, "Multicultural Education and School Reform," in *Multicultural Education: A Global Approach*, edited by Don Bragaw and W. Scott Thomson (New York: American Forum for Global Education, 1992), p. 315.

122. See Cochran-Smith, "Standing at the Crossroads," p. 9.

123. Kubow and Fossum, *Comparative Education*, p. 298.

124. Merryfield, "Learning from Current Practice," p. 3.

125. Merryfield (ed.), *Making Connections*, p. 239.

126. Karen Mundy and Lynn Murphy, "Transnational Advocacy, Global Civil Society? Emerging Evidence from the Field of Education," *Comparative Education Review* 45, No. 1 (2001): 86, 91, 97–99, 104–111, 121, 125.

127. *Ibid.,* 126; also see Sleeter, "Teaching Globalization," pp. 6–7.

128. http://www.campaignforeducation.org/aboutus/ Accessed August 3, 2008.

129. Massialas, "Issues-Centered Content Selection," p. 46.

130. Merryfield, "Pedagogy for Global Perspectives," p. 263. In cultivating transnational functional competence among K–12 students, "ongoing, responsible social action ... is the ultimate goal of all social issues instruction." Massialas, "Issues-Centered Content Selection," p. 49. In Geneva Gay's words, students must learn to "become change agents committed to promoting greater equality, justice, and power balances among ethnic groups." Gay, *Culturally Responsive Teaching,* pp. 34, 214.

131. Gay, *Culturally Responsive Teaching,* p. 34.

132. Merryfield (ed.), *Making Connections,* p. 189.

Notes for Chapter 6

1. Brustein interview, December 11, 2007.

2. Quoted in Brademas, Kolb, and Mockett, *Education for Global Leadership,* p. 6. Another survey respondent offered that U.S. MBA students are strong technically, but shortchanged cross-culturally and "linguistically deprived." A human-resource manager responded that MBA curricula are not designed to "create the global worker."

3. Bartlett, Ghoshal, and Birkinshaw, *Transnational Management,* p. 757.

4. Cited in Biddle, *Internationalization,* p. 59. In 2008, Duke's Fuqua School of Business announced that it was ready to become a transnational institution. Its transnational expansion plan called for the establishment of overseas campuses in partnership with the Graduate School of Management at St. Petersburg State University and other higher-education institutions in Dubai, Shanghai, New Delhi, and London. The objective of this initiative, according to Dean Blair Sheppard, is to transform the Fuqua School of Business into "the first truly global business school, shaped and driven by the fundamental issues of our time." Aisha Labi, "Duke's Business School Plans Overseas Campuses," *Chronicle of Higher Education,* September 26, 2008, p. A24.

5. See Rosenau, *et al., Cutting Edge of Globalization.*

6. Gretchen Lang, "Foreign Postings Beckon to the Young," *International Herald Tribune,* March 25–26, 2006, p. 18.

7. Brademas, Kolb, and Mockett, *Education for Global Leadership,* p. 22.

8. Marquardt and Berger, *Global Leaders for the 21st Century,* pp. 99–101.

9. Examples are the University of North Carolina's Kenan-Flagler Center for Sustainable Enterprise, the University of Michigan's Erb Institute for Global Sustainable Enterprise, and the Yale Center for Business and the Environment. Claudia H. Deutsch, "A Threat so Big, Academics Try Collaboration," *New York Times,* December 25, 2007, p. C2.

10. See, for instance, Leigh S. Shaffer, "Maximizing Human Capital by Developing Multicultural Competence," *NACADA Journal* 18, No. 2 (1998): 22; Joe Nocera, "China Needs Old Boys with M.B.A.'s," *New York Times,* April 19, 2008, pp. B1, B8. In December 2008, recruiters from 27 of China's financial firms aimed to fill 170 senior risk-management positions with "people with a global view" during a transnational recruiting tour. Jimmy Wang, "Chinese Recruiters Look Abroad for Diversity and Expertise," *New York Times,* December 26, 2008, pp. B1, B6.

11. Brademas, Kolb, and Mockett, *Education for Global Leadership,* p. 6.

12. Task Force for Transnational Competence, *Towards Transnational Competence,* pp. 104–105.

13. Peter H. Koehn, "Peaceful and Sustainable Development? Middle-Management Entrepreneurship and Transnational Competence in China." *East Asia* 24, No. 3 (Fall 2007): 259–262.

14. Erik Vance, "College Graduates Lack Key Skills, Report Says," *Chronicle of Higher Education,* February 2, 2007, p. A30; Karin Fischer, "'Flat World' Lessons for Real-World Students," *Chronicle of Higher Education,* November 2, 2007.

15. Marquardt and Horvath, *Global Teams,* p. 102.

16. Allan Bird and May Mukuda, "Expatriates in Their Own Home: A New Twist in the Human Resource Management Strategies of Japanese MNCs," *Human Resource Management* 28, No. 4 (Winter 1989): 449.

17. Ron Turko, "Experience with Africa Business Schools," (memorandum to Joyce Cacho and others, 19 March 2008), p. 1.

18. See Koehn, "Peaceful and Sustainable Development?" pp. 256–259, 263.

19. The term "transpatriate" more accurately than "expatriate" reflects the contemporary transnational firm's practice of deploying employees "from all parts of the world … to all other parts of the world." Adler and Bartholomew, "Managing Globally Competent People," p. 60.

20. See Brademas, Kolb, and Mockett, *Education for Global Leadership*, p. 19. Another survey of international-business representatives showed that small-, medium-, and large-scale company leaders see the need for improved international expertise across the board. Richard W. Moxon, Elizabeth A.C. O'Shea, Mollie Brown, and Christoffer M. Escher, "Changing U.S. Business Needs for International Expertise," in *Changing Perspectives on International Education*, edited by Patrick O'Meara, Howard D. Mehlinger, and Roxana M. Newman (Bloomington: Indiana University Press, 2001), pp. 143, 151.

21. Edwin L. Miller, "Preparing Globally Competent Business Students," in *Educational Exchange and Global Competence*, edited by Richard D. Lambert (Portland, ME: Council on International Educational Exchange, 1994), p. 90.

22. Moxon, , "Changing U.S. Business Needs for International Expertise," p. 153.

23. See Biddle, *Internationalization*, p. 60.

24. TC education could be integrated, for instance, in the key MBA course modules being developed by the International Finance Corporation's Global Business School Network for the Ghana Institute of Management and Public Administration. See Turko, "Africa Business Schools," p. 2.

25. John Tagliabue, "In Hiring, Europeans Go Global," *New York Times*, June 4, 2008, p. C10; Louise Story, "Seeking Leaders, U.S. Companies Think Globally," *New York Times*, December 12, 2007, p. A24. The business consequences of lack of transnational analytic competence on the part of employees can be serious. For instance, at Vesta Corporation, a multinational electronic-payment firm headquartered in Portland, cultural misunderstandings have delayed business deals and caused tensions among workers with different backgrounds according to CEO Douglas M. Fieldhouse. Fischer, "'Flat World' Lessons."

26. Gretchen Weber, "English Rules," *Workforce Management* 83 (May 2004): 49.

27. John Salt, "The Business of International Migration," in *International Migration into the 21st Century*, edited by M.A.B. Siddique (Cheltenham, UK: Edward Elgar, 2001), p. 95.

28. Lang, "Foreign Postings," p. 18.

29. Salt, "Business of International Migration," p. 96.

30. Lang, "Foreign Postings," p. 18; Bird and Mukuda, "Expatriates in Their Own Home," p. 448.

31. Task Force for Transnational Competence, *Towards Transnational Competence*, pp. 27, 36.

32. Salt, "Business of International Migration," pp. 95–96.

33. Thomas L. Friedman, "Learning to Keep Learning," *New York Times*, December 13, 2006, p. A33; Marquardt and Berger, *Global Leaders*, p. 103.

34. Marquardt and Berger, *Global Leaders*, p. 172; Shaffer, "Maximizing Human Capital," p. 24.

35. Bird and Mukuda, "Expatriates in Their Own Home," p. 444; J. Stewart Black, Allen J. Morrison, and Hal B. Gregersen, *Global Explorers: The Next Generation of Leaders* (New York: Routledge, 1999), p. 169.

36. Marquardt and Horvath, *Global Teams*, p. 13.

37. Charlick, interview.

38. Black, Morrison, and Gregersen, *Global Explorers*, pp. 168–169.

39. Brademas, Kolb, and Mockett, *Education for Global Leadership*, p. 6.

40. *Ibid.*

41. *Ibid.*, p. 47.

42. *Ibid.*, p. 19; Nicholas, Radja, and Schembri, "Professionalizing Education Programmes," p. 163.

43. Perrow, *Next Catastrophe*, pp. 258–259, 301.

44. Black, Morrison, and Gregersen, *Global Explorers*, pp. 158–159; Shaffer, "Maximizing Human Capital," p. 21; Charlick, interview.

45. Along with foreign-language proficiency, "critical-thinking skills" (including being able to distinguish the decisive parts of a proposition, discerning fact from fiction, and knowing how to ask the right questions) are at the "top" of William Brustein's list for MBA graduates. Brustein interview.

46. Juma and Yee-Cheong, *Innovation*, p. 128.

47. Marquardt and Berger, *Global Leaders*, p. 19. Learning to employ networking technology to keep abreast of emerging economic opportunities is a particularly valuable component in the education of business professionals in low-income countries. Juma and Yee-Cheong, *Innovation*, p. 48.

48. On the concept of organizational culture, see Geert Hofstede, *Culture's Consequences: Comparing Values, Behaviors, Institutions, and Organizations across Nations*, 2nd edition (Thousand Oaks: Sage Publications, 2001), p. 391.

49. See Margaret E. Alldredge and Kevin J. Nilan, "3M's Leadership Competency Model: An Internally Developed Solution," *Human Resource Management* 39, Nos. 2 and 3 (Summer/Fall 2000): 139, 142–143; Michael G. Harvey and David A. Griffith, "Developing Effective Intercultural Relationships: The Importance of Communication Strategies," *Thunderbird International Business Review* 44, No. 4 (July–August, 2002): 461, 465.

50. Nicholas, Radja, and Schembri, "Professionalizing Education Programmes," pp. 162–163.

51. The Thunderbird graduates also reported that they used cultural knowledge more frequently than foreign-language skills in their professional work (44 percent indicated "daily"). Christine U. Grosse, "The Competitive Advantage of Foreign Languages and Cultural Knowledge," *Modern Language Journal* 88, No. 3 (2004): 359, 363–364.

52. Moran, Harris, and Moran, *Global Leadership Strategies*, p. 29.

53. Alldredge and Nilan, "3M's Leadership Competency Model," p. 142; Shaffer, "Maximizing Human Capital," p. 22; Moran, Harris, and Moran, *Global Leadership Strategies*, p. 241.

54. Bird and Mukuda, "Human Resource Strategies of Japanese MNCs," p. 448.

55. The classic work by Geert Hofstede (*Culture's Consequences*) posits five binary dimensions on which national cultural differences affect business relationships: power distance, uncertainty avoidance, individualism versus collectivism, masculinity versus femininity, and long-term versus short-term orientation. For a critique of Hofstede's scheme based on postcolonial sensibility, see Martin Fougere and Agneta Moulettes, "The Construction of the Modern West and the Backward Rest: Studying the Discourse of Hofstede's *Culture's Consequences*," *Journal of Multicultural Discourses* 2, No. 1 (2007): 1–18. On the limited utility of essentialized and static conceptions of culture, see Wang, "Intercultural Dialogue and Understanding," p. 58.

56. Moran, Harris, and Moran, *Global Leadership Strategies*, p. 252.

57. Brustein interview.

58. Even Hofstede (*Culture's Consequences*, p. 443) acknowledges that one "should proceed with utmost modesty in using data about national cultures to predict the behavior of individuals, because values and talents vary widely within cultures...."

59. Moran, Harris, and Moran, *Global Leadership Strategies*, p. 30; Dwivedi, *et al.*, "Understanding Different Management Paradigms," p. 332.

60. In particular, given "the current global environment where India and China are becoming strong emerging economies it becomes a strategic necessity to understand these management styles in order to foster innovation and superior, effective operations." Dwivedi, *et al.*, "Understanding Different Management Paradigms," pp. 320, 334. On the dynamic contribution to economic development of "East Asian entrepreneurship" and management capacity for pragmatic synthesis, see Geert Hofstede and Michael H. Bond, "The Confucius Connection: From Cultural Roots to Economic Growth," *Organizational Dynamics* 16 (Spring 1988): 17–21.

61. Kwok Leung, Rabi S. Bhagat, Nancy R. Buchan, Miriam Erez, and Christina B. Gibson, "Culture and International Business: Recent Advances and Their Implications for Future Research," *Journal of International Business Studies* 36, No. 4 (July 2005): 364–365.

62. Ibid., pp. 365–366. For a discussion of the moderating influence of team cohesion and technological uncertainty, see pp. 366–368.

63. Marquardt and Berger, *Global Leaders*, p. 50.

64. Marquardt and Horvath, *Global Teams*, p. 102.

65. Moran, Harris, and Moran, *Global Leadership Strategies*, pp. 252, 288–289.

66. See Black, Morrison, and Gregersen, *Global Explorers,* pp. 122–124; Marquardt and Berger, *Global Leaders,* p. 105. Jan Selmer investigated the extent to which Swedish top managers could identify the work values of Hong Kong subsidiary middle managers with respect to goals and interests, rewards, and interpersonal relationships. The results showed that the top managers demonstrated considerable transnational empathy in key value areas and serious misperceptions in others. Jan Selmer, "What Do Expatriate Managers Know About Their HCN Subordinates' Work Values: Swedish Executives in Hong Kong," *Journal of Transnational Management Development* 2, No. 3 (1996): 5–14.

67. Moran, Harris, and Moran, *Global Leadership Strategies,* p. 236.

68. *Ibid.,* p. 122.

69. *Ibid.,* p. 29; Shaffer, "Maximizing Human Capital," p. 22.

70. Carlos E. Cortes and Louise C. Wilkinson, "Developing and Implementing a Multicultural Vision," in *Contemporary Leadership and Intercultural Competence: Exploring the Cross-Cultural Dynamics Within Organizations,* edited by Michael A. Moodian (Los Angeles: Sage, 2009), p. 28.

71. *Ibid.*; Marquardt and Berger, *Global Leaders,* p. 19; Black, Morrison, and Gregersen, *Global Explorers,* p. 127; Moran, Harris, and Moran, *Global Leadership Strategies,* pp. 252, 288–289. The ability to manage hybrid identities and adapt successfully to transnational conditions demonstrated by many Chinese transmigrants offers one example for business students to consider in connection with developing transnational emotional competence. See Bernard P. Wong, *The Chinese in Silicon Valley: Globalization, Social Networks, and Ethnic Identity* (Lanham: Rowman & Littlefield, 2006).

72. Moran, Harris, and Moran, *Global Leadership Strategies,* p. 241; Nancy J. Adler, *From Boston to Beijing: Managing with a World View* (Cincinnati, OH: South-Western, 2002), p. 99.

73. Christopher A. Bartlett and Sumantra Ghoshal, "Tap Your Subsidiaries for Global Reach," in *Transnational Management: Text, Cases, and Readings in Cross-Border Management,* edited by Christopher A. Bartlett, Sumantra Ghoshal, and Julian Birkinshaw (Boston: McGraw Hill, 2004), p. 418.

74. Marquardt and Berger, *Global Leaders,* p. 19.

75. Cited in Friedman, "Learning to Keep Learning," p. A33.

76. Adler and Boyacigiller, "Global Management in the 21st Century," p. 551.

77. Moran, Harris, and Moran, *Global Leadership Strategies,* p. 241.

78. Friedman, *The World Is Flat,* p. 545.

79. See Bergman, *et al.,* "Exploration of Future Service Innovations," pp. 121, 126, 130, 135, 137; Dwivedi, *et al.,* "Understanding Different Management Paradigms," pp. 333-334.

80. Bartlett, Ghoshal, and Birkinshaw, *Transnational Management,* pp. 457–458.

81. Adler and Bartholomew, "Managing Globally Competent People," p. 58.

82. Bartlett, Ghoshal, and Birkinshaw, *Transnational Management,* pp. 457, 461, 670–671.

83. Friedman, *The World Is Flat,* p. 439.

84. Scott E. Page, interview, in Dreifus, "Diversity = Productivity," p. D2.

85. Moran, Harris, and Moran, *Global Leadership Strategies,* pp. 30, 228, 248; Marquardt and Horvath, *Global Teams,* pp. 10, 102.

86. Barbara F. Schaetti, Sheila J. Ramsey, and Gordon C. Watanabe, "From Intercultural Knowledge to Intercultural Competence: Developing an Intercultural Practice," in *Contemporary Leadership and Intercultural Competence: Exploring the Cross-Cultural Dynamics Within Organizations,* edited by Michael A. Moodian (Los Angeles: Sage, 2009), p. 134.

87. Marquardt and Berger, *Global Leaders,* p. 105.

88. See Story, "Seeking Leaders," pp. A1, A24.

89. Marquardt and Berger, *Global Leaders,* p. 176.

90. *Ibid.*

91. Marquardt and Horvath, *Global Teams,* p. 19.

92. Brustein interview.

93. Weber, "English Rules," p. 49. However, when recruiting foreign nationals for headquarters assignments, Japanese companies prefer candidates who are proficient in Japanese or "at least comfortable enough with the language that they could acquire proficiency during their time in Japan." Bird and Mukuda, "Expatriates in Their Own Home," pp. 444, 448. In contrast, employees of 45 different nationalities and almost as many first languages worked at Sony's Berlin headquarters in 2004. One business observer concludes that, in this case at least, "the cost and effort associated with trying to teach everyone German

when a lot of them will be moving on to other assignments in a matter of months probably doesn't make a lot of sense." Cited in Weber, "English Rules," p. 49.

94. Sandra L. McKay, *Teaching English As an International Language: Rethinking Goals and Approaches* (Oxford: Oxford University Press, 2002), p. 5. On the preponderant use of English on the Web and among Internet users, see John Paolillo, "Language Diversity on the Internet," in *Measuring Linguistic Diversity on the Internet* (Montreal: UNESCO Institute for Statistics, 2005), pp. 57, 60.

95. Cited in Francis X. Rocca, "Educating Europe's Best and Brightest," *Chronicle of Higher Education,* June 21, 2002, pp. A43–A44.

96. As a consequence of more students around the world learning to conduct business in English, "its position as the language of commerce solidifies." Weber, "English Rules," p. 49. English has held or continues to hold the status of an official language in more than seventy countries and is a required foreign language in many others. McKay, *Teaching English As an International Language,* pp. 5–11. In the Asia-Pacific region, "the age at which English is a compulsory subject in most of the countries has shifted down in recent years, a shift that is predicated on the importance of English as a global language." Nunan, "Impact of English As a Global Language," p. 605; also see pp. 595–604.

97. Shaffer, "Maximizing Human Capital," p. 24; Weber, "English Rules," p. 48.

98. Brustein interview.

99. At present, however, English remains the target language in both countries. Weber, "English Rules," p. 49. English textbooks are popular at China's universities, "especially in the disciplines of medicine, engineering, business management, and public management." Kinglun Ngok, "Globalization and Higher Education Reform in China," in *Globalization: Educational Research, Change and Reform,* edited by Nicholas S. Pang (Hong Kong: Chinese University Press, 2006), p. 89.

100. Grosse, "Competitive Advantage," pp. 356–357, 363.

101. Brustein interview. He adds that graduates of MBA programs who cannot converse in the mother tongue of their business colleagues "are going to lose out in terms of being able to get into the kinds of conversations and pick up the nuances that those who do have that proficiency will be able to do."

102. Weber, "English Rules," pp. 48, 50.

103. Most notably, see Brademas, Kolb, and Mockett, *Education for Global Leadership,* p. 2; also see Moran, Harris, and Moran, *Global Leadership Strategies,* p. 289. The Committee for Economic Development's report adds that the employees of firms operating in the United States will need second-language skills "to serve culturally diverse domestic customers." Brademas, Kolb, and Mockett, *Education for Global Leadership,* p. 11. Robert Charlick (interview) reports that business recruiters expect graduates to arrive with foreign-language capability since many firms are unwilling to invest in language training. Also see Weber, "English Rules," p. 50.

104. Cited in Weber, "English Rules," p. 48; also see p. 47.

105. Miller, "Preparing Globally Competent Business Students," p. 96.

106. See Schneider, "Transpatriate Success Factors," pp. 13, 28, 74.

107. Weber, "English Rules," p. 50. Miller concludes that "the faculty must decide about the advisability of requiring students to acquire fluency in another language in contrast to taking additional internationally oriented courses." Miller, "Preparing Globally Competent Business Students," p. 96. In this connection, it is relevant to note that the CIBER business-school faculty who responded in the study conducted by Moxon and colleagues gave foreign-language proficiency the lowest average rating of the eight skills assessed for importance both for U.S. managers overseas and for international managers working in U.S. offices. Moxon, *et al.,* "Changing U.S. Business Needs for International Expertise," pp. 149–150.

108. Also see Weber, "English Rules," p. 50; Bird and Mukuda, "Expatriates in Their Own Home," p. 449; Moran, Harris, and Moran, *Global Leadership Strategies,* p. 36.

109. Shaffer, "Maximizing Human Capital," pp. 22–24.

110. Also see Moran, Harris, and Moran, *Global Leadership Strategies,* p. 36; Shaffer, "Maximizing Human Capital," p. 23.

111. Marquardt and Horvath, *Global Teams,* p. 32.

112. Moran, Harris, and Moran, *Global Leadership Strategies,* p. 29.

113. Marquardt and Horvath, *Global Teams,* p. 32.

114. Shaffer, "Maximizing Human Capital," p. 23.

115. See Phyllis B. Ngai and Peter H. Koehn, "Cross-Cultural Management: The Pitfalls of Unspoken Signals," *World Executive's Digest* (January 1998): 49–50.

116. Adler, *From Boston to Beijing*, pp. 86–87.

117. Harvey and Griffith, "Developing Effective Intercultural Relationships," p. 472.

118. Marquardt and Horvath, *Global Teams*, pp. 32–33, 55, 94.

119. Bird and Mukuda, "Expatriates in Their Own Home," p. 444.

120. Adler and Boyacigiller, "Global Management in the 21st Century," p. 551.

121. Adler and Bartholomew, "Managing Globally Competent People," p. 53; Adler and Boyacigiller, "Global Management in the 21st Century," p. 551. Both management practitioners and CIBER faculty ranked interpersonal skills highest in importance for work in overseas subsidiaries and in the multinational home office in the Moxon, *et al.* study ("Changing U.S. Business Needs for International Expertise," pp. 148–150).

122. Alldredge and Nilan, "3M's Leadership Competency Model," p. 139; Roy J. Lewicki, Daniel J. McAllister, and Robert J. Bies, "Trust and Distrust: New Relationships and Realities," *Academy of Management Review* 23, No. 3 (1998): 438.

123. Alldredge and Nilan, "3M's Leadership Competency Model," p. 139. Increasingly, moreover, the performance of multinational teams is "critical to success in the global marketplace." Brademas, Kolb, and Mockett, *Education for Global Leadership*, p. 6.

124. McCloud, "Globalisation in Higher Education," p. 7.

125. Vance, "College Graduates Lack Key Skills," p. A30.

126. Marquardt and Berger, *Global Leaders for the 21st Century*, p. 19.

127. Moran, Harris, and Moran, *Global Leadership Strategies*, p. 29; Bartlett, Ghoshal, and Birkinshaw, *Transnational Management*, p. 670.

128. Black, Morrison, and Gregersen, *Global Explorers*, p. 124; Lewicki, McAllister, and Bies, "Trust and Distrust," p. 438. Marquardt and Horvath (*Global Teams*, p. 82) maintain that "the successful global team requires a high level of trust among its members."

129. Lewicki, McAllister, and Bies, "Trust and Distrust," p. 439 [their emphasis]. These authors add that creating and maintaining trust in contemporary business relationships requires considerable skill because "the challenges of speed, quality, and global reach, which require trust, also have precipitated distrust, through corporate restructuring, downsizing, and fundamental violations of the psychological contracts connecting individuals with organizations."

130. *Ibid.*, p. 446.

131. Marquardt and Horvath, *Global Teams*, p. 82. Mobile project managers, who might move four times a year, have little time to form social relationships. Lang, "Foreign Postings Beckon to the Young," p. 18.

132. Marquardt and Horvath (*Global Teams*, p. 82) emphasize the need to create "swift trust" because members of transnational business teams usually "do not have a chance to build trust in a gradual, cumulative fashion." Also see Moran, Harris, and Moran, *Global Leadership Strategies*, p. 241.

133. Black, Morrison, and Gregersen, *Global Explorers*, pp. 124, 127. In his interview, Brustein pointed to the smile that comes across people's faces when they encounter a foreign counterpart who has taken the time to study their language, culture, or history. Also see Brademas, Kolb, and Mockett, *Education for Global Leadership*, p. 7.

134. Lewicki, McAllister, and Bies, "Trust and Distrust," p. 446; Harvey and Griffith, "Developing Effective Intercultural Relationships," p. 464.

135. Marquardt and Berger, *Global Leaders for the 21st Century*, p. 105.

136. Harvey and Griffith, "Developing Effective Intercultural Relationships," p. 460.

137. Task Force for Transnational Competence, *Towards Transnational Competence*, p. 39; Moran, Harris, and Moran, *Global Leadership Strategies*, pp. 228, 241.

138. Marquardt and Horvath, *Global Teams*, p. 16.

139. The ability to work smoothly with local staff in overseas subsidiaries is a widely desired functional skill. See, for instance, Bird and Mukuda, "Expatriates in Their Own Home," p. 444.

140. Bird and Mukuda, "Expatriates in Their Own Home," p. 448.

141. Tagliabue, "In Hiring, Europeans Go Global," pp. C1, C10.

142. Foreign-born CEOs, including three from India and one each from Morocco and Egypt, ran 15

of the top 100 U.S. firms in 2007. Story, "Seeking Leaders," p. A24. On upper-echelon prospects in head offices for non-Japanese managers, see Bird and Mukuda, "Expatriates in Their Own Home," p. 451.

143. In the Netherlands, about half of all board members are not Dutch. Tagliabue, "Europeans Go Global," p. C10.

144. Bartlett, Ghoshal, and Birkinshaw, *Transnational Management,* p. 669.

145. The IMF's diversity management strategy aims to maximize the skill mix present among its members and workforce; valuable approaches for transnational functional-competence learners include maintaining a balanced distribution of diverse staff in all grades and career streams, equal treatment, zero tolerance for discrimination, valuing and respecting each team member, provision of guidance, support, and constructive feedback, and rewards based on individual effort and team performance. Richard D. Erb, "Diversity at the IMF" (presentation at the University of Montana, April 2, 2007). Also see Adler and Boyacigiller, "Global Management in the 21st Century," p. 551; Adler, *From Boston to Beijing,* pp. 138–140; Christopher A. Bartlett and Sumantra Ghoshal, *Managing Across Borders: The Transnational Solution* (Boston: Harvard Business School Press, 1998), p. 76.

146. Crandall and Mensah, "Crisis Management and Sustainable Development," p. 20.

147. Marquardt and Horvath, *Global Teams,* pp. 19, 47, 51. Robert Moran and colleagues (*Global Leadership Strategies,* p. 3) maintain that managing cultural diversity skillfully is a "business imperative."

148. Bartlett and Ghoshal, *Managing Across Borders,* p. 76.

149. Marquardt and Horvath, *Global Teams,* pp. 55, 103-104; Moran, Harris, and Moran, *Global Leadership Strategies,* p. 252.

150. Parnell, "Sustainable Strategic Management," p. 41.

151. Crandall and Mensah, "Crisis Management and Sustainable Development," p. 31.

152. Emily Eakin, "How to Save the World? Treat It Like a Business," *New York Times,* December 20, 2003, p. A19. For instance, the functionally competent graduate of a TC-focused MBA program will work on finding microfinance solutions to the Millenium Development Goal (MDG) challenge of providing safe drinking water. See Deutsch, "A Threat so Big, Academics Try Collaboration," p. C1.

Notes for Chapter 7

1. Shuman, *et al.,* "ABET 'Professional Skills,'" p. 43.

2. Hirleman, interview, November 30, 2007.

3. William M. Sangster, "Engineering Education Faces the Challenge of Internationalization," in *Educational Exchange and Global Competence,* edited by Richard D. Lambert (Portland, ME: Council on International Educational Exchange, 1994), pp. 121–122. The traditional engineering method involves drawing a boundary around a problem and applying mathematical theories to find a solution. Gary L. Downey, *et al.* (12 co-authors), "The Globally Competent Engineer: Working Effectively with People Who Define Problems Differently," *Journal of Engineering Education* 95, No. 2 (April 2006): 108.

4. Downey, *et al.,* "The Globally Competent Engineer," p. 109.

5. National Academy of Engineering, *Educating the Engineer of 2020,* p. 24. Gretchen Kalonji argues that the early years of the engineering curriculum too often are disconnected from student interests, passions, and imaginations as well as "from the broader picture of what engineering education could be, and should be, about." Gretchen Kalonji, "Capturing the Imagination: High-Priority Reforms for Engineering Educators," in National Academy of Engineering, *Educating the Engineer of 2020: Adapting Engineering Education to the New Century* (Washington, DC: National Academies Press, 2005), p. 147.

6. B.I. Allert, D.L. Atkinson, E.A. Groll, and E.D. Hirleman, "Making the Case for Global Engineering: Building Foreign Language Collaborations for Designing, Implementing, and Assessing Programs," *Online Journal of Engineering Education* 2, No. 2 (2007); Downey, *et al.,* "The Globally Competent Engineer," p. 107; Allan and Chisholm, "Achieving Engineering Competencies," p. 151. Hirleman (interview) believes, however, that most engineering students "still don't quite see how the world is changing so fast, see the effects of globalization, and see how important it is that they very seamlessly function on international teams across large divides in culture." Hirleman's assessment is supported by the small percentage of engineering students in the United States who seek international enrollments (less than 3 percent in 2003) and in Europe who participate in ERASMUS programs (1 percent). Downey, *et al.,* "The

Globally Competent Engineer," p. 113. On the other hand, 37 percent of the international students in the United States in 2006 were studying science, engineering, technology, or mathematics. Peggy Blumenthal, Executive Vice President, Institute of International Education, report presented at the American Council on Education meeting, December 5, 2007.

The International Federation of Engineering Education Societies (IFEES), founded in 2006 by the American Society for Engineering Education, is "a global engineering education network that supports and enables interconnectivity between engineering education societies throughout the world." http://www.asee.org/international/index.cfm (accessed October 30, 2007).

7. John Grandin, transcript of telephonic interview with Peter Koehn, November 30, 2007.

8. Allert, *et al.,* "Case for Global Engineering."

9. National Academy of Engineering, *Educating the Engineer of 2020,* p. xi; also see p. 4.

10. *Ibid.,* p. 1.

11. The two main international systems for the professional registration of engineers are the Engineers Mobility Forum, associated with the International Professional Engineer (IntPE), and the European Federation of National Engineering Associations, associated with the European Engineer (EurEng). Allan and Chisholm, "Achieving Engineering Competencies," pp. 146–147, 151.

12. Juma and Yee-Cheong, *Innovation,* p. 90.

13. Somini Sengupta, "Skills Gap Threatens Technology Boom in India," *New York Times,* October 17, 2006, pp. A1, A6.

14. Gary L. Downey, "Are Engineers Losing Control of Technology? From 'Problem Solving' to 'Problem Definition and Solution' in Engineering Education," *Chemical Engineering Research and Design* 83, No. A6 (2005): 587.

15. Juma and Yee-Cheong, *Innovation,* p. 95.

16. Downey, "'Problem Definition and Solution' in Engineering Education," pp. 584–585, 589–590.

17. Downey, *et al.,* "Globally Competent Engineer," p. 110 [their emphasis].

18. Indeed, educators in chemical, civil, mechanical, and electrical engineering "around the world are now working hard to re-imagine the field in response to rapid technological change." Downey, "'Problem Definition and Solution' in Engineering Education," pp. 583–584; also see National Academy of Engineering, *Educating the Engineer of 2020,* p. xi.

19. Downey, "'Problem Definition and Solution' in Engineering Education," p. 592; also see Allan and Chisholm, "Achieving Engineering Competencies," p. 148. Hirleman (interview) envisions "three dimensional engineers" that possess technical, professional, and transnational or global skills. In our treatment, professional analytic competence encompasses transnational and other interpersonal skills.

20. National Academy of Engineering, *Educating the Engineer of 2020,* p. 55.

21. This includes identifying and analyzing areas of disagreement and conflict in the technical perspectives of engineers (and nonengineers). Downey, "'Problem Definition and Solution' in Engineering Education," p. 593.

22. Katehi, "Global Engineer," pp. 152–155.

23. Shuman, *et al.,* "ABET 'Professional Skills,'" p. 41 [their emphasis]. We prefer "technical" skills to the "hard" skills terminology used in the Shuman, *et al.,* article to avoid the diminishing insinuation of some educators that other ("professional") skills are "soft."

Sustainability is a major theme in Worchester Polytechnic Institute's global-studies program for engineers. Carlson, "Global Approach to Engineering," p. A33.

24. Allert, *et al.,* "Case for Global Engineering;" National Academy of Engineering, *Educating the Engineer of 2020,* p. 8.

25. Complexity "is the enemy of both reliability and security, engineers are fond of saying. The more complex the system, the greater the chance of the unexpected interaction of components, even when they are not faulty in themselves." Perrow, *Next Catastrophe,* p. 260; also pp. 295, 301. In this work, Perrow explicates the risks of cascading failure in the chemical, nuclear, electric-power, and IT realms.

26. Downey, "'Problem Definition and Solution' in Engineering Education," p. 590.

27. Downey, *et al.,* "Globally Competent Engineer," p. 109.

28. Katehi, "Global Engineer," p. 154; Juma and Yee-Cheong, *Innovation,* p. 43.

29. Downey, "'Problem Definition and Solution' in Engineering Education," p. 591.

30. Shuman, *et al.*, "ABET 'Professional Skills,'" pp. 41, 44, 46. Motivated to enable and facilitate professional mobility by the Bologna Declaration, engineering educators in Europe have expanded the professional content of curricula. Downey, *et al.*, "Globally Competent Engineer," p. 109.

31. Shuman, *et al.*, "ABET 'Professional Skills,'" p. 46; Allert, *et al.*, "Case for Global Engineering." For instance, the TC curriculum sharpens student awareness that "the very act of drawing a boundary around a problem has non-technical, or political dimensions, depending on who controls the definition, because someone gains a little power and someone loses a little power." Downey, *et al.*, "Globally Competent Engineer," p. 115.

32. Downey, "'Problem Definition and Solution' in Engineering Education," p. 591.

33. Juma and Yee-Cheong, *Innovation*, p. 157.

34. National Academy of Engineering, *Educating the Engineer of 2020*, p. 11.

35. Shaw and Kim, *Education for Sustainable Development Practice*, p. 65.

36. Shuman, *et al.*, "ABET 'Professional Skills,'" p. 47; Grandin interview; Allan and Chisholm, "Achieving Engineering Competencies," p. 151; Allert, *et al.*, "Case for Global Engineering;" Downey, *et al.*, "Globally Competent Engineer," pp. 113–114.

37. Downey, "'Problem Definition and Solution' in Engineering Education," p. 593.

38. Hirleman interview.

39. Allan and Chisholm, "Achieving Engineering Competencies," p. 146.

40. Downey, "'Problem Definition and Solution' in Engineering Education," p. 590; National Academy of Engineering, *Educating the Engineer of 2020*, pp. 10, 52.

41. Allan and Chisholm, "Achieving Engineering Competencies," p. 146.

42. *Ibid.*, pp. 147–148; Carlson, "Global Approach to Engineering," pp. A33, A36. For instance, interdisciplinary courses at Colorado School of Mines and Virginia Tech University use cultural anthropology to inform engineering-design methodology. Allert, *et al.*, "Case for Global Engineering." Acquiring knowledge from engineers and nonengineers from other countries also helps to illuminate different approaches to technical engineering work. Downey, *et al.*, "Globally Competent Engineer," p. 110.

43. Allan and Chisholm, "Achieving Engineering Competencies," pp. 148–149, 151; Allert, *et al.*, "Case for Global Engineering."

44. Tammo Steenhuis, email response to Koehn's interview questions, November 20, 2007.

45. Allert, *et al.*, "Case for Global Engineering."

46. Downey, *et al.*, "Globally Competent Engineer," p. 110.

47. *Ibid.*; also see pp. 108, 114.

48. *Ibid.*, p. 108.

49. Allan and Chisholm, "Achieving Engineering Competencies," p. 148; Allert, *et al.*, "Case for Global Engineering;" Downey, *et al.*, "Globally Competent Engineer," p. 113.

50. Steenhuis interview.

51. Allert, *et al.*, "Case for Global Engineering."

52. *Ibid.*

53. Downey, "'Problem Definition and Solution' in Engineering Education," p. 588; also see National Academy of Engineering, *Educating the Engineer of 2020*, p. 10.

54. National Academy of Engineering, *Educating the Engineer of 2020*, p. 28.

55. *Ibid.*, p. xi.

56. Spencer Michels, "Engineers Lend Technical Aid to Developing Countries," PBS Online NewsHour Report, December 7, 2007 (http://www.pbs.org/newshour/bb/science/july-dec07/engineers_12-07.html, accessed May 16, 2008).

57. Downey *et al.*, "Globally Competent Engineer," p. 119.

58. *Ibid.*, p. 109.

59. *Ibid.*, p. 114; also see p. 109.

60. *Ibid.*, p. 110.

61. *Ibid.*, p. 115.

62. The mapping process includes identifying particularly contentious issues. Downey, "'Problem Definition and Solution' in Engineering Education," p. 591.

63. Downey, *et al.*, "Globally Competent Engineer," p. 115.

64. Allan and Chisholm, "Achieving Engineering Competencies," pp. 147, 151. Yating Chang (interview) adds that it is important that U.S. engineering students learn empathy skills so that when they are confronted by situations conditioned by poverty or famine in low-income countries, they realize that they are not dealing with an isolated issue, but with a global issue and a global challenge.

65. Hirleman interview.

66. *Ibid.*

67. Downey, *et al.*, "Globally Competent Engineer," p. 114.

68. Grandin interview; Shuman, Besterfield-Sacre, and McGourty, "ABET 'Professional Skills,'" p. 46; National Academy of Engineering, *Educating the Engineer of 2020*, p. 10.

69. Downey, "'Problem Definition and Solution' in Engineering Education," p. 591. Limitations include indeterminacy and uncertainty. Dean, "Handle with Care," p. D4.

70. This is an explicit objective of the University of Michigan's Program in Global Engineering. Downey, *et al.*, "Globally Competent Engineer," pp. 108, 119. Also see Allert, *et al.*, "Case for Global Engineering;" Michels, "Engineers Lend Technical Aid."

71. Downey, *et al.*, "Globally Competent Engineer," pp. 110–111.

72. Gary L. Downey and Juan C. Lucena, "Engineering Selves: Hiring In to a Contested Field of Education," in *Cyborgs & Citadels: Anthropological Interventions in Emerging Sciences and Technologies,* edited by Gary L. Downey and Joseph Dumit (Santa Fe, NM: School of American Research Press, 1997), p. 139.

73. Downey, *et al.*, "Globally Competent Engineer," p. 115.

74. Dan Hirleman, quoted in Carlson, "Global Approach to Engineering," p. A33.

75. Downey, "'Problem Definition and Solution' in Engineering Education," p. 585. Downey (p. 587) suggests, however, that many engineering programs, particularly in the global South, no longer highly value the development of innovative skills.

76. National Academy of Engineering, *Educating the Engineer of 2020*, p. 44 [emphasis in original].

77. Allert, *et al.*, "Case for Global Engineering."

78. Chang interview.

79. Chang interview. In Bustan, Afghanistan, for instance, villagers and members of the Afghan American diaspora constructed a school using traditional building techniques coupled with new roofing technology contributed by Engineers Without Borders. Jennifer M. Brinkerhoff, "Contributions of Digital Diasporas to Governance Reconstruction in Fragile States: Potential and Promise," in *Governance in Post-Conflict Societies: Rebuilding Fragile States,* edited by Derick W. Brickerhoff (London: Routledge, 2007), p. 192.

80. Allan and Chisholm, "Achieving Engineering Competencies," p. 151.

81. *Ibid.*, p. 148.

82. Hirleman interview.

83. Downey, "'Problem Definition and Solution' in Engineering Education," p. 591; Katehi, "Global Engineer," p. 152.

84. Including centers in Namibia, Costa Rica, Ireland, Hong Kong, Denmark, and Australia. Shuman, Besterfield-Sacre, and McGourty, "ABET 'Professional Skills,'" pp. 46–47.

85. Juma and Yee-Cheong, *Innovation*, p. 86.

86. *Ibid.*

87. Hirleman interview.

88. Shuman, Besterfield-Sacre, and McGourty, "ABET 'Professional Skills,'" pp. 41, 44. Engineering schools remain challenged to improve the oral and written communication skills of all graduates. Vest, "Educating Engineers for 2020," p. 160.

89. Grandin interview. About 20 percent of URI's incoming engineering students participate in the international engineering program. Most elements of URI's five-year program have been adopted at the University of Connecticut and at Rice University. Shuman, Besterfield-Sacre, and McGourty, "ABET 'Professional Skills,'" p. 46. To avoid adding a fifth year, Purdue's program requires 12 credits of a foreign language, but does not insist on fluency. Carlson, "Global Approach to Engineering," p. A34.

90. See his statement in Carlson, "Global Approach to Engineering," p. A34. This view is shared by engineering educators at the University of Michigan, who maintain that, even if students do not end

up working in a situation where their second (or third) language is spoken, "having a second language makes the student more likely to work well in any other culture." Shuman, *et al.,* "ABET 'Professional Skills,'" p. 47.

91. Grandin interview. He adds that U.S. nationals have the advantage in being able to use English around the world, but are "handicapped" when they are monolingual. Also see Allert, *et al.,* "Case for Global Engineering."

92. Grandin interview. While engineering students in (and from) many countries enter their professional program with second-language ability, most U.S.-origin students lack adequate advance preparation. See Sangster, "Engineering Education," p. 122.

93. Allert, *et al.,* "Case for Global Engineering," pp. 1–2.

94. Allan and Chisholm, "Achieving Engineering Competencies," p. 151.

95. *Ibid.*

96. Downey, "'Problem Definition and Solution' in Engineering Education," p. 592; Downey, *et al.,* "Globally Competent Engineer," p. 119.

97. Chang interview.

98. Allan and Chisholm, "Achieving Engineering Competencies," p. 147.

99. National Academy of Engineering, *Educating the Engineer of 2020,* pp. 10–11.

100. Biddle, *Internationalization,* p. 57.

101. Downey, "'Problem Definition and Solution' in Engineering Education," p. 593.

102. Hirleman interview.

103. Allan and Chisholm, "Achieving Engineering Competencies," p. 148.

104. The ability to perform effectively on multidisciplinary teams is one of six professional skills introduced by ABET as new engineering-accreditation criteria. Shuman, *et al.,* "ABET 'Professional Skills,'" p. 41.

105. Allan and Chisholm, "Achieving Engineering Competencies," p. 151.

106. Shuman, *et al.,* "ABET 'Professional Skills,'" pp. 44–45; Allan and Chisholm, "Achieving Engineering Competencies," pp. 146–147; Allert, *et al.,* "Case for Global Engineering."

107. Chang interview.

108. Downey, *et al.,* "Globally Competent Engineer," pp. 109–110.

109. *Ibid.,* p. 112; Downey, "'Problem Definition and Solution' in Engineering Education," p. 592.

110. Downey, "'Problem Definition and Solution' in Engineering Education," p. 591.

111. Allan and Chisholm, "Achieving Engineering Competencies," p. 147; Carlson, "Global Approach to Engineering," pp. A33, A36. Student comments on their Purdue/Karlsruhe GEARE experience reported in Allert, *et al.* ("Case for Global Engineering") confirm the importance of developing cross-national friendships and socializing during off-work hours. Steenhuis (interview) champions social interaction among engineering students with different backgrounds and experiences as a teaching tool in this connection.

112. Shuman, *et al.,* "ABET 'Professional Skills,'" pp. 44, 46; Carlson, "Global Approach to Engineering," p. A36.

113. Juma and Yee-Cheong, *Innovation,* p. xiii.

114. Shuman, *et al.,* "ABET 'Professional Skills,'" pp. 44–45.

115. Dean, "Handle with Care," p. D1.

116. Downey, "'Problem Definition and Solution' in Engineering Education," p. 593.

117. Shaw and Kim, *Education for Sustainable Development Practice,* p. 65.

118. Shuman, *et al.,* "ABET 'Professional Skills,'" p. 45. Vest agrees, and also comments on the general failure to engage students in thinking about professional ethics. Vest, "Educating Engineers for 2020," p. 160.

119. Katehi, "Global Engineer," p. 155.

120. Skill in addressing social concerns ranges from civic participation to contributing effectively to public-policy formulation. See National Academy of Engineering, *Educating the Engineer of 2020,* p. 4.

121. Katehi, "Global Engineer," p. 153; also p. 147.

122. Vest, "Educating Engineers for 2020," p. 166. Argentina's Universidad Catolica currently offers a Master's degree in Environmental Engineering and Sustainable Development. Shaw and Kim, *Education for Sustainable Development Practice,* p. 58.

123. Allan and Chisholm, "Achieving Engineering Competencies," 147. As Gretchen Kalonji points out, service projects offer engineers "multiple *opportunities for leadership*" [emphasis in original]. Kalonji, "Reforms for Engineering Educators," p. 148.

124. Shuman, *et al.*, "ABET 'Professional Skills,'" p. 45.

125. Juma and Yee-Cheong, *Innovation*, pp. 70, 74, 79.

126. Michels, "Engineers Lend Technical Aid." Engineers Against Poverty is a parallel nonprofit organization in the United Kingdom. Juma and Yee-Cheong, *Innovation*, p. 85.

127. Biographical Sketch, Bernard Amadei, at http://www.edc-cu.org/profileamadei.htm (accessed May 16, 2008).

128. *Coloradan* [University of Colorado alumni magazine] December 2007, p. 2.

129. Shuman, *et al.*, "ABET 'Professional Skills,'" p. 47. Also see Kalonji, "Reforms for Engineering Educators," p. 147. Among other advantages, adequate infrastructure contributes to the diffusion of technology. Juma and Yee-Cheong, *Innovation*, p. 79.

130. *Coloradan*, December 2007, p. 2. At MIT, one DtM team "designed a novel IV clamp to make treatment of cholera and other diseases more accessible in areas with few trained health workers." Juma and Yee-Cheong, *Innovation*, p. 86.

Notes for Chapter 8

1. Kendall, "Foreword," p. xi.

2. Finn and Jacobson, *Just Practice*, p. 17.

3. Transnational social-work activity includes professional exchange and multisited practice as well as the cross-border connections of domestic practice and advocacy. While some professionals specialize in working with migrants, international service, or transnational adoptions, all social workers "encounter international issues in carrying out their professional responsibilities." Healy, *International Social Work*, pp. 10, 313. Transnational social-work practice also can be linked to human dimensions of development work. See Lara Herscovitch and Lynne Healy, "International Relief and Development Practice," in *International Social Work: Professional Action in an Interdependent World,* by Lynne M. Healy (Oxford: Oxford University Press, 2008), pp. 260–283. We treat most social-work/development connections in the next chapter.

4. Healy, *International Social Work*, p. 286.

5. *Ibid.*, p. 5; Healy, "International Social Work Curriculum," p. 26.

6. See Herscovitch and Healy, "International Relief and Development Practice," p. 283. According to Healy (*International Social Work*, p. 230), "social work's optimism and emphasis on possibilities are important commonalities" everywhere.

7. Kendall, "Foreword," p. xi.

8. In Europe, where educational preparation must meet EU standards in order for social workers to practice professionally in other member countries, schools have increased the international content of their curricula. Several schools of social work in Norway and Denmark have introduced specialized tracks in international social work. In 2008, however, Lynne Healy wrote that "the current content of social work education [in Denmark] may not prepare professionals adequately for work with ethnic minority youth, although programs are beginning to focus more attention on immigrant populations." Healy, *International Social Work*, pp. 205, 350–353; Healy, "International Social Work Curriculum," p. 21.

9. Finn interview; Link and Ramanathan, "Introduction," p. 1; Healy, "International Social Work Curriculum," pp. 22–23. In her interview, Finn distinguished the University of California, Berkeley, and the University of Connecticut as U.S. leaders in *inter*national social-work education.

10. Elliott and Mayadas maintain that "the goals of social development are consistent with those of social work: to create planned social, economic, and institutional change with a view to improving the lives of individuals." Doreen Elliott and Nazneen Mayadas, "Infusing Global Perspectives into Social Work Practice," in *All Our Futures: Principles and Resources for Social Work Practice in a Global Era,* edited by Chathapuram S. Ramanathan and Rosemary J. Link (Belmont: Brooks/Cole, 1999), p. 64. Social development "seeks to promote human well-being in association with a dynamic, ongoing process of economic development"; it "harnesses the power of economic development for social welfare purposes."

Centers for social development can be found in social-work programs at the City University of Hong Kong, LaTrobe University in Australia, and Washington University in St. Louis. James Midgley, "Social Development in Social Work: Learning from Global Dialogue," in *All Our Futures: Principles and Resources for Social Work Practice in a Global Era,* edited by Chathapuram S. Ramanathan and Rosemary J. Link (Belmont: Brooks/Cole, 1999), pp. 196, 193.

11. Midgley, "Social Development in Social Work," p. 194; Healy, "International Social Work Curriculum," pp. 22–23. The content of most international courses in EU schools of social work also tends to be Euro-centric. The University of East London's alternative model emphasizes migration, poverty, and cross-cultural work. Healy, "International Social Work Curriculum," p. 21.

12. Healy, "International Social Work Curriculum," p. 25.

13. Finn and Jacobson, *Just Practice,* p. xvii.

14. Healy, *International Social Work,* p. 7.

15. *Ibid.,* pp. 12, 347.

16. Finn and Jacobson, *Just Practice,* pp. 265, 362.

17. Finn interview.

18. Finn and Jacobson, *Just Practice,* pp. 43, 425.

19. *Ibid.,* p. 425.

20. Finn interview; Healy, *International Social Work,* p. 202; Finn and Jacobson, *Just Practice,* pp. 43, 362.

21. Finn and Jacobson, *Just Practice,* p. 419.

22. Finn interview; also see Finn and Jacobson, *Just Practice,* p. 47.

23. Herscovitch and Healy, "International Relief and Development Practice," pp. 279, 283; Jones and Kumssa, "Professional Growth in the Global Context," p. 217.

24. Jones and Kumssa, "Professional Growth in the Global Context," p. 208.

25. Koester interview.

26. Elliott and Mayadas, "Infusing Global Perspectives into Social Work Practice," p. 65.

27. Healy, *International Social Work,* p. 361.

28. Finn interview.

29. Healy points out that "cultural knowledge applied indiscriminately [to members of a group without individualization] is as damaging as no cultural information." Healy, "International Social Work Curriculum," pp. 296, 26.

30. See Dennis Saleebey, "Introduction: Power in the People," in *The Strengths Perspective in Social Work Practice,* edited by Dennis Saleebey (Boston: Pearson, 2006), p. 6; Finn and Jacobson, *Just Practice,* pp. 43–45.

31. Finn and Jacobson, *Just Practice,* pp. 32, 222.

32. *Ibid.,* p. 425.

33. Finn interview.

34. Webb, *Social Work in a Risk Society,* p. 193.

35. Including environmental forces and the many situations where social outcomes are affected by poor nutrition, poor pre- and post-natal health care, and HIV-AIDS. Finn and Jacobson, *Just Practice,* p. 21; Koester interview.

36. Finn and Jacobson, *Just Practice,* p. 31 [our emphasis].

37. Peter Koehn, *Refugees from Revolution: U.S. Policy and Third-World Migration* (Boulder: Westview, 1991), pp. 142–143. See the helpful table (taken from Drachman) of critical considerations for each migration stage reproduced in Healy, *International Social Work,* p. 287.

38. On the role of ethnography in social-justice work, see Finn and Jacobson, *Just Practice,* p. 236.

39. On the influence of circular migration and transnational family ties, see Healy, *International Social Work,* pp. 288–289.

40. *Ibid.,* pp. 10–11; also p. 256.

41. *Ibid.,* Healy, *International Social Work,* pp. 290–292, 330. See Jesse Wolowoy, "Should You Implement a Law You Strongly Disagree With?" *PA Times* (February 2005): 16–17.

42. *Ibid.,* Healy, *International Social Work,* pp. 289–290.

43. *Ibid.,* pp. 305–306.

44. *Ibid.*, p. 304.

45. Finn and Jacobson, *Just Practice*, p. 233; Herscovitch and Healy, "International Relief and Development Practice," p. 278.

46. Finn interview.

47. Healy, *International Social Work*, p. 231.

48. See Finn and Jacobson, *Just Practice*, p. 403–405.

49. *Ibid.*, pp. 42, 425.

50. Koester interview.

51. *Ibid.*

52. Finn and Jacobson, *Just Practice*, pp. 42–43.

53. *Ibid.*, p. 233.

54. Saleebey, "Power in the People," pp. 13–14, 16, 19; Finn and Jacobson, *Just Practice*, pp. 234, 236, 266.

55. Finn and Jacobson, *Just Practice*, p. 235.

56. *Ibid.*, p. 25; Healy, *International Social Work*, p. 253. Healy (p. 256) illustrates the importance of retaining social connectedness by reference to work with a Cambodian or Ethiopian woman in a U.S. battered-women's program: "Counseling, while still respecting her dignity and right not to be abused, should also involve the client in a search for ways to maintain her connectedness. Otherwise, the outcome of intervention may be to protect her from abuse but also to diminish the value of life itself through severing of crucial close ties."

57. Finn and Jacobson, *Just Practice*, p. 136; Finn interview.

58. Cited in Bill Yellowtail, "The Dignity of Indian Self-sufficiency," *Montana's Agenda* 6, No. 2 (Autumn 2008): 3.

59. Koester interview.

60. Finn and Jacobson, *Just Practice*, p. 326.

61. *Ibid.*

62. Healy, *International Social Work*, p. 366. On the choice of "action" over "intervention" as a term imbued with meaning and dynamic potential, see Finn and Jacobson, *Just Practice*, p. 314.

63. Finn and Jacobson, *Just Practice*, pp. 266–267.

64. Finn interview.

65. Finn and Jacobson, *Just Practice*, p. 419.

66. Finn interview.

67. Healy, "International Social Work Curriculum," p. 26.

68. Healy, *International Social Work*, p. 5.

69. Koester interview.

70. Herscovitch and Healy, "International Relief and Development Practice," p. 278.

71. Finn interview.

72. Healy, *International Social Work*, pp. 296–297.

73. Finn (interview) adds that students must learn not to assume that silence means agreement.

74. Finn and Jacobson, *Just Practice*, p. 239.

75. Healy, *International Social Work*, p. 6.

76. *Ibid.*, p. 347.

77. Lynne Koester (interview) suggests that conflict resolution is a particularly important functional skill in transnational social-work contexts because "the potential for conflict is high due to different cultural outlooks."

78. Finn and Jacobson, *Just Practice*, p. 231.

79. *Ibid.*

80. Finn interview.

81. Finn and Jacobson, *Just Practice*, pp. 15, 231.

82. Saleebey, "Power in the People," p. 17.

83. Finn and Jacobson, *Just Practice*, p. 232; Healy, *International Social Work*, p. 295.

84. Finn and Jacobson, *Just Practice*, pp. 324–326.

85. Also see Healy, *International Social Work*, p. 5.

86. Our characterization of transnational performance also is influenced by the definition of social

work agreed upon in 2001 by the IASWW and the International Federation of Social Workers. See Finn and Jacobson, *Just Practice,* pp. 20, 25. Also see Healy, *International Social Work,* p. 202.

87. Midgley, "Social Development in Social Work," pp. 201, 203.

88. Healy, *International Social Work,* p. 75.

89. Finn and Jacobson, *Just Practice,* pp. 14–15. They add (p. 362) that "social policy issues are at the heart of social work practice" (also see Herscovitch and Healy, "International Relief and Development Practice," p. 277). While responsibility for social change and empowerment is accepted as a professional value among social workers throughout the world, the level of commitment varies. See Healy, *International Social Work,* pp. 230–231.

90. Healy, *International Social Work,* p. 334.

91. *Ibid.,* pp. 5-6.

92. Midgley, "Social Development in Social Work," p. 204.

93. Finn and Jacobson, *Just Practice,* pp. 136–137, 325; Healy, *International Social Work,* pp. 253–254.

94. Finn and Jacobson, *Just Practice,* p. 326.

95. See Peter H. Koehn, and Phyllis B. Ngai, "Citizenship Education for an Age of Population Mobility and Glocally Interconnected Destinies," *Finnish Journal of Ethnicity and Migration* 1, No. 1 (2006): 26–33; Finn and Jacobson, *Just Practice,* p. 136.

96. Finn interview.

97. Elliott and Mayadas, "Infusing Global Perspectives into Social Work Practice," p. 65; Midgley, "Social Development in Social Work," pp. 197, 204.

98. Finn and Jacobson, *Just Practice,* pp. 335, 346–347, 353–354, 363–366, 428; Healy, *International Social Work,* pp. 12, 204, 325.

99. Finn and Jacobson (*Just Practice,* pp. 315–316) add that "accompaniment demands ongoing critical attention to questions of power and the power differentials among the participants in the change process."

100. Healy, *International Social Work,* p. 318.

101. *Ibid.,* pp. 10, 330. See, for instance, Koehn, *Refugees from Revolution*; Peter H. Koehn, "Transnational Migration, State Policy, and Local Clinician Treatment of Asylum Seekers and Resettled Migrants: Comparative Perspectives on Reception-Centre and Community Health-Care Practice in Finland," *Global Social Policy* 6, No. 1 (2006): 21–56.

102. Healy, *International Social Work,* pp. 318–319.

103. Transnational networks can play a useful role, for instance, in connection with issues and malpractices surrounding transnational adoptions, children's services, and treatment of minorities. See Healy, *International Social Work,* pp. 304, 327.

104. At the transnational level, social-justice workers are likely form coalitions with immigrant-assistance groups, human-rights advocacy organizations, public-health workers, and labor and education organizations. Healy, *International Social Work,* pp. 326–327. Helpful guidelines for assembling coalitions and building alliances that can be adapted transnationally can be found in Mark S. Homan, *Promoting Community Change: Making It Happen in the Real World,* 3rd edition (Pacific Grove, CA: Brooks/Cole, 2004), pp. 383–384. Koester (interview) emphasizes the importance of bringing people to the table around common objectives "before conflict arises."

105. In 1995, for instance, an alliance of social workers from 27 countries convened in conjunction with the Fourth U.N. World Conference on Women held in Beijing. They adopted a resolution with recommendations for reducing gender-based violence that the IASSW, in its NGO consultative status, presented to official U.N. delegates. See Case 1.5 in Healy, *International Social Work,* p. 17.

106. Including online coalitions and partnerships among groups in wealthy and low-income countries. Healy, *International Social Work,* p. 347.

107. Ideas adapted from Finn and Jacobson, *Just Practice,* pp. 314–315, 428.

108. Herscovitch and Healy, "International Relief and Development Practice," p. 281.

109. Healy, *International Social Work,* pp. 15–17.

110. *Ibid.,* pp. 357, 347, 363; also Ramanathan and Link, "Future Visions for Global Studies in Social Work," p. 235.

Notes for Chapter 9

1. Shaw and Kim, *Education for Sustainable Development Practice,* pp. iii–iv.

2. Astrid E. Merget, "Times of Turbulence," *Public Administration Review* 63 (July/August 2003): 390–395.

3. Deutsch, "Academics Try Collaboration," p. C1.

4. Sustainability will be an added criteria in the (U.S.) Northwest Accrediting Agency's cycle of institutional reviews that begin in 2010.

5. Although more and more public officials frequently interact with foreign counterparts, the core curriculum in public administration (at least in the United States) remains overwhelmingly domestic in content. See Merget, "Times of Turbulence," p. 391. In his interview for this book, Philip Morgan, who taught at Indiana University for twenty years, confirmed that there is "very little in the way of development-studies or development-management courses" in the mainstream public-administration curriculums at the "big schools" and that "most of the NASPA [National Association of Schools of Public Administration] crowd are really doing American public administration." Although international development-studies programs in the United States suffered from budget cuts at the end of the 20th century (Spaulding, Mauch, and Lin, "Internationalization of Higher Education," pp. 205–206), they rebounded at the beginning of the new millennium and new programs, such as the International Development track in the University of Montana's MPA-degree program (http://www.cas.umt.edu/polsci/mpa.htm), have been introduced. Also see the International & Development Administration emphasis in Syracuse University's MPA program and the George Washington University's M.A. in International Development Studies program. In 2008, moreover, according to American Society for Public Administration (ASPA) President Harvey L. White, "ASPA is internationalizing public administration for academics, practitioners, and students in our profession" as part of its "Transformational Public Administration initiative." White, "Transformation, Internationalization and Globalization of Public Administration," p. 3. Recognition that transnational collaboration is imperative for practicing public administrators is also embedded in two recently published volumes in the field: Gilles Paquet's *The New Geo-Governance* and the *Handbook of Globalization, Governance, and Public Administration* edited by Ali Farazmand and Jack Pinkowski (Boca Raton, FL: CRC Press, 2007). However, Krishna Tummala, who has long been active in ASPA's comparative and development administration section, offered a cautionary appraisal at the beginning of 2008. According to Tummala (interview), the public-administration curriculum and literature remain "largely American-centered. While we talk of 'diversity' and ASPA is moving along with the international components, it is not clear exactly what their agenda is and what strategies they would like to pursue. I hope this does not remain as a slogan!"

6. See http://www.gdrc.org/sustdev/un-desd/intro_un-desd.html.

7. Including poverty reduction and increasing the long-term well-being of the poor, natural-resource and biodiversity conservation, disease control, and climate-change mitigation and adaptation. Shaw and Kim, *Education for Sustainable Development Practice,* pp. iii, 11, 13.

8. The Commission's review of relevant graduate-degree programs in Africa, Australia, East Asia, Europe, Latin America, North America, and South Asia revealed "no programs that systematically provide students with the relevant skills and knowledge in health sciences, natural sciences and engineering, social sciences, and management...." Shaw and Kim, *Education for Sustainable Development Practice,* pp. iii, 13, 15–16, 55, 57–58. Our consolidated treatment of sustainable-development professional education is consistent with three of the four primary fields (or spheres) addressed by the Commission. We devote the next chapter to a separate consideration of medicine and public health (the fourth field).

Building higher-education capacity to graduate competent sustainable-development professionals is most critically needed in low-income countries of the Global South. In Mamphela Ramphele's words, "it is the capability to create, access, and apply knowledge that determines how successfully a country can address the numerous development challenges it faces." Ramphele, "The University As an Actor in Development," p. 19. On current and anticipated transnational skill deficits in U.S. public and nongovernmental organizations, particularly among national government departments and agencies with far-reaching international missions and multilateral linkages, see Bikson, Treverton, Moini, and Lindstrom, *New Challenges for International Leadership,* pp. xv, xvii–xviii, 4–5.

9. Shaw and Kim, *Education for Sustainable Development Practice*, p. 24.

10. For the complete list of universities preparing to launch MDP programs in October 2008, see Shaw and Kim, *Education for Sustainable Development Practice*, Appendix E, p. 73. Since 1992, Ghana's University for Development Studies in the northern region has emphasized integrated development studies, including agricultural sciences and health sciences, in its preparation of primarily rural practitioners. Jose Zaglul and Daniel Sherrard, "Higher Education in Economic Transformation," in *Going for Growth: Science, Technology and Innovation in Africa*, edited by Calestous Juma (London: Smith Institute, 2005), pp. 39–40. Cornell University grants the Master of Professional Studies (MPS) degree to graduates of its International Agriculture and Rural Development, Agricultural and Life Sciences (with a Peace Corps option), and International Development programs. http://ip.cals.cornell.edu/academics/.

11. Moreover, the Commission's communicative-skill curricular recommendations are basically limited to second-language learning. See Shaw and Kim, *Education for Sustainable Development Practice*, pp. 34–35. In contrast, the Elliott School at the George Washington University emphasizes skill development in transnational team work, leadership, and negotiation; cross-cultural communication, media and public relations; and grant-proposal preparation. http://www.gwu.edu/~elliott/academicprograms/mipp/skills.cfm.

12. See Thomas Faist, "Transstate Spaces and Development: Some Critical Remarks," in *Rethinking Transnationalism: The Meso-Link of Organizations*, edited by Ludger Pries (London: Routledge, 2008), pp. 75, 77; Xiao-huang Yin and Peter H. Koehn, "Immigrant Transnationals and U.S. Foreign Relations," in *A Companion to American Immigration*, edited by Reed Ueda (Oxford: Blackwell Publishers, 2006), pp. 77–105.

13. See Shaw and Kim, *Education for Sustainable Development Practice*, pp. 14, 38. Many 21st-century careers in sustainable development will involve geographical and organizational mobility. Salt, "The Business of International Migration," p. 95; Bikson, Treverton, Moini, and Lindstrom, *New Challenges for International Leadership*, p. xviii. The United Nations Development Programme (UNDP), for instance, generally expects its staff to move at least every four years.

14. Bikson, Treverton, Moini, and Lindstrom, *New Challenges for International Leadership*, p. xiv.

15. Shaw and Kim, *Education for Sustainable Development Practice*, pp. 14, 19. Among transnational boundary spanners, possessing an area of expertise or a special technical skill serves "as a kind of passport of legitimacy for engaging with people from other organizations—harnessing the power that is associated with knowledge." Williams, "Competent Boundary Spanner," p. 119. This view is shared by Stephen Siebert, who heads the University of Montana's International Natural Resource Management Master's degree program. Stephen Siebert, personal interview, August 22, 2008.

16. Bikson, Treverton, Moini, and Lindstrom, *New Challenges for International Leadership*, pp. 25–26. Moreover, no one is "smart enough" to know everything that practitioners "are going to have to know in 2030" (Kellogg interview). Developing social networks is an important strategy in ongoing knowledge acquisition and learning. Folke, Colding, and Berkes, "Synthesis," p. 373.

17. See Berkes, Colding, and Folke, "Introduction," pp. 2, 5–6, 22.

18. Effective networking is a key ingredient facilitating the exchange of relevant information across boundaries. Williams, "Competent Boundary Spanner," pp. 110, 115, 117.

19. Folke, Colding, and Berkes, "Synthesis," pp. 353, 381.

20. Herscovitch and Healy, "International Relief and Development Practice," p. 261; Peter H. Koehn (ed.), *Final Report of the International Symposium "Refugees and Development Assistance: Training for Voluntary Repatriation"* (Missoula, MT: Office of International Programs, the University of Montana, 1994).

21. Folke, Colding, and Berkes, "Synthesis," p. 375.

22. Including abiotic and biotic disturbances. See Johan Colding, Thomas Elmqvist, and Per Olsson, "Living with Disturbance: Building Resilience in Social-Ecological Systems," in *Navigating Social-Ecological Systems: Building Resilience for Complexity and Change*, edited by Fikret Berkes, Johan Colding, and Carl Folke (Cambridge: Cambridge University Press, 2003), p. 163; Berkes, Colding, and Folke, "Introduction," p. 14.

23. Asset identification often encompasses local ecological knowledge and traditional agricultural and risk-spreading practices, such as advanced Polynesian polyculture. Colding, Elmqvist, and Olsson, "Living with Disturbance," pp. 165, 179; Folke, Colding, and Berkes, "Synthesis," p. 374.

Ghana's University for Development Studies encourages students "to internalize the importance of local knowledge and to find ways of combining it with science" and emphasizes participatory rural appraisal. Zaglul and Sherrard, "Higher Education in Economic Transformation," pp. 40, 44. According to Stephen McCool, eco-tourism expert, resource-conservation consultant with UNESCO, and Emeritus Professor, the University of Montana (interview returned by email in August 2008), it is important that students of sustainable development learn to appreciate other ways of knowing and to recognize "the validity and utility of locally generated experiential knowledge in making decisions about natural resources." McCool maintains that professional schools of natural resources too often marginalize and limit the use of knowledge generated by ways of knowing that are not based on Western-scientific methods.

24. Shaw and Kim, *Education for Sustainable Development Practice*, p. 70. Micro-enterprise lending is a specialized skill course in the curriculum for international-development professionals offered at the George Washington University's Elliot School. http://www.gwu.edu/~elliott/academicprograms/mipp/skills.cfm.

25. This discussion is adapted from Shaw and Kim, *Education for Sustainable Development Practice*, p. 11 (see pp. 20–25, 61–64, 66–68 for further details regarding the potential contributions of these fields).

26. For instance, by appropriately utilizing the ecological, agricultural, demographic, infrastructural, and social data gathered through GIS technology in needs assessment, risk analysis, project selection and implementation, and monitoring and evaluation. Shaw and Kim, *Education for Sustainable Development Practice*, p. 22. Similarly, "spatial information collected by satellite or airborne remote sensing can be used to understand the capability of the land to support economic activity and water use" and to "help ensure that natural resources are used efficiently and sustainably." Juma and Cheong, *Innovation*, p. 59.

27. At present, "very few professionals are trained and prepared" in this way. Shaw and Kim, *Education for Sustainable Development Practice*, pp. 17–18. Costa Rica's EARTH University delivers a curriculum that aims to educate leaders who will promote sustainable development throughout Central and South America. Within an overall context of globalization, the curriculum emphasizes agriculture and integrates a number of disciplines to support learning the concept of holistic practice. See Juma and Cheong, *Innovation*, p. 97.

28. See, for instance, Berkes, Colding, and Folke, "Introduction," p. 10.

29. Paul F. Steinberg, "Understanding Policy Change in Developing Countries: The Spheres of Influence Framework," *Global Environmental Politics* 3, No. 1 (February 2003): 21; also see Roberts and Parks, *Climate of Injustice*, p. 240; Jennifer Brinkerhoff and Derrick Brinkerhoff, "Preparing People for International Public Service in a Changed World: The Continued Relevance of the MPA," *PA Times International Supplement,* March 2006, p. 6.

30. Morgan interview.

31. Siebert interview. Ali Farazmand of Florida Atlantic University (interview) stresses the importance of forward thinking and crisis planning in analytic preparation: "A top chess player, like Kasparov or Fischer, will think 19 or 20 steps ahead of time. That's what distinguishes them.... Can we do this in public management?"

32. Farazmand interview.

33. See, for instance, Peter H. Koehn, "Fitting a Vital Linkage Piece into the Multidimensional Emissions-Reduction Puzzle: Nongovernmental Pathways to Consumption Changes in the PRC and the USA," *Climatic Change* 77 (2006): 385–396.

34. McCool interview.

35. Acker interview.

36. Morgan interview.

37. Tummala interview. Also see Daniel J. Kealey, *Cross-Cultural Effectiveness: A Study of Canadian Technical Advisors Overseas* (Hull, Quebec: Canadian International Development Agency, 1990), pp. 5, 7, 10, 53.

38. Tummala interview.

39. Brinkerhoff and Brinkerhoff, "Continued Relevance of the MPA," p. 6; McCool interview.

40. McCool interview. Also see Kealey, *Cross-Cultural Effectiveness,* pp. 7, 41–42, 54, 60; Susan A.

Moore, Roger C. Severn, and Rebecca Millar, "A Conceptual Model of Community Capacity for Bio-diversity Conservation Outcomes," *Geographical Research* 44, No. 4 (December 2006): 368.

41. Morgan interview.

42. Tummala interview.

43. Kealey, *Cross-Cultural Effectiveness,* pp. 48, 54, 60–61.

44. Tummala interview.

45. Berkes, Colding, and Folke, "Introduction," p. 10.

46. Acker interview.

47. This insight comes from Robert Charlick (interview).

48. Williams, "Competent Boundary Spanner," pp. 110–111; Kealey, *Cross-Cultural Effectiveness,* p. 53.

49. Folke, Colding, and Berkes, "Synthesis," pp. 353–354.

50. Karen Brock and Jethro Pettit maintain that "it is in the unique experiences of development practitioners, and the sense they make of those experiences, that the catalysts of future innovations are to be found." Karen Brock and Jethro Pettit, "Introduction," in *Springs of Participation: Creating and Evolving Methods for Participatory Development,* edited by Karen Brock and Jethro Pettit (Warwickshire, UK: Practical Action Publishing, 2007), pp. 14, 6.

51. Paquet, *New Geo-Governance,* p. 9.

52. Tummala interview; Shaw and Kim, *Education for Sustainable Development Practice,* p. 28.

53. Juma and Cheong, *Innovation,* p. 51.

54. Folke, Colding, and Berkes, "Synthesis," p. 375. Such learning platforms could facilitate the transnational dissemination of information regarding local community innovations. Perez and Bhandarkar, *Innovation for Sustainable Development,* p. 6.

55. See the discussion of APLU's international research and development projects database found in Peter H. Koehn, Montague Demment, and Anne-Claire Hervy, "Enhancing Higher Education's Engagement in International Development: Africa-U.S. Partnerships," *Journal of the World Universities Forum* 1, No. 6 (2008): 130–134.

56. Berkes, Colding, and Folke, "Introduction," p. 13; Colding, Elmqvist, and Olsson, "Living with Disturbance," p. 181; Shaw and Kim, *Education for Sustainable Development Practice,* p. 63.

57. Folke, Colding, and Berkes, "Synthesis," pp. 371–373.

58. Berkes, Colding, and Folke, "Introduction," pp. 21–23; Colding, Elmqvist, and Olsson, "Living with Disturbance," pp. 163–165. Adaptation "may concentrate on reducing the impacts of change, or it may take advantage of new opportunities created by change." Folke, Colding, and Berkes, "Synthesis," p. 375; also p. 355.

59. Social and ecological resilience are vital components of sustainability because "loss of resilience leads to reduced capacity to deal with change." Likewise, species that appear to be redundant, and overlapping social practices and institutional functions, "may become of critical importance for regenerating and reorganizing the system after disturbance and disruption." Folke, Colding, and Berkes, "Synthesis," pp. 354–355, 361–363.

60. Acker interview.

61. *Ibid.*

62. Charlick interview.

63. Morgan interview; Shaw and Kim, *Education for Sustainable Development Practice,* p. 14.

64. Morgan interview.

65. Resource-mobilizing ability is enhanced by strong proposal-writing skills. Shaw and Kim, *Education for Sustainable Development Practice,* p. 23.

66. Colding, Elmqvist, and Olsson, "Living with Disturbance," p. 164.

67. Williams, "Competent Boundary Spanner," pp. 110, 119.

68. Berkes, Colding, and Folke, "Introduction," p. 21.

69. This idea comes from Shaw and Kim, *Education for Sustainable Development Practice,* p. 27.

70. Williams, "Competent Boundary Spanner," p. 115; also see Shaw and Kim, *Education for Sustainable Development Practice,* p. 70; Brinkerhoff and Brinkerhoff, "Continued Relevance of the MPA," p. 6.

71. Kellogg interview.

72. Sandra L. McKay, *Teaching English As an International Language: Rethinking Goals and Approaches* (Oxford: Oxford University Press, 2002), p. 17.

73. In addition, the proposed curriculum for global MDP programs requires that students "demonstrate basic proficiency in a non-native language." Shaw and Kim, *Education for Sustainable Development Practice*, p. 25.

74. Morgan interview.

75. Charlick, Morgan, Tummala, Kellogg interviews.

76. Morgan interview.

77. McCool interview.

78. Tummala interview. Earl Kellogg (interview), whose background in rural development includes work in Thailand, Nigeria, Zambia, and Kenya, shares Tummala's perspective on the importance of making some effort to learn your counterparts' language.

79. Bikson, Treverton, Moini, and Lindstrom, *New Challenges for International Leadership*, pp. 25, 27.

80. Charlick interview.

81. *Ibid.*

82. Brinkerhoff, "Contributions of Digital Diasporas," pp. 192–196, 200.

83. Bikson, Treverton, Moini, and Lindstrom, *New Challenges for International Leadership*, p. 49.

84. Acker interview.

85. Williams, "Competent Boundary Spanner," p. 115; Kealey, *Cross-Cultural Effectiveness*, p. 10. McCool's conceptualization of active listening includes processing what has been said and feeding it back to the person who said it (McCool interview). Active listening yields valuable early understandings and helps one avoid actions that would violate prevailing organizational or cultural norms.

86. Kellogg interview. Also see Williams, "Competent Boundary Spanner," p. 116.

87. Sarkissian, *Kitchen Table Sustainability*, pp. 115–116.

88. See Kealey, *Cross-Cultural Effectiveness*, p. 5.

89. *Ibid.*, pp. 5–7.

90. Williams, "Competent Boundary Spanner," p. 110.

91. Kealey, *Cross-Cultural Effectiveness*, pp. 6, 47–48.

92. See, for instance, James Pfeiffer, "International NGOs and Primary Health Care in Mozambique: The Need for a New Model of Collaboration," *Social Science & Medicine* 56, No. 4 (February 2003): 731, 737.

93. Morgan interview.

94. Kealey, *Cross-Cultural Effectiveness*, p. 53. Kellogg (interview) stresses "genuineness" in being "approachable and friendly and open."

95. Kellogg (interview) believes that educators need to help young learners understand that building transnational personal and professional networks and relationships is a "life-long" undertaking.

96. Kealey, *Cross-Cultural Effectiveness*, p. 61; Williams, "Competent Boundary Spanner," pp. 111, 116–117; Juma and Cheong, *Innovation*, p. 16. Morgan (interview) believes that trust building requires much more effort on the part of U.S. students today than it did twenty years ago because the people sustainable-development professionals will be working with are "much more skeptical of working with Americans."

97. Kealey, *Cross-Cultural Effectiveness*, pp. 15, 48; Williams, "Competent Boundary Spanner," p. 115; Marquardt and Berger, *Global Leaders*, p. 63. James Pfeiffer ("International NGOs," p. 738) thoughtfully recommends that "the compound residence model should be rejected (except in genuinely dangerous conflict situations in emergency work) since it sends a message of exclusion and creates so much local resentment."

98. Williams, "Competent Boundary Spanner," p. 116.

99. Kellogg interview.

100. See Brinkerhoff, "Contributions of Digital Diasporas," pp. 193, 200.

101. Morgan interview; Shaw and Kim, *Education for Sustainable Development Practice*, p. 68.

102. Morgan interview.

103. Kealey, *Cross-Cultural Effectiveness*, p. 54; Shaw and Kim, *Education for Sustainable Development Practice*, pp. 22, 68; Folke, Colding, and Berkes, "Synthesis," p. 356; Herscovitch and Healy, "International

Relief and Development Practice," p. 263; McCool interview. Required resources often are fragmented and spatially dispersed. Williams, "Competent Boundary Spanner," p. 105.

104. Bikson, Treverton, Moini, and Lindstrom, *New Challenges for International Leadership*, pp. xv, 4; Wilson interview; Williams, "Competent Boundary Spanner," p. 109.

105. Shaw and Kim, *Education for Sustainable Development Practice*, pp. 22, 17, 70; Siebert interview.

106. Williams, "Competent Boundary Spanner," pp. 117–118; Brinkerhoff and Brinkerhoff, "Continued Relevance of the MPA," p. 6; Shaw and Kim, *Education for Sustainable Development Practice*, p. 70; Folke, Colding, and Berkes, "Synthesis," p. 356; Sarkissian, *Kitchen Table Sustainability*, pp. 197, 296; Acker and McCool interviews. Professionals should be skilled at defusing interpersonal, interstitutional, transdisciplinary, and transnational conflicts. Charlick interview.

107. Williams, "Competent Boundary Spanner," p. 116.

108. Shaw and Kim, *Education for Sustainable Development Practice*, pp. 12, 18, 25, 70.

109. *Ibid.*, p. 33.

110. *Ibid.*, p. 67.

111. Berkes, Colding, and Folke, "Introduction," p. 15; Colding, Elmqvist, and Olsson, "Living with Disturbance," p. 181; Folke, Colding, and Berkes, "Synthesis," pp. 354, 356, 361.

112. The curriculum at the Elliot School includes coursework in advocacy and lobbying.

113. Juma and Cheong, *Innovation*, p. 96.

114. Zaglul and Sherrard, "Higher Education in Economic Transformation," p. 39.

115. McCool interview; Berkes, Colding, and Folke, "Introduction," p. 23. On ways of framing co-benefits in the interests of climatic stabilization and population health, see Peter H. Koehn, "Underneath Kyoto: Emerging Subnational Government Initiatives and Incipient Issue-bundling Opportunities in China and the United States," *Global Environmental Politics* 8, No. 1 (Fall 2007): 53–77.

116. Folke, Colding, and Berkes, "Synthesis," p. 382.

117. *Ibid.*, p. 381. A model of far-reaching and interconnected transnational advocacy is Oxfam's Global Action Plan in support of education for all. See Mundy and Murphy, "Transnational Advocacy," pp. 104–105. Oxfam's "ultimate goal is to redress the power imbalances that limit the poor from accessing ... [public] goods and services while empowering them to defend their economic and social rights." Offenheiser and Jacobs in Abhijit V. Banerjee, *Making Aid Work* (Cambridge: MIT Press, 2007), p. 101.

Notes for Chapter 10

1. This chapter draws, in part, on Peter H. Koehn, "Globalization, Migration Health, and Educational Preparation for Transnational Medical Encounters," *Globalization and Health* 2, No. 2 (January 30, 2006): 1–16.

2. Ronald M. Harden, "International Medical Education and Future Directions: A Global Perspective," *Academic Medicine* 81, No. 12 (Supplement December 2006): S27.

3. Paul K. Drain, Aron Primack, Hunt D. Dan, Wafaie W. Fawzi, King K. Holmes, and Pierce Gardner, "Global Health in Medical Education: A Call for More Training and Opportunities," *Academic Medicine* 82, No. 3 (March 2007): 226.

4. Eric Houpt, Richard D. Pearson, and Thomas L. Hall, "Three Domains of Competency in Global Health Education: Recommendations for All Medical Students," *Academic Medicine* 82, No. 3 (March 2007): 223.

5. Laurie Garrett, "The Return of Infectious Disease," in *Plagues and Politics: Infectious Disease and International Policy,* edited by Andrew T. Price-Smith (London: Palgrave, 2001), pp. 185–186.

6. Houpt, Pearson, and Hall, "Three Domains of Competency," p. 224.

7. Nina Bernstein, "Record Immigration Is Changing the Face of New York's Neighborhoods," *New York Times,* January 24, 2005, p. A16.

8. See Robert Pear, "Payments to Help Hospitals Care for Illegal Immigrants," *New York Times,* May 10, 2005, p. A12. In 2004, immigrants and their children (about 16 percent of the total U.S. population) constituted about 30 percent of the country's uninsured population. Michael A. Godkin,

Judith A. Savageau, and Kenneth E. Fletcher, "Effect of a Global Longitudinal Pathway on Medical Students' Attitudes Toward the Medically Indigent," *Teaching and Learning in Medicine* 18, No. 3 (2006): 226.

9. Sara Glasgow and Dennis Pirages, "Microsecurity," in *Plagues and Politics: Infectious Disease and International Policy,* edited by Andrew T. Price-Smith (London: Palgrave, 2001), pp. 196, 203; also Andrew T. Price-Smith, *The Health of Nations: Infectious Disease, Environmental Change, and their Effects on National Security and Development* (Cambridge: MIT Press, 2002), pp. 41, 165.

10. Lance Saker, Kelley Lee, Barbara Cannito, Anna Gilmore, and Diarmid Campbell-Lendrum, *Globalization and Infectious Diseases: A Review of the Linkages* (Geneva: World Health Organization, 2004), pp. 35, 37.

11. Danielle Grondin, Jacqueline Weekers, Mary Haour-Knipe, Akram Elton, and Julia Stukey. "Health—An Essential Aspect of Migration Management," in *World Migration 2003: Managing Migration Challenges and Responses for People on the Move,* edited by Thomas L. Weiss (Geneva: International Organization for Migration, 2003), p. 85.

12. Koehn, "Global Health and Human Rights," pp. 1045–1073.

13. Derek Yach and Douglas Bettcher, "The Globalization of Public Health I: Threats and Opportunities," *American Journal of Public Health* 88, No. 5 (May 1998): 735.

14. Michael Godkin, "International Medical Education at UMass Medical School" (unpublished and undated document emailed to Peter Koehn).

15. HIV/AIDS researchers are devoting increased attention to the role of social disruption and migration to "hot spot" environments in fueling the epidemic. Christopher J. Smith and Xiushi Yang, "Examining the Connection Between Temporary Migration and the Spread of STDs and HIV/AIDS in China," *China Review* 5, No. 1 (Spring 2005): 130–131; Kelley Lee and Anthony Zwi, "A Global Political Economy Approach to AIDS: Ideology, Interests and Implications," in Kelley Lee (ed.), *Health Impacts of Globalization: Towards Global Governance* (London: Palgrave Macmillan, 2003), p. 18.

16. Smith and Yang, "Examining the Connection," p. 126.

17. *Ibid.,* pp. 115–116, 122–123, 131.

18. Godkin, "International Medical Education."

19. Harden, "International Medical Education," p. S22; Toole, "Forced Migrants," pp. 198–199.

20. Jill E. Korbin, "Cultural Issues in Pediatric Care," in *Nelson Textbook of Pediatrics,* 17th edition, edited by Richard E. Behrman, Robert M. Kliegman, and Hal B. Jensen (New York: Saunders, 2004), p. 10; Janny Scott, "Life at the Top in America Isn't Just Better, It's Longer," *New York Times,* May 16, 2005, pp. A1, A18–19; Lee and Zwi, "A Global Political Economy Approach ," p. 19. In the United States alone, "an estimated 800,000 lives have been lost due to racial or ethnic health disparities in the past 10 years." Smith, *et al.,* "Recommendations for Teaching," p. 662.

21. World Health Organization and World Bank, *Dying for Change: Poor People's Experience of Health and Ill-Health* (Washington, DC: WHO and the Bank, 2002), pp. 4, 6–8.

22. Richard D. Smith and Landis MacKellar, "Global Public Goods and the Global Health Agenda: Problems, Priorities and Potential," *Globalization and Health* 3, No. 9 (2007).

23. Raymond Bissonette and Cynde Route, "The Educational Effects of Clinical Rotations in Non-industrialized Countries," *Family Medicine* 26 (April 1994): 229.

24. Howard Waitzkin, *The Politics of Medical Encounters: How Patients and Doctors Deal with Social Problems* (New Haven: Yale University Press 1991), p. 5; Wear, "Insurgent Multiculturalism," p. 552.

25. Brenda L. Beagan, "Teaching Social and Cultural Awareness to Medical Students: 'It's All Very Nice to Talk About It in Theory, But Ultimately It Makes No Difference,'" *Academic Medicine* 78, No. 6 (June 2003): 611–614.

26. Wear, "Insurgent Multiculturalism," p. 551; Wear, "Respect for Patients," p. 97; Smith, *et al.,* "Recommendations for Teaching," p. 655; Desiree Lie, John Boker, and Ella Cleveland, "Using the Tool for Assessing Cultural Competence Training (TACCT) to Measure Faculty and Medical School Perceptions of Cultural Competence Instruction in the First Three Years of the Curriculum," *Academic Medicine* 81, No. 6 (June 2006): 562–563; Joseph R. Betancourt, Alexander R. Green, J. Emilio Carrillo, and Elyse R. Park, "Cultural Competence and Health Care Disparities: Key Perspectives and Trends," *Health Affairs* 24, No. 2 (March/April 2005): 501.

27. Daniel George, Iahn Gonsenhauser, and Peter Whitehouse, "Medical Professionalism: The

Nature of Story and the Story of Nature," in *Professionalism in Medicine: Critical Perspectives,* edited by Delese Wear and Julie M. Aultman (New York: Springer, 2006), pp. 71–72.

28. Ronald Labonte and Ted Schrecker, "Globalization and Social Determinants of Health: Introduction and Methodological Background," *Globalization and Health* 3 (June 2007): 5.

29. Ilona S. Kickbusch, "New Players for a New Era: Responding to the Global Public Health Challenges," *Journal of Public Health Medicine* 19, No. 2 (1997): 173.

30. Currently, in many health-profession schools in the South, "instead of working competencies, production of health professionals is based on certification or Western medical standards. The result is a greater proportion of graduates focused on professional status and income generation, which further increases potential out-migration to wealthier countries." Mullan, Panosian, and Cuff, *Healers Abroad,* pp. 24, 27, 145.

31. Mary C. Beach, Somnath Saha, and Lisa A. Cooper, *The Role and Relationship of Cultural Competence and Patient-Centeredness in Health Care Quality* (New York: The Commonwealth Fund, October 2006); Lie, Boker, and Cleveland, "Using TACCT," p. 563.

32. Robert C. Like, "Graduate and Undergraduate Cultural Competence Education" (PowerPoint presentation at the International Workshop on Culturally Appropriate Health Care by Culturally Competent Health Professionals, Caesarea, Israel, October 9, 2007), slide 10; Pelletier, "N.J. Mandates." Social-work education is treated in Chapter 8.

33. Joseph R. Betancourt, Joel S. Weissman, Minah K. Kim, Elyse R. Park, and Angela W. Maina, *Resident Physicians' Preparedness to provide Cross-Cultural Care: Implications for Clinical Care and Medical Education Policy* (New York: The Commonwealth Fund, May 2007), p. ix.

34. Harden, "International Medical Education," p. S27.

35. Derek Yach and Douglas Bettcher, "The Globalization of Public Health II: The Convergence of Self-Interest and Altruism," *American Journal of Public Health* 88, No. 5 (May 1998): 738.

36. Betancourt, Green, Carrillo, and Park, "Cultural Competence," p. 502. In a 2003 survey, however, residents in emergency medicine and general surgery were especially likely to report having "very little instruction in cross-cultural skills," and one-fourth of all responding residents felt unprepared to treat new immigrants. Betancourt, Weissman, Kim, Park, and Maina, *Resident Physicians' Preparedness,* p. vii.

37. Compare, for instance, the approaches adopted and skills covered in CC programs at the University of California, Irvine, School of Medicine; the University of Massachusetts Medical School's Pathway on Serving Multicultural and Underserved Populations; and the Department of Family Medicine at UMDNJ–Robert Wood Johnson Medical School. Lie, Boker, and Cleveland, "Using TACCT," p. 558; Godkin, Savageau, and Fletcher, "Global Longitudinal Pathway," pp. 227–228; Like interview; http://www2.umdnj.edu/fmedweb/chfcd/INDEX.HTM. During the 2006–2007 academic year, RWJMS's new longitudinal Patient-Centered Medicine course devoted twenty-two formal curriculum hours to cultural competence. Robert C. Like, "Cultural Competency Education: UMDNJ–Robert Wood Johnson Medical School" (unpublished document emailed to Peter Koehn, November 2007). Also see Herbert Swick and Peter Koehn, "Preparing Transnationally Competent Physicians for Migrant-Friendly Health Care: New Directions in U.S. Medical Education," in *Proceedings of the Hospitals in a Culturally Diverse Europe Conference on Quality-Assured Health Care and Health Promotion for Migrants and Ethnic Minorities, Amsterdam, December 9–11, 2004.* www.mfh-eu.net/conf/results/. In response to accreditation requirements recently implemented by the Accreditation Council on Graduate Medical Education, new curricula and training standards "have begun to emerge, although none are widely accepted yet." Smith, *et al.,* "Recommendations for Teaching," p. 655. For a promising effort to design a unified CC framework for residency training and graduate medical education, see Robert C. Like, R. Prasaad Steiner, and Arthur J. Rubel, "Recommended Core Curriculum Guidelines on Culturally Sensitive and Competent Health Care" mhtml:file//Pub_NIHP/Workshops/CulturallyAppropriate_2007/Background Reading.

38. Betancourt, *et al.,* "Cultural Competence," p. 502.

39. Communicative competence is a particularly highly developed skill area in cultural-competence education. See, for instance, the resources available through Georgetown University's National Center for Cultural Competence at http://www11.georgetown.edu/research/gucchd/nccc. Indeed, the academics interviewed in 2002 by Betancourt and colleagues "viewed cultural competence as the development of

a skill set for more effective provider-patient communication." Betancourt, Green, Carrillo, and Park, "Cultural Competence," p. 501.

In a personal communication with one of the authors (email to Peter Koehn dated November 27, 2007), Robert Like reports that "we unfortunately don't yet have a 'transnational competency curriculum' per se at RWJMS but instead define cultural competency/diversity in a broader way than is often done. I believe that our content overlaps in part with much of what you've described in your various articles. There are ongoing discussions about incorporating more education/training about global/international health issue [sic] into the medical school curriculum in the future."

40. http://www.aamc.org/meded/tacct/start.htm.

41. However, none of the TACCT skills address creative competence.

42. Steven L. Kantner, "Global Health Is More Important in a Smaller World," *Academic Medicine* 83, No. 2 (February 2008): 116.

43. AAMC class of 2006 graduation questionnaire results cited in Godkin, "International Medical Education"; also see Drain, *et al.*, "Global Health in Medical Education," p. 227; Mullan, Panosian, and Cuff, *Healers Abroad*, p. 15. In 2005–2006, nearly half of the graduating medical students at the University of Massachusetts had participated in an overseas learning experience (in twenty-three, mostly low-income, countries). Godkin, "International Medical Education"; Godkin, Savageau, and Fletcher, "Global Longitudinal Pathway," p. 227. The American Medical Association's International Health Database lists more than thirty worldwide university sites and twenty residencies with international opportunities. http://www.ama-assn.org/ama/pub/category/print/12675.html (accessed November 16, 2008).

44. Drain, *et al.*, "Global Health in Medical Education," p. 227.

45. In 2006, medical schools at Vanderbilt University, University of New South Wales, Harvard University, and Duke University, among others, undertook major global-health initiatives. With funding from the NIH's Fogarty Center, a number of new and innovative interdisciplinary programs were launched in 2007. These initiatives, which are in the process of designing coordinated multidisciplinary curriculums, include programs at Pennsylvania State University ("training a new cadre of health scientists and practitioners as well as mining and petroleum engineers to holistically address the root causes of poverty, inequity, and disease in Africa"), Weill Medical College of Cornell University, and the University of Washington (medicine, public health, law, and arts and sciences). A few schools have established programs that specifically train medical students for transnational health careers. Many others have introduced a course or seminar on global health. Drain, *et al.*, "Global Health in Medical Education," p. 227; Jessica Evert, *Developing Global Health Curricula: A Guidebook for US Medical Schools* (Reston, VA: International Federation of Medical Students' Associations—USA, 2006), p. 31.

46. These include programs at Simon Fraser University, the University of Massachusetts–Amherst, the University of Montana's new global and rural health–oriented MPH, UCLA's specialization in global health within its MPH, and the University of Wisconsin–Madison's international health concentration. The London School of Economics offers Masters degrees in International Health Policy and in Development and Health. Evert, *Developing Global Health Curricula*, p. 20.

47. See Ravi Narayan and Claudio Schuftan, "The People's Health Movement: A People's Campaign for 'Health for All—Now,'" in Richard L. Harris and Melinda Seid (eds.), *Globalization and Health* (Leiden: Brill, 2004), pp. 236–240.

48. See, for instance, Amber S. Batata, "International Nurse Recruitment and NHS Vacancies: A Cross-Sectional Analysis," *Globalization and Health* 1, No. 7 (2005); Nerissa N. Koehn, G.E. Fryer Jr., R.L. Phillips, John B. Miller, and L.A. Green, "The Increase in International Medical Graduates in Family Practice Residency Programs," *Family Medicine* 34, No. 6 (June 2002): 429–435.

49. In Europe, Finnish medical schools generally have been accepting of transnational education initiatives, while those in Greece and the United Kingdom have not. Harden, "International Medical Education," p. S24.

50. Harden, "International Medical Education," pp. S25–S26, S22. Harden focuses on medical schools, but his argument can be more widely applied.

51. Programs in sixteen countries that participate in the International Virtual Medical School share learning resources. In Malaysia, students complete two and a half years of education at the International Medical University in Kuala Lumpur and then finish their medical degree at one of twenty-two partner

schools in North America, Australasia, and Europe. Harden, "International Medical Education," pp. S25–S26.

52. *Ibid.*, pp. S26–S27.

53. Audiey Kao and Jennifer Reenan, "*Wit* Is Not Enough," in *Professionalism in Medicine: Critical Perspectives,* edited by Delese Wear and Julie M. Aultman (New York: Springer, 2006), pp. 217, 222.

54. Milstein, *Hygeia's Constellation,* pp. 2, 8, 11. On the utility of transdisciplinary integration and using dynamic feedback models to analyze "mutually reinforcing causal feedback among afflictions, living conditions, and public strength [to act and alter]," see pp. 37–38, 42.

55. Kent Buse, Nick Drager, Suzanne Fustukian, and Kelley Lee, "Globalisation and Health Policy: Trends and Opportunities," in *Health Policy in a Globalising World,* edited by Kelley Lee, Kent Buse, and Suzanne Fustukian (Cambridge: Cambridge University Press), p. 273.

56. Houpt, Pearson, and Hall, "Three Domains of Competency," pp. 222–224.

57. Alexander R. Green, Joseph R. Betancourt, and J. Emilio Carillo, "Integrating Social Factors into Cross-Cultural Medical Education," *Academic Medicine* 77, No. 3 (2002): 193–197; Ray M. Fitzpatrick, Anthony P. Hopkins, and Olivia Harvard-Watts, "Social Dimensions of Healing: A Longitudinal Study of Outcomes of Medical Management of Headaches," *Social Science & Medicine* 17, No. 8 (1983): 505; Like, "Recommended Core Curriculum Guidelines," p. 294.

58. Betancourt, Weissman, Kim, Park, and Maina, *Resident Physicians' Preparedness,* p. ix. Students quickly discover that shared ethnicity does not necessarily mean shared culture. For an example, see "TB & Cultural Competency," *Northeastern Regional Training and Medical Consultation Consortium* 6 (June 2007): 4.

59. Like, "Graduate and Undergraduate Cultural Competence Education," slide 30.

60. This skill incorporates the "ability to understand critical issues in transnational research." Escobar interview. TACCT skills in "demonstrated knowledge of epidemiology" and "understanding of population health variability" are embedded in this TC analytic domain. See Lie, Boker, and Cleveland, "Using TACCT," p. 559.

61. The Global Health Education Consortium provides a rich set of web-based resources and information on global health issues. http://www.globalhealth-ec.org/GHEC.

62. Like, "Recommended Core Curriculum Guidelines," p. 294.

63. B.D. Smedley, A.Y. Stith, and A.R. Nelson (eds.), *Unequal Treatment: Confronting Racial and Ethnic Disparities in Health Care* (Washington, DC: National Academy Press, 2003), p. 205; Like interview.

64. Moustafa Bayoumi, "Confessions of an Arab Mind," *Missoulian,* July 13, 2004, p. A4.

65. Kate Gerrish, Charles Husband, and Jennifer Mackensie, *Nursing for a Multi-Ethnic Society* (Buckingham: Open University Press, 1996), p. 34.

66. Like, "Recommended Core Curriculum Guidelines," p. 292.

67. Buse, Drager, Fustukian, and Lee, "Globalisation and Health Policy," pp. 259, 263–267.

68. See Like, "Recommended Core Curriculum Guidelines," p. 292; Peter H. Koehn and Kirsti Sainola-Rodriguez, "Clinician/Patient Connections in Ethnoculturally Nonconcordant Encounters with Political-Asylum Seekers: A Comparison of Physicians and Nurses," *Journal of Transcultural Nursing* 16, No. 4 (Oct. 2005): 298–311.

69. TACCT skill in "understanding social determinants of health" is embedded in this TC analytic domain. See Lie, Boker, and Cleveland, "Using TACCT," p. 560.

70. Mary E. Duffy, "A Critique of Cultural Education in Nursing," *Journal of Advanced Nursing* 36, No. 4 (2001): 489.

71. Waitzkin, *Politics of Medical Encounters,* pp. 276, 4, 11.

72. Ilona Kickbusch and Kent Buse, "Global Influences and Global Responses: International Health at the Turn of the Twenty-First Century," in *International Public Health: Diseases, Programs, Systems, and Policies,* edited by Michael H. Merson, Robert E. Black, and Anne J. Mills (Gaithersburg: Aspen Publishers, 2001), pp. 713, 724; Anthony B. Zwi and Derek Yach, "International Health in the 21st Century: Trends and Challenges," *Social Science & Medicine* 54, No. 11 (2002): 1617.

73. These include "the industrialization of food production, the growth of sophisticated supply chain management on a global scale, ... the growing concentration of global food manufactures as a result of mergers and acquisitions, and the rapid growth of supermarkets in the developing world." Magnusson,

"Non-Communicable Diseases." Also see Corinna Hawkes, "Uneven Dietary Development: Linking the Policies and Processes of Globalization with the Nutrition Transition, Obesity and Diet-Related Chronic Diseases," *Globalization and Health* 2, No. 4 (2006).

74. Koehn, *Refugees from Revolution*, pp. 40–45, 58-98, 392–394, 400–405.

75. Derrick Silove, "The Challenges Facing Mental Health Programs for Post-Conflict and Refugee Communities," *Prehospital and Disaster Medicine* 19, No. 1 (2004): 93.

76. Jennifer Clapp, "The Distancing of Waste: Overconsumption in a Global Economy," in *Confronting Consumption*, edited by Thomas Princen, Michael Maniates, and Ken Conca (Cambridge, MA: MIT Press, 2002), pp. 155–176.

77. The latter ability is recognized as a vital component of residency training and graduate medical education by the Society of Teachers of Family Medicine's Group on Multicultural Health Care and Education. Like, "Recommended Core Curriculum Guidelines," p. 291; also Like interview. TACCT skills in "identifying physician biases that affect clinical care," "recognizing how physician biases affect care," and "describing potential ways to address bias" are embedded in this TC analytic domain. See Lie, Boker, and Cleveland, "Using TACCT," p. 559.

78. Marjorie Kagawa-Singer and Shaheen Kassim-Lakha, "A Strategy to Reduce Cross-Cultural Miscommunication and Increase the Likelihood of Improving Health Outcomes," *Academic Medicine* 78, No. 6 (2003): 579.

79. Including the influence of intergenerational health inequities. Milstein, *Hygeia's Constellation*, pp. 44–45.

80. Including the relationship of disparities in health care to health disparities. Smith, *et al.*, "Recommendations for Teaching," pp. 656, 658. TACCT skills in "identifying patterns of national data on disparities," "concretizing epidemiology of disparities," "describing patterns of health care disparities," "identifying and discussing key areas of disparities," "discussing barriers to eliminating health disparities," and "recognizing disparities amenable to intervention" are embedded in this TC analytic domain. See Lie, Boker, and Cleveland, "Using TACCT," pp. 559–560.

81. This theme provides the basis for collaborative initiatives undertaken by the Global Health Sciences program at the University of California, San Francisco. Sarah B. Macfarlane, Nina Agabian, Thomas E. Novotny, George W. Rutherford, Christopher C. Stewart, and Haile T. Debas, "Think Globally, Act Locally, and Collaborate Internationally: Global Health Sciences," *Academic Medicine* 83, No. 2 (February 2008): 177–178.

82. See Philip Kasinitz, "Race, Assimilation, and 'Second Generations,' Past and Present," in *Not Just Black and White: Historical and Contemporary Perspectives on Immigration, Race, and Ethnicity in the United States,* edited by Nancy Foner and George M. Fredrickson (New York: Russell Sage Foundation, 2004), p. 286.

83. See, for instance, Peter H. Koehn, "Transnational Migration, State Policy, and Local Clinician Treatment of Asylum Seekers and Resettled Migrants: Comparative Perspectives on Reception-Centre and Community Health-Care Practice in Finland," *Global Social Policy* 6, No. 1 (2006): 21–56.

84. K. Allden, "The Indochinese Psychiatry Clinic: Trauma and Refugee Mental Health Treatment in the 1990s," *Journal of Ambulatory Care Management* 21, No. 2 (1998), p. 32; also see Waitzkin, *The Politics of Medical Encounters*, pp. 3, 8, 14; Ellen Rosenberg, Claude Richard, Marie-Therese Lussier, and Shelly N. Abdool, "Intercultural Communication Competence in Family Medicine: Lessons from the Field," *Patient Education and Counseling* 61 (May 2006): 244.

85. Joan G.Lipson and Afaf I. Meleis, "Research with Immigrants and Refugees," in Ada Sue Hinshaw, Suzanne L. Feetham, and Joan L.F. Shaver (eds.), *Handbook of Clinical Nursing Research* (Thousand Oaks: Sage, 1999), p. 89.

86. Milstein, *Hygeia's Constellation*, pp. 42–43.

87. *Ibid.*, p. 43.

88. *Ibid.*, pp. 44, 53.

89. *Ibid.*, p. 60.

90. TACCT skills in "recognizing patients' healing traditions and beliefs," "identifying how ethnicity, race, and culture relate to health," and "describing challenges in cross-cultural community" are embedded in this TC analytic domain. See Lie, Boker, and Cleveland, "Using TACCT," p. 559.

91. These insights come from Robert Like. See Pelletier, "N.J. Mandates."

92. See Peter H. Koehn, "Transmigration, Transnational Competence, & Global Health" (PowerPoint presentation at the 2nd Tampere Symposium on Global Health Research, September 5, 2008), slides 4, 5, 12, 21, 24, 29–31; Peter H. Koehn and Marja Tiilikainen, "Migration and Transnational Health Care: Connecting Finland and Somaliland," *Siirtolaisuus—Migration* 34, No. 1 (2007): 2–9.

93. Gerrish, Husband, and Mackensie, *Nursing for a Multi-Ethnic Society,* p. 36; Jennie Popay and Gareth Williams, "Public Health Research and Lay Knowledge," *Social Science and Medicine* 42, No. 5 (1996): 760–762; Rosenberg, Richard, Lussier, and Abdool, "Intercultural Communication Competence," p. 237; Pelletier, "N.J. Mandates."

94. Melanie Tervalon and Jann Murray-Garcia, "Cultural Humility Versus Cultural Competence: A Critical Distinction in Defining Physician Training Outcomes in Multicultural Education," *Journal of Health Care for the Poor and Underserved* 9, No. 2 (1998): 121.

95. See Peter H. Koehn, "Improving Transnational Health-Care Encounters and Outcomes: The Challenge of Enhanced Transnational Competence for Migrants and Health Professionals," in *Proceedings of the Hospitals in a Culturally Diverse Europe Conference on Quality-assured Health Care and Health Promotion for Migrants and Ethnic Minorities, Amsterdam, December 9–11, 2004.* www.mfh-eu.net/conf/results/.

96. J. Shapiro and P. Lenahan, "Family Medicine in a Culturally Diverse World: A Solution-Oriented Approach to Common Cross-Cultural Problems in Medical Encounters," *Family Medicine* 28, No. 4 (1996): 251–252, 254–255; Kagawa-Singer and Shaheen Kassim-Lakha, "A Strategy to Reduce Cross-Cultural Miscommunication," p. 582.

97. See Koehn and Swick, "Medical Education for a Changing World," pp. 552–553.

98. See M. Eastmond, "Nationalist Discourses and the Construction of Difference: Bosnian Muslim Refugees in Sweden," *Journal of Refugee Studies* 11, No. 2 (1998): 162–163, 178.

99. Genogram construction enriches the ethnographic interview. In the process of constructing genograms, one is able to identify "patterns of physical illness in families and the chains of losses, bereavements, abuse and violence both within the family and towards the community." Alice Cook and Rhiannon England, "Pain in the Heart: Primary Care Consultations with Frequently Attending Refugees," *Primary Care Mental Health* 2 (June 2004): 110–111.

100. Anne Fadiman, *The Spirit Catches You and You Fall Down: A Hmong Child, Her American Doctors, and the Collision of Two Cultures* (New York: Farrar, Straus and Giroux, 1997), pp. 28, 259.

101. Eastmond, "Nationalist Discourses," pp. 177–179.

102. TACCT skills in "valuing the importance of diversity in health care" and "respecting patient's cultural beliefs" are embedded in this TC emotional domain. See Lie, Boker, and Cleveland, "Using TACCT," pp. 559–560.

103. J. Zweifler and A.M. Gonzalez, "Teaching Residents to Care for Culturally Diverse Populations," *Academic Medicine* 73, No. 10 (1998): 1058.

104. Betancourt, Green, Carrillo, and Park, "Cultural Competence," p. 501. More than half of the residents surveyed in 2003, for instance, indicated that they had received minimal training in identifying patient mistrust. Betancourt, Weissman, Kim, Park, and Maina, *Resident Physicians' Preparedness,* p. vii.

105. Charlie Davison, Stephen Frankel, and George D. Smith, "The Limits of Lifestyle: Re-Assessing 'Fatalism' in the Popular Culture of Illness Prevention," *Social Science and Medicine* 34, No. 6 (1992): 679–684.

106. TACCT skill in "valuing curiosity, empathy, and respect" is embedded in this TC emotional domain. See Lie, Boker, and Cleveland, "Using TACCT," p. 559.

107. Escobar interview.

108. See A. E. Nunez, "Transforming Cultural Competence into Cross-Cultural Efficacy in Women's Health Education," *Academic Medicine* 75, No. 11: 1072.

109. See Anna M. Napoles-Springer, Jasmine Santoyo, Kathryn Houston, Eliseo J. Perez-Stable, and Anita L. Stewart, "Patients' Perceptions of Cultural Factors Affecting the Quality of Their Medical Encounters," *Health Expectations* 8 (2005): 13; Peter H. Koehn, "Medical Encounters in Finnish Reception Centres: Asylum-Seeker and Clinician Perspectives," *Journal of Refugee Studies* 18, No. 1 (2005): 56–61.

110. D. Buchwald, P.V. Caralis, F. Gany, E.T. Hardt, T.M Johnson, M.A. Mueche, and R.W. Putsch,

"Caring for Patients in a Multicultural Society," *Patient Care* 28, No. 11 (1994): 105–123; Korbin, "Cultural Issues in Pediatric Care," p. 11.

111. Also see Like, "Graduate and Undergraduate Cultural Competence Education," slide 30.

112. For instance, many "refugee patients and their families bring to health consultation stories of incredible human resilience in the most extreme circumstances" (Stanton, *et al.*, 2000, p. 27).

113. A. Bandura, "Exercise of Personal and Collective Efficacy in Changing Societies," in *Self-Efficacy in Changing Societies*, edited by A. Bandura (Cambridge: Cambridge University Press, 1995), pp. 25–28, 35; R. Schwarzer and R. Fuchs, "Changing Risk Behaviors and Adopting Health Behaviors: The Role of Self-Efficacy Beliefs," in *Self-Efficacy in Changing Societies*, edited by A. Bandura (Cambridge: Cambridge University Press, 1995), pp. 262–268, 277, 280.

114. Anna R. McPhatter, "Cultural Competence in Child Welfare: What Is It? How Do We Achieve It? What Happens Without It?" *Child Welfare* 76, No. 1 (1997): 269.

115. Ellen A. Lothe and Kristin Heggen, "A Study of Resilience in Young Ethiopian Famine Survivors," *Journal of Transcultural Nursing* 14, No. 4 (2003): 314.

116. Escobar interview; Smith, *et al.*, "Recommendations for Teaching," p. 654; Like, "Recommended Core Curriculum Guidelines," p. 292. TACCT skills in "engaging in reflection about one's own beliefs" and "valuing the need to address personal bias" are embedded in this TC emotional domain. See Lie, Boker, and Cleveland, "Using TACCT," p. 559.

117. Tervalon and Murray-Garcia, "Cultural Humility Versus Cultural Competence," pp. 118–119; Like interview.

118. Escobar interview. TACCT skill in "valuing eliminating disparities" is embedded in this TC emotional domain. See Lie, Boker, and Cleveland, "Using TACCT," p. 560.

119. Kristin Akerjordet and Elisabeth Severinsson, "Emotional Intelligence: A Review of the Literature with Specific Focus on Empirical and Epistemological Perspectives," *Journal of Clinical Nursing* (2007): 1410.

120. Herbert M. Adler, "The Sociophysiology of Caring in the Doctor-Patient Relationship," *Journal of General Internal Medicine* 17 (November 2002): 874–881.

121. H.R. Searight, "Bosnian Immigrants' Perceptions of the United States Health Care System: Qualitative Interview Study," *Journal of Immigrant Health* 5, No. 2 (2003): 87–93.

122. Milstein, *Hygeia's Constellation*, pp. 22, 52, 58.

123. See Korbin, "Cultural Issues in Pediatric Care," p. 12.

124. Center for Mental Health Services, 2001, pp. III5, 10; Tervalon, "Components of Culture," p. 573; Fadiman, *The Spirit Catches You*, pp. 266–268; Larry D. Purnell and Betty J. Paulanka, "Purnell's Model for Cultural Competence," in *Transcultural Health Care: A Culturally Competent Approach*, edited by Larry D. Purnell and Betty J. Paulanka (Philadelphia: F.A. Davis, 1998), p. 43.

125. Craig R. Janes, "Going Global in Century XXI: Medical Anthropology and the New Primary Health Care," *Human Organization* 63, No. 4 (2004): 467.

126. Escobar interview.

127. Arthur Kleinman, Leon Eisenberg, and Byron Good, "Culture, Illness, and Care: Clinical Lessons from Anthropologic and Cross-Cultural Research," *Annals of Internal Medicine* 88 (1978): 251.

128. Waitzkin, *The Politics of Medical Encounters*, pp. 9, 23.

129. Janes, "Going Global," p. 468.

130. Kenneth Fox, "Provider-Patient Communication in the Context of Inequalities," in *Child Health in the Multicultural Environment*, edited by Esther Silverman (Columbus, OH: Ross Products Division, Abbott Laboratories, 2000), p. 27; also see Debra L. Roter and Judith A. Hall, *Doctors Talking with Patients/Patients Talking with Doctors: Improving Communication in Medical Visits* (Westport, CT: Auburn House, 1992), p. 5; Smedley, Stith, and Nelson, *Unequal Treatment*, pp. 141, 200.

131. Kao and Reenan, "*Wit* Is Not Enough," p. 218.

132. See, for instance, Fischer, "'Flat World' Lessons."

133. See Kreps, "Communication and Racial Inequities in Health Care," p. 8.

134. Napoles-Springer, Santoyo, Houston, Perez-Stable, and Stewart, "Patients' Perceptions of Cultural Factors," p. 5.

135. See Zweifler and Gonzalez, "Teaching Residents," pp. 1058, 1060. It is not surprising, therefore, that the value placed on learning another language diminished among students who participated in the

University of Massachusetts Medical School's Global Multiculturalism Track. See Michael A. Godkin and Judith Savageau, "The Effect of a Global Multiculturalism Track on Cultural Competence of Preclinical Medical Students," *Family Medicine* 33, No. 3 (2001): 185. Smith and colleagues ("Recommendations for Teaching," pp. 658–659) suggest that foreign-language training remains useful "for those training or practicing in certain geographic areas or with specific populations." Escobar (interview) recommends that additional language learning be weighed heavily as a qualification for *entry* into health-profession programs.

136. Nina Bernstein, "Language Gap Called Health Risk in E.R.," *New York Times*, April 21, 2005, p. C20.

137. Cynthia E. Roat (executive producer), *Communicating Effectively Through an Interpreter* (Seattle: The Cross Cultural Health Care Program, 1998); Smedley, Stith, and Nelson, *Unequal Treatment*, p. 192. In the 2003 national survey of resident physicians in their final year of training supported by the Commonwealth Fund, 22 percent of the respondents felt unprepared to work effectively with patients possessing limited English proficiency and more than half (53 percent) reported poor access to interpreters. Weissman, Kim, Park, and Maina, *Resident Physicians' Preparedness*, p. vii.

138. Melanie Tervalon, "Components of Culture in Health for Medical Students' Education," *Academic Medicine* 78, No. 6 (June 2003): 572–573; Weissman, Kim, Park, and Maina, *Resident Physicians' Preparedness*, p. ix. TACCT skills in "listing effective ways of working with an interpreter" and "identifying and collaborating with an interpreter" are embedded in this TC communicative domain. See Lie, Boker, and Cleveland, "Using TACCT," p. 560.

139. The latter is particularly important when care receivers are not literate. Smith, *et al.*, "Recommendations for Teaching," p. 658.

140. Like, Steiner, and Rubel, "Recommended Core Curriculum Guidelines," p. 294.

141. Howard Waitzkin, "Doctor-Patient Communication: Clinical Implications of Social Scientific Research," *JAMA* 252, No. 17 (November 2, 1984): 2445.

142. Kao and Reenan, "*Wit* Is Not Enough," p. 213.

143. K.H. Kavanagh, "Transcultural Perspectives in Mental Health," in *Transcultural Concepts in Nursing Care*, 3rd edition, edited by M.M. Andrews and J.S. Boyle (Philadelphia: Lippincott, 1999), p. 245; also see Tervalon and Murray-Garcia, "Cultural Humility versus Cultural Competence," p. 119.

144. Napoles-Springer, Santoyo, Houston, Perez-Stable, and Stewart, "Patients' Perceptions of Cultural Factors," p. 13; Kreps, "Communication and Racial Inequities in Health Care," p. 5; Like, Steiner, and Rubel, "Recommended Core Curriculum Guidelines," p. 294. TACCT skills in "asking questions to elicit patient preferences," "eliciting information in family-centered context," and "elicit[ing] a cultural, social, and medical history" are embedded in this TC communicative domain. See Lie, Boker, and Cleveland, "Using TACCT," pp. 559–560.

145. TACCT skill in "nonjudgmental listening to health beliefs" is embedded in this TC communicative domain. See Lie, Boker, and Cleveland, "Using TACCT," p. 559.

146. M.R. DiMatteo, "Health Behaviors and Care Decisions," in *Handbook of Health Behavior Research II: Provider Determinants*, edited by D.S. Gochman (New York: Plenum Press, 1997), p. 8; Waitzkin, *The Politics of Medical Encounters*, p. 273. TACCT skill in "valuing the link between communication and care" is embedded in this TC communicative domain. See Lie, Boker, and Cleveland, "Using TACCT," p. 559.

147. On the latter, see Kreps, "Communication and Racial Inequities in Health Care," pp. 7–8.

148. Milstein, *Hygeia's Constellation*, pp. 37, 50.

149. For instance, TC-prepared physicians integrate evidence-based insights regarding the influence of ethnocultural practices/predispositions, class, migration, trauma, and access into patient-specific health-status hypotheses and effective health-care responses.

150. Izadnegahdar, *et al.*, "Global Health in Canadian Medical Education," p. 193.

151. See Roter and Hall, *Doctors Talking with Patients*, pp. 46–49.

152. Marc Lacey, "In Africa, Guns Aren't the Only Killers," *New York Times*, April 25, 2005.

153. Grondin, *et al.*, "Health ," pp. 90–91.

154. *Ibid.*, p. 91.

155. See, for instance, Cook and England, "Pain in the Heart," p. 111.

156. In this respect, TC functional education draws upon *cheng*, a core doctrine of professional ethics

in traditional Chinese medicine that calls for "genuine and deep compassion for human pain, suffering, and distress" and endeavoring to treat all patients equally, as if each was one's close relative. Jing-Bao Nie, "After *Cheng* (Sincerity): The Professional Ethics of Traditional Chinese Medicine," in *Healing As Vocation: A Medical Professionalism Primer,* edited by Kayhan Parsi and Myles N. Sheehan (Lanham, MD: Rowman & Littlefield, 2006), p. 67.

157. One way for physicians to develop rapport with patients on quality-of-life issues is to be open about the challenge of balancing optimal service to the patient with one's own self-care and family needs. See James W. Lomax, "Building the Foundation," *Psychiatry* 70, No. 3 (Fall 2007): 212.

158. See "TB & Cultural Competency," p. 5; Godkin and Savageau, "Effect of a Global Multiculturalism Track," p. 185; Napoles-Springer, Santoyo, Houston, Perez-Stable, and Stewart, "Patients' Perceptions of Cultural Factors," pp. 13–14; Kao and Reenan, "*Wit* Is Not Enough," p. 213. Developing one's capacity to handle the resulting, often painful, level of intimacy is rarely explored in mainstream medical education. Cook and England, "Pain in the Heart," p. 111.

159. Duffy, "Cultural Education in Nursing," p. 491.

160. G. Flores, "Culture and the Patient-Physician Relationship: Achieving Cultural Competency in Health Care," *Journal of Pediatrics* 136, No. 1 (2000): 16; Kleinman, Eisenberg, and Good, "Culture, Illness, and Care," p. 257. In many low-income countries, family members perform the roles of nurses and hospital cooks (among others). Bissonette and Route, "Nonindustrialized Countries," p. 230.

161. Thom, Tirado, Woon, and McBride, "Cultural Competency Training Curriculum"; Like, "Recommended Core Curriculum Guidelines," p. 294. TACCT skill in "negotiating and problem-solving" is embedded in this TC function domain. See Lie, Boker, and Cleveland, "Using TACCT," p. 560.

162. Smith, *et al.,* "Recommendations for Teaching," p. 659.

163. Like interview; Mark Kuczewski, "The Problem with Evaluating Professionalism," in *Professionalism in Medicine: Critical Perspectives,* edited by Delese Wear and Julie M. Aultman (New York: Springer, 2006), p. 196.

164. See Betancourt, Green, Carrillo, and Park, "Cultural Competence," p. 503.

165. Few current medical-school curriculums target the elimination/reduction of disparities as a professional goal or focus on teaching students how to help address inequities. Smith, *et al.,* "Recommendations for Teaching," pp. 655–656, 659.

166. George, Gonsenhauser, and Whitehouse, "Medical Professionalism," p. 73.

167. See Waitzkin, *The Politics of Medical Encounters,* pp. 11, 23, 25, 39.

168. "In our 21st century world," George, Gonsenhauser, and Whitehouse maintain ("Medical Professionalism," p. 68), "medical schools must help students extrapolate a concern for the individual patient to the environment in which those patients live." For instance, the UMDNJ–Robert Wood Johnson Medical School offers a second-year rotation for family-medicine residents in medically underserved urban areas that is aimed at enhancing "skills in providing culturally sensitive, community-oriented primary care to a diverse and indigent population." Like, "Cultural Competency Education," p. 3. The major community-service projects initiated for poor residents by Global Longitudinal Pathway students at the University of Massachusetts include an exercise-buddy program for diabetic patients, a weekly free clinic for Portuguese- and Spanish-speaking immigrants, a health-education newsletter in Portuguese and Spanish, and school mentoring for refugee children. Godkin, Savageau, and Fletcher, "Global Longitudinal Pathway," p. 231; Godkin, "International Medical Education."

169. Like, "Recommended Core Curriculum Guidelines," p. 295. TACCT skills in "collaborating with communities to address needs," "describing methods to identify community leaders," and "proposing a community-based health intervention" are embedded in this TC function domain. See Lie, Boker, and Cleveland, "Using TACCT," pp. 559–560.

170. "TB & Cultural Competency," p. 5.

171. Kasinitz, "Race, Assimilation," p. 286; Donelle M. Barnes, Cara Harrison, Richard Heneghan, "Health Risk and Promotion Behaviors in Refugee Populations," *Journal of Health Care for the Poor and Underserved* 15, No. 3 (2004): 353–354.

172. Like, "Recommended Core Curriculum Guidelines," p. 292; Like interview. TACCT skills in "demonstrating strategies to address/reduce bias," and "recognizing and managing the impact of bias" are embedded in this TC function domain. See Lie, Boker, and Cleveland, "Using TACCT," pp. 559–560.

173. See Like, "Recommended Core Curriculum Guidelines," p. 295.

174. See Paul Farmer, *Infections and Inequalities: The Modern Plagues* (Berkeley: University of California Press, 1999), pp. 10–12, 15, 252; G. Pappas, "Some Implications for the Study of the Doctor-Patient Interaction: Power, Structure, and Agency in the Works of Howard Waitzkin and Arthur Kleinman," *Social Science and Medicine* 30, No. 2 (1990): 202; Smedley, Stith, and Nelson, *Unequal Treatment,* pp. 35–36, 185; Zwi and Yach, "International Health in the 21st Century," p. 1616; Silove, "Challenges Facing Mental Health," p. 95; Narayan and Schuftan, "The People's Health Movement ," pp. 238–239.
175. See Buse, Drager, Fustukian, and Lee, "Globalisation and Health Policy," p. 278; Magnusson, "Non-Communicable Diseases"; Milstein, *Hygeia's Constellation,* pp. 51, 78.
176. http://www.psr.org/site/PageServer?pagename=Social_Justice.
177. http://www.missoulamedicalaid.net/.
178. Siegel and Narayan, "Unite for Diabetes Campaign."
179. http://www.oxha.org/initiatives/cih.
180. Smith and Yang, "Examining the Connection," p. 132.
181. Janes, "Going Global," pp. 467–468.
182. Shapiro and Lenahan, "Family Medicine in a Culturally Diverse World," p. 250.

Notes for Chapter 11

1. William K. Cummings, "Transnationalism and Transnational Competence," in *Transnational Competence: Rethinking the U.S.-Japan Educational Relationship,* edited by John N. Hawkins and William K. Cummings (Albany: State University of New York Press, 2000), p. 8.
2. Brademas, Kolb, and Mockett, *Education for Global Leadership,* p. 26.
3. Merryfield, "Framework for Teacher Education," p. 20; Shaw and Kim, *Education for Sustainable Development Practice,* p. 55.
4. Given the rapid rate at which some technical knowledge and skills become obsolete, lifelong learning ability is "a most precious asset for the future." http://www.gdrc.org/sustdev/un-desd/intro_un-desd.html. Accessed October 2, 2008.
5. William I. Brustein, "Paths to Global Competence: Preparing American College Students to Meet the World," *IIE Network* (2005): 1–2. http://www.iienetwork.org/page/84657/.
6. See Carter, "Multiculturalism, Diversity, and Global Competence," p. 57.
7. Kenneth Prewitt, "Redefining International Scholarship," in *Changing Perspectives on International Education,* edited by Patrick O'Meara, Howard D. Mehlinger, and Roxanna Ma Newman (Bloomington: Indiana University Press, 2001), p. 85.
8. See Richard D. Lambert, "Domains and Issues in International Studies," in *Changing Perspectives on International Education,* edited by Patrick O'Meara, Howard D. Mehlinger, and Roxanna Ma Newman (Bloomington: Indiana University Press, 2001), p. 37.
9. Teichler, *Requirements of the World of Work,* p. 24.
10. Humphrey Tonkin, "Higher Education and Global Competence: Diversity, Technology, Global Resources," in *Educational Exchange and Global Competence,* edited by Richard D. Lambert (Portland, ME: Council on International Educational Exchange, 1994), pp. 181, 185.
11. Weber, "Framework for Teaching and Learning," p. 201.
12. NASULGC, *Expanding the International Scope of Universities,* p. 15.
13. Donald Killick, "World-Wide Horizons: Cross-Cultural Capability and Global Perspectives—Guidelines for Curriculum Review," in *Internationalising Higher Education,* edited by Elspeth Jones and Sally Brown (London: Routledge, 2007), pp. 207–208; Dena R. Samuels, "Teaching About Hate Crimes: Broadening the Scope," in *Teaching About Ethnoviolence and Hate Crimes: A Resource Guide,* edited by Abby Ferber and Kimberly Holcolm (Washington, DC: American Sociological Association, 2007), p. 161.
14. These pairings, of course, include matches of domestic and international students. See Elspeth Jones and David Killick, "Internationalisation of the Curriculum," in *Internationalising Higher Education,* edited by Elspeth Jones and Sally Brown (London: Routledge, 2007), p. 113; Peter H. Koehn, "Convergence of International and Multicultural Education: The Socio-Political Context," *International Education Forum* 12 (Spring 1992): 14; De Vita, "Taking Stock," p. 165; Allen, "Role of Faculty in International

Education," p. 2. Transnational group projects provide opportunities to hone skills in team building/leading and intercultural communication/negotiation.

15. Carter, "Multiculturalism, Diversity, and Global Competence," p. 57; Allen, "Role of Faculty in International Education," p. 2.

16. The transnational classroom is well-suited for dialogue and shared TC learning as participants "challenge and critique their own and each other's previously tightly held assumptions about learning, teaching and knowledge." Leask, "Teaching for Learning in the Transnational Classroom," p. 128. In contrast to globalized online educational programs, however, TC coursework and pedagogy must be adapted and tailored to local contexts and specific student needs. Christopher Ziguras, "The Cultural Politics of Transnational Education: Ideological and Pedagogical Issues for Teaching Staff," in *Teaching in Transnational Higher Education: Enhancing Learning for Offshore International Students*, edited by Lee Dunn and Michelle Wallace (New York: Routledge, 2008), pp. 48–49, 52.

17. Lev Gonick, "Creating Active Learning Spaces in the Digital Age," in *The New International Studies Classroom: Active Teaching, Active Learning*, edited by Jeffrey S. Lantis, Lynn M. Kuzma, and John Boehrer (Boulder: Lynne Rienner, 2000), pp. 172–173.

18. Killick, "World-Wide Horizons," pp. 207–208, 210, 212.

19. Including cross-impact analysis and comparison of likely outcomes. See Longstreet, "Alternative Futures," p. 323.

20. Jeffrey W. Seifert and G. Matthew Bonham, "Learning Through Digital Technology: Video-conferencing, Text Chat, and Hypertext," in *The New International Studies Classroom: Active Teaching, Active Learning*, edited by Jeffrey S. Lantis, Lynn M. Kuzma, and John Boehrer (Boulder: Lynne Rienner, 2000), p. 206.

21. Goleman, *Working with Emotional Intelligence*, p. 329.

22. Gonick, "Creating Active Learning Spaces," p. 173.

23. Cases usually are presented as written texts, "but they can also take the form of oral presentations, film or video clips, newspaper articles, and CD-ROM and Internet sources." Jeffrey S. Lantis, Lynn M. Kuzma, and John Boehrer, "Active Teaching and Learning at a Critical Crossroads," in *The New International Studies Classroom: Active Teaching, Active Learning*, edited by Jeffrey S. Lantis, Lynn M. Kuzma, and John Boehrer (Boulder: Lynne Rienner, 2000), p. 5.

24. Lantis, Kuzma, and Boehrer, "Active Teaching and Learning," p. 5.

25. Killick, "World-Wide Horizons," pp. 207–209.

26. Shaffer, "Maximizing Human Capital," pp. 22–23.

27. Alexander Thomas, "Scientific and Practical Aspects of Cross-Cultural Cooperation and Management in the Context of European Integration," *Studia Psychologica* 40, Nos. 1–2 (1998): 75–76.

28. Hirshberg, "Teaching Compassionate Social Studies," p. 180.

29. See Sylvia Hurtado, Jeffrey Milem, Alma Clayton-Pedersen, and Walter Allen, *Enacting Diverse Learning Environments: Improving the Climate for Racial/Ethnic Diversity in Higher Education* (Washington, DC: Graduate School of Education and Human Development, George Washington University, 1999), pp. 88–89.

30. Hirshberg, "Teaching Compassionate Social Studies," pp. 184, 191.

31. Shaffer, "Maximizing Human Capital," p. 23.

32. Videotaped playbacks offer a useful role-play feedback mechanism. On the multiple advantages of the role-play method, including heightened self-confidence, see Mak, Westwood, Ishiyama, and Barker, "Learning Sociocultural Competencies for Success," pp. 368–370.

33. In its report, *Global Competence and National Needs: One Million Students Studying Abroad*, the Lincoln Commission recently proposed a bold vision for the United States: send one million students to study abroad annually in a decade. See http://www.nasulgc.org/NetCommunity/Page.aspx?pid=731&srcid=1103. In all professional programs, committed and capable host institutions are the key to successful exchange partnerships. Nancy Wessel, "Integrating Service Learning into the Study Abroad Program: U.S. Sociology Students in Mexico," *Journal of Studies in International Education* 11, No. 1 (Spring 2007): 80. Cummings (interview) correctly points out that study-abroad experiences where U.S. faculty "essentially take somebody overseas to an American village" are far more limited than "getting right into a foreign university ... [and/or] into some community-development project."

34. Bikson, Treverton, Moini, and Lindstrom, *New Challenges for International Leadership,* pp. 50–51.

35. Parker, Ninomiya, and Cogan, "Educating World Citizens," p. 129.

36. Carter, "Multiculturalism, Diversity, and Global Competence," p. 57. Local experiences take on transnational dimensions in the wake of population mobility. See Kanter, "Global Health ," p. 116.

37. Wessel, "Integrating Service Learning," p. 76.

38. Marquardt and Berger, *Global Leaders,* p. 181.

39. The following discussion draws heavily upon Marquardt and Berger, *Global Leaders,* pp. 182–186.

40. According to Marquardt and Berger (*Global Leaders,* p. 185), "making connections, analyzing seemingly contradictory data, and seeking new possibilities rather than old answers are inherent parts of the action learning process."

41. *Ibid.,* p. 185.

42. Wear and Aultman critique the "fixation with assessment" and the "constant surveillance for evidence or lack of professionalism" that characterizes the "audit culture" of contemporary academic medicine. They warn that "the richness, complexity, and contradictions of professionalism in medicine are being flattened into categorical attitudes or behaviors that evaluators (whose professionalism is rarely assessed) can check." Delese Wear and Julie M. Aultman, "Introduction," in *Professionalism in Medicine: Critical Perspectives,* edited by Delese Wear and Julie M. Aultman (New York: Springer, 2006), p. vii. For another telling critique, see James F. Pontuso and Saranna R. Thornton, "Is Outcomes Assessment Hurting Higher Education?" *Thought & Action* 24 (Fall 2008): 61–69. TC assessment procedures should be designed in ways that minimize the administrative burden on raters.

43. See Knight, "Internationalization of Higher Education," p. 15.

44. Martin-Kniep, "Assessing Teachers," pp. 104–105, 108.

45. Gay, *Culturally Responsive Teaching,* p. 214; Bruno Art, Leen De Roo, Sara Willems, and Jan De Maeseneer, "An Interdisciplinary Community Diagnosis Experience in an Undergraduate Medical Curriculum: Development at Ghent University," *Academic Medicine* 83, No. 7 (July 2008): 679. Given the flexible multilocational emphasis of TC preparation, we favor the development of proficiency in a language other than one's primary language prior to admission into a professional program—that is, at secondary-school or first-degree levels. Also see Brademas, Kolb, and Mockett, *Education for Global Leadership,* p. 26.

46. Collins, Czarra, and Smith, "Global and International Studies Education," p. 238; Merryfield and Wilson, *Teaching Global Perspectives,* p. 126.

47. Downey, *et al.,* "Globally Competent Engineer," pp. 110, 113. For the authors' pre/post essay assignment and scoring rubric used in assessing students' analytic skills, see pp. 116–117.

48. Downey, *et al.,* "Globally Competent Engineer," pp. 110, 113.

49. Downey, "'Problem Definition and Solution' in Engineering Education," p. 593.

50. Also see Deardorff, "Identification and Assessment of Intercultural Competence," p. 257.

51. Goleman, *Working with Emotional Intelligence,* p. 277.

52. Craig Kissock, "Student Teaching Overseas," in *Preparing Teachers to Teach Global Perspectives: A Handbook for Teacher Educators,* edited by Merry M. Merryfield, Elaine Jarchow, and Sarah Picket (Thousand Oaks: Corwin Press, 1997), p. 124.

53. Martin-Kniep, "Assessing Teachers," pp. 101–104; Shuman, Besterfield-Sacre, and Mc Gourty, "ABET 'Professional Skills,'" pp. 50–51. In evaluating transboundary team projects in TC engineering programs, attention is devoted to the innovativeness and contextual appropriateness of the overall design as well as to presentation effectiveness. Shuman, Besterfield-Sacre, and Mc Gourty, "ABET 'Professional Skills,'" p. 50.

54. Martin-Kniep, "Assessing Teachers," p. 108.

55. See Walter C. Parker, "Assessing Student Learning of an Issue-Oriented Curriculum," in *Handbook on Teaching Social Studies,* edited by Ronald W. Evans and David W. Saxe (Washington, DC: National Council for the Social Studies, 1996), pp. 283–285; Shuman, Besterfield-Sacre, and Mc Gourty, "ABET 'Professional Skills,'" p. 50. For an excellent portfolio format specifically designed to assess the global-education skills of students learning to be teachers, see Martin-Kniep, "Assessing Teachers," p. 110. On digital portfolios, see Gonick, "Creating Active Learning Spaces," p. 179.

56. Killick, "World-Wide Horizons," p. 211. Critical-incident reporting can be used in this connection, provided that evaluators focus on major omissions or incidents of negative behavior rather than on documenting minor transgressions and that it is accompanied by detailed and specific feedback responses. See Kuczewski, "Problem with Evaluating Professionalism," p. 192.

57. Including, in the case of medical students, confidential 360-degree evaluations by other allied health professionals, peers, real and standardized (simulated) patients. Kao and Reenan, *"Wit* Is Not Enough," p. 229; David C. Leach, Patricia M. Surdyk, and Deirdre C. Lynch, "Practicing Professionalism," in *Healing As Vocation: A Medical Professionalism Primer,* edited by Kayhan Parsi and Myles N. Sheehan (Lanham, MD: Rowman & Littlefield, 2006), p. 5; also see Kuczewski, "Problem with Evaluating Professionalism," p. 192. David Thom and Miguel Tirado found patient reports of physician transcultural communicative competence to be "associated more strongly with processes and outcomes of care [including trust and satisfaction] than physician self-report ..." David H. Thom and Miguel D. Tirado, "Development and Validation of a Patient-Reported Measure of Physician Cultural Competency," *Medical Care Research and Review* 63, No. 5 (October 2006): 650, 647.

58. Shuman, Besterfield-Sacre, and Mc Gourty, "ABET 'Professional Skills,'" p. 50.

59. Kuczewski, "Problem with Evaluating Professionalism," p. 194.

60. Allan and Chisholm, "Achieving Engineering Competencies," p. 149.

61. Kenneth Cushner and Richard W. Brislin, *Intercultural Interactions: A Practical Guide* (Thousand Oaks, CA: Sage, 1996), p. 3; Kao and Reenan, *"Wit* Is Not Enough," p. 228.

62. The National Academy of Engineering (*Educating the Engineer of 2020,* p. 53) recommends that, when conducting outcomes-based accreditation reviews, "ABET should ensure that evaluators look for innovation and experimentation in the curriculum...."

63. For instance, Kuczewski and colleagues ("Can Justice Be Taught," pp. 80–81, 90) suggest that professional programs be graded on the extent to which faculty and administrators demonstrate the premium the institution places on social justice and advocacy for those most in need.

64. Including exit interviews with students, written course and experiential-learning evaluations, and "openly shared discussions that help to evaluate the various features of the program and to refine it further for the future." Allert, *et al., "*Case for Global Engineering," p. 12.

65. Killick, "World-Wide Horizons," p. 210; NASULGC, *Expanding the International Scope of Universities.* p. 14; Deardorff, "Identification and Assessment of Intercultural Competence," pp. 250–252, 257.

66. Downey, "'Problem Definition and Solution' in Engineering Education," p. 594.

67. Gay, *Culturally Responsive Teaching,* p. 209.

68. Merryfield, "Framework for Teacher Education," pp. 12, 20. Teacher-education programs in Finland, Hong Kong, Australia, the Netherlands, France, Germany, and Taiwan, among others, have introduced in-depth pedagogical study. Linda Darling-Hammond, "Teaching As a Profession: Lessons in Teacher Preparation and Professional Development," *Phi Delta Kappan* 87, No. 3 (November 2005): 238.

69. Merryfield, "Learning from Current Practice," pp. 5, 7.

70. Many of these components are adapted from Geneva Gay's recommendations for multiculturally responsive pedagogy. See Gay, *Culturally Responsive Teaching,* pp. 212–214, 31.

71. Merryfield and Wilson, *Teaching Global Perspectives,* pp. 18–19; Merryfield, "Framework for Teacher Education," p. 6; Mungo, "Training Teachers for Cultural Diversity," p. 225. Rather than isolated in an elective or add-on course, transnational perspectives are treated as lenses through which all subject matter and the "extra" curriculum is approached. See Merryfield (ed.), *Making Connections,* p. 14; Wells, "The Global and the Multicultural," p. 142. As the Delaware K-20 International Education Capacity Study concluded, opportunities to explore the lives of the vast majority of people who live beyond the borders of one's country "exist within every subject area." O'Malley, *et al., Report,* p. 50. For instructional ideas, see Merryfield and White, "Issues-Centered Global Education," pp. 178, 180–183. For an illustration of how "intercultural synergy," a TC creative skill, can be infused across the teacher-education curriculum, see Ngai, "Reinforcing Curriculum and Program Reform Proposal," pp. 326–327.

72. Parker, Ninomiya, and Cogan, "Educating World Citizens," p. 132; Merryfield, "Pedagogy for Global Perspectives," p. 255; Merryfield, "Framework for Teacher Education," p. 11; Cummings interview; Wang, "Intercultural Dialogue," p. 64. Group projects that involve domestic and foreign

students simultaneously enhance transnational-communication skills. Transnational collaboration on curriculum-development projects strengthens functional skill. Merryfield, "Framework for Teacher Education," pp. 10–11, 13.

73. In this emotion- and creativity-provoking pedagogical tool, "each member of the pair takes a different point of view from the other; then they alternately write lines that juxtapose how each sees the issue or experiences the situation." Sleeter, "Teaching Globalization," p. 8.

74. Merryfield and White, "Issues-Centered Global Education," p. 183; Merryfield, "Pedagogy for Global Perspectives," p. 257; Hey, "Teaching About the Third World with Cases," pp. 57, 59, 61; Cummings interview.

75. Merryfield, "Learning from Current Practice," p. 7.

76. Merryfield, "Global Educator," p. 20; Merryfield and White, "Issues-Centered Global Education," p. 182; Merryfield, "Framework for Teacher Education," pp. 9–10; Merryfield, "Learning from Current Practice," pp. 3–4, 6, 9; Cheng, "New Teacher Education," p. 55. Cummings (interview) has found that an overseas experience of "some intensity" at an early age contributes immensely to "developing the foundations for empathy." Ngai (interview) sees transnational efficacy, a key emotional skill, enhanced when preservice and in-service teachers succeed in overcoming intercultural challenges through face-to-face interactions in partnerships with one's neighbors. Also see Phyllis Ngai and Karen Allen, *A Process Guide for Realizing Indian Education for All: Lessons Learned from Lewis & Clark Elementary School* (Helena, MT: Office of Public Instruction, 2007). Merryfield ("Framework for Teacher Education," p. 10) observes that "teachers who have experienced another culture are more likely to perceive the power and potential of being connected to another part of the world and are also more likely to find ways in their daily instruction to teach local/global interconnectedness and perspective consciousness to their students." At Ohio State University, the Social Studies and Global Education program draws upon the ethnic diversity of the city of Columbus in arranging intercultural-interaction experiences. Merryfield (ed.), *Making Connections*, p. 189. "Reflective" intercultural e-learning offers another promising TC pedagogical tool. Ngai interview.

77. Darling-Hammond, "Need to Invest," p. B20. Merry Merryfield ("Framework for Teacher Education," p. 10) adds that "we find that preservice teachers are more likely to become accomplished global educators when they learn to teach in the classrooms of teachers who are involved every quarter in having their students interact with and learn from diverse groups of people."

78. Ngai interview; Cummings interview; Merryfield, "Framework for Teacher Education," p. 11.

79. Merryfield, "Framework for Teacher Education," pp. 12, 14; Massialas, "Issues-Centered Content Selection," p. 49; Martin-Kniep, "Assessing Teachers," p. 116.

80. Gay, *Culturally Responsive Teaching*, p. 209.

81. Merryfield, "Pedagogy for Global Perspectives," p. 255; Gay, *Culturally Responsive Teaching*, p. 209. The master teachers considered exemplary global educators by sixteen school districts in Merry Merryfield's 1991–1994 study "used themes such as religious conflict, cultural change, or globalization in an integrated multidisciplinary approach." They also emphasized face-to-face experiential intercultural learning. Merryfield, "Pedagogy for Global Perspectives," pp. 259, 249, 269.

82. Cushner, "Intercultural Education," pp. 362, 369; Kenneth Cushner and Sharon Brennan (eds.), *Intercultural Student Teaching: A Bridge to Global Competence* (Lanham, MD: Rowman and Littlefield, 2007); Kissock interview. On Minnesota-based student-teaching-abroad programs, see Kissock, "Student Teaching Overseas," pp. 125–126. The International Education program at the George Washington University encourages overseas internships, research partnerships, and action-learning experiences. In some courses, professors guide students in developing policy-options reports, implementation plans, and monitoring and evaluation schemes. Cummings interview.

83. Mehaffy, "Educating a New Generation of Globally Competent Teachers," pp. 129–130. Also Wells, "The Global and the Multicultural," p. 148; Merryfield, "Framework for Teacher Education," p. 20.

84. Miller, "Preparing Globally Competent Business Students," p. 93; Biddle, *Internationalization*, p. 60; Brustein interview.

85. Marquardt and Horvath, *Global Teams*, p. 149.

86. Turko, "Africa Business Schools," p. 2.

87. Janet Hulstrand (ed.), *Proceedings of the Forum on Study Abroad & Economic Competitiveness*

held at the National Press Club, February 15, 2007 (Washington, DC: Commission on the Abraham Lincoln Study Abroad Fellowship Program and NASULGC, 2007), pp. 34–35.

88. Brustein interview.

89. Efforts to utilize the Internet as a vehicle for business-management education are currently in the experimental stages. Turko, "Africa Business Schools," p. 4.

90. William Brustein (interview) is "a strong advocate of creative capstone experiences."

91. Brustein interview; Brademas, Kolb, and Mockett, *Education for Global Leadership*, p. 22.

92. Turko, "Africa Business Schools," p. 4.

93. University of Washington MBA students currently collaborate with local business employees on transnational projects. Brademas, Kolb, and Mockett, *Education for Global Leadership*, p. 22. TC programs with resources can adapt a learning tool from EARTH University's entrepreneurial-project program. They can provide students with a loan to design a unique project, conduct feasibility and market studies, and establish and run their own transnational business. Juma and Yee-Cheong, *Innovation*, p. 97.

94. Fischer, "'Flat World' Lessons."

95. Downey, "'Problem Definition and Solution' in Engineering Education," p. 592.

96. These suggestions are modeled, in part, on courses offered at Old Dominion University. See Shuman, Besterfield-Sacre, and Mc Gourty, "ABET 'Professional Skills,'" p. 47.

97. Downey, "'Problem Definition and Solution' in Engineering Education," p. 592; Downey, *et al.*, "Globally Competent Engineer," p. 119; Allert, *et al.*, "Case for Global Engineering," p. 8.

98. See Juma and Yee-Cheong, *Innovation*, p. 93.

99. Allan and Chisholm, "Achieving Engineering Competencies," p. 149; National Academy of Engineering, *Educating the Engineer of 2020*, pp. 54–56; Allert, *et al.*, "Case for Global Engineering," p. 2; Downey, "'Problem Definition and Solution' in Engineering Education," p. 593.

100. Shuman, Besterfield-Sacre, and Mc Gourty, "ABET 'Professional Skills,'" p. 46.

101. Hirleman interview.

102. Downey, *et al.*, "Globally Competent Engineer," p. 114; Grandin interview.

103. Shuman, Besterfield-Sacre, and Mc Gourty, "ABET 'Professional Skills,'" p. 45.

104. *Ibid.* These authors note (p. 45) that "activities that are lower in fidelity are typically more structured and easier to administer, but may be perceived as less relevant by the student, resulting in the experience having less of a learning impact."

105. Shuman, Besterfield-Sacre, and Mc Gourty, "ABET 'Professional Skills,'" p. 45.

106. Hirleman interview; Downey, *et al.*, "Globally Competent Engineer," pp. 111–112; Carlson, "Global Approach to Engineering," p. A36.

107. Kalonji, "Reforms for Engineering Educators," pp. 147–150.

108. In Worcester Polytechnic Institute's program, about half of each graduating class collaborates with NGOs on projects initiated by local organizations in countries such as Morocco, Namibia, and Thailand. Carlson, "Global Approach to Engineering," p. A36.

109. Chang interview; Allert, *et al.*, "Case for Global Engineering," p. 7.

110. Online is the emphasis at Carnegie Mellon University. Carlson, "Global Approach to Engineering," p. A34.

111. Dan Hirleman, "Global-HUB: A Virtual Community for Global Engineering Education, Research, and Collaboration" (unpublished project summary, NSF 07-558).

112. Hirleman interview. Also see Allert, *et al.*, "Case for Global Engineering," pp. 9–10.

113. Downey, *et al.*, "Globally Competent Engineer," pp. 112–113.

114. Hirleman interview; Carlson, "Global Approach to Engineering," p. A34.

115. Downey, *et al.*, "Globally Competent Engineer," p. 111.

116. By 2007, about 20 percent of Purdue's 280 engineering graduates participated in an overseas learning experience (up from 3 percent in 1999). Hirleman interview. Under URI's program, fourth-year students study language and engineering at partner universities in Germany, France, Mexico, Spain, and China. Carlson, "Global Approach to Engineering," p. A34.

117. Hirleman interview. Also see Allert, *et al.*, "Case for Global Engineering," pp. 4, 11.

118. Shuman, Besterfield-Sacre, and Mc Gourty, "ABET 'Professional Skills,'" p. 46.

119. Hirleman interview.

120. Nader, "International Opportunities."

121. Grandin interview.

122. In the GEARE program, Purdue and exchange students complete a summer internship "before progressing to an international assignment with the same company." Allert, *et al.*, "Case for Global Engineering," p. 11; Carlson, "Global Approach to Engineering," p. A36. Hirleman reports that GEARE graduates are in "ultrahigh demand" among employers. Carlson, "Global Approach to Engineering," p. A33.

123. Transnational service learning for engineering students can involve assignments with NGOs, underserved communities, or a rural village in a low-income country. Shuman, Besterfield-Sacre, and Mc Gourty, "ABET 'Professional Skills,'" p. 51.

124. Allan and Chisholm, "Achieving Engineering Competencies," pp. 150–151.

125. Downey, *et al.*, "Globally Competent Engineer," p. 112.

126. Chang interview.

127. Finn interview.

128. *Ibid.*

129. Herscovitch and Healy, "International Relief and Development Practice," p. 273.

130. Finn interview.

131. Midgley, "Social Development in Social Work," p. 194. Most U.S. schools of social work only inconsistently place a handful of students in international field-practicum situations. Healy, *International Social Work*, p. 348.

132. Jones and Kumssa ("Professional Growth in the Global Context," p. 213) point out that "including students in [research] projects familiarizes colleagues abroad with the students' potential, sometimes opening the way for ... job placements."

133. In another example, "the School of Social Work in Esbjerg, Denmark, is part of a multicountry linkage focused around issues of aging and social work." Healy, *International Social Work*, p. 345.

134. Healy, *International Social Work*, p. 353.

135. Finn interview.

136. Profoundly beneficial overseas placements require careful preparatory work and the nurturing of strong inter-institutional linkages and mutually meaningful partnerships. Healy, *International Social Work*, pp. 348–349, 352–353; Healy, "International Social Work Curriculum," p. 25; Finn interview.

137. Healy, *International Social Work*, p. 350.

138. Wessel, "Integrating Service Learning," pp. 77, 87.

139. Finn interview.

140. Shaw and Kim, *Education for Sustainable Development Practice*, pp. 33–35.

141. *Ibid.*, p. 36.

142. Morgan (interview) notes that students of sustainable development now are able to reach out directly to Romania's Ministry of Environment online without needing to find a vertical way to gain access.

143. Shaw and Kim, *Education for Sustainable Development Practice*, p. 6.

144. David Schodt, "Using Cases to Teach Analytical Skills," in *The New International Studies Classroom: Active Teaching, Active Learning*, edited by Jeffrey S. Lantis, Lynn M. Kuzma, and John Boehrer (Boulder: Lynne Rienner, 2000), pp. 65–67; Morgan interview.

145. Farazmand interview; Morgan (interview) gives "high marks to role play."

146. Sarkissian, *Kitchen Table Sustainability*, p. 105.

147. Charlick interview; Shaw and Kim, *Education for Sustainable Development Practice*, p. 26. Acker (interview) emphasizes the importance of learning partnership-building skills in project exercises. In cooperation with an umbrella organization of development-focused NGOs in the Washington, DC, area, students enrolled in the Monterey Institute's graduate program in international policy complete an intensive workshop called the "development project." Monterey also offers a development-administration practicum that involves collaborative action research with an organization in the greater urban area. Morgan interview.

148. Shaw and Kim, *Education for Sustainable Development Practice*, p. 27.

149. Kellogg interview.

150. Through a partnership with Middlebury College, Monterey's students now hone their language

skills by participating in immersion programs at one of twenty-two locally operated language centers around the world. Morgan interview.

151. Kellogg interview. Morgan (interview) describes Monterey's six-month International Professional Service Semester as "the ultimate internship." Students have "a real [entry-level] job in a real global governance type agency [e.g., Organization for Migration, WTO, IUCN] in any of their desired fields." Under this program, Monterey faculty members mentor students before they leave, their managers mentor them while they are in their professional positions, and they return to Monterey for a wrap-up seminar in July.

152. Kellogg (interview) emphasizes the value of attachments with NGOs because, increasingly, they are assuming responsibility for providing key public services; they are "extraordinarily powerful in terms of policy impacts"; and they often are "creative and imaginative in terms of new solutions and ideas."

153. Shaw and Kim, *Education for Sustainable Development Practice*, p. 30.

154. Juma and Yee-Cheong, *Innovation*, p. 97.

155. Shailaja Neelakantan, "A Young University in India Focuses on Real-World Industry and Sustainability," *Chronicle of Higher Education*, January 9, 2009, p. A20.

156. Zaglul and Sherrard, "Higher Education in Economic Transformation," pp. 39–40.

157. *Ibid.*, pp. 40, 47.

158. David Doukas argues for a thematic course that commences in the first year of medical school and is sustained through graduation on the grounds that assigning curriculum time to a course with its own grading demonstrates to students that administrative authorities have deemed the skills addressed to be worthy of mastery. David J. Doukas, "Professionalism: Curriculum Goals and Meeting Their Challenges," in *Professionalism in Medicine: Critical Perspectives*, edited by Delese Wear and Julie M. Aultman (New York: Springer, 2006), p. 55.

159. Betancourt, Weissman, Kim, Park, and Maina, *Resident Physicians' Preparedness*, p. viii; Like, Steiner, and Rubel, "Recommended Core Curriculum Guidelines," p. 296.

160. "Poorly designed and pedagogically flawed courses" dampen demand among medical students. Kao and Reenan, *"Wit* Is Not Enough," pp. 213–214.

161. It is important for role modeling that TC education involve "deans, department chairs, program directors, and faculty and administrators who are perceived as accomplished." Kuczewski, "Problem with Evaluating Professionalism," p. 195.

162. See Lomax, "Building the Foundation," p. 212; Like, "Cultural Competency Education," p. 1. Ho and colleagues found role-play practice to be effective in eliciting the perspectives and concerns of diverse patients and in exploring social factors in a non-Western setting. Ming-Jung Ho, Grace Yao, Keng-Lin Lee, Mary C. Beach, and Alexander R. Green, "Cross-Cultural Medical Education: Can Patient-Centered Cultural Competency Training Be Effective in Non-Western Countries?" *Medical Teacher* 30 (2008): 719–720. Virtual patients can be programmed to present transnational cases. See David Debolt, "Virtual Patients Help Real Professors Teach Medicine," *Chronicle of Higher Education*, December 12, 2008, p. A6.

163. Rosenberg and colleagues ("Intercultural Communication Competence," p. 237) point out that Balint groups currently do not routinely address the role of physician ethnocultural identity in clinical relationships or develop transnational-communicative skills.

164. These could be modeled on the University of Massachusetts' two-year preceptorships, where Pathway students shadow physicians at a site populated by underserved and multinational patients. Godkin, Savageau, and Fletcher, "Global Longitudinal Pathway," p. 228.

165. Like, Steiner, and Rubel, "Recommended Core Curriculum Guidelines," p. 296; Like, "Cultural Competency Education," p. 3; Betancourt, Weissman, Kim, Park, and Maina, *Resident Physicians' Preparedness*, p. ix; Kuczewski, "Problem with Evaluating Professionalism," p. 196.

166. Smith, *et al.*, "Recommendations for Teaching," p. 660; Lomax, "Building the Foundation," p. 211. The early-start feature of student-patient transnational interactions builds on Harvard University Medical School's successful "new pathway" program. See Maggie Moore-West, Martha Regan-Smith, Allen Dietrich, and Donald O. Kollisch, "Innovations in Medical Education: Enhancing Humanism through the Educational Process," in *Educating Competent and Humane Physicians*, edited by Hugh C. Hendrie and Camille Lloyd (Bloomington: Indiana University Press, 1990), pp. 146, 165.

167. Central to these discussions will be observations of disparities in health and health care, and

ways to eliminate them. Joseph R. Betancourt, "Eliminating Racial and Ethnic Disparities in Health Care: What Is the Role of Academic Medicine,"*Academic Medicine* 81, No. 9 (September 2006): 791.

168. Kao and Reenan, "*Wit* Is Not Enough," p. 223.

169. Jack Coulehan, "You Say Self-Interest, I Say Altruism," in *Professionalism in Medicine: Critical Perspectives,* edited by Delese Wear and Julie M. Aultman (New York: Springer, 2006), pp. 107, 116.

170. Laura J. Fochtmann, "Professionalism and the Heisenberg Uncertainty Principle," in *Professionalism in Medicine: Critical Perspectives,* edited by Delese Wear and Julie M. Aultman (New York: Springer, 2006), p. 246.

171. Kao and Reenan, "*Wit* Is Not Enough," pp. 214, 225.

172. Harden, "International Medical Education," p. S24. Across the United States, roughly one-third of psychiatry residents are graduates from overseas. Lomax, "Building the Foundation," p. 212. The University of California, San Francisco, and Muhimbili University of Health and Allied Sciences in Tanzania have established a partnership that supports institution-wide exchanges among students, faculty, and senior administrators. Macfarlane, *et al.,* "Think Globally, Act Locally, and Collaborate Internationally," p. 177.

173. Harden, "International Medical Education," pp. S25–S26.

174. Like interview.

175. Kao and Reenan, "*Wit* Is Not Enough," p. 223. In an existing model that could incorporate TC training, the Sewankambo Clinical Scholars Program links five clinicians at the Makerere University Faculty of Medicine "with at least one internationally recognized investigator who commits to providing five years of substantive ongoing mentoring." Sande and Ronald, "The Academic Alliance," p. 183.

176. Thomas S. Inui, "Educating for Professionalism at Indiana University School of Medicine," in *Professionalism in Medicine: Critical Perspectives,* edited by Delese Wear and Julie M. Aultman (New York: Springer, 2006), pp. 174–175.

177. Beagan, "Teaching Social and Cultural Awareness to Medical Students," p. 612; Lie, Boker, and Cleveland, "Using TACCT," p. 558; Kuczewski, "Problem with Evaluating Professionalism," p. 195.

178. Herbert M. Adler, "The Sociophysiology of Caring in the Doctor-Patient Relationship," *Journal of General Internal Medicine* 17 (November 2002): 878. Increasingly, managed-care providers recognize that providing such quality attention more effectively contains health-care costs than does limiting services. Center for Mental Health Services, *Cultural Competence Standards.*

179. Betancourt, Weissman, Kim, Park, and Maina, *Resident Physicians' Preparedness,* p. 10; Like, Steiner, and Rubel, "Recommended Core Curriculum Guidelines," p. 296; Sande and Ronald, "The Academic Alliance," p. 183.

180. Group community-service projects at the University of Massachusetts commence in the second year of medical school. However, each student enrolled in the medical school's Global Multiculturalism Track visits regularly with a local family whose background and language are of interest during the first year of studies. Through these interactions, students are expected to learn about "the family's culture and health beliefs, their problems adjusting to the United States, their experiences with health care in the country of origin and in the United States, and linguistic [and financial] and cultural barriers to services in the United States." Godkin and Savageau, "Effect of a Global Multiculturalism Track," p. 179. Service projects include in-school HIV education, flu-shot programs, mentoring, and soup kitchens. Godkin, Savageau, and Fletcher, "Global Longitudinal Pathway," p. 228. On the University of Florida College of Medicine's placement of first-year students in underserved rural and urban situations where they participate in addressing community-health problems, see Richard A. Davidson, "Community-Based Education and Problem Solving: The Community of Health Scholars Program at the University of Florida," *Teaching and Learning in Medicine* 14, No. 3 (2002): 178–181. Part of the third-year family-medicine clerkship at Robert Wood Johnson Medical School is devoted to community-service learning with an underserved population. Learning activities have included presenting nutrition demonstrations for preschoolers, offering health workshops at drug-treatment and correctional facilities and a middle school, and working with people with dementia. Like, "Cultural Competency Education," p. 1. George, Gonsenhauser, and Whitehouse ("Medical Professionalism," p. 68) emphasize the importance of providing ample time for meaningful reflection on field experiences along with "communal sharing of successes, failures, frustrations, value-judgments, and insecurities through storytelling...."

181. Including trained medical interpreters, cultural brokers, health-education information in multiple languages aimed at people with limited health literacy, staff TC training, and programs designed to increase the TC skills of patients. Betancourt, Weissman, Kim, Park, and Maina, *Resident Physicians' Preparedness*, p. ix; Peter H. Koehn, "Improving Transnational Health-Care Encounters and Outcomes: The Challenge of Enhanced Transnational Competence for Migrants and Health Professionals," in *Proceedings of the Hospitals in a Culturally Diverse Europe Conference on Quality-Assured Health Care and Health Promotion for Migrants and Ethnic Minorities, Amsterdam, December 9–11, 2004.* www.mfh-eu .net/conf/results/ (2005).

182. Kanter, "Global Health," p. 116.

183. Peter H. Koehn, "Transnational Migration, State Policy, and Local Clinician Treatment of Asylum Seekers and Resettled Migrants: Comparative Perspectives on Reception-Centre and Community Health-Care Practice in Finland," *Global Social Policy* 6, No. 1 (2006): 38–39, 45.

184. Also see Sande and Ronald, "The Academic Alliance," pp. 181–182. At Ghent University in Belgium, medical students team with Master's of Social Work (MSW) students to identify the range of professionals and services involved in providing health care, develop a community diagnosis, and formulate community-health-promotion interventions. Art, *et al.*, "An Interdisciplinary Community Diagnosis Experience," pp. 675–680.

185. Kuczewski, "Problem with Evaluating Professionalism," p. 196.

186. Godkin and Savageau, "Effect of a Global Multiculturalism Track," pp. 178–179.

187. A study of sixty U.S. students from three medical schools who participated in the International Health Fellowship Program (six- to eight-week field experiences in developing countries) found that participants markedly improved their transnational analytic, communicative, and functional skills. Cynthia Haq, Deborah Rothenberg, Craig Gjerde, James Bobula, Calvin Wilson, Lynn Bickley, Alberto Cardelle, and Abraham Joseph, "New World Views: Preparing Physicians in Training for Global Health Work," *Family Medicine* 32, No. 8 (2000): 568–570. Qualitative data indicate that U Mass Pathway participants who experienced a rotation in a low-income country or with the Indian Health Service report enhanced transnational emotional skills (empathy, motivation to serve). Godkin, Savageau, and Fletcher, "Global Longitudinal Pathway," pp. 228, 231.

188. Drain, *et al.*, "Global Health in Medical Education," pp. 227–228.

189. Bissonette and Route, "Nonindustrialized Countries," p. 229. These authors report data (p. 230) from a study of University of Buffalo medical students who completed rotations in developing countries indicating that "the discipline imposed by practice in a spartan environment invigorates reliance on basic clinical [judgment and] skills...."

Notes for Chapter 12

1. Ross E. Dunn, "Growing Good Citizens with a World-Centered Curriculum," *Educational Leadership* 60, No. 1 (October 2002): 13.

2. Kao and Reenan, "*Wit* Is Not Enough," p. 226.

3. See, for instance, George, Gonsenhauser, and Whitehouse, "Medical Professionalism," p. 71.

4. Biddle, *Internationalization*, p. 15.

5. Charles Ping ("Educational Imperatives for a New Era," p. 3) explains that transformational leadership involves vision, vigor, understanding the particular capacities and circumstances of one's university, and the ability to "capture others in a common cause."

6. Downey, *et al.*, "Globally Competent Engineer," p. 111; Biddle, *Internationalization*, p. 40. Responses from chief international officers indicate that *faculty* constitute a prime initiator of international research and development activity at 90 percent of the U.S. universities and colleges reporting in a 2007 survey. Only senior international program leaders come close as program catalysts. Peter H. Koehn, Kerry D. Bolognese, and Darla K. Deardorff, "International Development and Campus Internationalization: The AIEA/NASULGC Initiative" (PowerPoint presentation, 2008 AIEA Conference roundtable, Washington, DC, February 19, 2008), slide 11.

7. Downey, *et al.*, "Globally Competent Engineer," p. 111.

8. See Shaw and Kim, *Education for Sustainable Development Practice*, p. 24.

9. Jeffrey Froyd, "The Engineering Education Coalitions Program," in National Academy of Engineering, *Educating the Engineer of 2020: Adapting Engineering Education to the New Century* (Washington, DC: National Academies Press, 2005), p. 96.

10. Like (interview) confirms this assessment. Also see Nicole Saba and Timothy F. Brewer, "Beyond Borders: Building Global Health Programs at McGill University Faculty of Medicine," *Academic Medicine* 83, No. 2 (February 2008): 185.

11. Kellogg interview; Brustein interview. Many of the initiatives reported in Chapter 11 offer evidence that resources are available for innovative approaches that enhance TC professional education.

12. Biddle, *Internationalization*, pp. 35, 39, 112; Graves, *et al.*, "Legislation As Intervention," p. 360; Peter H. Koehn, Darla K. Deardorff, and Kerry D. Bolognese, "Enhancing International Research and Development-Project Activity on U.S. Campuses: The Senior International Officer Perspective" (unpublished paper).

13. On the growing involvement of China's universities in entrepreneurial undertakings, see Peter H. Koehn, "Globalization, Decentralization, and Public Entrepreneurship: Reorienting Bureaucracy in the People's Republic of China," in *Handbook of Bureaucracy and Its Alternatives*, 2nd edition, edited by Ali Farazmand (New York: Marcel Dekker, in press, 2009).

14. In this connection, for instance, APLU has proposed that the U.S. government provide $50 million in support of long-term capacity-building partnerships involving African and U.S. universities, and devote $20 million to expanding the role of higher education in combating AIDS, malaria, and tuberculosis. McMurtrie, "Universities Look to Obama," p. A25.

15. Godkin and Savageau, "Effect of a Global Multiculturalism Track," p. 186.

16. Most specifically, the Task Force recommended that the Department of Education's Title VI program emphasize TC initiatives in "such field as business and engineering." Task Force for Transnational Competence, *Towards Transnational Competence*, p. 122. We also endorse the more recent recommendation of the Committee for Economic Development that additional funding be supplied for teacher professional development in international studies, provided that TC preparation is included in any new initiative. See Brademas, Kolb, and Mockett, *Education for Global Leadership*, pp. 26, 2.

17. Like interview.

18. In medical schools, for instance, "there is little chance that … improvements and innovations will take root" without "the support of academic health center presidents, chiefs, deans, and division leaders." Betancourt, "Eliminating Racial and Ethnic Disparities," p. 791. Also see Shuman, Besterfield-Sacre, and Mc Gourty, "ABET 'Professional Skills,'" p. 47; Reimers, "'Global Competency' Is Imperative," p. A29.

19. Biddle, *Internationalization*, p. 120.

20. Kissock interview.

21. Hirleman (interview) mentions this environmental constraint in connection with engineering education. Betancourt and colleagues ("Cultural Competence," p. 500) refer to the perception among some managed-care providers that cultural-competence training is "soft science." Edwin Miller ("Preparing Globally Competent Business Students," p. 89) notes that some business-school faculty members "are unsympathetic to the importance of an international or global perspective in the curriculum."

22. See, for instance, Shaw and Kim, *Education for Sustainable Development Practice*, p. 38. NASULGC's 2004 "Call to Leadership" (p. 40) recommends the strategic hiring of a visible team of supportive administrators, staff, and faculty.

23. Biddle (*Internationalization*, p. 39), paraphrasing a University of Michigan department chair.

24. Also see Betancourt, "Eliminating Racial and Ethnic Disparities," p. 791.

25. William I. Brustein, "Paths to Global Competence: Preparing American College Students to Meet the World" (Washington, DC: NASULGC, Commission on International Programs, Document Library, August 28, 2007), p. 6.

26. Miller, "Preparing Globally Competent Business Students," p. 90; Biddle, *Internationalization*, p. 112; Saba and Brewer, "Beyond Borders," p. 185.

27. Roland Case and Walter Werner, "Building Faculty Commitment for Global Education," in *Preparing Teachers to Teach Global Perspectives: A Handbook for Teacher Educators*, edited by Merry M. Merryfield, Elaine Jarchow, and Sarah Picket (Thousand Oaks: Corwin Press, 1997), p. 206; Miller, "Preparing Globally Competent Business Students," p. 94; Like interview.

28. Kao and Reenan, "*Wit* Is Not Enough," p. 215.
29. And students. See the next section.
30. Escobar interview. Tummala (interview) regards "faculty availability" as the "greatest limitation" on the capacity to implement a TC program in sustainable development. Finn (interview) concurs that most social-work programs lack a "critical mass of folks" with the required level of experience and critical insight to launch TC programs successfully.
31. Allen, "Role of Faculty in International Education," p. 1.
32. Like (interview) suggests that some medical-school faculty members would be uncomfortable incorporating TC-skill learning in their work with students because they have not received training in transnational competence and/or lack associated group-facilitation and reflection skills. Steenhuis (interview) maintains that teachers who have not spent considerable time abroad will find it difficult to prepare engineering students with transnational skills. Katherine Kendall ("Forward," p. ix) similarly attributes the neglect of international dimensions in social-work curricula primarily to faculty members' lack of "knowledge drawn from first-hand experience in other lands." And Edwin Miller ("Preparing Globally Competent Business Students," p. 94) observes that "some [business] faculty will feel threatened by the thought of incorporating an international dimension into their professional competence…."
33. Miller, "Preparing Globally Competent Business Students," pp. 89, 94. In certain cases, faculty resistance to adopting core dimensions of the TC program can be attributed to entrenched parochialism (Farazmand interview).
34. Biddle, *Internationalization*, p. 60; Fischer, "'Flat World' Lessons." This perspective is widespread among faculty in professional programs. Like (interview) cites "limited time in an already crowded medical school curriculum and competition with other subjects that people feel need to be covered" as a factor that is likely to restrain faculty from enthusiastically embracing the adoption of a TC curriculum. Also see Graves, *et al.*, "Legislation As Intervention," p. 359; Wells, "The Global and the Multicultural," p. 142. Grandin (interview) mentions that "there is so much more we'd like to do" at the University of Rhode Island, but the international engineering program leaders are most seriously constrained by lack of time, given the tight and rigorous engineering curriculum.
35. Miller, "Preparing Globally Competent Business Students," p. 93.
36. *Ibid.*
37. Downey, "'Problem Definition and Solution' in Engineering Education," p. 592.
38. Healy, "International Social Work Curriculum," p. 26.
39. Miller, "Preparing Globally Competent Business Students," p. 96.
40. See Biddle, *Internationalization*, p. 61; Allen, "Role of Faculty in International Education," p. 3.
41. As Jones and Kumssa ("Professional Growth in the Global Context," p. 212) point out, "faculty development is almost always a prerequisite for student development." Miller ("Preparing Globally Competent Business Students," p. 93) maintains that "faculty development is the key" to developing the "global competence" of business-school graduates. Betancourt and colleagues (*Resident Physicians' Preparedness*, p. 10) state that "faculty development … in cross-cultural education is essential to the teaching and mentoring of residents in cross-cultural care." Wells ("The Global and the Multicultural," p. 148) recommends that "teacher education programs should provide (and/or require) professional development concerning the opportunities and challenges of joining the global and the multicultural in teacher education."
42. Karin Fischer, "Professors Get Their Own Study-Abroad Programs," *Chronicle of Higher Education*, October 31, 2008, p. A34.
43. Jones and Kumssa, "Professional Growth in the Global Context," pp. 208–209.
44. Like, "Cultural Competency Education," p. 1; Miller, "Preparing Globally Competent Business Students," p. 94; Smith, *et al.*, "Recommendations for Teaching," p. 660; Allen, "Role of Faculty in International Education," p. 3.
45. Turko, "Africa Business Schools," p. 2.
46. Merryfield, "Learning from Current Practice," p. 9; Allen, "Role of Faculty in International Education," p. 2.
47. Merget, "Times of Turbulence," p. 391. On the value of skill-enhancing fellowships for clinician educators, see Lomax, "Building the Foundation," p. 213. Allen ("Role of Faculty in International

Education," p. 2) recommends that an extended experience living and working in another country occur early in the academic career of faculty. The Fulbright program provides opportunities for rewarding professional-learning experiences overseas for U.S. faculty at all stages of their academic career.

48. McCool interview.

49. Case and Werner, "Building Faculty Commitment," pp. 203, 205.

50. Allen, "Role of Faculty in International Education," p. 3.

51. Also see Case and Werner, "Building Faculty Commitment," pp. 204, 206.

52. *Ibid.,* p. 202. See, for instance, the role of the Emory Global Health Institute in promoting initiatives in global health among Emory University's faculty. Jeffrey P. Koplan and Rebecca L. Baggett, "The Emory Global Health Institute: Developing Partnerships to Improve Health Through Research, Training, and Service," *Academic Medicine* 83, No. 2 (February 2008): 128–133.

53. The 2007 Changing Academic Professions survey found that faculty members who have spent three or more years overseas are far more likely to incorporate international themes in their teaching in comparison with professors who have spent little time abroad. Fischer, "U.S. Faculty Members Lag on Global Engagement," p. A37.

54. Godkin, Savageau, and Fletcher, "Global Longitudinal Pathway," p. 231; Case and Werner, "Building Faculty Commitment," p. 202; Biddle, *Internationalization,* pp. 35, 39; Fischer, "'Flat World' Lessons."

55. Charlick interview.

56. Also see O'Malley, Miller, and Wang, *Delaware K-20 International Education Capacity Study,* p. 50.

57. Biddle, *Internationalization,* p. 61; Allen, "Role of Faculty in International Education," p. 3.

58. Biddle, *Internationalization,* pp. 39–40.

59. Kalonji, "Reforms for Engineering Educators," p. 149.

60. Miller, "Preparing Globally Competent Business Students," p. 94; Brustein interview; Allen, "Role of Faculty in International Education," p. 3.

61. Brustein interview; Fischer, "'Flat World' Lessons."

62. See Case and Werner, "Building Faculty Commitment," p. 205; Kao and Reenan, "*Wit* Is Not Enough," p. 214. However, there are indications of growing student interest in transnational education. See Sandra Egege and Salah Kutieleh, "Dimming Down Difference.... ," in *Teaching in Transnational Higher Education: Enhancing Learning for Offshore International Students,* edited by Lee Dunn and Michelle Wallace (New York: Routledge, 2008), pp. 74, 76. In addition, U.S. internal-medicine program directors cited a shortage of qualified faculty and not lack of resident interest as a barrier to teaching about health disparities. Smith, *et al.,* "Recommendations for Teaching," p. 655.

63. Like (interview), with reference to the medical-school curriculum (also see Betancourt, "Eliminating Racial and Ethnic Disparities," p. 791). On the little "space" that exists in teacher-education curriculums, see Case and Werner, "Building Faculty Commitment," p. 203.

64. Allert, *et al.,* "Case for Global Engineering," p. 1. Charlick (interview) believes that students enrolled in Cleveland State University's 36-credit-hours Masters' degree program, many of whom also are working, would be intimated by the thought of adding additional coursework.

65. Allert, *et al.,* "Case for Global Engineering," p. 1; Carlson, "Global Approach to Engineering," p. A36; Drain, *et al.,* "Global Health in Medical Education," p. 228.

66. Case and Werner, "Building Faculty Commitment," p. 203.

67. Kao and Reenan ("*Wit* Is Not Enough," p. 226), with reference to medical students.

68. In the United States, the proposed Paul Simon Study Abroad Foundation could play an important role in connection with financing overseas skill-learning experiences by needy students enrolled in professional programs. At many universities, moreover, student advocacy will generate institutional budgetary support. Based, in part, on evidence that its medical school's Global Multiculturalism Track had a strong positive influence on enrollment decisions, the University of Massachusetts decided to fund the program, including stipends for student participation in overseas experiences, internally once external funding had evaporated. Godkin and Savageau, "Effect of a Global Multiculturalism Track," p. 186; Godkin, Savageau, and Fletcher, "Global Longitudinal Pathway," p. 231.

Index

nonverbal communication, 14, 50, 62
North-South relations, 38
Norway, 169n8
nutrition, 39

O
Obama, Barack, xii, 33
off-campus learning, 112
operational skills, 14–16
overseas work placements, 119, 120, 122
Oxfam, 52
Oxford Health Alliance, 108

P
pandemic diseases, 39
Parks, Bradley, 38
parochialism, 28
partnerships, 4, 52, 73
patient-centered learning, 101
Paul Simon Study Abroad Foundation, xi, 200n68
pedagogical tools
for business education, 115–116
for engineering education, 116–118
for health education, 121–122
for social-justice education, 118–119
for sustainable-development practice, 119–121
for teacher education, 114–115
person-to-person relationships, 2
perspective taking, 48
Pew Center on Global Change, 28–29
Physicians for Social Responsibility, 107
population flows, 24
porosity, 23–24
professional associations, xviii–xix, 3
professional competence, 2
professional connections, 4
professional education, 18–21
professional mobility, xvi
professionals, xvii–xviii, xx–xxi
professional schools, xviii–xix
project/task competence, 9, 14–16
public administration, 173n5
public health, 38–40
public-private partnerships, 25–26

Purdue University, 70, 71, 72

Q
Qin-Hilliard, Desiree Baolian, 45

R
Ramphele, Mamphela, xvi
rapport building, 15
Reimers, Fernando, 1
relationship building, 81, 92, 106
research projects, 110
resilience, 103
resources, 125
Roberts, Timmons, 38
role plays, 111

S
Saleebey, Dennis, 81
Sarkissian, Wendy, 18
self-awareness, 88
self-confidence, 12
self-efficacy, 49, 79
service learning, 119
Shapiro, Steve, 52
Sheppard, Sheri, 19
Shuman, Larry, 65
Singapore, 28
skill revolution, 1–4
Smith, Amy, 32
Smith, Andrew, 27
social capital, 3
social entrepreneurship, 64
social justice, transnational, 82–83
social-justice education
analytic competence and, 76–78
communicative competence and, 80–81
creative competence and, 79–80
emotional competence and, 78–79
functional competence and, 81–83
pedagogical tools for, 118–119
TC framework for, 75–83
social-justice work, 33–35
social/power context, 8
Social Science Research Council, 3
social-work education, xix

Acknowledgments

Intellectually, *Transnational Competence* is built on inspiration from diverse sources. Colleagues from multiple disciplines and nationalities, particularly the transnationally competent among them, helped illuminate the way. Former students, including those who are now practicing in the professions we are concerned with in this book, provoked our thinking on the subject both in class and after graduation. We are especially indebted to the professional-program experts who shared their insights on challenges and curriculum possibilities with us in extensive interviews.

Personally, we acknowledge the cheerful patience of family members during the demanding times of research and writing. Phyllis's constructive criticism of an early draft of Chapter 5 was particularly helpful, as was the support and encouragement she provided on numerous occasions along the way. Perhaps most meaningful, the early stages of this project brought us together for four memorable months in Washington, D.C., when Justin, Jason, Phyllis, and Peter occupied the guest wing of the Rosenau ninth-floor 26th Street apartment overlooking Georgetown and shared a kitchen and meals with Jim.

We also acknowledge with special gratitude the project support granted by the Association of Public and Land-Grant Universities (APLU) and the sustained encouragement provided by the APLU's Vice President International, Kerry Bolognese, during Peter's autumn 2007 tenure as faculty fellow. Dean Gerald Fetz and President George Dennison of the University of Montana made it possible for Peter to accept the fellowship offer. And a 2008 spring-semester sabbatical award from the university allowed him to make substantial progress at the writing stage.

Two University of Montana students played important parts in this book project. Katie Stevenson helped identify potential interest in Transnational Competence through a meticulous web-based search of programs, courses, and individual faculty members. Montana James capably transcribed our interviews with professional-education innovators. And, we are deeply appreciative of the valuable guidance provided at key stages by Jennifer Knerr at Paradigm Publishers and the diligent and expeditious copyediting provided by Laura Esterman.

Peter Koehn, Missoula, Montanna
Jim Rosenau, Washington, D.C.

About the Authors

Peter H. Koehn is Professor of Political Science, the University of Montana's founding Director of International Programs and Distinguished Scholar for 2005, a Fulbright New Century Scholar, and APLU's first faculty fellow. He has taught at universities in Ethiopia, Nigeria, Namibia, Eritrea, China, and Hong Kong. His publications include six books, more than forty chapters, and more than fifty articles in refereed journals. At Montana, Koehn directs the International Development Studies minor. His teaching portfolio includes courses in rural and global health (MPH program), sustainable climate policies (China and the United States), development administration, and African politics. His recent scholarship centers on migration health and climate stabilization.

James N. Rosenau holds the distinguished rank of University Professor of International Affairs at George Washington University. This honor is reserved for the few scholar-teachers whose recognition in the academic community transcends the usual disciplinary boundaries. Professor Rosenau has held a Guggenheim Foundation Fellowship and is a former president of the International Studies Association. He is a renowned international political theorist with a record of publication and professional service that is acknowledged worldwide. He is the author of some 140 articles and author or editor of more than 40 books, including *Turbulence in World Politics: A Theory of Change and Continuity* (1990), *Governance Without Government: Order and Change in World Politics* (1992), *Along the Domestic-Foreign Frontier: Exploring Governance in a Turbulent World* (1997), *Information Technologies and Global Politics: The Changing Scope of Power and Governance* (2002), *Distant Proximities: Dynamics Beyond Globalization* (2003), *The Study of World Politics* (2 vol., 2006), and *People Count! Networked Individuals in Global Politics* (2008).